LATIN AMERICAN CINEMA

Latin American Cinema

Stephen M. Hart

REAKTION BOOKS

For Dany

Published by Reaktion Books Ltd
33 Great Sutton Street
London EC1V 0DX, UK
www.reaktionbooks.co.uk

First published 2015

Printed and bound in China

A catalogue record for this book is available from the British Library

ISBN 978 1 78023 365 9

Contents

Introduction

This book grew out of a hunch – highlighted by my experience teaching documentary filmmaking at summer schools held at the Escuela Internacional de Cine y Televisión in San Antonio de los Baños in Cuba since 2006 – that Latin American film has as much to do with the step-changes in film technology as it does with the historical and political reality it memorializes. Or, to put it another way, that film historians have to be as sensitive to the implications of major paradigm shifts which have occurred in camera technology – such as the use of the hand-held camera in the 1950s or the emergence of digital film at the end of the 1990s – as they are alert to the major historical changes that occurred in Latin America in the twentieth century (such as the rise of dictatorship in the 1970s and 1980s, and the radical political polarizations that took place as a result in the political space of a number of Latin American nations). This hunch was partly based on Lev Kuleshov's argument that the best type of approach to film is one that blends theory with practice. As Kuleshov suggests, teaching film craft 'without being cognisant of fundamental cinematic theories demeans film craft to the mere level of an amateur workshop. Likewise, studying film history and theory without a corresponding experience in the elemental aspects of filmmaking leaves theoretical research without a solid basis, forcing students to plunge into abstraction.'[1] This book extends Kuleshov's thesis by arguing, for example, that to ignore the evolving technology by which, at a given time and in a given place, the image was captured, edited and produced is to run the risk of producing 'timeless' and 'static' interpretations of films. This basic insight has been used in this book as a key to reassess the ways in which we think about the evolution of film as a discursive, investigative and imagistic medium.

Occasionally film historians look at the history of film as if it were a sideshow appended to the grand narrative of nations having wars with each other, and thus produce chapters entitled, by way of example, 'Post-World War II Film'. While, in some isolated cases, film may have coincided with enormous upheavals in history, in many others it did not. Film, indeed, has its own history. Thus the creation of cross-cutting by D. W. Griffith in his film *A Corner in Wheat* (1909), such that the wealth of the upper classes is contrasted with the poverty of the lower classes, was arguably just as important for the evolution of film as the brutal historical sequence of the First World War. Likewise the hand-held camera in the 35mm Canadian film *Les Raquetteurs* ('The Snowshoers', directed by Michel Brault and Gilles Groulx) which was used to film the convention of snowshoers held in Sherbrooke, Quebec, in February 1958, demonstrated the new flexibility of the camera to mingle in with the public, almost as if it were another spectator within the crowd that had gathered to witness the events. Filming with a hand-held camera was an innovation destined to have far-reaching consequences for the way in which filmmakers subsequently saw their craft. It radically democratized film, allowing for the creation of a living, 'breathing' camera.

The advent of digital film 30 years later – *Idioterne* ('The Idiots', 1998), directed by Dogme 95 Danish film director Lars von Trier, was the first film to be filmed entirely on a digital camera (a Sony DCR-VX1000) – led to one of the most radical changes ever experienced in the film industry. The digital camera in the new millennium, given its flexibility, low costs, portability and the fact that you can see immediately what you are recording, offered the opportunity for thousands to create new narratives about the world we live in. It signalled the birth of a post-35mm universe which eschewed the grand narrative of national destiny or world wars, focusing instead on the everyday lives of the world's citizens. It also introduced a new vision of the world. Since the digital camera never 'cuts' the film in the way the analogue film editor did, it allows the universe to be seen as an unbroken continuum. This continuum is perceived not only through time but also through space. Thus the traditional tripartite division of filmic space (foreground, mid-ground, background), which is itself based on a theatrical paradigm, no longer holds in the digital world. The digital turn, indeed, led to new ways of formulating the space and time of the universe, questioning the past–present–future formula of time as much as it interrogated the foreground–mid-ground–background paradigm of space.

Latin American film has not, of course, remained impervious to major paradigm shifts such as these. As I hope to demonstrate in this book, Latin American film has reacted to the invention of the hand-held camera and digital film in innovative ways. In 2007 three Mexican directors, Alejandro González Iñárritu, Alfonso Cuarón and Guillermo del Toro, were able to attract sixteen Oscar nominations between them (the Mexicans were therefore in second place, jointly tied with the United Kingdom behind the United States in first place).[2] A number of film critics at the time asked how this came about. The answer to this question lies not only in the meteoric careers of the 'Three Amigos', as they are known in Hollywood, but in the history of the seismic shifts within Latin American cinema whose strata over time finally produced cinematographic 'diamonds'. The success of Latin American cinema in the twenty-first century springs from the pioneering steps taken by film directors such as Fernando Birri, Julio García Espinosa and Tomás Gutiérrez Alea in the 1950s and 1960s, around whom the Nuevo Cine Latinoamericano (New Latin American Cinema) movement came to coalesce. As Birri once suggested to me in an interview, twenty-first-century filmmakers in Latin America are 'standing on our shoulders'.[3]

This book attempts to trace connections such as these – how, for example, the 'grit' of New Latin American Cinema led to the 'slick grit' of 'New' New Latin American Cinema – and it soon became clear that the best way to answer the question was by conducting a longitudinal study of Latin American film from its origins to the present. In order to do so this study draws on a number of essential books published on the subject, ranging from the early classics such as Michael Chanan, *The Cuban Image* (1985), Julianne Burton, *Cinema and Social Change in Latin America: Conversations with Filmmakers* (1986), Randal Johnson, *The Film Industry in Brazil* (1987) and John King, *Magical Reels* (1990), to important recent studies such as Deborah Shaw, *Contemporary Cinema of Latin America: Ten Key Films* (2003), Lisa Shaw and Stephanie Dennison, *Latin American Cinema: Essays on Modernity, Gender and National Identity* (2005), Lúcia Nagib, *Brazil on Screen: Cinema novo, New Cinema, Utopia*

(2007), Joanna Page, *Crisis and Capitalism in Contemporary Argentine Cinema* (2009), Demetrios Matheou, *The Faber Book of New South American Cinema* (2010), Laura Podalsky, *The Politics of Affect and Emotion in Contemporary Latin American Cinema: Argentina, Brazil, Cuba and Mexico* (2011), Jens Andermann, *New Argentine Cinema* (2012) and Cynthia Tompkins, *Experimental Latin American Cinema: History and Aesthetics* (2013).[4] The analysis of this archive of celluloid film can provide what Laura Mulvey has called a 'historically unprecedented "time machine"' of the past.[5] As she goes on to suggest:

> The celluloid cinema may be there evidentially, a flawed but still indexical record of its movement, but also, and perhaps more crucially, it offers a more abstract, imaginative, means for reflecting on time itself. By a knight's move across into a different technological medium, it allows reflection on how time is inscribed into culture and politics and how it gets lost in the elusiveness of history.[6]

This book seeks to create its own knight's move by providing a new analysis of Latin American film as seen through the looking glass of the major step-changes in film technology. Other books have focused on the historical backdrop to the films, their production, how they are funded, and the stars who have delighted audiences.[7] This book, however, looks at the films themselves, analysing how their message is expressed – through technology, techniques and 'tricks of the trade'. By providing an in-depth, chronological study of Latin American cinema, from the early silent film era in the late nineteenth century to its boom in the early twenty-first, it seeks to provide some answers to the conundrum of the success of contemporary Latin American cinema.

This study of Latin American cinema, from its inauspicious beginnings in 1896 until the present day (2013), with Guillermo del Toro and Alfonso Cuarón successfully directing new-look sci-fi movies with an auteurish flourish, focuses on the main paradigm shifts marking its evolution.[8] It has not been possible, for obvious reasons, to focus on every Latin American film made. The films chosen for analysis in this book have been included either because they have won awards or been commercially successful or because they are filmically significant. The readings offered here have deliberately avoided the sociological turn – namely, tying the meaning of the films too closely to the history of human society – preferring instead to contextualize these films within the history of the camera-eye.

1

Inauspicious Beginnings (1895–1950)

Images in movement

As the philosopher Gilles Deleuze has argued, the earliest stage of film, epitomized by Auguste and Louis Lumière's *L'Arrivée d'un train en gare de La Ciotat* ('Arrival of a Train at La Ciotat Station', 1895), was characterized by 'images in movement'. The 'cinématographe' – an early moving image projector to which we owe the word 'cinema' itself – was given its first public demonstration by the Lumière brothers in the Grand Café, Paris, on 28 December 1895, when they screened their film. There are reports of the audience running out of the Grand Café in horror when they saw the train approaching. As Paola Marrati suggests:

> In the early days of cinema, before the introduction of the mobile camera, the frame was defined in relation to a unique, frontal point of view: the spectator. In this context the shot was a purely spatial determination indicating the distance between the camera and the objects filmed, from the close-up to the long shot. At this stage, these first images produced by the cinema are not by their nature different from those in the theatre, for instance. They are what Deleuze calls *images in movement.*[1]

In this 'primitive cinema' phase, to use Deleuze's terminology, film was defined and mediated by the fixed frontal camera which would record objects in real time, rather like a cameraman simply filming some actors on a stage in a theatre. Filming, as a result of being still tied in performance terms to the mechanics of the theatre, sought to amaze audiences with the screening of movement, ranging from the arrival of a train at La Ciotat station as mentioned above, or events such as people leaving a factory or a church, or the moving pictures of sports events. Given the portability of the 'cinématographe' – it weighed less than 20 lb (9 kg) – the Lumière brothers sent their cameramen around the world to give demonstrations of their new invention. In Rio de Janeiro, Brazil, the first screening of what was then called the 'Omnigrapho' took place on 8 July 1896 at 57 rua do Ouvidor.[2] On 28 July 1896, *L'Arrivée d'un train en gare de La Ciotat* was screened in the Odeon Theatre in Buenos Aires, and subsequently at the Cinematógrafo Lumière, 9 Plateros Avenue, in Mexico City in August 1896; the cameraman was Gabriel Vayre.[3] The first film screenings took place in Lima, Peru, on 2 January 1897 and in Havana, Cuba, on 24 January 1897.[4]

Film soon developed into the screening of actualities, such as an official function attended by a state dignitary, as well as other newsworthy events. Examples of some of these early *actualité*-type films in Latin America are *Un célebre especialista sacando muelas en el Gran Hotel Europa* ('A Celebrated Specialist Pulling Teeth at the Gran Hotel Europa', dir. Guillermo and Manuel Trujillo Durán, Venezuela, 1897) and *Carrera de bicicletas en el velódromo de Arroyo Seco* ('Bicycle Race at the Arroyo Seco Velodrome', dir. Félix Oliver, Uruguay, 1898). It was not long, though, before audiences were craving more interesting material than a train arriving at a station or a dentist's antics. During the Mexican Revolution (1911–19), the flamboyant revolutionary Pancho Villa signed a contract with Mutual Film Corporation for $25,000, giving in exchange permission for the battles he waged to be filmed and broadcast in the United States, even agreeing to have his dawn executions filmed. As he promised the cameraman:

> Don't worry Don Raúl. If you say the light at four in the morning is not right for your little machine, well, no problem. The executions will take place at six. But no later. Afterwards we march and fight. Understand?[5]

Movement-image

The screening of actualities led – again quite rapidly – to a number of experiments with the new medium of moving images. It was once photographers began to explore different ways of playing back and recombining the recorded images that the seventh art of the silver screen was born: montage. It was arguably with Georges Méliès' 30-scene, fifteen-minute narrative film *Le Voyage dans la lune* ('Journey to the Moon', 1902) that montage emerged most famously into filmic discourse, notably in the sequence in which the spaceship is depicted landing in the moon's eye. Though Méliès' editing was rudimentary it was the first hint of what Deleuze called the creation of 'movement-images', of a new sense of narrativity. As Marrati suggests:

> In primitive cinema, as in natural perception, movement depends on a body that is displaced through a space that is itself fixed. Movement remains attached to moving bodies; it does not emerge in itself. The emancipation of movement, its appearance in a pure state, so to speak, would come to be one of cinema's great achievements, but it would only happen progressively, with the introduction of the mobile camera and montage.[6]

Film in Latin America, as elsewhere in the world, gradually developed from the screening of actualities to the creation of realist narratives. Over time a number of montage techniques were developed, such as film continuity (Edwin S. Porter), cross-cutting (D. W. Griffith) and point-of-view shots (Vitagraph), and this progression from actualities to realist film involved an 'emancipation of movement', to use Deleuze's term, which was expressed specifically as a transition from image-in-movement to movement-image.[7] The earliest narrative (movement-image) films were documentaries about famous individuals, such as *El fusilamiento de Dorrego* ('Dorrego's Execution', dir. Mario Gallo, Argentina, 1908), *Paz e amor* ('Peace and Love', dir. Alberto Botelho, Brazil, 1910), *A vida do Cabo João Cândido* ('The Life of Commander João Cândido', dir. unknown, Brazil, 1910) and *Revolución orozquista* ('Pascual Orozco's Revolution', dir. Alva brothers, Mexico, 1912).

This group of documentaries was followed by a number of fiction narrative films such as *El automóvil gris* ('The Grey Car', Mexico, 1919), *El húsar de la muerte* ('The Hussar of Death', Chile, 1925), *Luis Pardo* (Peru, 1927), *Brasa dormida* ('Sleeping Ember', Brazil, 1928), *Del pingo al volante* ('From the Country to the Town', Uruguay, 1929) and *La*

Venus de nácar ('The Venus of Mother of Pearl', Venezuela, 1932) which explore montage innovatively and embody the movement-image characteristic of classical-realist cinema as analysed by Deleuze in which the characters are embedded within a situation which has its own momentum. As Deleuze suggests, in classical-realist cinema 'objects and settings already had a reality of their own, but it was a functional reality, strictly determined by the demands of the situation . . . The situation was, then, directly extended into action and passion'.[8] The situations portrayed in realist cinema were subject to sensory-motor schemata which were 'automatic and pre-established', articulating a visible cause and effect relationship between the situation and the character's actions.[9] As Deleuze further suggests, 'The space of a sensory-motor situation is a setting which is already specified and presupposes an action which discloses it, or prompts a reaction which adapts to or modifies it.'[10]

An excellent early example of the movement-image narrative style in Latin America is *El automóvil gris*, directed by Enrique Rosas, the earliest silent film to emerge from Mexico, first screened in Mexico City on 11 December 1919. The film was originally intended as a documentary about the lives of a group of crooks who were targeting upper-class households in Mexico City in 1915. A local detective, Juan Manuel Cabrera, agreed to have Enrique Rosas follow him in his investigations. Enrique Rosas, however, decided to depart from the original documentarist approach, working with actors to reconstruct the robberies. The film began to reconstruct the scene of the crime, rather like an embryonic version of *Crimewatch*.

In the first scene we see the gang members swear an oath of allegiance to one another. Then we see a young girl kidnapped off the streets and bundled into the 'grey car' that becomes almost the protagonist of the crime. The event is pre-prepared by the creation of cinematic tension; we watch the girl walk past the car and then we see the gang jump out, pounce and bundle her into the car. In the following scene we see the forced entry into a house, the bullying of the women until they reveal where the money and the jewels are, the hurried escape and the sharing-out of the loot. As this first episode demonstrates, *El automóvil gris* works like a fiction film because it creates tension between interlocking episodes; the divvying-up of the loot is full of tension because the young girl who has been kidnapped is the *novia* (girlfriend) of one of the members of

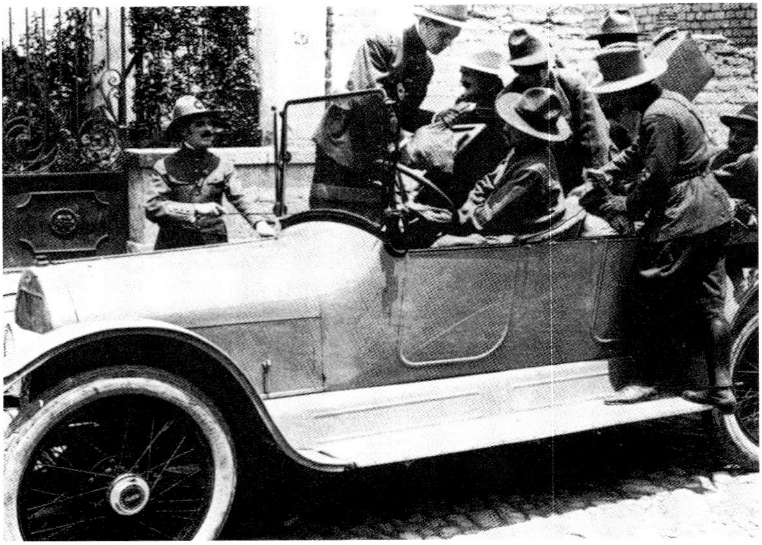

The grey car in *El automóvil gris* (1919).

the gang, and she sees him when she looks through a crack in the door. *El automóvil gris* has an excellent sense of continuity and dramatic tension; it is an action-based drama more than a piece of journalism. And yet the documentarism of its genesis came back to haunt the film in its closing sequence in which we see the actual criminals – who had been captured and convicted – lined up against a wall and shot dead by firing squad. The film demonstrates the osmotic nature of the medium at this early period in Latin America. Enrique Rosas was director, screenwriter, cameraman and producer. But just as importantly, *El automóvil gris* demonstrates that the mixture between fiction and documentary was already in the DNA of the Latin American cinematic tradition by 1919. It was a legacy which would prove to be one of the distinctive characteristics of Latin American film.

Six years later, a very significant silent film was made in Chile, differing from the Mexican film in that it was an excavation of the historical past of that Latin American country. *El húsar de la muerte*, which premiered on 24 November 1925 in Santiago, was directed by Pedro Sienna. He also starred in the film, which tells the story of the adventures of the guerrilla leader, Manuel Rodríguez (1785–1818), during the Reconquista up until his death in 1818. The 65-minute film was reconstructed in 1962 and 1995 by the film unit at the University of Chile and is now considered a 'national monument'. Unlike the history books that focus on the liberation of Chile via the figures of José de San Martín and Bernardo O'Higgins, this silent film tells the story via the perspective of the guerrilla leader, Manuel Rodríguez. Though José de San Martín does appear in the film Bernardo O'Higgins is airbrushed out of the frame, perhaps not surprisingly since the two men did not always see eye to eye. (After the Battle of Chacabuco in 1817, for example, won by José de San Martín, O'Higgins ordered Rodríguez's arrest, and Rodríguez only managed to escape his prison sentence as a result of San Martín's intervention.)

The film opens with the rout of the Chilean troops by the Spanish army at the Disaster of Rancagua in 1814. While the royalists are celebrating, Rodríguez sends them a message: 'No alegrarse demasiado. Se acerca la hora de la libertad. Mueran los tiranos ¡Viva la patria!' (Don't get too happy. The hour of freedom is approching. Down with tyrants. Long live our motherland!) Rodríguez rallies the Chilean troops, encouraging them to fight a rear-guard action against the Spanish, and he begins to take on various disguises, allowing him to travel around Santiago undisturbed. The royalist captain, Vicente San Bruno, is portrayed as disturbed by this via montage; the captain hangs his head in his hands when he imagines Rodríguez in his various disguises, as presented by some (rudimentary) cross-cutting between the captain's face and Rodríguez's different disguises. The film also adds a star-crossed love motif to the plot, having Rodríguez fall in love with the daughter of the Marquis of Aguirre, their union 'forbidden' since it cuts across political lines (the

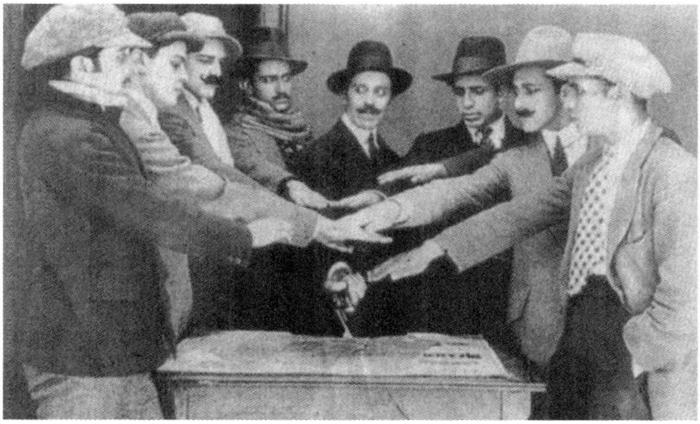

The hoodlums swear allegiance in *El automóvil gris*.

Marquis of Aguirre, as his title suggests, is a royalist). Rodríguez's popularity among the lower classes is suggested by the introduction of a boy *guerrillero* called 'El Huacho Pelao' (The Ragamuffin Soldier) who is so fed up with being bullied by the Spanish troops that he decides to fight for Rodríguez. The film has all the types of 'errors' associated with early twentieth-century filmmaking (dialogue intertitles not synchronized with actors' dialogue, non-adherence to the 180-degree rule, abrupt transitions between events and over-reliance on subtitles to relate significant events, such as Rodriguez's death) – but it has raw energy, especially evident in scenes such as the discovery by Captain San Bruno that Rodríguez is hiding in the Aguirre residence, protected by Carmen, and the simple circumstances of Rodríguez's burial by some humble peasants. The final scene suggests most clearly that this film offers a man-in-the-street version of Chile's independence. It also shows the osmotic nature of the various roles associated with filmmaking in Latin America in the 1920s since Pedro Sienna was director, screenwriter and star actor of the film.

Another silent film of this period which focuses, like *El húsar de la muerte*, on a popular folkloric figure, was *Luis Pardo* (1927, directed by Enrique Cornejo Villanueva), which told of the life and adventures of Luis Pardo Novoa ('El Bandolero' [The Bandit], 1874–1909), a Robin Hood-type from Ancash in Peru who fought against the oppression of the common people in the large estates which spread across the Andres. Most of the surviving footage shows Luis Pardo's skirmishes before his eventual death at the hands of Leguía's troops. *Brasa dormida* (1928), directed by Humberto Mauro and arguably Brazil's most famous silent film, tells the tale of Luis Soares (played by Luis Soroa), a dissipated youth living in Rio de Janeiro who is rejuvenated though his work at a sugar factory in the interior and his love of the owner's daughter, Anita Silva (played by Nita Ney). It is beautifully shot.

Osmosis from without

It was inevitable, given its rudimentary nature at this time, that Latin American cinema should be overwhelmed by foreign imports, by osmosis from without. Sergei Eisenstein's famous film about the Mexican Revolution, *¡Que viva Mexico!* (1931; reconstructed by Grigori Alexandrov in 1979) epitomizes Latin American culture of the early 1930s, a work in progress created by external osmosis. The film was funded in 1931 by the distinguished socialist writer Upton Sinclair and his wife, who were keen to encourage the famous Soviet film director to produce a revolutionary film about Mexico. But after the initial three months had run out, and Eisenstein was clearly not close to producing a finished product, Sinclair decided to withdraw the funding. As he later explained:

> What first led us to distrust him [Eisenstein] was that when the money was spent he wrote us that we'd have to send more or we'd have no picture . . . He kept that up, over and over, and we realized that he was simply staying in Mexico at our expense in order to avoid having to go back to Russia.[11]

As a result Eisenstein and Sinclair fell out, and Sinclair kept the raw footage Eisenstein had been sending him, and subsequently refused to allow Eisenstein to edit the film. Some of the negatives were sold by Sinclair, who was trying to recoup some of the capital he had raised for the venture, and released piecemeal as *Thunder over Mexico* (1933; based on the 'Maguey' sequence), *Eisenstein in Mexico* (1934), *Death Day* (1934; based on the Epilogue) and *Time in the Sun* (1939). Eisenstein was upset by this betrayal. When asked years later by Jan Leyda why he had not directed any major film since *¡Que viva México!*:

> he gave me the most genuinely anguished look I ever saw on his face and shouted at me: 'What do you expect me to do? How can there be a new film when I haven't given birth to the last one?' And he clutched his belly with an equally painful gesture.[12]

It is clear that Eisenstein went to Mexico because, like a number of artists and intellectuals of the time, including D. H. Lawrence, Aldous Huxley and Graham Greene, he felt drawn to the country as an image of an alternative to Europe.[13] Despite its truncated status, *¡Que viva Mexico!* is an extraordinary film which proved highly influential in Latin America. Eisenstein was hostile to the advent of sound in the cinema and in 1928 he, Grigori Alexandrov and Vsevolod Pudovkin co-signed a manifesto rejecting 'sound cinema'; sound, they argued, would 'degrade' cinema and make it too similar to the theatre.[14] Eisenstein was more interested in exploring the artistry of the image and his film has some breathtaking cinematography.

The film's 1979 reconstruction by Grigori Alexandrov divides the film into six sections. The most striking feature of the first sequence, the prologue, which focuses on pre-Columbian architecture, is an attempt to bring out the visual similarities between the profiles on the monuments and modern-day models. The second section, 'Sandunga', is set in Tehauntepec in southern Mexico and tells the story of a young woman, Concepción, who is saving up for her dowry which will allow her to marry the man of her dreams, Abundio. At one point we see her combing her hair. Subsequently, a voice-over explains that her dowry is a necklace made of gold coins. A still image of the necklace – shown in a crescent shape – then dissolves by virtue of a visual rhyme to reveal a man in a hammock, the focus of her desire. The third section, 'Fiesta', focuses on the Virgin of Guadalupe and on bullfighting in order to draw out the conflict which is at the heart of Mexican society in Eisenstein's view. Though sketchy in terms of plot, the choreography is exquisite. The fourth section, 'Maguey', is the most accomplished of the sequences, and the only one with any semblance of a coherent plot. Sebastián and María are about to marry but the local custom ('derecho de pernada', *ius primae noctis*)

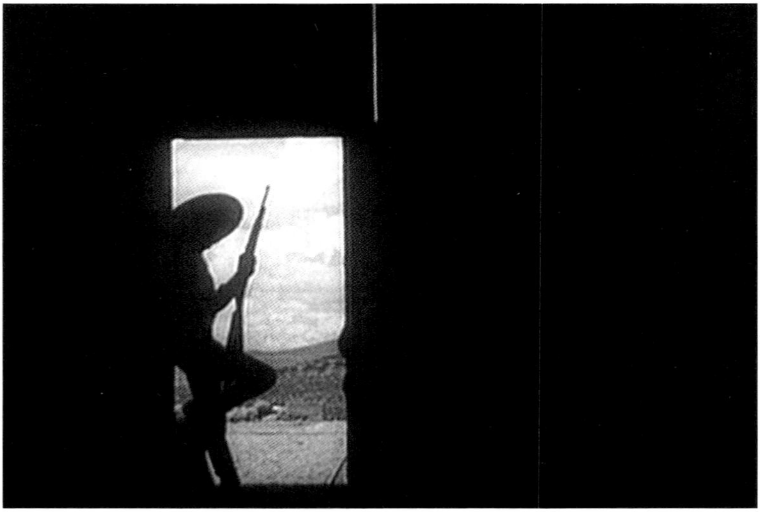

Soldier in a doorway in Eisenstein's *¡Que viva México!* (1931).

Clash of cultures in *¡Que viva México!*

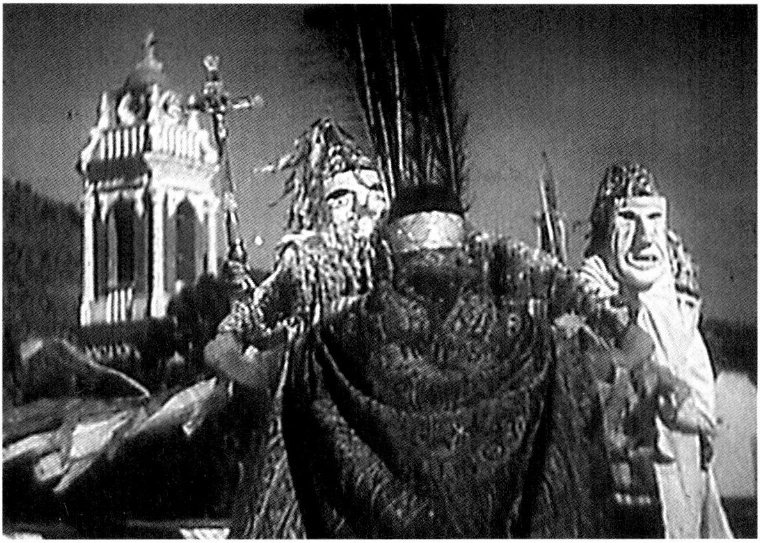

means that María must visit the local landowner. She is raped, Sebastián tries to avenge her lost honour, and he and two accomplices are buried with their torsos revealed before being trampled to death by horses. During the gunfight between Sebastián, his accomplices and the landowner, a highly choreographed sequence of shots underlines the metaphorical connections between the maguey cactus and the workers' blood. Exchange of fire is cross-cut with images of the cactus being destroyed and its sap dripping out. This connection between blood and sap is used to enhance the notion of exploitation. The sap, which the peasants have to suck laboriously from the cactus plants in order for it to be fermented and then drunk by the rich, provides an example of how the workers are used as an agent of their own oppression. Later on, the same image of the sap is used to underline the notion of Mexico 'fermenting' during its Revolution.

The fifth section, the 'Soldadera' sequence, only existed in draft form, as did the sixth section, the epilogue, which, though truncated, is suggestive in that it overlays a religious, cultural ceremony, the Day of the Dead, with political significance. Rather than simply rehearsing the Aztec notion of the continuity of life and death, Eisenstein uses the masks which characterize the celebrations of the Day of the Dead to make a political point. When the masks are cast off, some reveal the face of smiling young boys, while others show the skull of a socially doomed class, the military and the gendarmes. It is not insignificant that one of the people chosen to represent this class is wearing spurs, namely, the social class which in the pre-Revolutionary era had raped humble women such as María and murdered men such as Sebastián if they dared to rebel. The epilogue concludes with the shot of a face of a smiling young boy, a symbol of the future of Mexico in the post-Revolutionary era.

Eisenstein saw *¡Que viva México!* in terms of a woven garment, the Mexican *sarape*:

> A sarape is the striped blanket that . . . every Mexican wears. So striped and violently contrasting are the cultures in Mexico running next to each other and at the same time being centuries away . . . we took the contrasting independent adjacence of its violent colours as the motif for constructing our film: 6 episodes following each other.[15]

Though the six sections are distinct in many ways – focusing in turn on a pre-historical matriarchal society, the Spanish influence in Mexican culture (specifically Catholicism and bullfighting), the oppression of the Mexican working classes by the landowners in the pre-Revolutionary era, female agency within the Mexican Revolution – there are a number of common strands which suggest that Eisenstein was attempting to produce a unified artistic vision of Mexico. The Christological resonance of the final scene of the 'Maguey' sequence in which the three men are trampled to death, for example, was meant to be counterbalanced with the depiction of the re-enactment of Christ's passion in the third section (as in the later scene, there are three Christ figures, and the ropes used in each sequence mutually reinforce their interconnectedness). Eisenstein's notes suggest that he intended to splice the depiction of Sebastián's death with images of the Corpus Christi but because he was unable to edit the film, this remained an intention rather than an accomplishment.[16] The importance of *¡Que viva México!* is that it allows us to enter into the laboratory of a genius before he worked his magic. For this reason alone the footage is intrinsically valuable.

Death in a cactus
in *¡Que viva México!*

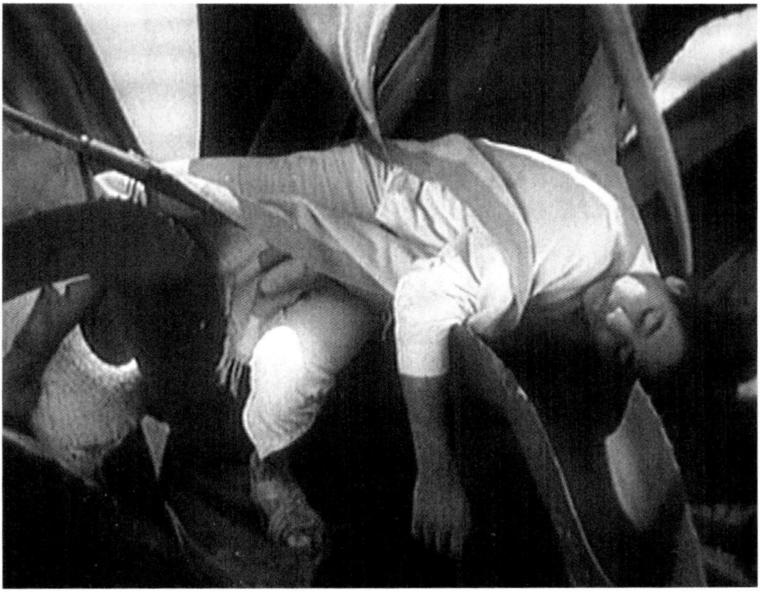

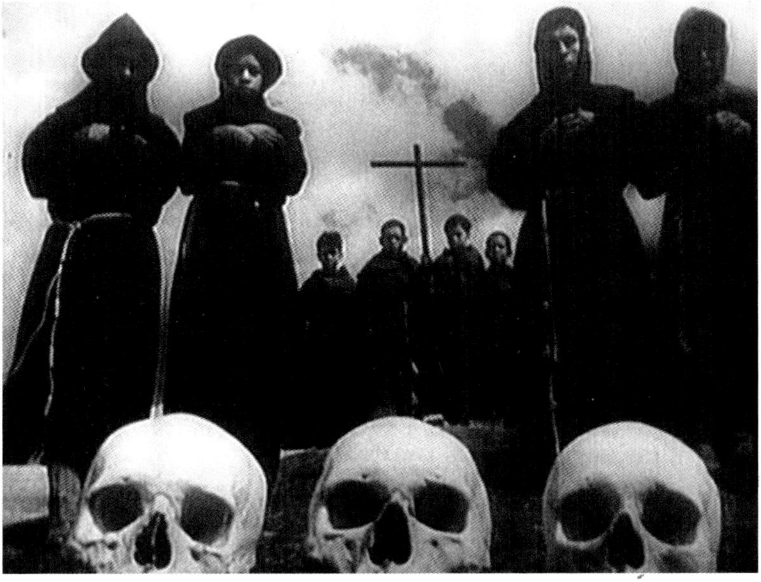

Religion and death
in *¡Que viva México!*

Sound and image

The 1930s, of course, were the decade in which sound began to infiltrate the otherwise image-centric world of film, producing new hybrid discourses. An early example was *La Venus de nácar* (1932), a seven-minute film made in Venezuela which told the story of the birth of the Venus of mother-of-pearl.

The establishing shot is of a young girl who sees her mother's pearls, remarks how beautiful they are and is told by her mother that mother-of-pearl has a story to it, at which point the story unfolds. A pearl fisherman catches a pearl, from which there emerges Venus who begins to dance seductively for him until he takes her off to a cave. Though hailed as the first example of sound cinema in Venezuela it should be noted that the sound component in *La Venus de nácar* signals the introduction of synchronic music used to accompany the dancing, rather than dialogue (the film uses intertitles to express the dialogue between mother and daughter). It would be another six years before Venezuela had a film with optical sound: *Tobago* (1938).

Indeed, it was not long before the sound heard in Latin American films was real sound rather than a synchronic music track. And the sound that audiences first heard – in Latin America as elsewhere – was the performance of vocal artists. If home-grown films were to be made, the safest route was

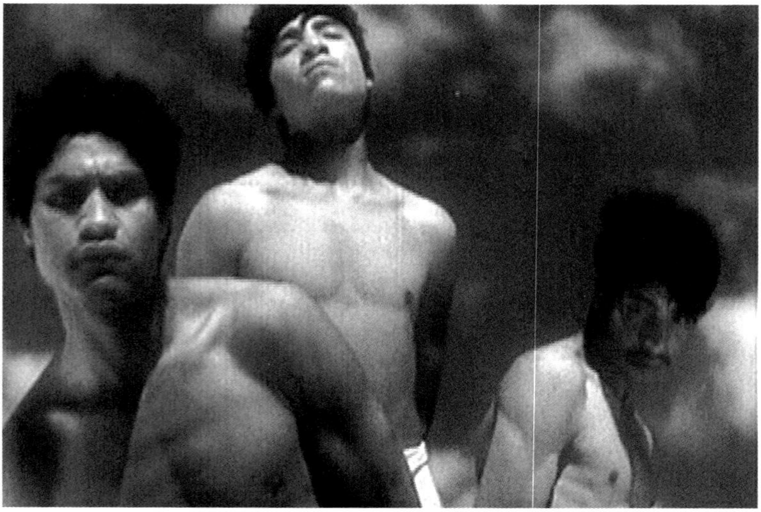

The three sacrificial victims in *¡Que viva México!*

to mimic foreign models – which meant a larger audience could be achieved eventually – and then add some home-grown ingredients. One of the best examples of this import-driven formula was the genre of the Mexican melodrama which dominated the scene from the mid-1930s until the early 1950s.[17] The Mexican film industry used the Hollywood notion of building a film around a star and a show and focused very much on the entertainment value of the film. The Hollywood musical, for example, which itself 'typically features musical and dance numbers woven around a backstage plot', is characteristic of an era which was still focused on the movie as a record of a cultural event, such as a Broadway show, which could be presented to a still larger audience.[18] The film was, in effect, still using the language of theatre in order to present its product to the larger world. The Mexican melodramas of the time followed the pattern, simply substituting American songs with Mexican *rancheras*, popular songs about how good life was back on the ranch.[19] *Allá en el Rancho Grande* ('Back Home on the Big Ranch', 1936), directed by Fernando de Fuentes, for example, inaugurated what became known as the Golden Age of Mexican cinema. The plot of the film is built around the rivalry between the owner of the Rancho Grande, Don Felipe (René Cardona) and an itinerant ranch hand and crooner, José Francisco (Tito Guízar), for the affections of Cruz (Esther Fernández). Don Felipe is persuaded by Angela (Emma Roldán) to 'buy' Cruz for 100 pesos but he desists once he discovers that Cruz is engaged to José Francisco. At various junctures in the film the plot pauses in order to allow Tito Guízar the opportunity to sing 'Allá en el rancho grande', following in the popular U.S. tradition of the filmed vaudeville performance.

One striking feature of *Allá en el Rancho Grande* was its working of the dilemma of the plot – would José Francisco still want to marry Cruz if she had succumbed to Don Felipe's advances the night before? – into the singing competition between José Francisco and a rival singer, which leads to José Francisco dramatically demanding that his rival say in prose what he has just said in song (that Cruz had lost her honour). The film has recourse to humour to vary its tone, mainly via Angela's partner, Florentino (Carlos López 'Chaflán'), whose drunken antics and irreverent comments provide a balanced counterpoint to the seriousness of the romantic drama. *Allá en el Rancho Grande* became the prototype of the *comedia ranchera*, and also led to the launching of Tito Guízar's

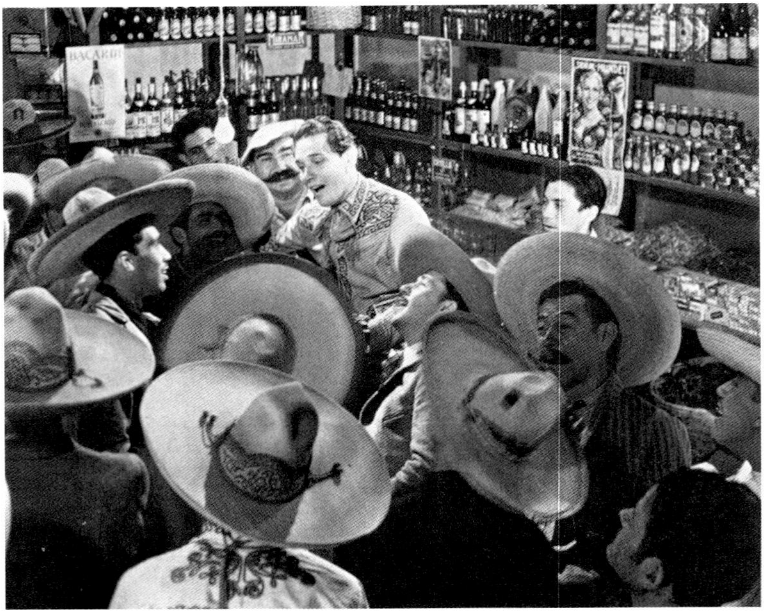

Tito Guízar (centre) in a scene from *Allá en el Rancho Grande* (1936).

career as a vocal artist as well as recognition for the cinematographer, Gabriel Figueroa.

During this period of the Golden Age of Mexican cinema a number of stars were born, such as the beautiful Dolores del Río and the equally ravishing María Félix. Mexico was beginning to assert its dominance in the internal Latin American market (in 1939 it had managed only 39 films compared to Argentina's 50, but in 1950 Mexico produced 125 films, more than double Argentina's 56). *Flor silvestre* ('Wildflower', 1943), directed by Emilio Fernández and starring Dolores del Río and Pedro Almendariz, tells the story of the Mexican Revolution via a Mexican mother (played by Dolores del Río). A runaway box office success, the film used the tried and tested formula inherited from Hollywood and then Mexicanized, and combined Dolores del Río's feminine beauty with Gabriel Figueroa's cinematographic aestheticism – a winning formula for the times.

In Brazil a similar phenomenon emerged, that of the *chanchada*, which was partially based on the Hollywood musical, dominating Brazilian film production from the 1930s until the 1950s.[20] Both the *comedia ranchera* and the *chanchada* can be seen as symptoms of a culture struggling to find its voice beneath the pressure of acculturation from without. It is clear that the Mexican melodramas and the Brazilian *chanchadas*, in that they were both essentially re-vampings of the Hollywood idiom, led to commercial success but also to an artistic cul-de-sac. They were always going to be the poor cousins, and Mexican melodramas eventually dried up, or rather they went underground in order to resurface in a new mass medium, television, and specifically the *telenovelas* (soap operas) which captivated audiences around the world in the 1980s and '90s. In the same way the Brazilian *chanchada* re-emerged years later in the form of the rather racy *pornochanchada*.[21]

By the 1940s and '50s, however, commercial film directors were attempting to develop a new language for film, seeking to present it as a new, unique art form, one which went beyond its theatrical roots to embrace what Deleuze would one day define as the 'emancipation of movement'. But by this time the vehicle by which it could come into being – film studios, actors, film production, trained camera teams and even in some cases a developed TV culture which could act as a safety net, inter alia – was already being controlled from elsewhere. This is why the first stirrings of a cineaste tradition, paradoxically enough, came via foreigners such as the Soviet Sergei Eisenstein and the Spaniard Luis Buñuel. Though they were cultural ventriloquists, these film directors brought a breath of fresh air to the evolving tradition of Latin American cinema.

Luis Buñuel's *Los olvidados* ('The Young and the Damned', 1950) was a landmark of Latin American cinema. In the 1940s, after a bad experience in Hollywood, Buñuel travelled to Mexico City and began making films; the best of this period was undoubtedly *Los olvidados*. Made on schedule in twenty-one days, it had a robust storyline about criminals in an urban setting which has led some critics to see the film as a revamping of a picaresque tale.[22] While acclaimed at the Cannes Film Festival (it won first prize for *mise en scène* in 1951), its uncompromising view of the down-and-outs of Mexico City aroused fierce reactions from some Mexicans: 'Many organizations, including labor unions, demanded my expulsion, and the press was nothing short of vitriolic in its criticism. Such spectators as there were left the theatre looking as if they'd just been to a funeral.'[23] The reaction was, indeed, so hostile that Buñuel had originally been obliged to create a more palatable ending for the film; the alternative conclusion, which was found at the UNAM Film Warehouse in 2002, has recourse to poetic justice in that Pedro (the protagonist) kills El Jaibo (the villain of the piece), retrieves the money entrusted to him by the director of the Reformatory and returns it to him.[24]

Los olvidados brought about a significant paradigm shift in Latin American film as Buñuel introduced a different mindset – European, Surrealist. At the beginning of the 1950s Mexican cinema was still playing out the last runs of its Golden Age years, in which men were strong, women beautiful and love a word with a romantic aura. This was, perhaps, the main reason for the shock, since the characters in Buñuel's film are anything but stars. In fact it would be difficult to think of a film in which the characters are less star-like; it is, as Octavio Paz pointed out, a 'star-less film'.[25] Both El Jaibo and Ojitos were played by non-actors, after all. But its un-star-like quality went deeper than this. There were simply no redeemable characters in this film, with the possible exception of Julián (Javier Amezcúa), who is consigned to the oblivion of death early on in the film. El Jaibo is instantly recognizable as the archetypal young villain, a Mexican version of Hollywood's Babyface.

Even the characters we expect to be good are corrupt. We expect sympathy to be engineered on behalf of Carmelo (played superbly by Miguel Inclán) when he is cruelly beaten up by the local gang, spearheaded

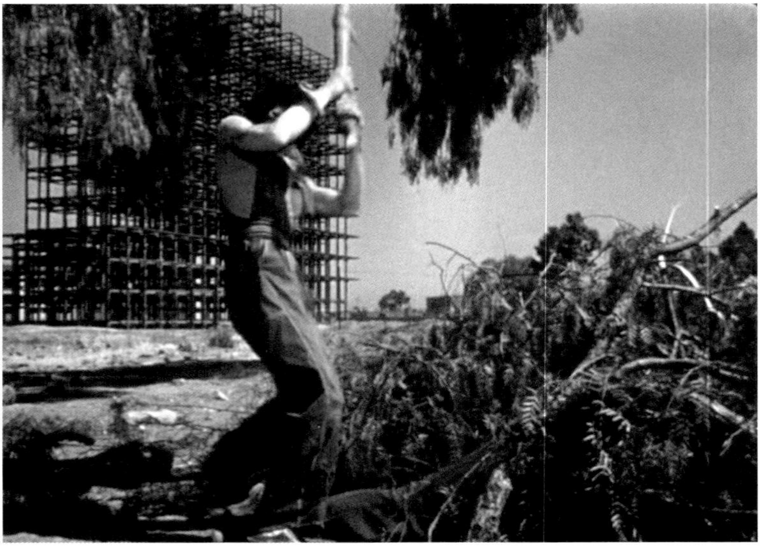

El Jaibo attacks Julián in Buñuel's *Los olvidados* (1950).

by El Jaibo, early on in the film. But then, later on, he shows himself to be just as quick to kick others when they are down given half a chance. A latent paedophile, he tries to grope the young girl, Meche (Alma Delia Fuentes) when she sits on his lap, and he jumps at the chance to turn in El Jaibo to the police later on in the film. Pedro's mother, Marta (Estela India) also deviates from contemporary film mores. Carlos Monsiváis notes how women were depicted in films of the Golden Years:

> For a married woman, monogamy is the only guarantee of your existence; for a single woman, your honour is your only justification; for the prostitute, tragedy is your punishment and your only chance for glory; for the daughter, in your hymen I have deposited my honour and your future.[26]

Yet Marta disrupts the codes of melodrama; she is beautiful, sensual and prepared to have a sexual relationship with El Jaibo just, it appears, for the hell of it. In one of the most disturbing scenes of the film, the dream sequence, she offers her son some meat, and if we accept Peter Evans's convincing interpretation that she is offering him her 'torn vagina', then she is offering sex to her son.[27] The moral of the film, furthermore, rather than enacting catharsis or promoting social justice, appears to be simply the working out of the inevitable consequences of evil.

One reading of the film would suggest that it is akin to a sociological study, showing the grittier side of life in the slums of Mexico City. In fact, Buñuel spent a number of months travelling around the shanty towns of Mexico City, watching, listening and thinking about the subject of his film:

> For the next several months, I toured the slums on the outskirts of Mexico City – sometimes with Fitzgerald, my Canadian set designer, sometimes with Luis Alcoriza, but most of the time alone. I wore my most threadbare clothes; I watched, I listened, I asked questions. Eventually, I came to know these people, and much of what I saw went unchanged into the film.[28]

On the face of it, therefore, we might see *Los olvidados* as offering a closely observed picture of the world. But, alongside this notion of sociological

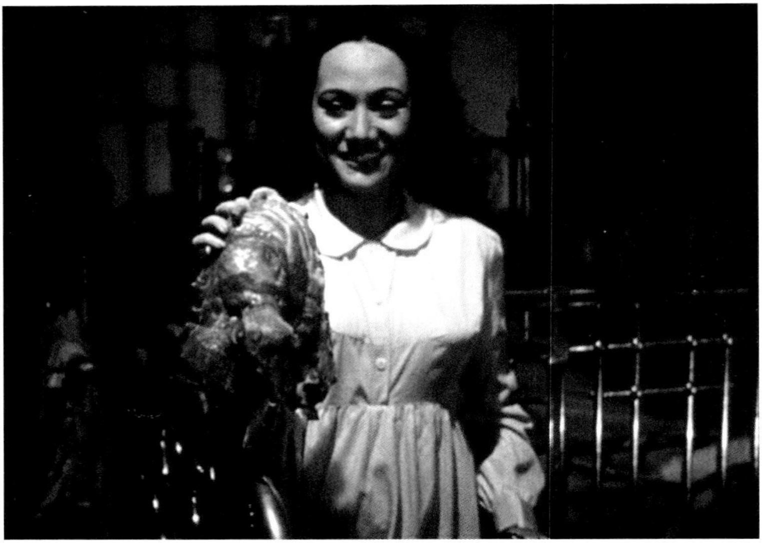

Pedro's mother offers him meat in a dream in *Los olvidados.*

transparency, the use of the motif of blocking and concealment suggests that other factors are at work in Buñuel's film. El Jaibo conceals the rock he will use to kill Julian in a sling. When El Jaibo has to flee from the police, he chooses to hide away in a disused slum by the railways. When Pedro is caught up to by El Jaibo, the latter emerges from his hiding place in the shadows.

Pointing in a similar direction, the dwellings inhabited by the various people in the story – Meche, Carmelo – are always depicted in semi-darkness. This could be an example of verisimilitude (the houses of the lower classes in the 1950s in Mexico City did not enjoy the luxury of electricity) but it is remarkable how consistently Buñuel chooses to depict interiors as dark and threatening, so much so that it becomes a leitmotif of the film. As Deleuze suggests, Buñuel 'injects the power of repetition into the cinematographic image'.[29] Thus the overwhelming nocturnal atmosphere of *Los olvidados* has striking parallels with those films noirs of the late 1940s – precisely the years when Buñuel was in Hollywood prior to going to Mexico – in which the city is a 'place of crime, corruption, and darkness', *The Big Sleep* (1946), *The Killers* (1946) and *Out of the Past* (1947) being classics of the genre.[30] What is so original about Buñuel's rewriting of the film noir trope is that he took its vocabulary of darkness and violence, but at the same time avoided the urban anomie of the prototype, instead tying his vision specifically to Mexico City, which is recognizable in all the location shots. As Michael Wood suggests, 'Like Godard's Paris, Buñuel's Mexico City is permanently being built.'[31] This darkness is also expressed concretely in Carmelo's physical blindness.

The ambiguity of the use of the blindness motif is suggested in the scene towards the end of the film where Pedro attacks his peers in the reform school and subsequently, out of frustration, two hens. It is at this point that the viewer realizes that the cycle of violence has passed from one generation to the next and, furthermore, that Pedro cannot escape El Jaibo's evil influence. An unusual feature of this scene occurs when the camera lens is suddenly brought into focus and gets splattered by the egg yolk hurled angrily at it by Pedro. Marcel Oms describes this scene in terms of aggression against bourgeois perceptions of reality.[32] It can also legitimately be seen as that juncture when the subaltern attempts to destroy the control that the camera-eye exerts over the characters' lives, breaking down the system whereby art produces scopophilic pleasure, allowing, just for a moment, the violence of the subaltern to be expressed precisely because it fights against disclosure. There is thus a tension operating within *Los olvidados* whereby it mimics the positivistic essentialism of the sociologist who exposes poverty on a superficial scale, while simultaneously hinting that the consciousness of the subaltern will always remain hidden, even when it is being disclosed.[33]

Eisenstein's *¡Que viva México!* and Luis Buñuel's *Los olvidados* set down the foundation on which later cineastes would build. Despite Hennebelle and Gumucio-Dagrón's suggestion that, for example, 'Mexican cinema was unable to assimilate the cardinal virtues of Buñuel's work', these early filmic experiments were important for the creation of later films.[34] They became the bedrock in which Latin American film directors would thrive.

2

Nuevo Cine Latinoamericano and the 'Time-image' (1951–1975)

The European 'antibody'

After the Second World War, Europe developed new cinematic 'anti-bodies' which counteracted Hollywood's dominance. European avant-garde film, particularly Italian neo-Realism and the French New Wave, inspired a new type of cinema in Latin America, the so-called Nuevo Cine Latinoamericano (New Latin American Cinema). In the new formula of neo-Realism,[1] film directors turned for inspiration to everyday reality, they shot 'on location', used non-professional actors, and their films – Roberto Rossellini's *Roma, città aperta* ('Open City', 1945), Luchino Visconti's *La terra trema* ('The Earth Trembles', 1945) and Vittorio De Sica's *Ladri di biciclette* ('Bicycle Thieves', 1948) – had an edgy, documentary feel about them. Following hard on the heels of Italian neo-Realism came the French New Wave. André Bazin crystallized the key concept of the movement when he coined, in 1948, the term *caméra-stylo* ('camera-pen') to describe the role of the film director, who was seen more as a creative writer than camera technician. Centred around the influential film review *Cahiers du Cinéma*, founded in 1951, a new concept of the film director was born, christened *la politique des auteurs* ('auteurs' policy'), according to which film was seen as a medium bearing the personal imprint, or signature, of the film director's world view.[2] A landmark year for the movement was 1959: François Truffaut's *Les Quatre cents coups* ('The Four Hundred Blows') and Alain Resnais' *Hiroshima, mon amour* ('Hiroshima, my Love') came out, and Jean-Luc Godard's *À bout de souffle* ('Breathless') was released the following year. Seemingly overnight, a new cinematic style had come into being; relying on location shooting with hand-held cameras, as well as elliptical editing favouring the long take and composition-in-depth, the French New Wave constituted a radical departure from the action-image then favoured by Hollywood.

The transition from documentary to feature film

A clear line of artistic descent can be traced from Italian neo-Realism to Cuba, as evident in the early careers of two important Cuban filmmakers, Julio García Espinosa and Tomás Gutiérrez Alea.

Following García Espinosa's lead, Gutiérrez Alea (often known by his nickname, Titón) decided in the early 1950s to travel to Rome to enrol on a course at the Centro Sperimentale di Cinematografia which, at the time, was a hotbed for neo-Realist filmmaking as well as theory. Alea described his experience in a letter to German Puig, dated 22 November 1951: his studies were 'impressive and comprehensive'; he had started his film exercises in earnest and had met Vittorio De Sica.[3] Having access to luminaries of the time such as Vittorio De Sica, whose *Ladri di biciclette*, which had been released only three years before in 1948 and which had established Italian neo-Realism as a thriving new filmic genre, was clearly inspirational for the young Cuban film enthusiast. Together Gutiérrez Alea and Julio García Espinosa learned how to create cinema in Italy, and they took this new-found knowledge back with them to Cuba.

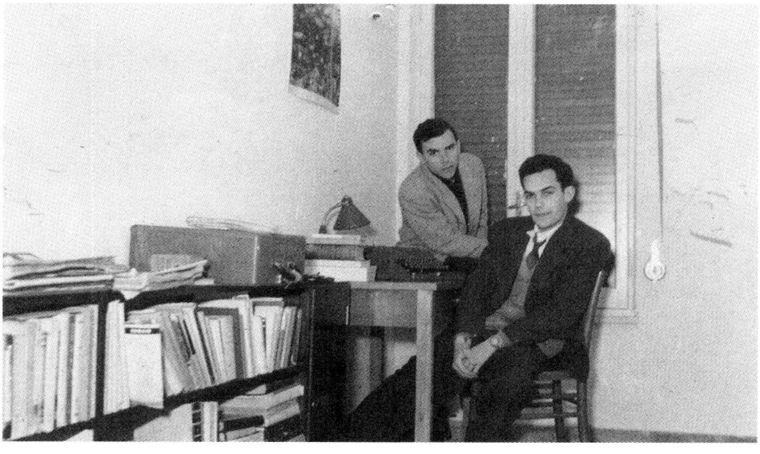

Julio García Espinosa with fellow filmmaker Titón in Rome in the early 1950s.

Shortly after their return to Cuba, Gutiérrez Alea and García Espinosa collaborated on a documentary film, *El Mégano*, based on the working lives of charcoal workers in the marshlands of Ciénaga to the south of Havana. The film is intriguing because it mixes observational documentary – for example, the depiction of the removal of the wood from the river, its transport to the charcoal ovens, the burning of the wood, the shacks that the workers live in – with fiction, in the sense that the film dramatizes a conflict between the landowner and the workers who decide to rebel as a result of their exploitation, as expressed by the worker who calls a meeting to say that the situation cannot go on, and who screws up the paper in his hand at the conclusion of the film.[4]

The film was released in 1955 and, though it was a documentary rather than a feature film, it bore the hallmark of neo-Realism in its depiction of everyday reality, of poverty among the disadvantaged classes, and its use of non-professional actors. Soon after being screened at the University of Havana, the film came to the attention of the Servicio de Inteligencia Militar of Batista's government; it was impounded by the military and García Espinosa was held in custody. He was told to hand in the film within 24 hours.[5] He and Titón, concerned that they would lose the film for ever, went to deposit it at the Asociación de Críticos de Radio, Televisión y Cine (ACRTC), thinking it would be safe there. But they were wrong. When García Espinosa went to see Colonel Castaño,

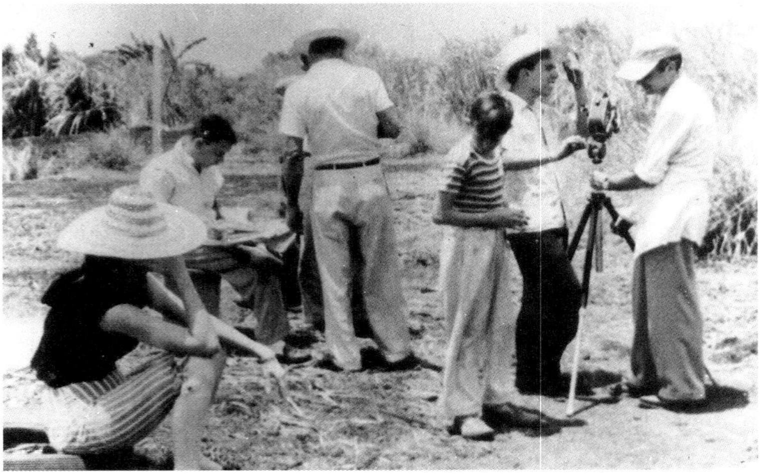

García Espinosa with the cameraman Jorge Haydú (Alfredo Guevara is sitting down) on the set of *El Mégano* (1955).

Workers battling through the swamps in *El Mégano* (1955).

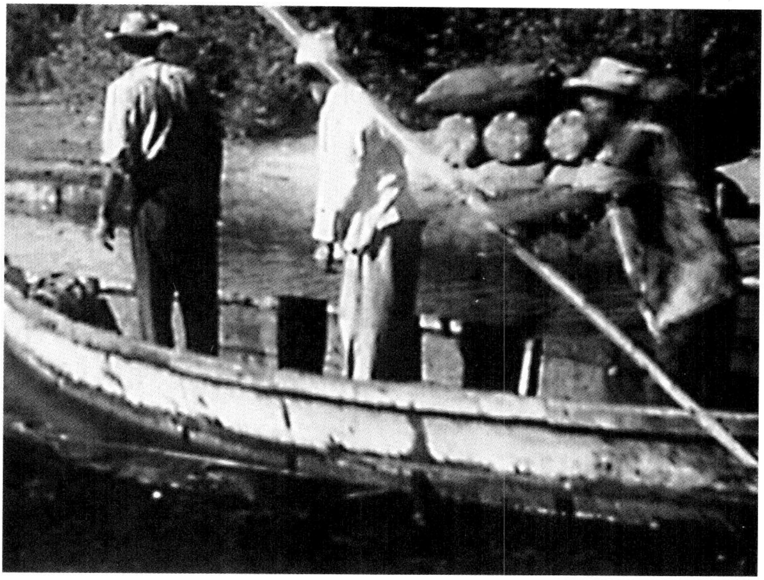

he refused to accept the excuse that the film had been left at the ACRTC, and demanded it be handed over to the military authorities. García Espinosa had no choice and he deposited the film within 24 hours.[6] With the benefit of hindsight it is now clear that *El Mégano* was the blueprint for the politicized formula of filmmaking which would come to fruition in the post-1959 film produced in Cuba with a transparent political ideology.

Cuba was not the only place where these new ideas, inspired by Italian neo-Realism, were taking root. An important new voice in documentary film emerged in Argentina in 1958 with the release of Fernando Birri's *Tire dié*, which is now recognized as one of the classics of Latin American documentary. Along with García Espinosa's *El Mégano* (1955), this work set a mould for Latin American cinema which departed sharply from the Hollywood-inspired films dominating the viewer's imagination in the 1950s, both in the United States and elsewhere. The most important difference is that we are exposed in this film to the have-nots of society, the people normally forgotten by the silver screen, or sometimes domesticated in order to make them palatable for discreet consumption. This is a gritty documentary with a social message, shot

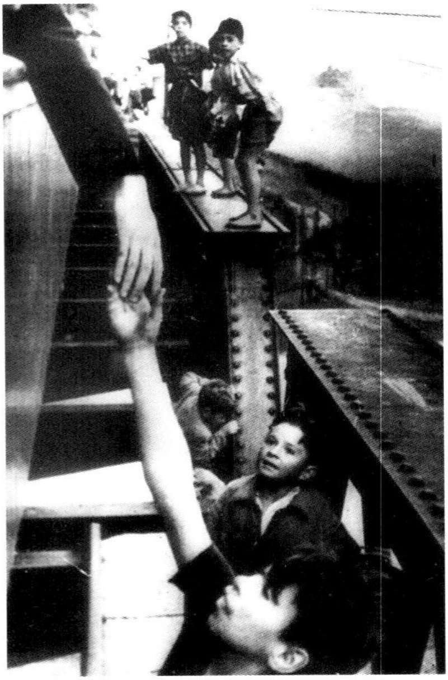

The destitute children in Fernando Birri's *Tire dié* (1958).

with a hand-held camera. It is not entertainment. Following in Brecht's footsteps, *Tire dié* evokes a distancing effect with regard to its viewers, making us think rather than cry. It is reality rather than fiction. Nevertheless, it does use some of the stock-in-trade of the feature film (the use of suspense, for example, since we have to wait until two-thirds of the way through the film before the train finally appears).

The voice-over often takes over a few seconds after we hear the interviewees begin to speak. This is because the original recording was too imperfect for professional use, as Birri has himself acknowledged. This might be seen as a defect of the film, but alternatively it could be seen as an early example of what García Espinosa would later define as Latin America's 'imperfect cinema'; that is, cinema which was not as glossy or as well filmed or as well produced as a standard Hollywood film, but which nevertheless was able to make an important social point despite its material and technical imperfections. Indeed, some would argue that the signifier of the celluloid is making just such a point. Its poverty is a concrete image of Latin America's poverty. A slick image would have defeated the point.

Birri creates contrast and conflict by having the government rhetoric and bird's-eye shot of Santa Fe contrast poignantly with the down-to-earth reality of the inhabitants of the *barriadas* near the railway line. He gives us the names of the people he interviews, refusing to allow them to become statistics. A true documentarist, he allows us to see the material culture that envelops them, how they earn their money, the shacks where they live. He uses suspense effectively, only allowing the train to arrive when the scene has very deliberately been set. He allows the social message to evolve from the events filmed and the words spoken by the protagonists rather than in the clumsy overlay of a narrator. The voice-over is either used ironically (such as during the opening aerial views of the city) or it is there to transcribe what the protagonists say. Birri does not talk; he lets reality speak for itself.

Perhaps most importantly, the documentary has a clear direction; it sets the scene, builds up a contrast, interviews a set of protagonists, stays on message (how the train dominates their lives), moves towards a climax (the entry of the train) and then allows the story to wind down as the train is seen departing. There are some nicely framed mood shots of children running towards the train, running along the bridge structure, and lots of energy in the footage of the children running alongside the train. There are also some impressive ideological montage shots, such as when the children picking through the trash are compared visually with the pigs eating slops, inevitably prompting comparison with the leftovers (the coins) that the children pick off the floor. The main message is that these children and the community to which they belong are the forgotten, undocumented underbelly of Argentine society, a group the government and the middle classes would prefer to ignore. One of the protagonists says: '*mentira el gobierno*' ('government lies'). This is the main message of the film. But it is made obliquely through realities rather than through commentary. Given the fact that there are so many close-ups of the children as they watch the train depart, it gradually dawns on the viewer that we are the ones in the train, the spectators of this poverty; we are the ones who have paid a dime to see this social spectacle, the voyeurs of this pain.

It is arguable that many of these experiments – for experiments they were – would have disappeared without trace were it not for a political event that changed the face of Latin American politics forever. The Cuban Revolution of 1959 provided a new political horizon in

Latin America. Régis Debray has argued, for example, that the Cuban Revolution was, in effect, a 'revolution in the revolution'.[7] As Robert Young has suggested, it brought about

> a fundamental break with the increasingly bankrupt role of bureaucratic communist parties controlled by Moscow and the achievement of a new form of socialism founded on the revolutionary agency of local people, in the first instance the peasantry rather than the urban proletariat . . . The Cuban Revolution showed that a different sort of revolution was possible.[8]

As one of the intellectual leaders of the Cuban Revolution, Che Guevara, suggested, Marxism was now to be seen as a political philosophy based on the human: 'It was love of man, of humanity, the desire to combat the distress of the proletariat, the desire to fight poverty, injustice, suffering, and all the exploitation of the proletariat, that gave rise to Marxism.'[9]

The Cuban Revolution was, indeed, to have a far-reaching effect on the evolution of cinematic language in Latin America. Fidel Castro followed Lenin's line that cinema is 'the most important of the arts' and established the Instituto Cubano del Arte e Industria Cinematográficos (ICAIC, Cuban Film Institute). As a state-funded cultural institution it helped formulate a new image of Latin American reality, one which was specifically not constrained by the ideological baggage of colonialism. The Cuban Film Institute brought together a number of key cultural figures, including Tomás Gutiérrez Alea, Julio García Espinosa and others such as Humberto Solás, Alfredo Guevara and Enrique Colina. Following the Soviet model, it used documentaries to educate the masses, producing what was in effect transculturated agitprop, but it was also involved in promoting the Cuban film industry. Octavio Cortázar remembers how in 1966 in Imías, a small town in the southeast of Cuba, he saw a group of farm labourers, many of them on horseback, watching a Charlie Chaplin film in the 'transportable cinema' (*unidad de cine móvil*) set up there, an event which persuaded him to make his own documentary, *Por primera vez* ('For the First Time').[10]

García Espinosa, for his part, has described what the situation was like in pre-Revolutionary Cuba; the Hollywood film industry called the shots:

The founders of the ICAIC in the 1960s.

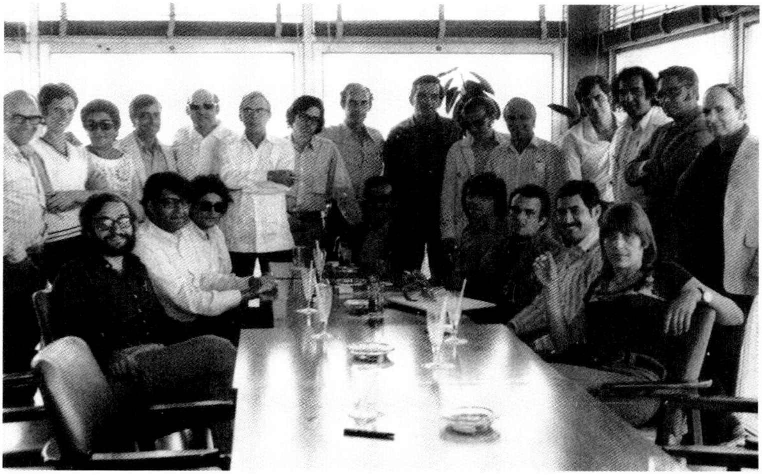

> If we wanted one of their hits they would force us to take nine other films of lower quality. The glossy-produced films with big budgets were always put in the best cinemas, so Latin American films screened in the less well-kept theatres. The public therefore assumed their own films were inherently inferior.[11]

After the Revolution, however, García Espinosa and his colleagues informed the Hollywood studios that they would be showing more Latin American and Cuban films than previously: 'The studios said that we were forcing films on the public that they didn't want to see and that cinema attendance would fall. This didn't happen. Attendances stayed the same. We broke the myth.'[12]

The first feature films produced by ICAIC were directed by García Espinosa and Titón, because they were the only two with any concrete experience of filmmaking – *Historias de la Revolución* ('Stories of the Revolution') by Titón, and *Cuba baila* ('Cuba Dances', 1960) by García Espinosa.[13] Both Titón and García Espinosa made these films in order to provide a template for other aspiring filmmakers of the time. There was no time to set up a school formally. The young film directors had to learn on the job in order to record the reality that was unfolding before their eyes. *Cuba baila* was the first feature film produced by ICAIC. Set in Cuba's pre-Revolutionary era, it tells the story of the trials and

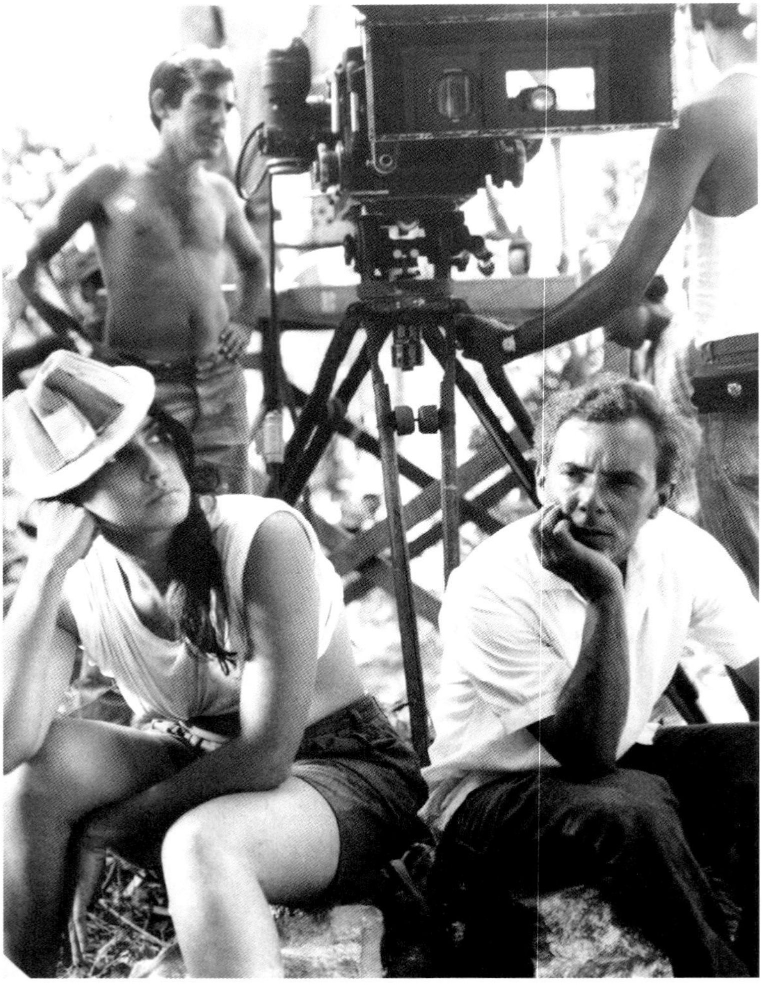

García Espinosa on set in Cuba with his wife, Adelaida Raymat.

tribulations suffered by a married couple, Ramón and Flora, who are desperate to keep up with the Joneses by holding a lavish *quinceañera* party for their daughter, Marcia.[14]

Some of the lessons learned through the film-making of García Espinosa, Gutiérrez Alea and Birri spilled over into the rest of Latin America. In Brazil a group of young film directors and theorists coalesced around a journal, *Metropolitano*, which was modelled on Bazin's *Cahiers du Cinéma*. Indeed, one of the first signs of the dawn of a truly independent Latin American cinema emerged in Brazil in the early 1960s in the form of its so-called Cinema Novo (New Cinema). Brazilian 'New Cinema' also drew inspiration from Italian neo-Realism and the French New Wave. Low-budget, independent films were shot on location with non-professional actors, in an attempt to encapsulate a new, authentically Brazilian *politique des auteurs* which pointedly flew in the face of the *chanchada*, memorably dismissed by Glauber Rocha as 'Public Enemy No. 1'.[15] Films such as *Ganga dumba* (1963) by Carlos Diegues, *Deus e o diabo na terra do sol* ('Black God, White Devil', 1964) and *Terra em Transe* ('Land in Anguish', 1967) by Glauber Rocha, *Os fuzis* ('The Guns', 1964) by Ruy Guerra and *Vidas secas* ('Barren Lives', 1963) and *Fome de amor* ('Hunger for Love', 1968) by Nelson Pereira dos Santos, were recognized as independent, autochthonous versions of Latin American reality. Though initially inspired by contemporary European films, Cinema Novo had more of a political edge for, as Diegues scornfully observed: 'We were making political films when the New Wave was still talking about unrequited love.'[16] Perhaps just as importantly, the film directors were keen to theorize about what they were doing; Diegues, Rocha and Pereira dos Santos were, in effect, producing meta-film just as much as film. Rocha's famous phrase, '*uma idéia na cabeça e uma câmera na mão*' ('an idea in your head and a camera in your hand'), became almost a leitmotif of the times.

Deus e o diabo na terra do sol (1964, directed by Glauber Rocha), which won the International Review Prize in Cannes, is a powerful film. Set in the 1940s it tells the story of a ranch hand, Manuel (Geraldo Del Rey), who explodes when his boss tries to cheat him of his earnings; he kills him and escapes with his wife, Rosa (Yoná Magalhães). Now an outlaw, Manuel joins up with a self-proclaimed saint who condones violence; some of the (unadorned) torture scenes which ensue are gut-wrenching. Rosa also turns to killing and, at the conclusion of the film, the pair are seen fleeing from the law. Drawing upon the struggle between the state and the *sertanejos*, which occurred at the end of the nineteenth century and which was at the heart of Da Cunha's classic work *Os Sertões* ('The Devil to Pay in the Backlands'), *Deus e o diabo na terra do sol* is a meditation on the never-ending struggle between two cultural options, offering a pessimistic vision of whether these two cultural lifestyles can ever be harmonized within state discourse.

The film came out in 1964, the year of the Brazilian coup engineered by Governor José de Magalhães Pinto of Minas Gerais state and Marshal Humberto de Alencar Castelo Branco, chief of staff of the army. Though the film is cast in the past anterior it also allegorizes the contemporaneous political rift which had been occurring in Brazil since the early 1960s between the military and the 'communist infiltration'. That conflict is best understood in the light of Rocha's theory of 'Uma estetica da Fome' (1967). Rocha argued:

> Cinema Novo teaches that the aesthetics of violence are revolutionary rather than primitive. The moment of violence is the moment when the colonizer becomes aware of the existence of the colonized. Only when he is confronted by violence can the colonizer understand, through horror, the strengths of the culture he exploits.[17]

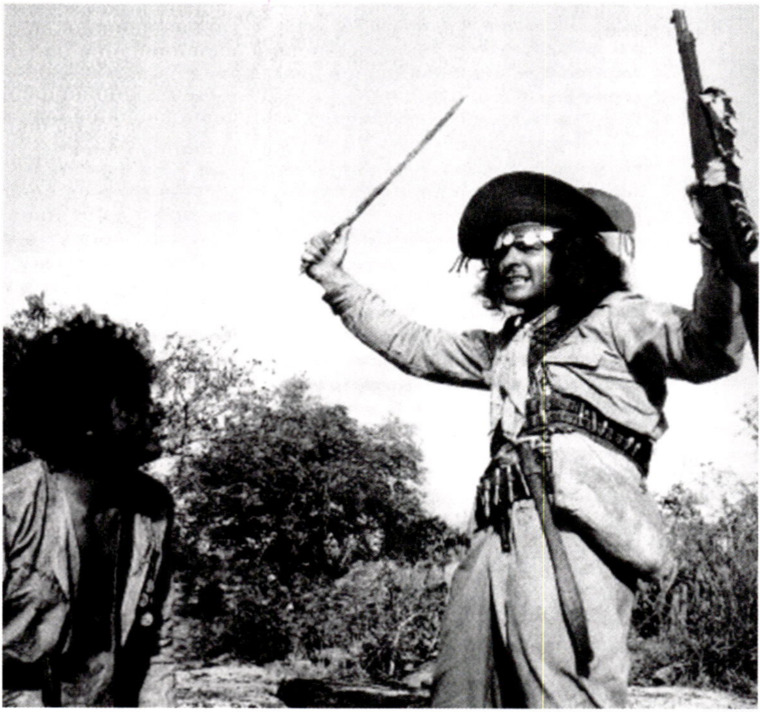

Manuel in Glauber Rocha's *Deus e o diabo na terra do sol* (1964).

In his essay Rocha argues that Latin America's colonized status leads to mutual miscomprehension in the relationship between Brazil and its colonizers, to formalist exoticisms which vulgarize social problems. This leads Brazilian art to be, as he argues, either sterile or hysterical. It is sterile when it attempts to ape the soi-disant universalism of Western art, when it creates official art, monsters created by university discourse. It is hysterical when it expresses social indignation about Brazil's subaltern status; but here it often descends into political sectarianism and pornographic anarchism.

Rocha rejects both sterility and hysteria, advocating the aesthetics of hunger, which forces the colonizing powers to watch people eating earth, killing in order to eat, fleeing in order to eat, miserabilism rather than watching rich bourgeois people eating well in São Paulo. New Cinema is therefore an attack on 'digestive cinema', on cinema as entertainment. This hunger and this ugliness in Cinema Novo is only understood as a tropical surrealism by Europeans, and provokes a sense of shame in Brazilians. The New Brazilian Cinema's aesthetics of violence is revolutionary in that it is only by raising consciousness about its violence that Latin America can make colonizers understand, 'via horror', to use Rocha's words, the strength of the culture they exploit. Rocha's depiction of the *sertão* in *Deus e o diabo na terra do sol* proved itself to be a benchmark motif of subsequent Brazilian film.[18]

A film released in the same year as *Deus e o diabo na terra do sol*, but which had none of its immediate impact, was *Soy Cuba* ('I Am Cuba'), directed by Mikhail Kalatozov (1964; script by Enrique Pineda Barnet), now considered a classic on the Cuban Revolution, especially because of Sergey Urusevsky's cinematography. The plot is straightforward enough, with the first two sections describing oppression in pre-Revolutionary Cuba and the last two portraying the people's rebellion against Batista. Part I tells the story of María who, despite her love for her Cuban fruitseller boyfriend, Rene, has to prostitute herself in a nightclub full of rich Americans. Part II is about a sugar cane farmer, Pedro, who is told that his land has been sold to the United Fruit Company; in desperation he sets fire to the crops and his house. Part III shows the Revolution exploding at the University of Havana while in Part IV the rebellion reaches fever pitch in the Sierra Maestra. The ordinariness of the plot is at odds with the extraordinarily virtuoso camerawork. In one continuous long take

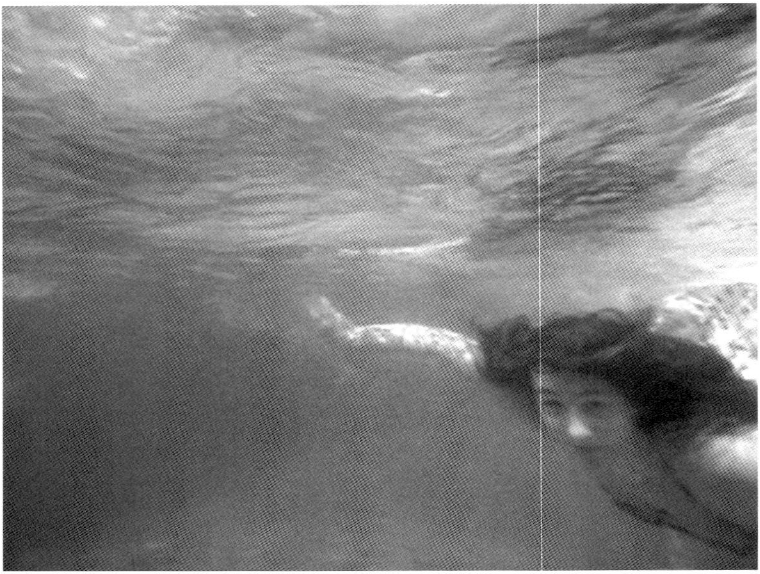

The camera goes underwater in *Scy Cuba* (1964).

early on in the film the hand-held camera records a beauty contest taking place in the Hotel Nacional and then descends slowly down one side of the building until it ends up in the swimming pool and then drops below the surface of the water to film a bathing beauty. In Part III, the camera moves at street level through the funeral procession of a student, Enrique, who was shot by the police, and then ascends to the top of the building and 'floats' between two buildings, moving among some tobacco workers before exiting through a window to witness the scenes of mourning below – the camera appears to be flying. The film uses infrared film provided by the Soviet military,[19] and this provides sharp contrasts between whites and blacks, particularly in the landscape shots. Occasionally this contrast is enhanced by movement. In Part II, when Pedro begins to set fire to the sugar cane the camera begins to swivel round jerkily and a blur of slashing machete knife strokes is thereby created.

But perhaps the most extraordinary feature of *Soy Cuba* is the use of a wide-angle convex lens which makes foreground objects more striking while maintaining focus for distant objects. Combined with some of the crane shots and the infrared photography, the effect created is one of abnormal distance from the phenomenal world, as if it were seen for the

The camera hovers in the air above the funeral cortège in *Soy Cuba.*

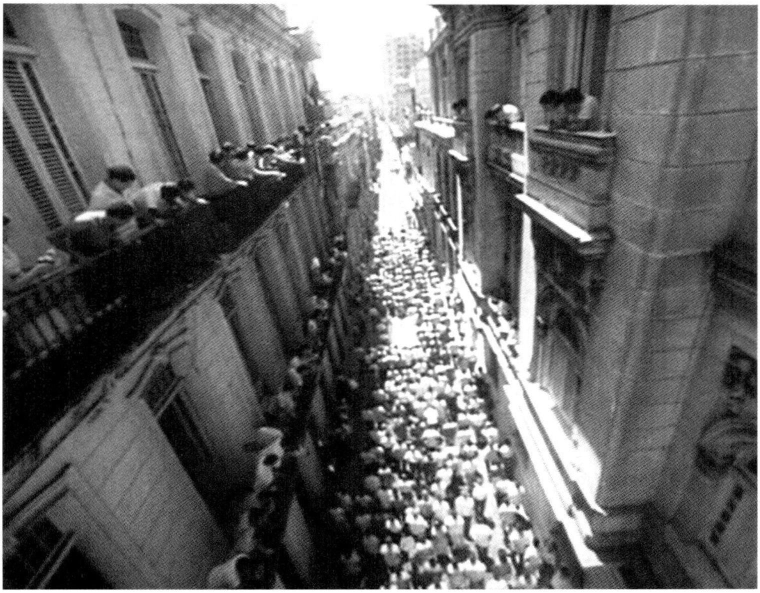

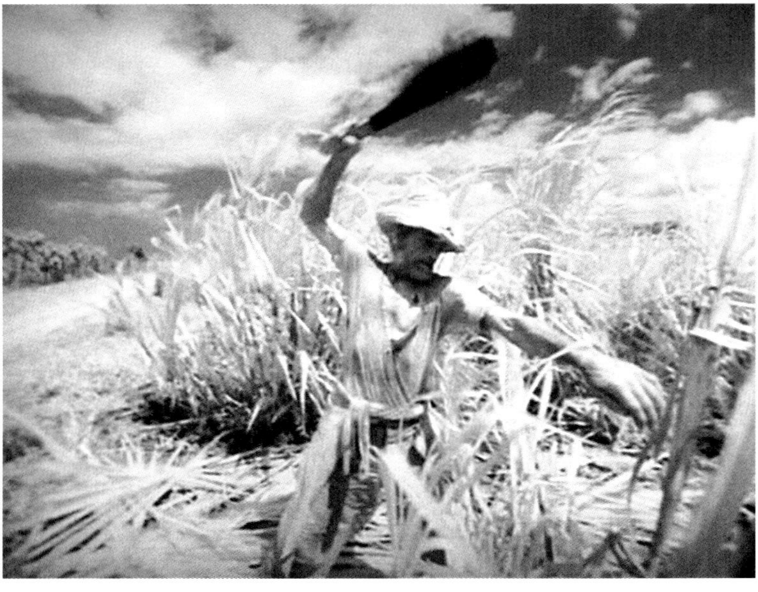

The sugar cane worker rebels against social injustice in *Soy Cuba.*

first time, thereby echoing the Formalist technique of 'ostranenie'. Occasionally the frame is tilted. The combination of cinematographic techniques such as these – ranging from the tilted frame to the floating camera – leads to uncertainty about where the ground is and unsettles the viewer. A tour de force, *Soy Cuba* was rejected when released in 1964 by Cubans for its simplistic portrayal of Cuban oppression and by Soviet audiences because of its empathy with pre-Revolutionary Cuba, but was re-launched as a result of the enthusiastic support of directors such as Martin Scorsese and Francis Ford Coppola who saw it when it was screened at the 1993 San Francisco Film Festival, and subsequently promoted as a 'forgotten classic'. Perhaps more importantly, *Soy Cuba* should be seen as the missing link of Cuban cinema; it taught the hero of *Memorias del subdesarrollo*, Sergio Corrieri, how to act, and the film equipment – which included not only cameras but also a crane – brought to Cuba by Mikhail Kalatozov, was left in Cuba after filming was completed and was subsequently put to good use by ICAIC's budding film directors, one of whom was Tomás Gutiérrez Alea.[20]

Nuevo Cine Latinoamericano: theory and praxis

One of the most distinctive features of the Nuevo Cine Latinoamericano was its theoretical underpinning. For their part, Fernando Solanas and Octavio Getino, in an important manifesto, 'Towards a Third Cinema', advocated a new cinema which threw off the shackles of colonial oppression both in ideological and industrial terms and, in the process, they became important spokesmen for anti-colonialist film directors all around the world:

> The anti-imperialist struggle of the peoples of the Third World and of their equivalents inside the imperialist countries constitutes today the axis of the world revolution. *Third cinema* is, in our opinion, the cinema that *recognises in that struggle the most gigantic cultural, scientific, and artistic manifestation of our time*, the great possibility of constructing a liberated personality with each people as the starting point – in a word, the decolonisation of culture.[21]

A more vivid catchword, perhaps, than 'third cinema' was 'imperfect cinema', a term coined by the Cuban film director, Julio García Espinosa in 1969. In a wide-ranging essay, 'For an Imperfect Cinema', García Espinosa contrasted the gritty, more realist cinema emerging from Cuba with the slick, commercially effective but ideologically barren film coming out of Hollywood:

> Imperfect cinema is no longer interested in quality or technique. It can be created equally well with a Mitchell or with an 8mm camera, in a studio or in a guerrilla camp in the middle of the jungle. Imperfect cinema is no longer interested in predetermined taste, and much less in 'good taste'. It is not quality which it seeks in an artist's work. The only thing it is interested in is how an artist responds to the following question: What are you doing in order to overcome the barrier of the 'cultured' elite audience which up to now has conditioned the form of your work?[22]

Just as radical was the theoretical position taken up by the Bolivian film director, Jorge Sanjinés. In a concise and punchy essay, 'Problems of Form and Content in Revolutionary Cinema', Sanjinés rejected the ideology and content of imperialism and advocated a cinema which is revolutionary, collective and people-centred: 'Revolutionary cinema, as it reaches maturity, can only be collective, just as the revolution itself is collective.'[23] Latin American Film gradually began to play a central role in the evolution of a new concept of Third World Film during the 1960s and 1970s.

In his essay 'Cinema and Underdevelopment', Birri, for example, argued that underdevelopment is an intrinsic part of the fabric of Latin American culture, that it is caused by colonialism and that – up until then, namely, the 1960s – cinema inevitably shared the characteristics of this superstructure ('it presents us with a false image of both society, and our people').[24] Birri therefore called for a new type of documentary which would reverse this representational paradigm: 'It shows matters as they irrefutably are, and not as we would like them to be (or as, in good or bad faith, others would like to make us believe them to be).'[25] The Brazilian film director Glauber Rocha, in his essay 'The Aesthetics of Hunger', which has already been alluded to, argued from a similar postcolonial viewpoint ('Latin America remains a colony') to propose that Latin America is therefore characterized by 'philosophical undernourishment' and 'impotence'. As Rocha went on to suggest:

> It is for this reason that hunger in Latin America is not simply an alarming symptom; it is the essence of our society. Herein lies the tragic originality of Cinema Novo in relation to world cinema. Our originality is our hunger and our greatest misery is that this hunger is felt but not intellectually understood.[26]

A number of the essays published by Latin American film directors at the time sang from the same hymn sheet; they rejected the colonization of Latin America, whether by the multinationals or by the film industry, and advocated a radical de-colonization of Latin American reality. Perhaps just as importantly, they refused to examine film in isolation from its political context. Film, for the cineastes of the Nuevo Cine Latinoamericano, is always political.

With hindsight it is now clear that the various film festivals organized in the late 1960s were crucial to the formation of a sense of Latin American cultural identity, beginning with the Viña del Mar, Chile, festival held in 1967, followed by the festival in Mérida, Venezuela, in 1968, and then back again in Viña del Mar in 1969. At the time these were new venues for Latin American film directors to present their work, and they encouraged other budding film directors to try their luck. It soon became clear that Latin American film directors had something new to say, something which was intrinsic to their culture, which was recognized as different by Europeans, and – much more importantly – was understood by Latin Americans as expressing something fundamentally different about the way life was lived in the southern continent of the Americas.

Arguably, the most important film of the New Latin American Cinema was Gutiérrez Alea's *Memorias del subdesarrollo* ('Memories of Underdevelopment'). Whereas the majority of the films associated with Nuevo Cine Latinoamericano were revolutionary in terms of their politics but less innovative when it came to their filmic language, Gutiérrez Alea's film embodied revolution in both its use of media and in its politics. After his experience working on *El Mégano*, Gutiérrez Alea had decided that film was where his future lay. The revolution of 1959 allowed that desire to come to fruition since he was one of the individuals 'commissioned' by ICAIC to create a number of documentaries about the new social reality which the revolution was creating. But it was with *Memorias del subdesarrollo* that his work made an international impact. There were, of course, a number of techniques in this film which could be traced back to Gutiérrez Alea's apprenticeship in neo-Realism, including the use of the street as the set (evident in a number of the scenes in which the protagonist Sergio [Sergio Corrieri] meets and seduces Elena [Daisy Granados]), and the use of a hand-held camera (this is used to most striking effect in the bedroom scene in which Sergio 'hunts' Elena in a sequence leading up to her sexual conquest).

But there were also a number of scenes in the film which demonstrated that Titón was not simply revamping the Italian blueprint but instead reformulating its DNA in order to bring out new aspects which were more relevant and more appropriate for the Cuban national context. Thus Titón began evolving a new type of cinematic discourse in which documentary footage could be integrated into the fictional narrative of a feature film. The aim was to intensify and enhance the sense of the historicism of the narrative; it was a new technique absent from the original neo-Realist formula, but which went in the same historicizing direction. There are a number of these sequences in *Memorias del subdesarrollo*, the most significant relating to the narrative of the CIA-supported invasion of the Bay of Pigs, and including the film relating to the trials which occurred afterwards, as well as the documentary footage of the militarization of Havana, which occured as a result of the Missile Crisis of 1962.

Deleuze has identified neo-Realism as the point of crisis for classical cinema, and this crisis was expressed in five new characteristics of the image: 'the dispersive situation, the deliberately weak links, the voyage form, the consciousness of clichés, the condemnation of the plot. It is the crisis of both the action-image and the American Dream.'[27] What now defined neo-Realism was a build-up of 'purely optical situations (and sound ones, although there was no synchronized sound at the start of neo-realism), which are fundamentally distinct from the sensory-motor situations of the action-image in the old realism. It is perhaps as important as the conquering of a purely optical space in painting, with impressionism.'[28] This revolution of the 'optical space' had implications for the role of the protagonist in neo-Realist films:

> The character has become a kind of viewer. He shifts, runs and becomes animated in vain, the situation he is in outstrips his motor capacities on all sides, and makes him see and hear what is no longer subject to the rules of a response or an action. He records rather than reacts. He is prey to a vision, pursued by it or pursuing it, rather than engaged in an action.[29]

This also had implications for the relationship between the character in the neo-Realist film and his surroundings, for 'it is no longer a motor extension which is established, but rather a dreamlike connection through the intermediary of the liberated sense organs. It is as if the action floats in the situation, rather than bringing it to a conclusion or strengthening it.'[30] Finally, the neo-Realist film is one where, as Deleuze suggests, 'the character does not act without seeing himself acting, complicit viewer of the role he himself is playing'.[31]

It is not too far-fetched to argue that Deleuze's description of the typical protagonist of the neo-Realist film, in many respects, is a description of Sergio's dilemma as we witness the unfolding of his vision of the world in *Memorias del subdesarrollo*. Especially in the opening sequences of the film, Sergio's gaze appears to suggest that he is looking at Havana for the first time. He appears to be distanced, for example, from the experience of bidding his wife farewell, as if he were watching the event through the eyes of somebody else rather than himself. Sergio is a voyant rather than an actor and, as we discover later on, he appears even to be – to quote Deleuze's words – a 'complicit viewer of the role he himself is playing'.

Indeed Sergio is not only disconnected from space; he also appears to be disconnected from time. The title of the film, *Memorias del subdesarrollo*, alerts the viewer immediately to the fact that time is an intrinsic component of the experience recounted in the film. The first sequence – after the enigmatic establishing sequence in the nightclub when somebody gets shot, which actually does not establish anything – shows us Sergio at the airport bidding farewell to his wife and then on the bus going home. The idea of memory is instantiated when we suddenly see scenes from that recent past: we assume that Sergio is daydreaming on the bus and recreating in his mind what he has just experienced at Havana airport. This remembering of the past does not occur in a conventional sense –

for example, we perceive the character's eyes looking out of the window, then the frame dissolves, then we see the airport, which would be a paradigmatic way of introducing a memory of this kind. Rather, we are suddenly plunged into a remembered reality, and thus the present of the film (the reality we perceive when Sergio says goodbye at the airport) is suddenly revealed to be the past (Sergio is sitting on the bus remembering what his wife looked like when he said goodbye to her).

Or, is it? Is it the past as recollected via the present, or does the first sequence really happen prior to getting on the bus (in other words, Sergio just remembers a part of that recent experience)? The answer to this question is neither yes nor no; rather it is that the film thrives on this temporal ambiguity and, indeed, attempts to trick the reader into experiencing the present as the past and, by contrast, the past as the present. Indeed, this introduces a level of meta-cinema into the scene, since it foregrounds the present reality along with the act of remembering itself. It is possible to interpret the opening sequence as a set of disjointed flashbacks but, as the film subsequently demonstrates, Gutiérrez Alea's work deconstructs the performativity of the flashback and creates what Deleuze would call a 'time-image'; in other words, an image that simultaneously encapsulates time and reflects upon it. This is most obvious in the third section of the film. Sergio is walking around his Havana apartment overlooking the Malecón, recalling aspects of his relationship with his wife who has now departed for Miami. He goes through her drawers, reviewing her underwear, lipstick and clothes, while listening to her words as he recorded them at an unspecified time in the past. At one point he puts on her eyeglass and we see a frame of him wearing it.

Though the viewer has become accustomed during this third sequence of the film to the presence of Sergio's wife, this has only been through her voice; thus we 'experience' her aurally rather than visually. Suddenly, two seconds after putting on her eyeglass, we see her. As a result of this visual irruption of the past, the chronology of the scene is disturbed. Until this point the dividing line between the present and the past had been enunciated transparently. Sergio is in the present listening to the past as a result of operating a machine that had recorded his wife's voice. But this distinction is perturbed when we suddenly see a frame of the past – his wife adjusts her glasses to look back at him – and it is not clear how this memory of the past has emerged. Clearly, this is not a flashback in the sense of being a 'conventional extrinsic device', to use Deleuze's words. Were it a flashback the viewer would expect, if presented in conventional terms, an image of the past preceded by a dissolve frame indicating that the past will now emerge into the current narrative of the film. None of this happens. The film does not explain whether this frame is from Sergio's point of view, or POV shot (that is, a remembered POV) or a director's shot. While the viewer's first reaction is likely to be one of confusion, it is clear subsequently that Titón is attempting to allow the past to be experienced within the present of film, that is, inverting the normal protocol of film in which present is turned into past. Indeed, it is just as likely that this frame is an instantiation of the camera remembering its own past, as if the camera had become the protagonist of the film and could remember as if it possessed human agency.

The plot thickens two seconds later. Here the viewer sees a new frame in which we are back with Sergio who looks as if he is reacting to a fleeting glimpse of his wife. It is likely that a viewer without contextual knowledge would see this sequence as an example of the shot-reverse shot technique. The shot-reverse shot is a classic technique used in realist cinema, and characteristic of the action-image style. Typically it will occur in the present of the film when two people react to the signals of each other's face, which include speech as well as facial gesture, normally as part of a dialogue. And here we see Sergio, then his wife, then Sergio.

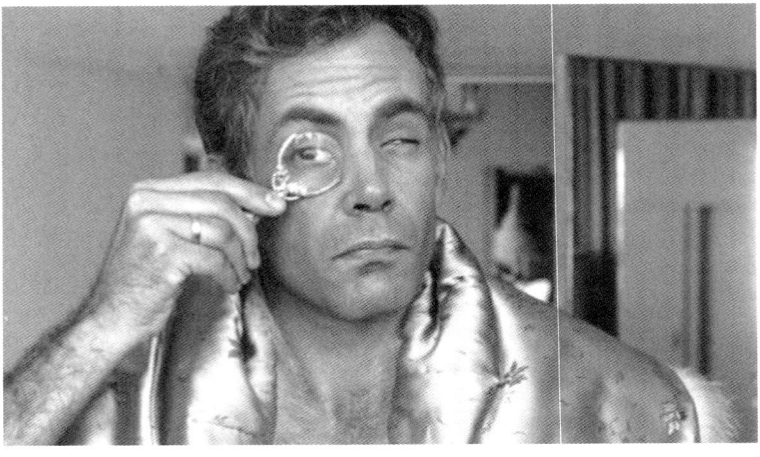

Time-image in *Memorias del subdesarrollo* (1968).

Time-image in *Memorias del subdesarrollo.*

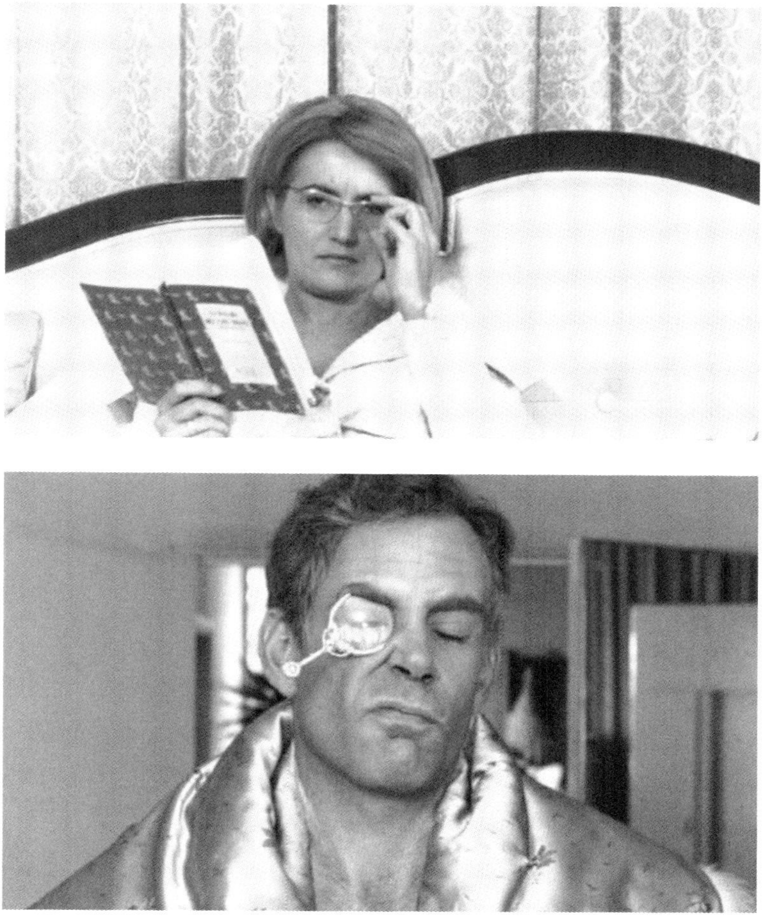

But the context already provided indicates to the viewer that this is an 'impossible' shot-reverse shot sequence since we saw Sergio's wife leaving for Miami in the first section of the film. This sequence, therefore, can only be a shot-reverse shot sequence in which the reverse shot is a memory of the past. It could not have occurred in one chronological sequence, and instead occurred in the space between present and past, as it were. Furthermore, to complicate things, it is not a recollection image or flashback such as we find, for example, in Hitchcock's *Vertigo*. It is a more dynamic, dialectical shuttling between past and present. Time has therefore entered the frame as a mediator of the shot-reverse shot sequence, and is in effect caught in dialectical suspension. The action image has been re-articulated to create a time-image, one in which time itself has been enunciated before the viewer's startled eyes. Titón has in effect used the time-image to create his own version of an algebra of memory, thereby adding a meta-cinematic patina to the image.

This meta-cinematic patina is evident in *Memorias del subdesarrollo*, not only on the level of the image but also on the level of plot and sequencing. Titón's film is, indeed, self-reflexive on a number of levels. In the round-table discussion about underdevelopment, for example, which Sergio attends with Elena, one of the round-table participants is Edmundo Desnoes, the author of the novel (*Inconsolable Memories*) on which the film is based. In effect, the film is playing with the difference between the real and the fictional, allowing one to feed into another in a way which is redolent of Pirandello's *Six Characters in Search of an Author*. Sergio is totally unconvinced by Desnoes's interventions, which shows a character 'standing up' to the individual who created him. The North American conferencee who stands up during the round-table debate and questions its effectiveness is none other than Jack Gelber, the author of the foreword to the English edition of the novel. Gelber is thus criticizing the book he helped to bring into being in English. This Unamunesque play of creator against the created is further complicated by the scene in which Sergio and Elena watch a series of risqué film clips with a film director at the Cuban Film Institute. The director concerned is none other than Titón himself. His subsequent comment to Sergio that he may well use the scenes in some concocted film later on is supremely ironic, since this is, after all, the film we – as viewers – are actually watching. These different scenes could all be interpreted as 'insider jokes' in which Titón is cocking a private snook at the audience, but they can also be seen as scenes in which Titón is drawing attention to the way in which art can reflect upon its origins, and 'recall' its own genesis.

The documentary *El chacal de Nahueltoro* (1969), directed by Chilean filmmaker Miguel Littín, told the story of Chile's first ever serial killer, José (or Jorge) del Carmen Valenzuela Torres, and it was an enormous success at the Second Festival of Latin American Film held in Viña del Mar in November 1969. A drifter, Valenzuela Torres, or the 'Jackal of

Nahueletoro', as he came to be known, had brutally clubbed to death a defenceless mother and her five children in Chillán in northern Chile in what was apparently a motiveless crime. News coverage of the event and the massive police search for him traumatized Chile at the time. Miguel Littín decided to reconstruct the tragedy using the documentary genre but he introduced some innovative twists. First, he allowed Valenzuela Torres to speak directly to the camera and, second, he used chronology creatively. There are basically four self-contained time worlds in Littín's documentary: (i) his early life as recounted in voice-over in confession mode; (ii) the reconstruction of the events leading up to the murder, along with the murder itself; (iii) his arrest, and abuse by the crowd; (iv) his life in prison after the trial in which he is sentenced to death, culminating in his execution. The film opens with a sequence depicting his arrest, and then tracks back into the events of his early childhood – recounted in voice-over – which are reconstructed up until the point of the murder. It takes up the narrative of the Jackal's life in prison during the period of rehabilitation, and concludes with his execution. During the narrative of his life, the film returns almost obsessively to the scene in which the Jackal is led away by police, signalled each time by the whine of the police siren. It is only at the end of the film when we see the Jackal being interviewed, making a final confession to a news reporter just before his execution, that we realize that the earlier reconstruction of his childhood was elicited at this point. The documentary, rather

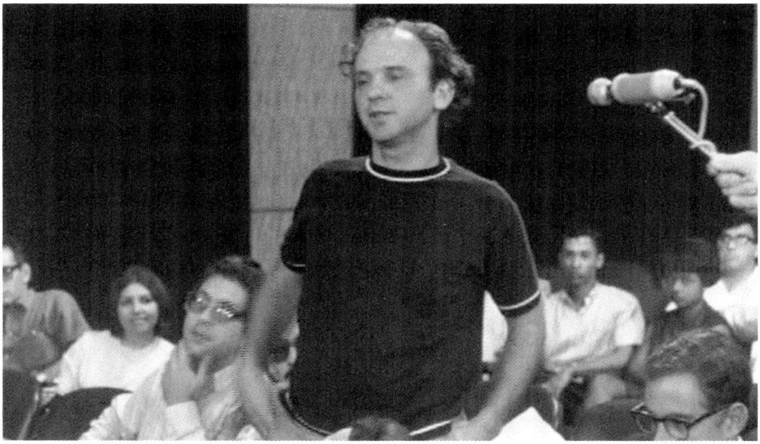

Jack Gelber, the U.S. translator of *Inconsolable Memories*, becomes a character in the film *Memorias del subdesarrollo*, which was based on the book he translated.

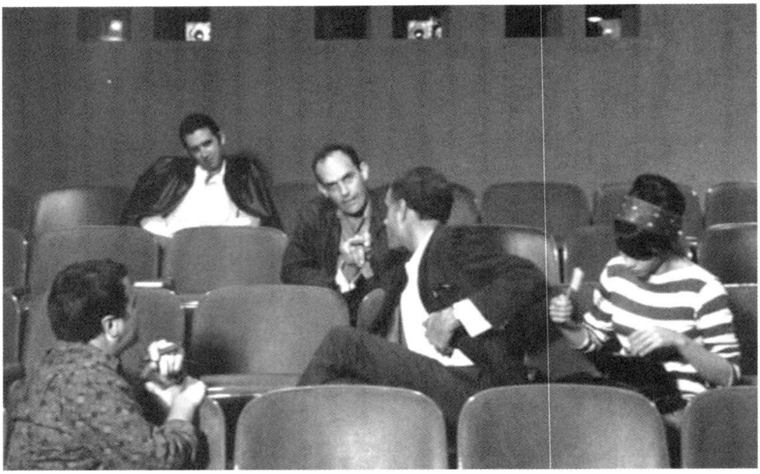

Sergio discusses film with the director of the actual film he is starrin in, Tomás Gutiérrez Alea, in *Memorias del subdesarrollo* (1968).

dramatically, takes its point of departure from the Jackal's last confession, a criminal's version of the last will and testament.

Inconsistencies are left in the narrative: at one point the Jackal says that he only used a stick on one of the daughters, but this account is contradicted by someone present who states that he is lying, and that she was strangled. Likewise, when describing the murder of Rosa, the mother, he again claims to have used a stick, but he also states that he was holding a knife at the time. The reporting style simply leaves these details as they are. One of the mysteries of the murder concerns the fact, classic in this kind of sensationalist tragedy, that there was no discernible motive. He mentions that he was drunk on the wine that Rosa had given him, and that she insulted him. No more details are given. And when this scene is reconstructed, we witness Rosa shouting, but the sound is cut, thereby enhancing the horror of the event. The murders are all the more powerful since the Jackal is unable to give any reason for them. The camerawork used to portray the murders in *El chacal de Nahueltoro* is versatile. At times the camera moves around wildly, and we lose focus, thereby echoing the savagery of the events themselves. At other times, we are invited as viewers to step into the mind of the murderer, since the murder scenes are reconstructed via the Jackal's point of view; occasionally the camera looks calmly at the children before they are killed, recalling the filmic perspective of early horror films such as *Dracula* (1931) and *The*

Wolf Man (1941). A chilling moment in the film is when Rosa, just before she is beaten to death, looks directly at the viewer.

Yawar Mallku ('The Blood of the Condor', 1969) is a classic Latin American film by the Bolivian film director Jorge Sanjinés. On the day of its premiere in La Paz (17 July 1969), the theatre where it was about to be shown, the 18 de Julio, was suddenly closed down as a result of the film's inflammatory subject-matter; a public riot ensued and, eventually, the authorities relented and allowed the film to be screened.[32] The film showed the trademark of Sanjinés's interest in politicized cinema. Though Sanjinés began his career with the desire to make 'film for film's sake', he gradually became more interested in creating a 'cinema for society', because art is an 'excellent instrument' with which to create a social consciousness; art plays a fundamental role in the process whereby society achieves a '*toma de conciencia*' ('reality check') of itself, drawing inspiration from Italian neo-Realism.[33] In contradistinction to Hollywood work practices (professional actors in carefully constructed sets), Sanjinés based his film on a real-life event, the covert sterilization of women in the Bolivian village of Kaata. Sanjinés went to the village with his camera crew consisting of himself, Ricardo Rada, Oscar Soria and Antonio Eguino, but he found that it was practically impossible to persuade any of the villagers to act in his film. They were far more concerned with

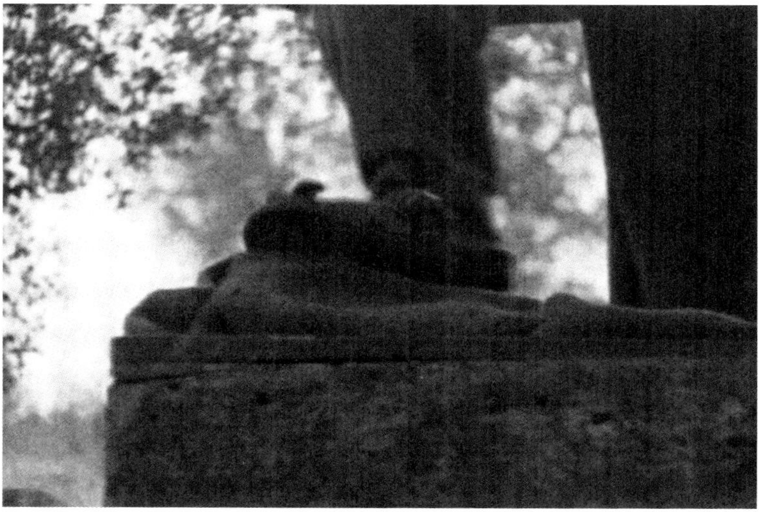

The execution scene in *El chacal de Nahueltoro* (1969).

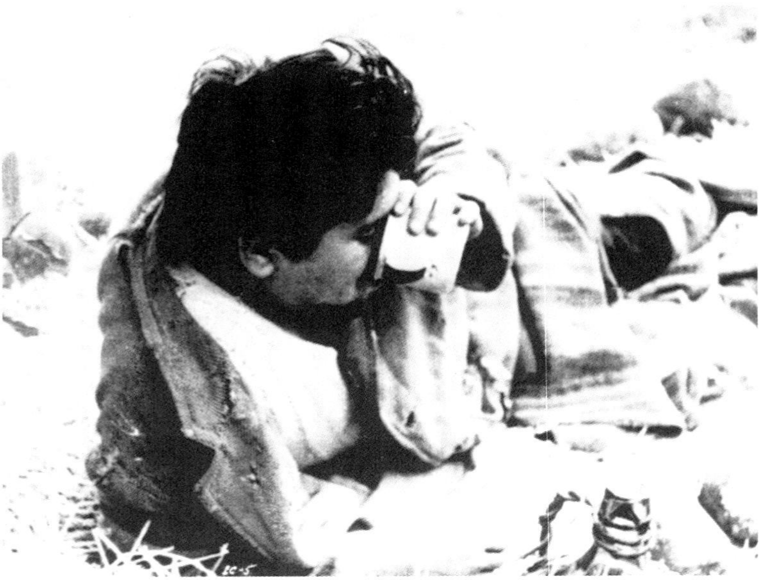

Nelson Villagra having a rest on set in Miguel Littín's *El chacal de Nahueltoro*.

reaping the harvest. Finally a coca leaves ceremony was held by the local *yatiri* (soothsayer) who sanctioned the project, and everything then went to schedule.

The three main protagonists of the film – Ignacio, Paulina and Sixto – were not professional actors. In fact *Yawar Mallku* has Ignacio, as communal leader of Kaata, in effect (like Visconti's postman) playing himself. The overall message of the film is that the Peace Corps is a malevolent Western influence in Latin America seeking to colonize under the guise of providing medical and economic assistance. As José Sánchez-H. points out: 'As a result of the denunciation made by *Yawar Mallku*, the Peace Corps was expelled from the country by President General Juan José Torres in 1971 and did not return to Bolivia until 1990.'[34] The final freeze-frame of the film, showing a group of the villagers holding their rifles aloft in a sign of obvious defiance, suggests that armed struggle is the only logical way forward for Bolivia – and indeed for Latin America. The allusion to Che Guevara, who died in Bolivia two years before the film was screened, could not be more transparent. While the film relies on traditional storytelling techniques – it tells the story of the tragedy experienced by a particular community via the representational narrative of one significant individual, Ignacio – it disrupts narratological linearity by combining cross-cutting with flashback, thereby drawing time into the DNA of the image and creating what Deleuze defines as a 'time-image'.

One significant flashback occurs, for example, when Sixto, faced with his brother, Ignacio, who has been shot and is bleeding to death, asks Paulina what happened. But *Yawar Mallku* does not use the flashback in a conventional fashion – that is, where the flashback is initiated, the film scrolls back to some significant moment in the past and then gradually moves in linear fashion back to the 'present' of the film when it was initiated. Rather, the flashback initiates a tightly choreographed see-saw effect between the present (Sixto wandering around La Paz looking for blood for his dying brother) and the past (a discrete set of events during which Ignacio discovers what is happening in the maternity clinic and rebels against the Western invaders). The film's cross-cuts become more intense as the plot proceeds, echoing the anxiety and suspense underlying Sixto's doomed search for blood, adding a sinister, proleptic mood to the film. Cross-cutting between present and past also allowed Sanjinés to build up connections between apparently unconnected events. When Sixto goes to the centre of La Paz, for example, he witnesses a military procession

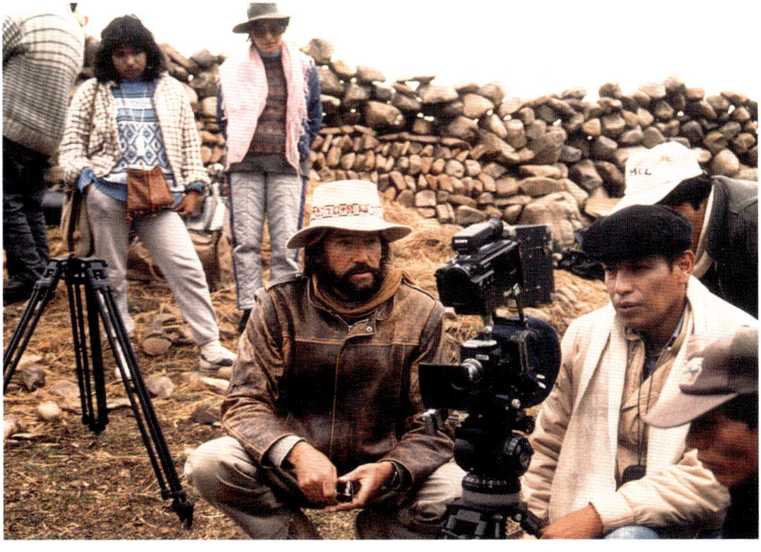

Jorge Sanjinés on set in Bolivia 1969.

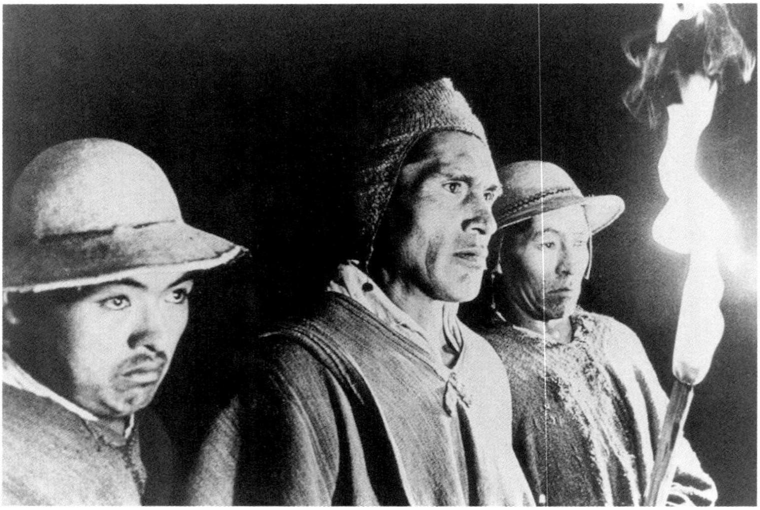

Ignacio prepares to take revenge on the gringos in *Yawar Mallku* (1969).

going past, and the camera focuses in close-up on a young girl who is also witnessing the procession; as if to underscore the sinister nature of the ceremony, we see she is crying. The camera then slips into the past time of the film, and the viewer now witnesses the commandant who is attempting to persuade the villagers that they should accept the gringos who have just arrived in town. The gringos hand out clothes for the children to wear. This scene – which might be interpreted at face value as an example of kindness towards others – is already overlaid by the scene of the young girl crying which immediately preceded it, and the gift acquires sinister overtones.

It is important to point out, however, that the use of the cross-cut in the context of the flashback was not seen at the time of the film's release as an unmitigated success. Sanjinés has stated in interviews that his aim in *Yawar Mallku* was to address the Aymara population of Bolivia rather than a Western audience. He discovered, soon after the film was released, that many Indians in the audience found the time shifts rather confusing. Here is Sanjinés's own verdict:

> When we filmed *Blood of the Condor* with the peasants of the remote Kaata community, we certainly intended that the film should be a political contribution, denouncing the *gringos* and

presenting a picture of Bolivian social reality. But our fundamental objective was to explore our own aptitudes . . . the spectators . . . complained later when the film was shown to them.[35]

Sanjinés decided, as a result of this experience, to reformulate his cinematic vision, and thus, in later films such as *El coraje del pueblo* ('The Courage of the People'), he decided against using the flashback. In this later film, he argued, he was able to integrate the vision of the people into the filmic narrative rather than tying some of the community's ideas to his personal vision: 'We, the members of the crew, became instruments of the people's struggle, as they expressed themselves through us!'[36] Some would argue that this was not necessarily a step forward, since few would suggest that *El coraje del pueblo* is a better film, either structurally or aesthetically, than *Yawar Mallku*. While it is legitimate to argue that the rapid cross-cutting between past and present in *Yawar Mallku* led to some confusion, it ultimately allowed the final scenes of the film to acquire their triumphant logic; by returning to his village to fight against the forces of imperialism, Sixto, not just metaphorically but literally, *becomes* Ignacio.

Political documentary, 1970–75

The landmark documentary *La batalla de Chile* ('The Battle of Chile', 1973) directed by Patricio Guzmán focused on the overthrow and assassination of Salvador Allende in Chile on 11 September 1973 by General Augusto Pinochet. Of the footage, 95 per cent was filmed directly by Guzmán and his camera team, the Equipo Tercer Año. The external footage which was incorporated into the documentary consisted of (i) the filming of his own death by Leonardo Henricksen; (ii) the filming of the jets flying over the presidential palace (which came from Pedro Chaskel who filmed them from his Cine Experimental offices); (iii) the bombing of La Moneda palace (which belonged to a German film collective, Hayowsky and Sceunmann Studios); and (iv) some stills derived from Noticiarios de Chile Films.[37] Everything else was filmed by Guzmán himself – this is made clear in the various images where we catch the sound engineer or Guzmán himself on camera. These scenes lend authenticity, providing an excellent example of the strengths of what Bill Nichols has called the interactive documentary.[38] Guzmán has described how the film developed:

> The 'screenplay' thus took on the form of a map, that we hung on the wall. On one side of the room, we listed the key points of the revolutionary struggle as we saw them. On the other side, we would list what we had already filmed . . . So we had the theoretical outline on the one side and the practical outline of what we had actually filmed on the other.[39]

By emphasizing five aspects of the economic life of the country (Hoarding and the Black Market, Parliamentary Boycott, Student Disturbances, The Trade Unions Go on the Offensive, The Copper Mine Strike), Part I of the documentary draws attention to the worsening relationship between the workers and their bosses, between Allende's government and the United States, and the struggle between the office of President Allende and the opposition-dominated Congress. But its most effective feature is the way that it manages – through the use of apparently unplanned interviews, the rawness of the emotions expressed, the abrupt camera movements – to suggest that a crucially important series of historical events is being recorded for posterity before our very eyes. Part II employs a chronological frame in order to structure its message. The struggle is Allende and the people versus the Christian Democrat Party and the military. It begins with footage of the first attack on La Moneda which occurred on 29 June 1973 and follows the dramatic events of the subsequent summer of discontent, with each new event punctuated by the date of its occurrence, and finally concludes with footage of the bombing of the presidential palace on 11 September. The focus of Part III is a reflection with the benefit of hindsight on the lessons learned during Salvador Allende's political experiment.

The most impressive feature of *La batalla de Chile* is the use of filmed interviews. In an interview with one of Allende's supporters who expresses her support for Alianza Popular, the hand-held camera moves effortlessly from her face to the ice-cream in her hand, providing a sense of unplanned spontaneity. The camera is 'curious' and becomes a roving eye keenly observing everything around it. At a later meeting of Allende sympathizers the camera flits from face to face, creating a fluid,

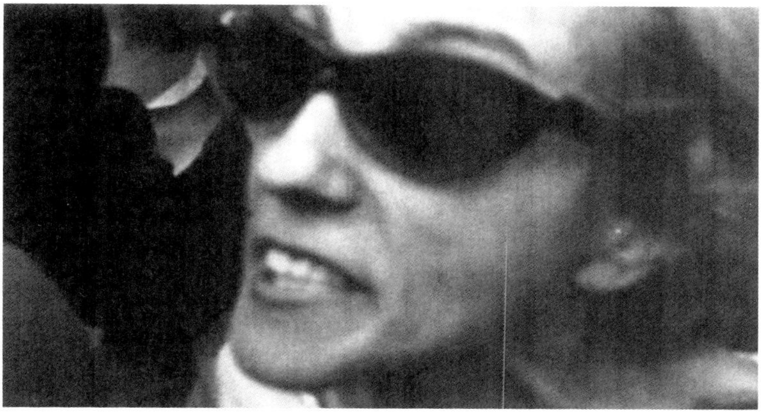

One of Pinochet's supporters in *La batalla de Chile* (1973).

dynamic sense of reality before our eyes. On another occasion we are led into the home of a Christian Democrat sympathizer; we see her coyly not wishing to answer all the interviewer's questions, and yet her coyness is belied by the wealth surrounding her. As a result of the camera panning around the room it seems almost redundant to ask her why she is in favour of the opposition. Objects speak louder than words.

One of the filmed incidents for which the documentary is justifiably famous is the 30-second sequence in which the cameraman, Leonardo Henricksen, filmed his own death, shot by one of Pinochet's soldiers. There are two versions of the same event. The version which occurs at the conclusion of Part I focuses on a soldier in a truck who notices the camera and begins firing; one of the bullets hits its target, and the camera falls to the ground and blurs over. The second version, which occurs at the beginning of Part II, shows the same soldier firing from the truck at the camera, but now it appears that the fatal bullet is fired not by the soldier but by his military superior. In an interview Guzmán explained why he decided to use both versions. The first, he says, is the unedited footage which was recovered after the event in Henricksen's camera. The second was footage which had been edited and was subsequently broadcast on national TV and on international media, and Guzmán suggested that, though it appears to have been edited, he decided to retain it because it showed that the real guilty party was not the soldier but his superior who had ordered him to open fire.[40] The first version had a 'raw' truth, the second a 'poetic' truth; not for nothing did Chris Marker work on

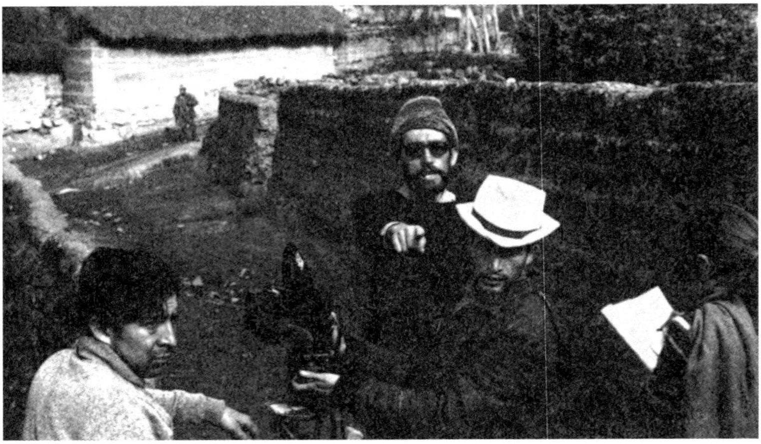

Jorge Sanjinés working with non-professional actors in Kaata, Bolivia, in 1969.

the editing of the film. One of the strengths of *La batalla de Chile* was, indeed, that it was able to combine the two levels – the 'raw' and the 'poetic' – thereby providing a blueprint for the future of the potential expressiveness of the documentary genre.[41]

3

Nation-image (1976–1999)

The emergence of the protagonist-as-nation genre – what I have called the 'nation-image' paradigm in this chapter – in Latin American film from the mid-1970s until the end of the millennium grew out of what might be called an 'officialist' reading of Latin America's historical reality, which was itself predicated on the 35mm film paradigm. In order to produce films such as *La historia oficial* ('The Official Version', 1984) and *La frontera* ('The Frontier', 1991), as well as justify the significant investment involved – especially in Latin America – it was important for films such as these to be seen as relevant to and, ideally, representative of the nation's citizens. And thus it was that the 35mm paradigm of the 1970s to 1990s tipped Latin American films into a tried and tested genre of the 'national drama'. This filmic stereotype proved to be resilient during this period. Even in the late 1990s the Argentine cultural critic Beatriz Sarlo found that Latin American films were viewed with 'sociological eyes'; a young Argentine film director Sarlo knew had screened his film at a European film festival and 'the critics at the festival told him that this type of film was European territory, and that they expected something more political from a Latin American film'.[1] Barred from artistry and railroaded into the political camp, Latin American film during this period made some important advances – María Luisa Bemberg's *Camila* (1984) was nominated for an Academy Award as Best Foreign Film and Luis Puenzo's *La historia oficial* won precisely this distinction in 1985[2] – but Latin American film was still unable to shake off its role as the echo chamber of what was happening elsewhere, in Hollywood or Europe.

The nation-image film, 1976–89

La última cena ('The Last Supper', 1976), Gutiérrez Alea's first venture into the world of Technicolor, sought to use the historical account of a slave revolt as a metaphor of Cuba in the 1970s. The basis of the historical account by Manuel Moreno Fraginals, is as follows:

> His Excellency the Count de Casa Bayona decided in an act of deep Christian fervour to humble himself before the slaves. One Holy Thursday he washed the feet of twelve negroes, sat them at his table, and served them food in imitation of Christ. But their theology was somewhat shallow and, instead of behaving like the Apostles they took advantage of the prestige they thus acquired in their fellow-slaves' eyes to organise a mutiny and burn down the mill. The Christian performance ended with rancheadores (hunters of escaped slaves) hunting down the fugitives and sticking on twelve pikes the heads of the slaves before whom His Excellency had prostrated himself.[3]

Gutiérrez Alea's film sought to interrogate the very nature of slavery:

> The aim is to question the distorted and prejudiced image of the slave which was created by the culture of the oppressor, as well as revealing in all its complexity the uneven and contradictory traits of the slave's personality, created as a result of his social subjugation: his simultaneously realistic and superstitious spirit, his mix of distrust and credulity.[4]

The film does this mainly through a gradual demystification of the character of the Count. Whereas the establishing scenes of *La última cena*, for example, allow the viewer to take up a sympathetic view of the Count (as opposed to the barbaric slaves, and the brutal Foreman), we gradually realize that his life is based on a facade. While his act of washing his slaves' feet seems to be based on humility, this is later shown to be merely a show when he reveals his merciless side and orders his 'disciples' shot, and their heads put on pikes to commemorate the foundation of a new church. In his *Dialéctica del espectador* ('The Viewer's Dialectic'),

Gutiérrez Alea discusses the two main inspirations for his work: Bertolt Brecht, from whom he derived the notion of the distancing-effect, and Sergei Eisenstein who inspired the idea of montage as conflict.[5] Titón, for example, uses these two techniques in order to force the viewer to reflect upon the contradiction at the centre of the Count's existence. There are two good instances in the film. The first occurs in the long drawn-out scene in which petals are spread on the floor, accompanied by loud rousing music, which comes just before the scene in which the Count washes the slaves' feet, echoing the Last Supper. The audience is drawn into the Count's mind: we see his highly emotional caressing of the flowers; the music drives up in a crescendo; we capture his sense of pain and delight as he contemplates the statue of Christ. We are brought down to earth with a bump, however, because the scene is followed by a long silence, which is then abruptly punctured by the sound of laughter of a slave as his feet are bathed, and tickled in the process. Another similarly bathetic scene occurs again when, during the Maundy Thursday evening meal, the Count tells the story of St Francis, which justifies suffering as the only true religion. Again his account is accompanied by grand, melodramatic music. Since we do not see anyone's face but the Count's, we assume that the slaves share his expression of love for others. The music is followed by an ominous silence. And then the slaves simply burst out laughing because they have been told to 'enjoy' their beatings. Another good example of ironic contrast occurs when the Count's story of the Last Supper is spliced with references to the Carabalí tribe who practise cannibalism. Contrasts between sequences of this kind are good examples of what Eisenstein meant by conflict within the work of art. They force the viewer to reassess his or her views about religion, mysticism and suffering. One is forced to perceive directly the conflict between the two worlds. We therefore experience the work of art dialectically.

Gutiérrez Alea uses the hand-held camera as an additional weapon of his demystificatory armour. His cameraman Mario García Joya was very helpful in this process, as Titón has suggested:

> His camera is very steady. In addition, Mayito uses some devices that he has invented. For instance, he or an assistant places a rod underneath the camera when it must be stationary, and that rod is removed when the camera must begin to move and follow

a character. His inventions work marvelously. You see a tremendous fluidity in these different mises-en-scène. I would go so far as to say that the fluidity is even more perfect than if he had used a Steadicam, because when a Steadicam is used the camera floats a bit.[6]

The film is skilful at presenting the social pyramid within Cuba in colonial times. At the pinnacle of the social pyramid is the Count, closely followed by his cruel foreman, Manuel. The priest and the sugar master act as intermediaries with the subaltern classes; the priest, for example, pleads with the Count to keep to his word about letting the slaves have Easter Day off, but to no avail. Don Gaspar, the educated French sugar master with a scientific mind, mocks the priest's statement to the effect that the slaves have witchcraft while the Church has truth, saying both systems deal in magic. He compares what he is doing (changing sugar beet into white refined sugar) to the Christian theory of redemption of souls (purged by suffering in the fires of hell). He also seems to be mocking, perhaps, the racist basis of the Church and society's views by drawing attention to the fact that he is producing white out of black. He tells the

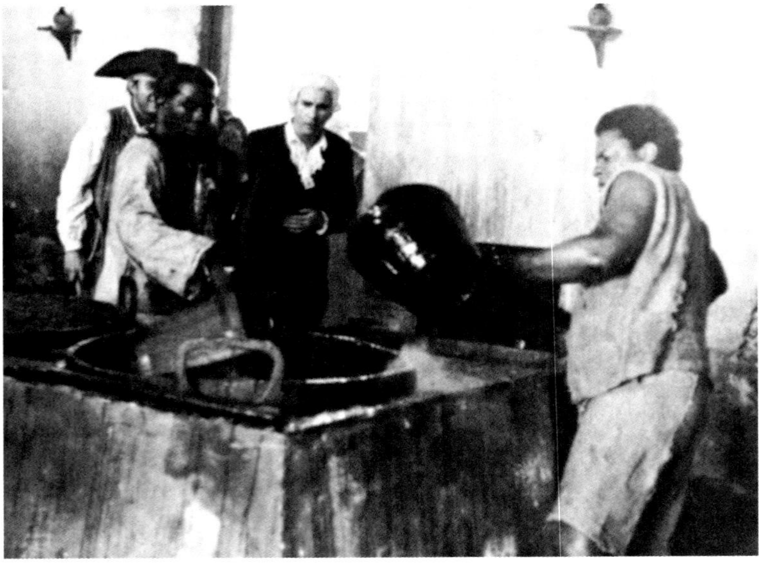

Workers making sugar in *La última cena* (1976).

priest that the real secret to the refining process is in the little bag that contains 'caca de poule' (humour at the priest's expense). Don Gaspar is a Voltaire-like figure, well aware of the excesses of colonial administration.

The slaves are also individualized, ranging from the old man, Pascual, who is powerless and could not accept freedom even if it were given to him; to the deferential subaltern, Edmundo, who works as the Count's personal servant, and refers to the other slaves as 'negroes'; Antonio, who is desperate to exchange his labours in the sugar cane fields for the easy life in the Big House as a domestic servant; the proud subaltern, Bangoché, from the Congo, a man who is now a slave but was once a king, and therefore has innate dignity; and the dancer who, as his story about the son who sells his father rather than being sold himself aptly illustrates, is the witty rather than rebellious subaltern, namely the slave who works the system rather than challenging its raison d'être. Sebastián reminds us of the personification of Caliban as described in Roberto Fernández Retamar's influential 1971 essay *Calibán*, since he is at once magical and rebellious. His association with magic is confirmed when he takes out a pouch containing powder which, he suggests, will ensure that he will not be caught, and blows it over the Count as if asserting his power over him. His rebelliousness is epitomized when, after being asked by the Count, '¿Quién soy, Sebastián?' ('Who am I, Sebastian?'), there follows a pregnant pause before Sebastián spits in the Count's face. The Count accuses him of being a Judas figure, and this is in a sense confirmed when he murders Manuel during the uprising (in other words, this scene recreates the 'murder' of 'Christ').

But Sebastián is more enigmatic than this. As Titón has pointed out:

> Sebastian, the rebellious negro, assimilates the count's language so as to be able to address the slaves as well: the myth of the body of Truth and the head of Lies is his response, which will cause the demise of the values and reasoning which the count presents as infallible.[7]

The African parable he tells his audience, which is about the struggle between 'Truth' and 'Lie', is a postcolonial version of the struggle between colonized and colonizing peoples which acts as a counter-response to the count's parable of human suffering:

> When Olofi made the world he made it complete with day and night, good and bad. Truth and Lie. Olofi was sorry for Lie, who was ugly, and gave him a machete to defend himself. One day Truth and Lie met and had a fight. Lie cut off Truth's head. Headless, Truth took Lie's head. Now Truth goes around with the body of Truth and the head of Lie.

In order to demonstrate this idea, Sebastián picks up the pig's head, which is on the table, and places it in front of his own. The clear message is that the Christian West has been passing off lies as truth in order to guarantee its ideological superiority over the rest of the world. Sebastián furthermore tells the group of slaves that he has magical powers which allow him to change into an animal or a tree – an idea reinforced by the final, uplifting sequence of the film. In that concluding sequence we see Sebastián running free through the jungle, and his flight is spliced with lush, flowing images of the jungle (a flying bird, a running river, running horses), and accompanied by stirring, triumphalist music. We do not know Sebastián's fate but these final images and sounds of the film suggest freedom and a return to the laws of nature, as if to suggest that Sebastián has finally escaped his political oppressors. *La última cena* has been interpreted by Jerome Branche as 'a metaphor for Cuba's present struggle against contemporary Yankee imperialism',[8] and the promotion of an Afro-Hispanic legacy in Cuba provided the film with a specific contemporaneous relevance.

Pixote: a lei do mais fraco ('Pixote: The Law of the Weakest', 1980), directed by the Brazilian director Héctor Babenco, was a gritty filmic mix of the fictional and the documentary. Babenco first wanted to make a true-to-life documentary about a particular reform school but when the school directors found out what he had in mind they refused to cooperate. Thus it was that Babenco decided to write a fictional treatment, and he based his account on José Louzeiro's documentary novel *Infância dos mortos* (1977).[9] Louzeiro's novel – strictly speaking a work of documentary fiction, the 'romance-reportagem' – was, as Randal Johnson has pointed out, based on a chilling event: dozens of imprisoned minors were taken from Rio de Janeiro prisons and pushed over a cliff near Camanducaia, a town in the state of Minas Gerais.[10] The film that Babenco eventually made was stark; *Pixote* can be described as the Brazilian version of

Buñuel's *Los olvidados*, since it offers a dispiriting vision of the lives of a number of young men who are outcasts in a large Latin American city (this time it is Rio de Janeiro) and whose lives soon lead to crime. The film opens by evoking the language of the documentary. As Marc Lauria points out:

> The film begins [in the version released in the U.S.] as a documentary. Babenco addresses the camera, and states that 50 per cent of the population in Brazil is under 21, and this includes three million homeless children. Brazilian law prevents anyone under the age of 18 to be prosecuted for criminal offences; older criminals prey on these youths. Babenco, standing in front of a slum area, then introduces Fernando Ramos da Silva, who lives there as 'Pixote' in the film proper.[11]

Babenco and Jorge Durán used Louzeiro's *Infância dos mortos* to create a screenplay that differed in some key respects from the original documentary novel. As Johnson points out, 'Pixote ("Pichote" in Louzeiro) is a minor character in Louzeiro's book who dies in the first chapter, gunned down as he and other marginalised children run through a cemetery to avoid being abused by pimps and drug pushers.'[12] A number of the film's episodes, such as the prostitution/hold-up racket, are taken straight from the novel, though it is a character called Dito who is the protagonist. The theme of the corruption of the authorities likewise originated in the book, and Sapato is a prime example of this. While he pretends to be on the boys' side, he does not attempt to punish the perpetrator of the rape committed during the night. The children are 'disappeared' as soon as there is a problem; they become pawns in a larger social power game. When Sapato says to Garatão that he will soon be eighteen, and that he 'doesn't exist', his words may be interpreted on a number of levels. First of all they are meant as encouragement in that Garatão's record will be wiped clean. But they also suggest that in society's eyes the delinquents really do not exist. On a third level, they are a chilling omen of what will happen to Garatão that night – he will be murdered. Sapato knows that this is going to happen and is a willing accomplice in the murder. Following in the footsteps of Italian neo-Realism, the children in *Pixote* were non-professional actors, and were given crash courses in acting before and during the shoot: 'Babenco trained each child from scratch, thereby avoiding the stereotypical mannerisms that likely would have come from using professional child actors.'[13] The actors were allowed to extemporize and change the script. As Babenco said, 'They gave me the right words, the right sentences.'[14] Sometimes their input even changed the perspective on a given episode; as a result of Fernando's input, for example, Pixote was drafted in as a witness to the sex scene between Chico and Sueli; in the original script he had been in another room.[15] As Marc Lauria puts it, 'Incidents in *Pixote* don't seem to be set up for the cameras; the film seems to follow the characters no matter what they do or say.'[16]

The film is split into two. In the first half we witness Pixote's life in the reformatory, and in the second we see the gang on the outside. Much of what was being worked out in the first part of the film (social culpability, police corruption and so on) is left unresolved. The culpability of the authorities, though underlined, never re-enters the frame, subverting the Hollywood formula in which evil is routinely punished with retribution. As in a picaresque novel where the energy is in the episodic, ever-moving nature of the narrative, Pixote simply moves on to pastures new. It is interesting that Roberto, the singer, should stay behind. He does so for empirical reasons in that he has a broken leg. But his refusal to leave can be interpreted on a symbolic level as well. For him, the world of the imagination – the world of the asylum and the institution palliated by unrealistic dreams – is better than the real world.

The film repeatedly re-enacts the drama of the dysfunctional family, focusing in particular on the absence of any positive female figures. Sexuality is never presented within a normative context. It appears either in the guise of prostitution – there are two prostitutes in the film, Deborah and Sueli, and both offer sordid views of sexuality – or male rape (as when Garatão rapes the young boy in the reformatory), or male–male sex (when Dito and Lila have sex soon after their arrival in São Paulo). Mothers are either absent (as in Pixote's case, since he does not know where his mother is, as his grandfather comments during the prison visit) or they are two-timers (as Dito's mother shows herself to be, when she seduces Sapato), or they are heartless prostitutes (as Sueli reveals herself to be, when she kills her foetus with a knitting needle). The protagonists, Pixote foremost among them, search for their mothers in different people, but find 'false' maternal figures. Lilica, for example, attempts to 'mother' Garatão and then Dito. Deborah attempts to mother Pixote (she asks him if he wants to come round and play with her son, thereby in effect mothering a motherless boy), and Sueli does the same. But this gesture always leads to failure or death. The relationship between Sueli and Pixote is the most poignant since there are a number of pointers that suggest that the mother–son relationship is central to the film's symbolics. In a visually unpleasant scene – the abortion in the toilet – Sueli says that the aborted child looks a bit like him. This scene is especially important since, as the concluding scene of the film makes clear, she pointedly refuses to be his mother. She sends him out into the world; he is, in a sense, not only a dead man walking (we are reminded of the pertinence of the title of the documentary novel on which the film is based – *Infância dos mortos*), but, as it were, an abortion walking. Sulia has, in fact, expelled Pixote from her home, her womb, and has condemned him to an early death.

As one might expect in such a gritty film, it is the grim harvester who provides the symbolic resonance behind the different scenes. There is, for example, a deliberate parallelism between the needle used by Garatão to torture Fumaça early on in the film and the needle which Sueli uses

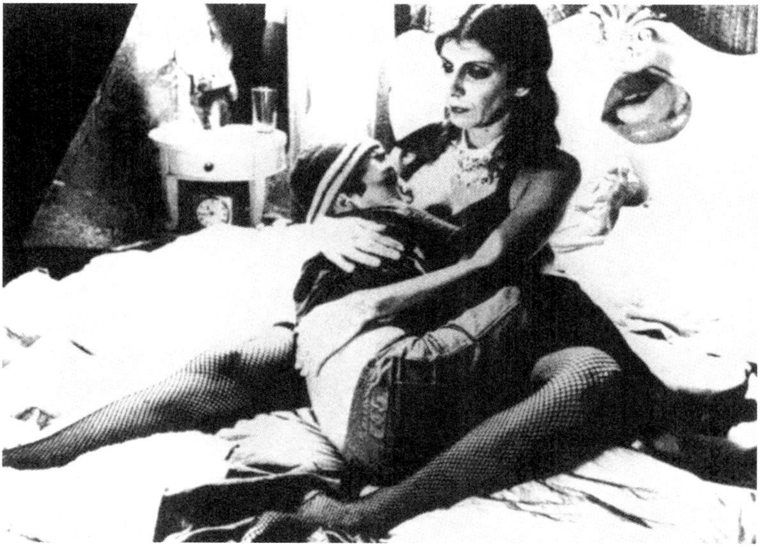

Suel breastfeeds the protagonist in Babenco's *Pixote* (1981).

to kill her unborn child. The torture of Fumaça thereby becomes, in retrospect, a grim omen of what is to follow. This parallelism has a number of implications for our interpretation of the film. Given that Garatão is a rapist, and given the phallic resonance of the needle, it is clear that a web of association is being built up that aligns male sexuality with torture, rape and death. This pessimistic assessment of human sexuality is balanced by the repetition of the motif of the absent mother. The terror of this film does not lie in what we have witnessed so much as in what we imagine will happen next. In the final haunting image we see Pixote walking along a railway track back to Rio de Janeiro, with a gun in his belt. Having murdered three people already, he is a 'hardened' criminal, though still a minor, experienced in violence, extortion, the use of firearms and with a worryingly precocious interest in sex. The fate of the lead actor in the film after its release in 1980 is testimony to its verisimilitude. Fernando Ramos da Silva, who played Pixote, was persistently harassed by the police, arrested on two occasions, tortured and, on 25 August 1987, gunned down by police.[17] The film *Quem matou Pixote?* ('Who Killed Pixote?', 1996), directed by José Joffily, was made about the life of the actor who was gunned down, revealing this to be a story that runs and runs. There is, indeed, no greater testimony to the true-to-life grittiness of Babenco's film.[18]

Camila (1984), directed by the Argentine María Luisa Bemberg, was one of the highlights of the 1980s. The story of the love affair at the core of the film was a contentious one which reflected badly on an important figure of Argentina's republican history (Juan Manuel de Rosas) as well as the Church. For that reason every director since then had been forbidden to tell the story of the love affair between Camila O'Gorman, the daughter of one of Argentina's richest landowners, and a local priest, Uladislao Gutiérrez, which occurred from 1847 to '48.[19] But Bemberg prevailed, and her re-enactment followed the historical account closely. The film shows Camila (Susú Pecoraro) seducing and eloping with the local priest, Ladislao (Imanol Arias), to Goya City where they live happily until discovered by Padre Gannon; they are subsequently captured and shot to death on General Rosas's orders, with the complicity of Camila's father, Adolfo (Héctor Alterio). Though *Camila* cost a mere $370,000 to make,[20] it became one of the biggest box office hits of all time in Argentina, surpassing takings of the recent

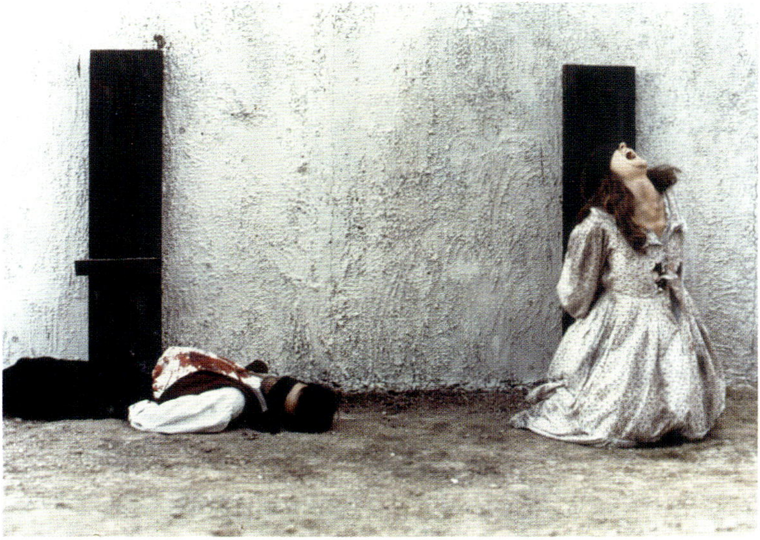

The execution of the lovers in *Camila* (1984).

Hollywood blockbuster *E.T.*, released in Argentina at the end of 1982. Bemberg's aim in filming *Camila* was to create an Argentine melodrama:

> [it] was shot in a highly romantic style because I felt that in that way I could really hit the audience, in the heart and in the pit of their stomach. Melodrama is a very tricky genre, because at any minute it can turn into something sentimental, which I detest. So it had all those little tricks, such as the handkerchief, the gold coin, the priest who's sick with love, and the thunder when God gets angry. They're all like winks at the audience.[21]

Camila, indeed, has all the hallmarks of what Warren Buckland has identified as the 'fallen woman melodrama', namely the melodramatic film which focuses on a woman who commits a sexual transgression, is expelled from the domestic space and is eventually punished with death.[22] There is a struggle in the film between Ladislao's more traditional notion of love (evident when he turns back to God) and Camila's more subversive view of love which, for her, is tied to the personal, the erotic. As Ruby Rich has suggested, Bemberg used 'seamless art cinema (lush, transparent, and perfect periodicity) in the service of a new idea'.[23]

Beneath its more obvious melodramatic level as a tragic love story set in mid-nineteenth-century Argentina, *Camila* allegorizes the events of the Guerra Sucia ('Dirty War') of the mid-1970s to early 1980s, in which thousands of political subversives were captured by the authorities and 'disappeared'. Bemberg has pointed to the dual level of the film in interviews: 'It's a very Romantic story in which fear and menaces are also present, something which we've very much lived with in Argentina and it's there, just beneath the surface.'[24] The film led to what has been called a 'collective catharsis'. As John King has pointed out, 'Over two million people wept at the story of Camila O'Gorman, which was their story.'[25] There is a sense, though, in which this film is also Bemberg's own story. Bemberg once declared that she became a film director because she wanted to give women the chance to speak rather than be spoken for: 'My films are an attempt to make women recognise themselves and learn more about themselves through the protagonists' predicament. This is my ethical commitment, helping them to be free.'[26] So the film is itself a blueprint for Bemberg's own rebellion against her family, her society and sexual oppression. In her films, Bemberg had said that she wanted to 'propose images of women that are vertical, autonomous, independent, thoughtful, courageous, spunky', and this is certainly the case with Camila.[27] After all, it is she who is portrayed as initiating the love affair. Traditional versions of the story had an innocent woman seduced by a lecherous priest. 'I think it was a good idea to have the priest seduced by the woman', remarked Bemberg wryly. 'It helped me with the Church.'[28]

Quite consistently throughout the film, Camila takes centre stage and thereby marginalizes Ladislao. When she discovers from the doctor, for example, that she is pregnant, we cut to a shot in which Camila is screaming through her prison bars to Ladislao that they have a child. The camera shows Ladislao's cell; we see him in long shot, hunched over, clearly oblivious to her words. Our sympathy is engineered for Camila during the prison sequences with a standard director's trick – the microphone is placed close to Susú Pecoraro's throat and we hear her nervous breathing and swallowing; the viewer is thereby transported inside the character's bodily space. The denouement of the film implies that the unborn child that Camila is carrying when she is executed allegorizes the fledgling nation of the 'unitarios' mercilessly crushed by Rosas's iron fist. The very presence of the voice-over – '*A tu lado, Camila*' (At your side, Camila) – which, as suggested above, is an overt allusion to a Romantic notion of post-corporeal love, itself suggests a transcendence of those powers which have crushed Camila's and Ladislao's vulnerable bodies. The film, therefore, has a positive political message. The way in which it actually came into being points not only to its political resonance but also to the sense in which its gestation period accompanied the birth of a new political era. As Lila Stantic recalls:

> It's 2.30 in the morning and I'm with María Luisa . . . Marta goes off and comes back a few minutes later with the papers under her arm. In banner headlines all the papers proclaim: 'Argentina has invaded the Malvinas' . . . We did not know that at this precise moment the right conditions were being created for María Luisa's third film, *Camila*. This is because almost all the critics agreed that in María Luisa's films to date (*Momentos* and *Señora de nadie*), there was no belief in the possibility of love. This machista interpretation of María Luisa's female characters led me, a few days later, to throw down the big challenge: 'Now you have to do a love story. You have to do a love story. You have to tell the story of Camila O'Gorman.'[29]

The filming of *Camila* began – significantly enough – on 11 December 1983, the day after Alfonsín became the first civilian president in almost a decade in Argentina, when the country finally emerged from the nightmares of the Guerra Sucia.[30] This day also happened by pure coincidence to be the anniversary of the time when Camila and Ladislao eloped (it was on the night of 11–12 December 1847). These omens were not fortuitous, perhaps. *Camila* presents a positive ideological statement given the structural significance of its ending. The transcendence of death by virtue of love suggested by the voice-over must logically be seen as an allegory of the transcendence of the dirt of war through the hope inspired by the new democracy ushered in by the demise of the Guerra Sucia. Camila's child – the body of Argentina – dies in her womb but the voice-over of love ('*A tu lado, Camila*') suggests hope for the future, 'another rhythm of breathing and loving'.[31] *Camila* was the Academy nominee

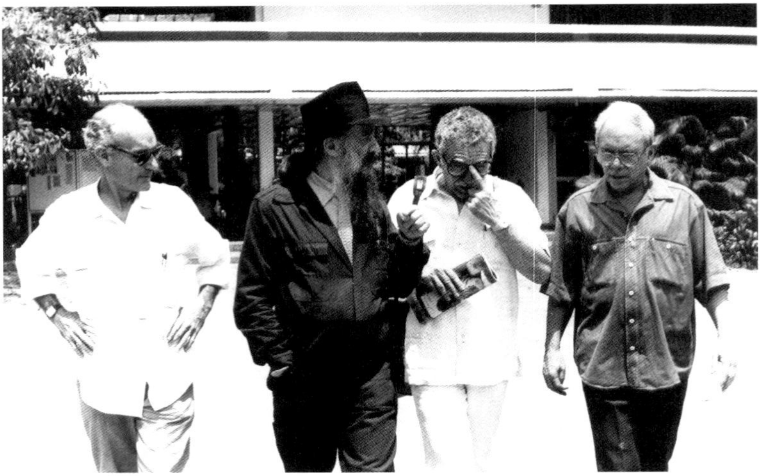

Titón, Birri, Gabo and García Espinosa founding the Escuela Internacional de Cine y Televisión in Cuba in 1985.

for Best Foreign Film, and as such put down a marker for Latin American film which proved auspicious.[32]

The following year, 1985, *La historia oficial,* directed by Luis Puenzo, became the first Latin American film to win an Academy Award for Best Foreign Film. It was as if the emperor's clothes that had adorned *Camila* in the previous year had now been stripped from Argentina's body politic – the truth of Argentina's Dirty War could now be told. As a result the Argentine film industry became famous overnight. *La historia oficial* specifically portrays and analyses the social conflict which produced the Guerra Sucia in Argentina from 1975 until 1982; it was a dirty war in which as many as 30,000 people were kidnapped and 'disappeared' (the so-called *desaparecidos*) by the military leaders. But rather than focus on the specifics of warfare between the military and the terrorists, Puenzo's film instead narrates the story of the abduction of the children of subversives who were adopted, once their parents had been 'disappeared', by higher echelons of the military establishment, and it does so by focusing on the drama of one particular child, Gaby. The action of the film centres on the gradual discovery by Alicia (Norma Aleandro), a history teacher in a secondary school, that the child her husband, Roberto (Héctor Alterio) – a high-ranking businessman with links to counter-espionage, the USA, and the military – gave to her some four or five years before the film narrative proper begins, was in fact illegally abducted from her 'subversive' parents just before they were murdered. The genre invented by Puenzo to tell his story in *La historia oficial* was thriller with a political twist. It was a genre in which Latin American film directors would before long demonstrate great dexterity.

The enunciation of the narrative was engineered through three superb acting performances – by Norma Aleandro (who won the Best Actress award at Cannes), Héctor Alterio and Chunchuna Villafane (who won Best Supporting Actress at the Chicago Film Festival). The last of these plays Ana, who has returned to Buenos Aires after a number of years in exile. The film contains a superb scene in which Ana, through her laughter then her tears, tells Alicia how she was tortured, while Alicia listens to her account in stunned disbelief. The curious thing about the scene is that though the actress Norma Aleandro is stunned by Ana's account of her exile it is, in some ways, the account of Norma's own life: she was forced into exile on 21 June 1976 by a bomb which exploded at 3 o'clock in the morning beneath her apartment, followed by a threat telling her to leave the country within 24 hours and that if she did not do so she and her family were running a grave risk.[33] The superb acting in *La historia oficial* was supported by the use of three cinematic devices which enhance the expression of suspense in the film: blocking, the long shot, and montage-in-depth. The establishing shot of the film, for example, gives a hint of what is to come. We witness the playing of the national anthem in the school playground at which Alicia and Benítez teach, but for those viewers who expect a Hollywood-style

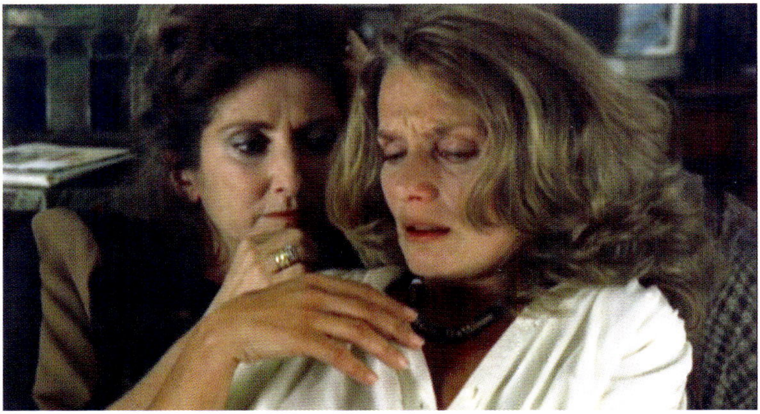

The anagnorisis scene in *La historia oficial* (1985), when Ana tells Alicia why she had to leave Argentina.

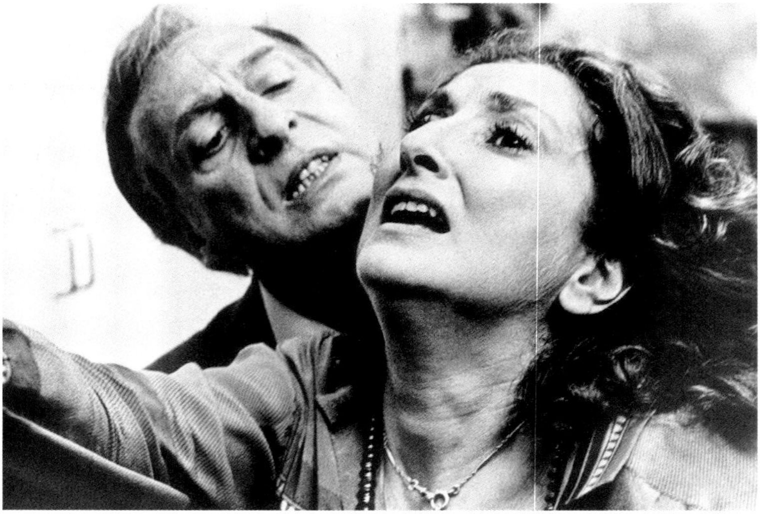

Roberto reveals he is a torturer in the final scene of *La historia oficial*

master shot the results are rather surprising. The film begins with the title ('La historia oficial') being ripped up, at which point the camera focuses on a loudspeaker, and then – in an obsessively deliberate way – on the individuals in the school playground, but our view is consistently blocked by the concrete structure of the roof behind which the camera is placed. This blocking shot – that is, there is something interrupting the vision of the spectator from the main action – is an early indication that we will be seeing a behind-the-scenes version of Argentine reality. This establishing shot, indeed, draws attention to one of the key techniques used in the film, namely, the snares which offer a tantalizing view of an event but do not tell us the whole truth,[34] in order to support the basic message of the film – that the state conceals its actions from its citizens' gaze. It is not coincidental, indeed, that the first time we see Roberto (soon after the establishing scene described above) he is not viewed openly but glimpsed obliquely. Our view of him is blocked by the wall behind which he scurries after entering the house. In pragmatic terms his actions are understandable since he is attempting to hide the doll he has bought for Gaby but, as the film progresses, the prevalence of blocking takes on a more sinister resonance. He is the character, after all, whom we know the least about. As we realize at the conclusion of the film when, quite out of the blue, he attacks his wife, his past may have been very murky indeed.

That Puenzo has deliberately chosen to block the viewer's perception at certain crucial junctures is suggested by what might at first seem innocuous decisions about *mise-en-scène*. Thus, when we see Roberto and Alicia in long shot leave the restaurant and walk along the pavement to their car (we hear their conversation, and can see that Alicia is visibly agitated about being insulted as a result of her infertility), it is striking that the camera tracks them from behind a hedge on the other side of the road; the long shot combined with the fact that we can hear their voices perfectly – as if they were close by – inevitably evokes the atmosphere of secrecy and covert spying, techniques that were part and parcel of the culture animating the Guerra Sucia.

Pointing in a similar direction to the use of blocking and the long shot is the use of montage-in-depth, which underlines the mystery of the state's machinations. The best example occurs when Alicia turns up unexpectedly at Roberto's office and witnesses a showdown between her husband and a business associate called Macchi. Macchi loses his temper and shouts at Roberto that he is not prepared to take the blame for the latter's misdemeanours. Roberto tries unsuccessfully to placate him, and we see Macchi being bundled into a nearby office. The following sequence of shots is seen via Alicia's point of view; the door is opened and then closed, and a final glimpse of what is going on in the room terminates when the lift door shuts. One of the men seems to have his hand around Macchi's neck: is he loosening his collar or strangling him? Because the scene in the office is portrayed as occurring in the most distant segment of cinematic space from the camera-eye – namely further away than the lift door, than the intervening space in the office and than the office door – it is difficult to pick out what precisely is happening. We find a similar exploration of cinematic space in the scene towards the end of the film set in Roberto's home when he is entertaining his American guests and Argentine business associates. The older American is complimenting Gaby; the younger American is on the phone trying to locate his wife who seems to have disappeared; Roberto is boasting about his prowess in the business world; and his two associates are playing pool. This sequence is characterized by deep focus cinematography in which 'a great deal of space is not only visible within a shot but also clearly in focus';[35] in particular three cinematic spaces – foreground, middle ground and background – are combined in such a way that the viewer used to the Hollywood formula of explicit foregrounding may be confused. Should we be listening to the Argentine men arguing about their pool game or listening to the younger American who is becoming increasingly agitated as his attempts to locate his wife prove unsuccessful? Where is Alicia? To further compound the viewer's disorientation, at one point in the sequence the 180-degree rule is broken, and we see the American behind rather than in front of Roberto. Though not as dramatic as the scene is which Macchi is bundled into a nearby office, this sequence demonstrates Puenzo's deliberate use of montage-in-depth in order to underline the theme of the deliberate blocking of the truth. Like the next-of-kin of the *desaparecidos*, we don't know what to look for or where to look.

Macu, la mujer del policía ('Macu, the Policeman's Wife', 1987), directed by the Swedish-Venezuelan Solveig Hoogesteijn, tells the story of Macu (María Luisa Mosquera), a pretty woman whose husband Ismael (Daniel Alvarado) is accused of murdering her lover Simón (Frank Hernández), along with his two friends. The film opens with the news that the three young men have disappeared; a police investigation begins which is intercut with a reconstruction of Ismael and Macu's courtship. Not only is Ismael an older man, but he first met Macu when she was a young child, the daughter of a woman he had an affair with. He was thus, in effect, 'grooming' Macu for later on. Based on the true story of a policeman, Argenis Rafael Ledezma, the so-called 'Monster of Mamera', who was jailed for murder in 1980 for 30 years, *Macu, la mujer del policía* is a brooding, atmospheric drama about sex, revenge, police corruption and paedophilia which reaches its inevitable climax when Macu testifies against Ismael.[36]

La boca del lobo ('The Lion's Den', 1988), directed by the Peruvian Francisco Lombardi, tells the story of the brutal struggle between the Sendero Luminoso (Shining Path) and the army in Peru which lasted throughout the 1980s and the beginning of the 1990s, and claimed more than 10,000 lives. Lombardi's film is set in a fictional, prototypical town in the Andes, Chuspi, and shows the struggle descending into the seventh circle of hell. A lieutenant, Basulto (Antero Sánchez) captures a Sendero Luminoso suspect, has him questioned and then decides to hand him over; their truck is attacked and Basulto and two of his men are cruelly murdered. A new tougher lieutenant, Iván Roca (Gustavo

Bueno) is sent in, and he begins terrorizing the local population, demanding information from the mayor, killing the cow of a villager he suspects of collusion, Faustino Sulca, and the film describes the descent into violence which leads to the rape of a young girl (Julia) by one of the recruits, followed by the machine-gunning of a number of the villagers next to a remote gulley. The strength of the film lies in its depiction of an absent enemy – the Sendero Luminoso are never seen – which makes of it something of a psychological thriller. The denouement shows the army turning in on itself; it concludes with a duel of Russian roulette between Iván Roca and Vitín Luna (Toño Vega), who beats the lieutenant but then decides to turn his back on the mindless violence perpetrated by the army.[37]

The life-as-journey movies of the 1990s

The 1990s opened with a sharp shock to the system of Latin America's film world. The decade was the 'era of de-nationalisation of the [large] screen', as Erica Segre suggests.[38] In Brazil in 1990, President Collor de Melho stopped all funding of the national Brazilian film industry, and as a result Embrafilme, the national film body, was forced to close its doors.[39] At the same time private investment was encouraged and, indeed, grew apace as the decade progressed. The picture was a similar one in Mexico. At an international film conference held in Cancun in 1993 a new law was promulgated (the so-called Nueva Ley Federal de Cinematografía) whereby the National Film Institute (IMCINE) would 'now only subsidize 60% of the costs of production', with the other 40 per cent to be raised by the director through private funding.[40] The release of *Como agua para chocolate* ('Like Water for Chocolate') in Mexico City in February 1993 was a test case of just how much the cinematic landscape had changed. Following the new law to the letter, Alfonso Arau's film had split public/private funding, which consisted of a state grant from IMCINE, along with private funds from Aviasco, a Mexican airline, the Mexican Ministry of Tourism and the State Government of Coahuila where the film is set.[41] It was an unprecedented success. *Como agua para chocolate* first became a hit with Latin American audiences before being exported abroad; it went on to be a Hollywood blockbuster.

The secret of its success – apart from its heady mixture of exoticism, sex and magical realism – was that, from the outset, it was a film that had its eyes firmly on its audience. *Como agua para chocolate* owed as much to the financial jolt that the Mexican economy received in the early 1990s as to the determination and perseverance of its director (Alfonso Arau) and author (Laura Esquivel). While a number of critics have pointed out that *Como agua para chocolate* offers up rather stereotypical images of men, women, Mexico and the United States, thereby pandering to some of the easy clichés of Hollywood's filmic idiom, there is no escaping the fact that it allowed Latin American cinema a new lease of life, a passport to being taken seriously as an artistic product on its own merits. That the success of *Como agua para chocolate* was not dependent on the Hollywood machine is suggested by the fact that it was not even nominated for Best Foreign Film. It had transcended the category. There were many, though, particularly those of the old school such as Arturo Ripstein, who disagreed with the new policy – Ripstein famously went to see President Zedillo in 1997 on behalf of IMCINE to complain about the lack of state funding: 'A country without film is a sad country' were his words – but the paradigm shift was leading to irreversible changes in the film industry in Latin America.[42]

Bemberg's *Yo, la peor de todas* ('I, the Worst of All', 1990) provides a twentieth-century reading of the life of a seventeenth-century Mexican nun, Sor Juana Inés de la Cruz (Assumpta Serna), her struggle with the archbishop (Lauturo Murúa) and her burgeoning love for the vicereine (Dominique Sanda). Bemberg used this story in order to create a new reading of feminist culture. In a lecture given in 1992 at the University of Warwick, Bemberg referred to the social conditioning which often holds women back:

> We are limited by psychological conditionings that conspire against women: an absence of inner confidence and the authority to restrict cultural models; an absence of the motivation needed to create art, like a competitive spirit, the urge to differentiate yourself through what you do, and a liking for complex issues. On top of this man has cannibalized womanhood and tries to speak for both.[43]

In her film Bemberg seeks to wrest culture back from its patriarchal mould, and the area in which she questions the official story of Sor Juana

Inés de la Cruz's life relates to her sexuality. There is no historical evidence of a sexual relationship having occurred between Sor Juana and the vicereine, Leonor María Carreto, Marchioness of Mancera, but Sor Juana did write some sonnets in her honour and, as Emilie Bergmann suggests, 'Although Paz insists she could not possibly have had homoerotic desires, her lesbianism is taken for granted by Latino/a and Spanish American lesbian and gay poets who have adopted her as their patron saint.'[44] A lesbian structure of feeling is suggested in two scenes in which we witness a declaration of love. In the first the vicereine looks into Sor Juana's eyes, asks her to loosen her bodice for her and then makes a number of innuendo-laden comments: '*qué bellas eres cuando te apasionas*' (how beautiful you are when you become passionate) and '*no se puede negar la naturaleza*' (you can't deny nature). The second, more forthright scene occurs when the vicereine, after her husband has allowed her to ignore the archbishop's prohibition to stay out of her library, asks her to take off her veil: '*quítate el velo. Es una orden*' (take off your veil. That's an order), after which she plants a delicate kiss on her lips. As Rosa Sarabia suggests, not only the vicereine but the viewer is thereby constructed as a voyeur of Sor Juana's beauty.[45] As Bemberg herself once suggested in an interview, there are so many 'splendid women' portrayed on the big screen that it would not be surprising if 'we all ended up being lesbians'.[46] Given that the vicereine is at one stage provided the fictitious name of María Luisa by the viceroy just as they are about to leave for Madrid, it is perhaps not to stretch the point too much to see the vicereine as a projection of Bemberg herself who wished to 'de-nun' Sor Juana. The gushing words uttered by the vicereine ('*¿Cómo es Juana, con ella misma, cuando está sola, cuando nadie la mira?*', What is Juana like, with herself, on her own, when nobody sees her?, and – after the veil is removed – '*esta Juana es mía, solamente mía*'; this Juana is mine, mine only) could also be the words of the artist, seeking in Pygmalion fashion to create a new image of womanhood for the modern day. In an interview Bemberg has suggested that she chose Assumpta Serna to play Sor Juana not only because of her beauty and poise but also because she would give the role a contemporary feel, which is what she wanted: 'You forget that the character is a nun because she gave the role a contemporary feel'.[47]

But just as intriguing as these scenes in which innuendo speaks volumes, are those in which the poems for which Sor Juana is famous are recited in voice-over, and are framed within a new context, thereby transforming them into examples of *littérature à clé*, with the key being the lesbian subtext. Perhaps the best example of this occurs when the sonnet 'Detente, sombra de mi bien esquivo . . .', a love poem traditionally seen as a stylistic exercise[48] but now imbued – given the view the camera provides of the vicereine just to the right of the frame – with the sense of being a love poem to the vicereine. This is also the meaning given to the poems by the small committee set up by the archbishop to determine what to do with Sor Juana. Though given a lead by Octavio Paz,[49] Bemberg pursues some imaginative juxtapositions which breathe a new, ambiguous light into what were seen as rhetorical exercises. It does not matter so much whether the interpretation is an historically justifiable one (Paz, for example, sees the love poems more in terms of feudal submission than of eroticism);[50] what is more important is that it allows Sor Juana's transgression to be understood in a more contemporary sense.

The setting of the film is sparse and minimalist, the colours used contrastive. The archbishop often appears surrounded by darkness, while Sor Juana and the convent are often bathed in light, thereby echoing the atmosphere of a baroque painting. As Bemberg said to Félix Monti when they were filming, 'Félix, remember Zurbarán's light.'[51] One critic has noted that, 'Through long, static, shots, confined staging, and minimized tracking, Bemberg creates a visual metaphor for the pervasive repression and claustrophobia of the times, as Sor Juana struggles to defy social convention and pursue an independent life as an intellectual and artist.'[52] The film was not made on location; instead Bemberg used a film set. The blues, greens and greys used to convey the convent give it, indeed, almost an art deco feel.[53]

La frontera ('The Frontier', 1991), directed by the Chilean film director Ricardo Larraín, is based on the actual mechanism whereby an individual who disagreed with Pinochet's regime – instituted in 1973 and continuing up until 1990 – was sent away to a remote part of the country such as the Dawson Islands in the Magellan Straits, becoming in effect a *relegado* (an internal 'exile'). Rather than focusing on physical torture or the murder of the *desaparecidos*, Larraín's film concentrates on a more subtle type of torture, one which concerns the basic problems of the everyday life of a *relegado* living in a remote unnamed village in southern Chile, as presented through the life of Ramiro Orellana (Patricio Contreras), in order to create a film in the political-absurdist mode. The progressively more absurd rules that the two officials invent in order to make Ramiro's life difficult – forcing him to sign an attendance book at regular intervals to prove that he has not absconded, as well as write out his name in capital letters to confirm the signature, even though there can be no doubt about his identity since, as Ramiro himself points out, there are no other *relegados* anywhere around – have a black humour about them. The camera uses a blue tint to underline the ubiquity of water, and thereby focus on the main image of oppression as experienced by the Chilean people – a slow, painful death by drowning. The blue tint also acts as an omen of the tidal wave which, like the apocalypse, destroys the life of the community. The tidal wave, though it has some Amerindian and biblical resonances, is more appropriately interpreted as a concrete embodiment of the uncontrollable forces of fascism – in Spain in the 1930s and in Chile in the 1970s – that invaded and destroyed people's lives (Maite and her father, Ignacio, are in some senses more desperate victims than Ramiro). A central image in *La frontera* which offers a counterpoint to that of the tidal wave is the statue of the founders of Chile which is rescued at the end and becomes a point of anagnorisis, in that it represents the 'Abrazo de Maipú' – the embrace between José de San Martín and Bernardo O'Higgins after the Battle of Maipú, which secured Chilean independence – symbolizing the bringing together of the two cultures – the Spanish and the Mapuche – rather than the destruction that fascism has brought about. This is in contrast to the official culture represented early on in the film by the absurd posing of the two detectives in front of the national flag for the 'family' snap. The true history of Chile – its authentic roots – has been buried under the tidal wave of fascism.

Perhaps more important than the film's rather obvious symbolism are its quirky, surrealist motifs, such as the diver who is seeking to avert the catastrophe of the tidal wave by finding the hole at the bottom of the ocean. In a world which has been rendered absurd by its political devastation, the diver's logic is as sensible as anyone else's. Since *La frontera* was released when Pinochet still possessed political power (he had stepped down from the presidency in 1990 as the result of a plebiscite but was still head of the armed forces), the director judiciously chose to make his point in a displaced rather than direct manner. Even so, the film ends on a clear message of repudiation. Ramiro is filmed repeating his denunciation

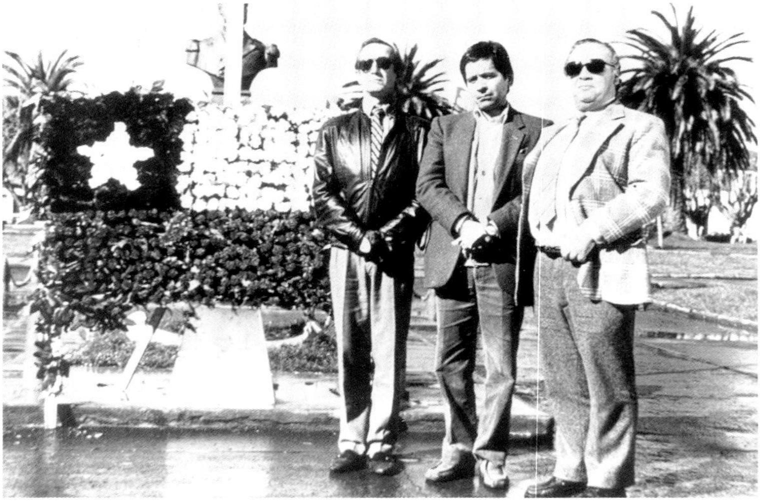

The 'family' snap in *La frontera* (1991)

to the press at the conclusion – the very words that got him into trouble in the first place.

El viaje ('The Voyage', 1992), by the Argentine director Fernando Solanas, is similar to *La frontera* in that it is a political-absurdist film about the desire to discover national identity. We follow Martín (Walter Quiroz), a hybridly ironic mix of Argentina's liberator José de San Martín, and prototypical revolutionary Ernesto 'Che' Guevara, as he journeys on his bicycle (rather than motorbike) through Argentina (the Straits of Magellan, Patagonia, Buenos Aires), the Andes, Machu Picchu, Cuzco and its Holy Temple, the Amazon, a goldmine in Brazil and finally Mexico. While searching for his father, Martín discovers that Latin America is drowning in debt – which is demonstrated naturalistically (matches are sold to him one at a time in the Peruvian Andes), graphically (Brazil's president as well as his advisors are trussed up) and metaphorically (Argentina is under water, clearly echoing Larraín's *La frontera*). The film begins as a self-discovery fable and gradually turns into a tale of the absurd: the weather forecast predicts the world will 'tilt', and then it appears to do so; because Argentina is under water, people have started selling 'plots of water'; the Argentine president is called Dr Rana (Dr Frog), suggesting that he will swim when others drown – an obvious dig at Carlos Menem; while in Brazil there is an External Debt truck which arrives in the Andes in order to demand contributions from the peasants through its loudspeakers. Though humorously melodramatic, *El viaje* was not to everyone's taste. There were those who pointed to its 'overt allegorical strategies'.[54] Others did not agree with Solanas's left-wing politics: 'Fernando Solanas's outspoken contempt for Carlos Menem's administration in Argentina nearly cost him his life – an assassination attempt confined him to a wheelchair for most of the post-production on *The Voyage*.'[55] The conclusion of *El viaje* – Martín appears to discover his father in Mexico, driving a truck carrying an enormous image of the Aztec god Quetzalcoatl, the Plumed Serpent – appears tacked on, and indeed it was since Solanas ran out of funding towards the end of the project and was only able to secure help from the Instituto Mexicano de Cinematografía on the condition that one of the filmed sequences would take place in Mexico.[56] The main moral of the *El viaje* – as suggested by its conclusion – is that Latin America should seek its cultural destiny not by espousing Western values but rather by delving into its Amerindian past.[57]

Cronos (1993), directed by Guillermo del Toro, is a vampire movie with a difference. The 'cronos', a gold contraption developed by an alchemist in Veracruz, Mexico, in 1536, containing a scarab whose sting brings eternal life, ends up in an antique shop in 1937. The antique owner is Jesús Gris (Federico Luppi) – a grey and therefore 'imperfect' Christ,[58] who suddenly finds that he regains his youthful looks after

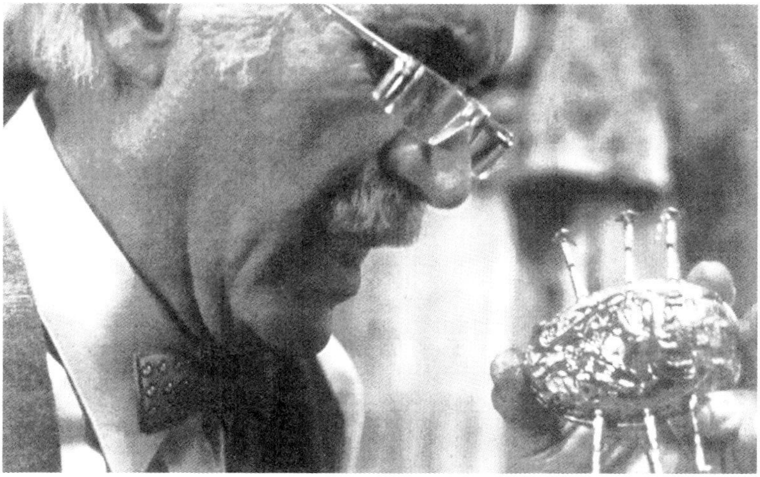

Jesús Gris looks closely at the 'cronos' in *Cronos*.

being stung by the contraption. There is, however, a nasty side effect in that he is also overcome by an uncontrollable desire to drink human blood. A local businessman, Dieter de la Guardia (Claudio Brook), suspecting that Jesús Gris now possesses the 'cronos', sends his psychotic nephew, Angel de la Guardia (Ron Perlman), to retrieve it. Casting an American actor as the villain of the film was a 'little wink' from del Toro to the audience since it was a reversal of the stereotypical evil Mexican in many U.S. movies.[59] Though pushed off a cliff in a car by the evil nephew and declared dead, Jesús Gris is resurrected, escaping in hilarious fashion from the morgue just before he is about to be cremated, and eventually kills the evil nephew as well as Dieter de la Guardia. He is cared for by his granddaughter, Aurora Gris (Tamara Shanath), but when Aurora is injured and he sees her blood, the scene is set for the final triumph of evil when he approaches her, echoing the iconic scene from James Whale's *Frankenstein* (1931) when Frankenstein's monster kills the young girl by the lake. (Guillermo del Toro mentions this scene in an interview as the prototypical scene of the horror film, the thrill of which he had always wanted to re-create in his own films.[60]) However, in a twist of the monster movie prototype, Jesús Gris refuses to kill her, and instead destroys the 'cronos' by smashing it with a rock. *Cronos* thus concludes on a note of redemption, and thereby in effect re-Catholicizes vampirism.[61]

Guillermo del Toro found it very hard to make *Cronos* because of spiralling production costs. When it first went into production it was officially Mexico's most expensive film with a budget of $1,500,000 (although it was soon overtaken by Arau's *Como agua para chocolate*) and it cost an extra $500,000 as a result of the interest payable on the original loan.[62] But the biggest obstacle was the reluctance of the Mexican Film Institute to fund the film. In the 1990s, as del Toro has pointed out, the film industry in Mexico was 'sadly very corrupt' in that there was an older generation of Mexican film directors who, because of government funding, were on their tenth or eleventh film (del Toro does not mention names but he is thinking of directors such as Arturo Ripstein whose eleventh film, *La mujer del puerto*, came out in 1991) while a younger generation (del Toro mentions his contemporaries Alfonso Cuarón and González Iñárritu) had to go through many years of 'internship' working for nothing on a number of films, including those of their friends. He and González Iñárritu often discussed their fear that theirs would be the 'skipped' generation.[63] But Del Toro was so persistent that after four years the Mexican Institute of Film eventually relented and allowed *Cronos* to go into production.

It was a labour of love. The cinematography, the camera angles and the editing all showed an attention to detail that was more in keeping with an art house film than a 'popular culture' movie about a Mexican vampire. The colour coding, for example, is used purposefully in *Cronos* to indicate the identity of different characters as well as the stages of the alchemical process. As del Toro has pointed out, there is an abundance of black in the film, reflecting the importance of black as the symbol of base matter in alchemy, and grey – as well as black and white – is often used to echo the protagonist's name (Jesús Gris) and suggest the drabness of his existence. Jesús Gris's house – and his wife – are colour-coded in warm earth tones while the villains are colour-coded in blues, cold greys, blacks and whites. Red, given its importance in the alchemical cosmology, is only used in connection with Aurora, who often wears very striking red dresses, although it also appears in association with Jesús and his shop at certain crucial junctures.[64] But when the final cut of *Cronos* was pre-screened, one of the heads of the Mexican Film Institute told the team that because the film was a vampire movie it would simply fade into obscurity in Mexico.[65] But *Cronos* went on to win nine out of the eleven Mexican academy awards, as well as the Critics' Week Prize at the Cannes Film Festival.[66]

The individual who dismissed *Cronos* as a vampire movie was wrong in that Guillermo del Toro's clever film could not be simply typecast in this way. *Cronos* mixes genres innovatively, combining the vampire movie formula with black comedy, leading to a blend of genres that del Toro, as he points out in an interview, has always aimed for in his Spanish-language films. This contrasts with his English-language films which, as he discovered to his personal cost when he later made *Mimic*, have to be less experimental because of the pressures of the Hollywood system.[67] The black humour in *Cronos* is death-fixated and intrinsically Mexican. As Guillermo del Toro has pointed out:

> The film is very Mexican in the sense that what is portrayed in it could only happen in Mexico. The undertaker who is chewing chewing gum and eats a banana . . . is so careless that he loses the

dead body . . . There is also the idea that death can be seen in such a natural way by a young girl. So it's a film of its time and place.[68]

Some details identify *Cronos* as a Mexican historical allegory. The branding iron mark which can be seen on Jesús Gris's hand at the beginning of the film, for instance, is a reference to the practice of the Inquisition in the early colonial days of New Spain (as Mexico was then known) of branding individuals regarded as potential heretics.[69] But *Cronos* is not only about Mexico's past, it is also about the 'horrors' of modern Mexico. The film was released in 1993 and, as del Toro has noted, the vampire motif had a political resonance:

> The insect was vampirizing the victim, the mechanism was vampirizing the insect, in turn the industrialists are vampirizing Mexico. I just wanted to create an ever-growing chain of vampirism in the movie. That's why you can see all the signs on the street and the newspapers in several languages, because this movie was made in a pre-NAFTA Mexico and NAFTA was seen by me as essentially a form of vampirism.[70]

It was meant as an allegory of what was occurring at that time on the political front in terms of NAFTA (the North American Free Trade Agreement) in which the United States was cast as the vampire-villain feeding off its victim, Mexico. The international acclaim received by *Cronos* in Cannes in 1993 as well as in other international festivals caught the Mexican authorities off balance and, in retrospect, was the first major step in the internationalization of Latin American cinema.

In many ways 1993 can be seen as the year in which Mexican cinema came of age. It was the time it achieved a profound impact on the festival circuit with *Cronos* as well as breaking into the commercial world of film with Arau's *Como agua para chocolate*. While Arau's film was conspicuous by its absence from the list of international awards – though it did win eleven Mexican Academy of Motion Pictures awards – it was the first film, as noted above, to demonstrate that Latin American cinema could punch above its weight in terms of box office success. *Como agua para chocolate* was screened continuously in Mexico City in six cinemas for six months.[71] In the seven months following its February 1993 release it made $6.1 million in Mexico, which at the time was the most ever made by a Latin American film.[72] It then made $21,665,468 in sales in the United States.[73] The film has a conventional plot based on the trials and tribulations of star-crossed lovers. The authoritarian Mamá Elena (Regina Tomé) offers the young suitor, Pedro (Marco Leonardi), her eldest daughter, Rosaura (Yareli Arizmendi), in marriage rather than her younger daughter, Tita (Lumi Cavazos), whom Pedro really loves. Pedro agrees to marry Rosaura just to be close to Tita. Pedro and Tita's love is finally allowed to blossom after Rosaura's death but their lovemaking leads to Pedro's death during orgasm, and Tita then commits suicide by eating matches.

Como agua para chocolate is, in essence, a feminine counter-version of the Mexican Revolution, offering a kitchen's-eye view of those turbulent years, at odds with the masculinized version that focuses on soldiers and battles. As Esquivel has said in an interview: 'The kitchen, to me, is the most important part of the house. It is a source of knowledge that generates life and pleasure.'[74] The most striking characteristic of the film, as its title suggests, is the use of food as a metaphor for human emotions.[75] There are various examples of this: Tita's tears which drop into the cake as it is prepared for Rosaura and Pedro's wedding meal produce a fit of vomiting in the guests; Tita's blood, mixed with rose petals, when added to the quails, produces an aphrodisiac reaction in those

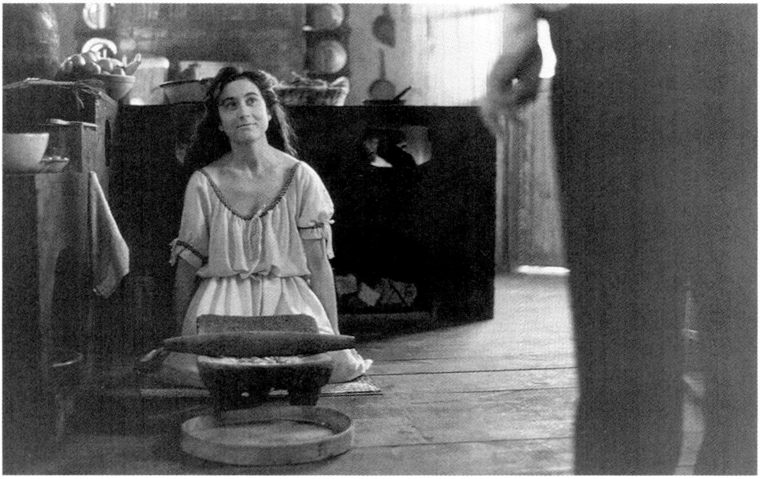

Tita looks adoringly at her beloved Pedro in *Como agua para chocolate* (1993).

who consume it, an idea that is repeated in the last chapter of the novel when Tita makes *chile en nogada* and unleashes an orgy of the senses. While the link between food and sex is a traditional one, *Como agua* manages to extend this association in unexpected ways. Perhaps the best illustration of this occurs when Tita has to sing to the beans to make them cook. In a house, so popular knowledge suggests, where there have been arguments, the food is 'annoyed' and therefore will not allow itself to be cooked. Most intriguing of all is the way in which the emotions are depicted as emanating from the body like a cloud, influencing everything in their path. Such is the cloud of rose perfume which emanates from Gertrudis's body and attracts Juan, the *villista*, to her, at which point, following a romantic stereotype, they sail off into the sunset on a horse.

Como agua was an undeniably popular film and, as Tomás Pérez Turrent put it, 'The response to the film by the world public was "chocolate" while the response of the critics was "water".'[76] John Kraniauskas argues that the film 'retreats from the masculinized terrain of high politics and the battlefield and concentrates our attention on the so-called private sphere of a household run by woman'.[77] In terms of its success at creating visual solutions to the plot, *Como agua* has a mixed scorecard. The parallelism between sadness and salt, as expressed through the central image of the tear, for example, appears in a set of successful visual solutions. Thus the film opens with a close-up of an onion, and this motif is explored through the tears that the foetal Tita is heard to shed in the womb, the salt in the amniotic fluids that gush over the kitchen table when she is born and the salt used in the meals – a set of associations paralleled in the subsequent scene when Tita's tears drop into the batter from which the wedding cake will be made. To counterbalance this, the visual expression of the parallelism between fire and love, such as when Gertrudis's shower bursts into flames, or when Tita and Pedro finally make love at the conclusion of the film, is less convincing. But the overall significance of *Como agua para chocolate* is clear; it was a stepping stone for Latin American cinema which showed that a Latin American film director could create a commercially successful film which spoke directly to audiences across the subcontinent mainly in the language of magical realism, and thereby plotted a new course between the Charybdis of Nuevo Cine Latinoamericano and the Scylla of state funding.[78]

The following year a film was released which, like *Como agua para chocolate*, used food as a metaphorical avenue with which to delve into deeper issues. Cuban director Tomás Gutiérrez Alea's *Fresa y chocolate* ('Strawberry and Chocolate', 1994) caused quite a stir when it first came out since it treated a subject hitherto taboo in Cuba: homosexuality. In Cuba the film was so popular that 'impatient crowds broke down a cinema's doors to see it'.[79] It showed continuously in Havana for eight months and 'became the first Cuban film to be nominated for an Academy Award as Best Foreign Film; the year before it won first prize at the Berlin Film Festival'.[80] The film is based on Senel Paz's novel *El lobo, el bosque y el hombre nuevo* ('The Wolf, the Woods, and the New Man', 1991). Gutiérrez Alea read the novel, saw its filmic potential and asked Paz to write him a script.[81] Like *La frontera* and *El viaje*, *Fresa y chocolate* sought to investigate the notion of nationhood through allegory spiced with humour. *Fresa y chocolate* portrays Cuba at a crossroads; it was released at a time when Cuba was beginning to experience the beginning of a deep and lasting crisis, the so-called 'Periodo Especial'. The film portrays the conflict between two opposing lifestyles. On the one hand we have David (Vladimir Cruz), a young idealistic member of the Communist Party, who is a little naive as his lack of knowledge about products such as whisky, and his ignorance of literary figures such as Mario Vargas Llosa and John Donne, suggest. On the other we have Diego (Jorge Perugorría), a tortured artist who is disillusioned with the Communist regime, fascinated with the foreign and the exotic, and – to boot – gay. The plot focuses on how these two contradictory notions of Cubanness are eventually brought together – epitomized by the hug between Diego and David at the end of the film.

Both Diego and David in a sense come nearer to each other politically, though this political rapprochement is represented in terms of physical attraction. Everyone, it seems, is in love with David. Diego, as the older, gay man, has completely fallen for David's innocent ways and his good looks. Nancy (Mirtha Ibarra) is also in love with him, and even prays to the African deities to allow her to keep him for just one year. Vivian (Marilyn Solaya) offers him love, and sex, even though she has recently married. Even his hardline Communist friend Miguel wants to keep him for himself and the Communist Party, and accuses him of being gay when he senses that he has begun to lose him towards the end of the

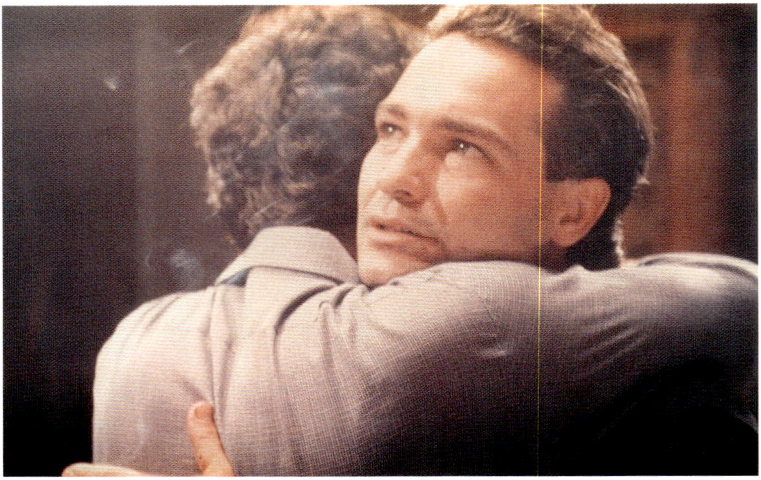

The famous hug in Tomás Gutiérrez Alea's *Fresa y chocolate* (1993).

film. David in a sense represents Cuba, and all of these different aspects of Cuba – the gay artist, the conventional young woman who plays safe, the ageing prostitute, the Communist youth – are 'in love' with David, and desire him. He seemingly holds the key to Cuba's future.

While it is possible to read *Fresa y chocolate* as a pro-gay film (in the sense that David, by hugging Diego at the conclusion of the film, appears to accept his gayness), a number of pointers in the film belie this reading. Gay sexuality, at a number of key junctures, is replaced by feminine sexuality in the film, thereby ostracizing homosexuality as a phantom presence which is always offstage. As Paul Smith suggests:

> By narrativizing explicitly, if discreetly, the oppression of homosexuals in Cuba, the film states a domesticated mise-en-scene in which the unspeakable horrors of the other scene (out of shot, behind the door) are allowed to emerge into visibility, but only on condition that they do not trouble the heterosexual spectator.[82]

This heterosexual normativization of homosexuality appears to be elicited triumphantly by the final, sexless hug of the film between Diego and David. But there is one discordant note in this apparently seamless heterosexualization of gay sexuality, and this is the scene in the shower in which Miguel – otherwise presented as the macho, homophobic Communist – in a gesture that seems very much out of character, pats David on the buttocks. Though this is the only point at which a same-sex gesture is hinted at, it is nevertheless significant that it should be initiated by the character whose actions and words up until this point suggest he is ruled by homosexual panic. This surely must be a deliberate wink at the viewer as well as a humorously ironic jibe at homosexual panic.

The viewer, knowing the anti-gay credentials of Fidel Castro, is bound to ask if Gutiérrez Alea was making an anti-Castro statement in this film. This was certainly the view taken by the author of the film preview which appeared in *Variety*: 'Filled with malicious swipes against the Castro regime, *Fresa y chocolate* is a provocative but very humane comedy about sexual opposites and, with proper handling, could attract the *Wedding Banquet* crowd in cinemas worldwide.'[83] Castro, indeed, was asked if he liked the film but he did not comment.[84] On one level, then, the film can be interpreted as an apology for the freedoms of the West. Diego's interest in John Donne and Mario Vargas Llosa, his taste for tea and whisky, are not presented as reprehensible in the film; indeed, it is David's naivety that is more susceptible of criticism. As Stephen Wilkinson suggests, the film 'seems to be making the point that Cuba and Revolution are very much the less for having lost the contribution that figures like Diego could make'.[85] With hindsight though, it is clear that *Fresa y chocolate* went further than this. The letters that have recently been published by Titón's widow, Mirtha Ibarra, suggest that he used the gay narrative as a vehicle to express his dissatisfaction with the government. Gutiérrez Alea, throughout his career, always asked hard questions of the regime, and indeed never shied away from criticizing certain reprehensible aspects of it. But this was always in the sense of constructive criticism rather than outright attack. In a letter Gutiérrez Alea wrote to Alfredo Guevara on 14 September 1977, he referred to the problems he had been facing in ICAIC:

> I do not find in the organisation to which I am linked professionally the necessary stimulus allowing me to develop my capacity to work effectively, and this at a time when furthermore I feel that I am achieving the right level of artistic maturity so I can give the very best of myself.

He also referred to the problems that had plagued him over the years:

> We now have the privilege of hindsight allowing us to look back and see that those errors and clumsy actions have proliferated abundantly during that period in all areas and especially in the cultural field where they have been nothing less than scandalous.[86]

If it is possible to extract the gay ingredient from Diego's dilemma as portrayed in *Fresa y chocolate*, it is not possible to do the same with regard to the artistic ingredient. Most of Diego's conversations with David, indeed, revolve around art. He has an intense relationship with Germán (Joel Angelino), but this is expressed as much through art as through homosexual love. It is Diego's artistic integrity which persuades him to write the letter that leads to the loss of his job. The strategy Diego uses, indeed, to seduce David is via art – namely, recreating a Lezama Lima meal as described in chapter VII of Lezama Lima's novel *Paradiso* (1966). *Fresa y chocolate* is, thus, not a pro-gay film. Alea agreed with Senel Paz, the screenplay writer, that 'the main theme of the film is not so much about homosexuality as about intolerance'.[87] All these pointers, as well as the fact that homosexuality is never visually articulated, suggest that Diego is more artist than gay man.[88]

Some of the difficulties in extrapolating the ideology of Gutiérrez Alea's film were brought home to me in the lively exchange which occurred between Mirtha Ibarra, his widow, and Edmundo Desnoes, the co-scriptwriter of *Memorias del subdesarrollo*, in a roundtable I chaired in the Bloomsbury Theatre on 10 November 2009, as part of the London World Film Festival. The disagreement focused on the use of the word 'contradictorio' (contradictory) with regard to Titón's work. Desnoes said the film was contradictory but Ibarra flatly disagreed, saying Titón would never have used such a term to describe his work. In the light of the letters, as well as the portrayal of Diego's artistic dilemma, it is likely that *Fresa y chocolate* is a coded film that expresses Gutiérrez Alea's last testimony about the struggles he had experienced as an artist expressing his vision of the world in Cuba.[89]

Espinosa's *Reina y Rey* (1994), a low-budget film inspired by one of the classics of Italian neo-Realism *Humberto D.* (1952), co-directed by Vittorio De Sica and Cesare Zavattini, and dedicated to the latter, manages to offer an allegory of post-Perestroika Cuba through the simple story of the friendship of an elderly woman, Reina, with her dog, Rey.[90] There is hardly any criticism on this film; as far as I am aware there are only two short reviews, one in the *New York Times* by Sandra Brennan, the other for *Vanity* by Lisa Nesselson.[91] As the first half of the film unfolds it becomes clear that the main dilemma Reina faces is whether she is able to keep her dog. There is so much poverty in Havana that everyone has had to give up their dogs and cats. Reina takes Rey to the *asilo canino* (dog kennels) but, horrified by what she sees – the gas chamber where the dogs are sacrificed – she cannot bring herself to hand him over. In a touch of black humour the chamber cannot be used because the kennels have run out of gas. It soon becomes clear that these apparently accidental or realist details are being used to build up a sense of modern-day Cuba as a concentration camp where people are dying.[92] As one character says to Reina when she is worried that Rey has not returned in the evening: '*los perros son como los seres humanos*' (dogs are like human beings). Underscoring the parallelism between human beings and dogs we note the title in which Rey functions almost as the surrogate husband of Reina. The world of the dogs throws light on human society in a number of ways. Apart from the *asilo canino,* we see stray dogs around Havana's streets or fighting for food on the local rubbish tip. It is important to note that Rey is fed on two occasions by *jineteras* who are walking along the Malecón, as if to suggest that his only source of food is via the illicit earnings of prostitution.

Yet Rey is not simply a synecdoche of the human condition, although he does have this role in the film. Reina would rather starve than give him up. When Rey disappears Reina becomes distraught, so much so that, as a neighbour remarks, she would never even consider leaving Cuba as long as there is the slightest possibility that Rey might come back. It is only once Reina finally accepts that Rey will not be coming back that she is enticed by the offer of her former boss, Carmen, to leave Havana and go and live with them in Miami. But when walking through Havana with Carmen and her husband, just as she has made up her mind, Rey suddenly appears. Reina turns back but does not see him since her view is blocked by some passers-by. Indeed Rey's symbolic function within the plot is underscored at the conclusion of the film. Inexplicably, Reina refuses at the last moment to go with Carmen, who drives off with her husband in their car to the airport and thence to Miami without her. A young man on a bike asks Reina if she is waiting for Rey, and she says she is. The film concludes with the word '*esperándolo*' (waiting for him), making it clear that Rey is a symbol of Cuba's future utopia. Reina, the film seems to be telling us, is waiting for a better future and in this she becomes paradigmatic of all Cubans. It is important to underscore that this longed-for future does not include the Americanization of Cuba. When Carmen and her husband arrive in Havana they turf Reina out of the bedroom, reclaim their former house and do all the touristy things such as drinking champagne at the Tropicana club. There, Carmen gets extremely drunk while her husband goes off with a black prostitute. To cap the colonialist metaphor they attempt to take Reina back to Miami since they know they will be able to exploit her good habits (hard work with little complaint). This is the point at which the film becomes an allegory for the feared future invasion of Cuba after Castro's death. The thought does not even cross Carmen's mind that Reina might not want to go to Miami. Carmen and Reina fall out when Reina says that her real name is Yolanda – at which point Carmen blows her top. This can be interpreted as the anagnorisis scene in which Reina's true Cuban revolutionary self is revealed. No longer the submissive maid, kowtowing to her rich superiors, Reina becomes Yolanda, the authentically Cuban and revolutionary woman.

Reina y Rey can, as suggested above, be seen as an allegory for the dilemmas faced by modern-day Cuba, or more particularly the Cuba of the 1990s. In a witty use of the language of film to make a semantic point, the first half is filmed in black and white in order to underline the drabness of Cuba with its poverty and endless queues, while the second half, from the point when the 'bosses' arrive from Miami, is filmed in colour. As García Espinosa has pointed out: 'The use of black and white was motivated by the desire to show in an oblique way the drabness of the old woman's life; the colour coincided with the appearance of the couple from Miami and underlies the false colour of their lives.'[93] Indeed, by breaking one of the cardinal rules of Hollywood filmmaking, Espinosa is able to make a clever point about how Cuban reality is schizoid. As one character says, 'All people in Miami do is think about people over here, while all people here do is think about people in Miami. Nobody's happy.' It is of course imperfect cinema, but imperfect cinema with a difference, since the signifier of the film – the decision to film in unadorned black and white – becomes a new political signifier. What better way of expressing the poverty of communism and the glitz of capitalism than to film in black and white first and then in colour?

But there is of course more to this than meets the eye. The technique was clearly inspired not only by *The Wizard of Oz* but also by the more subtle play between black-and-white and colour in Steven Spielberg's *Schindler's List*, which had come out the previous year in 1993, where the only object filmed in colour is the little girl's red coat as she is led off to her premature grave. As often occurs in Espinosa's films, there is a self-reflexive component to this artistic choice. Espinosa essentially deconstructs the positive value we normally associate with colour, for it becomes representative of the exploitative language of American capitalism. Miami, as it were, invades in colour. Thus, in the last scene when Reina decides not to go to Miami with her bosses, the colour of Cuba changes. Filmed with a blue lens, Reina's residence is now somewhere in between the black and white of Part I and the Technicolor of Part II. It is chiaroscuro of Cuba, waiting and hoping; '*esperándolo*'. We may recall that the anagnorisis scene occurs during the *apagón* (blackout). In effect, when the lights go out we are left with black and white. Colours recede from the film's mental screen. It is significant, too, that Reina's moment of defiance occurs when we see her in the shadows; we see her silhouette swaying backwards and forwards in the rocking chair, an image perhaps of 'dialectical' rebellion. The film offers a concrete embodiment of the dialectical tension of Cuba in the mid-1990s, caught between two discourses and two ways of being. Indeed, the chiaroscuro as filmic signifier suddenly turns into a political signifier before our very eyes. While *Reina y Rey* can, at a primary level, be seen as a homage to Italian neo-Realism, on closer inspection it reveals itself to be an artful interrogation of the different codes – black and white realism versus glitzy Americanism – which moves it beyond the dead-end rhetorics of neo-Realism. It is here that the stamp of Espinosa's arresting filmic vision – its dialectical chiaroscuro – may be divined.

Moebius (1996), by the Argentinian director Gustavo Mosquera, tells the story of the enigmatic disappearance of a train on the Buenos Aires underground. An investigator, Daniel Pratt, is called in to solve the mystery and he 'discovers' that a perimeter extension line – which was in the original plans for the underground drawn up by Pratt's topology professor, Hugo Mistein, but apparently not built – has mysteriously appeared, causing the network to behave like a Möbius strip. Pratt stumbles across a station called Borges, gets on a train and finds that it is the missing train carrying the disappeared people, and driven by his old topology professor. The train then accelerates along the Möbius strip to infinity. Though a little heavy-handed in terms of its allegorical dimension, *Moebius* offers a new sci-fi take on the 'disappeared' of Argentina's Dirty War.[94]

Central do Brasil ('Central Station', 1998), directed by Walter Salles, is the most reflective of the nation-image Latin American films of the 1990s. The search for national identity is articulated in a more layered manner than in *El viaje* and *La frontera* since it has been split between two characters, a middle-aged woman, Dora (Fernanda Montenegro), and a nine-year-old boy, Josué (Vinícius de Oliveira), who are thrown together by circumstance: Josué's mother, Ana (Soia Lira) dies in a car crash, having only just employed Dora as her scribe to pen a letter to her husband living in Estrela do Norte. Dora first of all takes Josué to an 'adoption agency' and is paid 1,000 reis for her efforts, but she is persuaded by her best friend Irene (Marília Pêra) that Josué might be killed and his organs sold. Dora returns to save him from his fate. At this point *Central do Brasil* turns from being a thesis-film about the fate of children in modern Brazil to become a road movie in which Dora and Josué search for their roots, a search that, especially as expressed by Josué, takes on a universal dimension.[95] As Walter Salles pointed out in an interview:

> With *Central Station*, the story was basically about the recuperation of one's identity and also, an investigation into the country's identity. In Portuguese, the words for father (*pai*) and country (*pais*) are almost the same. So the search for a father in *Central Station* is also a search for a country.[96]

As a result of this search, Josué is reunited with his half-brothers, Moisés (Caio Junqueira) and Isaías (Mateus Nachtergaele), Dora eventually comes to terms with her unrequited love for the father who rejected her, and Ana and her husband Jesus are united in letter if not in body (Dora leaves Ana's letter to Jesus on the mantelpiece next to Jesus's letter to Ana under their portrait).

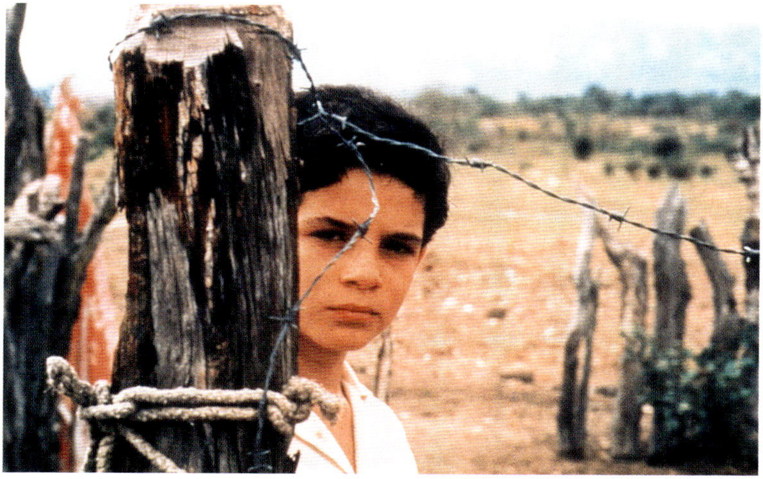

Josué is forlorn in *Central do Brasil* (1998) when he fails to find his father.

The film draws strength from its documentary roots (as Salles has pointed out, he made documentaries for about ten years before he took up making fiction films),[97] as suggested by the two letter-writing sequences in which we see a succession of faces narrating the details of their lives in the manner of a vox pop, and the spontaneous filming of a religious festival:

> So when we were location scouting I saw these religious processions and I really felt that that was so descriptive of what was inherent to that part of Brazil that we needed to plunge it in, so we rewrote the screenplay as we were filming it. I think with road movies, especially, you should leave the door open for things like that to happen. And also, you should be porous to the people that you encounter on the road. You have to be open to let those persons change you and change the fabric of the film.[98]

There are also some strong cinematographic solutions to support the evolution of the plot – the bars which crowd the frame in the early Rio scenes which express entrapment in the big city, Dora's helplessness expressed by the goat which limps with its front paws tied up past her when she is overwhelmed by despair at the bus station, and the shot of Dora crying and clinging to the bars of the bathroom window when she sees the *evangelista*'s truck drive off, abandoning her to her fate. Colours and focus are also used effectively. As Salles explains:

> What we aimed to do in this film was to lose the focus at the beginning, just focus on the human drama of the faces in the station, so that as the story gets closer and closer to the father, and by extension, the country, you start to see – through the changing depth of focus – that the reality and the country is actually a lot denser than you first thought. At the same time, the colour also changes – I don't know if you realised, but it's very monochromatic. We opted to use very brown colours at the beginning, and it's as if the characters are unable to see more than that. And the closer they get to the heart of the country, the more colours they start to perceive. So the idea of recuperating one's identity is linked to the idea of having a more wide-ranging sensorial palette as well.[99]

Last but not least, this film has a number of strong acting performances, particularly by Marília Pêra and Fernanda Montenegro, who was nominated for an Academy Award for Best Actress in a Leading Role. *Central do Brasil* was the most successful of the nation-image dramas of the 1990s in Latin America even if, in cinematic terms, it was in effect the end of the line for this particular genre.[100]

4
The Slick Grit of Contemporary Latin American Cinema (2000–2014)

This book has argued that Latin American film has experienced a number of paradigm shifts in which, following Gilles Deleuze's theorization, the movement-image that characterized early action-drama film was superseded by the time-image which emerged with the advent of neo-Realism. In *Cinema 2*, for example, Deleuze referred to the way in which neo-Realist cinema had led to a re-drawing of the boundaries between the real and the imaginary:

> As for the distinction between subjective and objective, it also tends to lose its importance, to the extent that the optical situation or visual description replaces the motor action. We run in fact into a principle of indeterminability, of indiscernibility: we no longer know what is imaginary or real, physical or mental, in the situation, not because they are confused, but because we do not have to know and there is no longer even a place from which to ask. It is as if the real and the imaginary were running after each other, as if each was being reflected in the other, around a point of indiscernibility.[1]

Whereas in the movement-image the imaginary was subservient to the real, the time-image led to a new parity between the real and the imaginary as if they were 'running after each other', to use Deleuze's words. It is important to recall that, despite the paradigm shift identified by Deleuze when realist cinema succumbed to neo-Realism (and the movement-image was superseded by the time-image), both types of film were analogue in the sense of creating an 'analogue' pre-digital image of reality. The process whereby the optical-sound space of cinema achieved a gradually increasing autonomy from the economy of the real as the century progressed increased in intensity exponentially as a result of the digital revolution. That revolution gave rise to a new motor driving the geometry of optical-sound space: digital technology. Indeed, the ease with which digital editing produced a new sound-look for digitally recorded reality led to a re-juggling of the relationship between the real and the virtual.

The digital-image

Although the first recorded attempt at building a digital camera took place as long ago as 1975,[2] it was only in 1998 that the first digital film was released.[3] The advantages of digital film – the drastically reduced costs of equipment as well as film, the portability of the cameras, the convenience of having the response to light determined automatically by the camera sensor, the ability to see the actual images that are captured immediately on the set, as well as the greater flexibility provided by digital post-production – led to more and more film directors turning away from 35mm to digital, including Danny Boyle (*Slumdog Millionaire*), Francis Ford Coppola (*Youth without Youth*), George Lucas (*Star Wars Episode II: Attack of the Clones*), Guy Ritchie (*Sherlock Holmes*), Michael Moore (*Bowling for Columbine*), Martin Scorsese (*George Harrison: Living in the Material World*), Lars von Trier (*Antichrist*), Robert Rodriguez (*Once Upon a Time in Mexico*) and Steven Soderbergh (*Che*). Indeed digital cinematography's acceptance was canonized in 2009 when *Slumdog Millionaire* became the first movie shot mainly in digital to be awarded the Academy Award for Best Cinematography. The highest-grossing movie in the history of cinema, *Avatar* (2009),[4] was not only shot on digital cameras but most of its box office earnings came no longer by film but by digital projection. Latin America has also been part of this shift towards the digital. In 2010 the Academy Award for Best Foreign Language Film was won by *El secreto de sus ojos* ('The Secret in Their Eyes'), which had been shot digitally.

What are the implications, we may well ask, of this shift towards the digital in the twenty-first century? Patricia Pisters in *The Neuro-Image:*

A Deleuzian Film-Philosophy of Digital Screen Culture (2012) has argued that the digital turn in culture at large is characterized by three trends: networked software cultures, deep remixability and database logic.[5] For his part, William Brown has argued in his important book *Film-Philosophy for the Digital Age: Supercinema* (2013) that the digital turn has had profound implications for the evolution of film in the twenty-first century. First, it has led to a new conception of space:

> Digital technology has brought about a conception of space in cinema that differs from that of the analogue. If limits in the size of film reels and the bulk of the camera have led mainstream narrative and analogue cinema to cut, then digital cinema seems to be predicated upon continuity . . . By showing space and all that fills it as a single continuum, as opposed to a space fragmented by objects, digital technology suggests the inherently connected nature of those objects and their surroundings.[6]

This has profound implications for the ways in which human beings interact with that space of their environment in the world of digital cinema, as Brown has argued:

> If space becomes indistinguishable from all that fills it, then this brings about a fundamental decentring of the figures that fill that space. That is, characters in digital cinema no longer stand out as unique agents against the space that surrounds them, but instead become inseparable from that space. The result of this 'decentring' is a minimizing of anthropocentrism in digital cinema. This logic is not only expressed by the way in which digital cinema increasingly features prominent characters of a nonhuman nature, but also by the way in which environments take on prominent roles in films, including mainstream films.[7]

This in turn has meant that the way time is projected in digital cinema has also been transformed:

> If digital cinema does not need to cut, thereby suggesting a continuity of space, and if analogue film was required to cut,

> then a similar logic applies to time . . . time becomes 'spatialized' in a certain way, such that we can pass from 'real' to 'imagined' or 'remembered' moments without necessarily seeing a marked division between them. In this way, time – both lived, 'real' time and imagined time – also form a continuum.[8]

As we shall see this sense of a new continuum within the projection of space and time in digital film is evident in Latin American film of the twenty-first century. It soon became clear, for example, with the release of *Amores perros* ('Love's a Bitch') by Alejandro González Iñárritu in 2000 that Latin American cinema had embarked on a new course which combined the political grit of its 1960s Nuevo Cine Latinoamericano roots with slick editing and acting performances that converted it into one of the major players of World Cinema in the new millennium. Latin American film has been able to attract new audiences because of a new, dynamic filmic mix; it combines the 'grit' associated with its heyday of the New Latin American Cinema of the 1960s and '70s – typified by directors such as Tomás Gutiérrez Alea, Julio García Espinosa, Jorge Sanjinés and Patricio Guzmán, renowned for their gritty, subaltern-focused view of the world – with the 'slick' camerawork of masters such as César Charlone (the cinematographer of *Cidade de Deus*) and Alejandro González Iñárritu. Films such as these used the innovations of digital editing to bold effect, and combined that wizardry with a fresh new type of acting; thus the actors of *Cidade de Deus* were 'real' gangsters of Rio de Janeiro (rather like the 'real' postman of Italian neo-Realism) who had been taught to act over the course of one year, and Gael García Bernal was a virtually unknown actor when he starred in *Amores perros*. The 'New' New Latin American film was typically located in a generic (often urban) non-national site akin to Deleuze's 'any-space-whatever',[9] thereby making a clean break with films of the 1990s which were located within a recognizably national space.

One additional feature of twenty-first-century films that distinguished them from their predecessors was that they were financed by private capital rather than state funds. Alejandro González Iñárritu sums up the new approach: he and his co-producer Guillermo Arriaga 'loathe the government-financed movie-making that seems to operate by the maxim: 'If nobody understands and nobody goes to see a movie, then it must mean it's a masterpiece.'[10] These characteristics – exploration of the digital image, the social grit of Nuevo Cine Latinoamericano, slick digital editing, the use of non-professional actors, location within a non-national space and private financing – were, as we shall see, the essential ingredients of the 'slick grit' of Latin American cinema in the twenty-first century.

Amores perros was a bracing start to the new millennium. It was the culmination of a process of private financing for filmmaking in Mexico which began in the early 1990s – it was jointly financed by two private companies, Altavista (86 per cent) and Zeta Films (14 per cent), the latter González Iñárritu's own production company – coupled with a new vision for the millennium.[11] It traced an abrupt departure from the nation-state and life-as-journey narratives that had peopled Latin American films in the 1990s, as epitomized by *La frontera* (1991), *El viaje* (1991) and *Central do Brasil* (1998), in which the protagonist's journey represented the nation's transition from one status to another. It is noticeable, for example, that there are no visible architectural landmarks in *Amores perros* to indicate that the film is set in Mexico. González Iñárritu clearly wanted to deconstruct the stereotype; as he suggested in an interview:

> I am not a Mexican with a moustache and a sombrero and a bottle of tequila . . . Nor am I a corrupt cop or a drug trafficker. There are millions like me. And this is the world I live in and the one I want to show.[12]

The reality represented as a result is contemporary, generic and urban.[13] The use of virtually unknown or non-professional actors also contributed to the contemporary generic feel of the film.[14]

The facial recognition effect, which comes from seeing a well-known actor, is a comfort zone for the viewer that *Amores perros* sought to break down. The other main difference was that *Amores perros* portrayed youth/teenager culture rather than, say, the middle-age culture evident, broadly speaking, in the three films mentioned above released in the 1990s. Especially in the first segment of *Amores perros*, the reflective consciousness is squarely located within a culture characterized by rebellion, lawlessness and violence, expressed as much by the brutal struggle

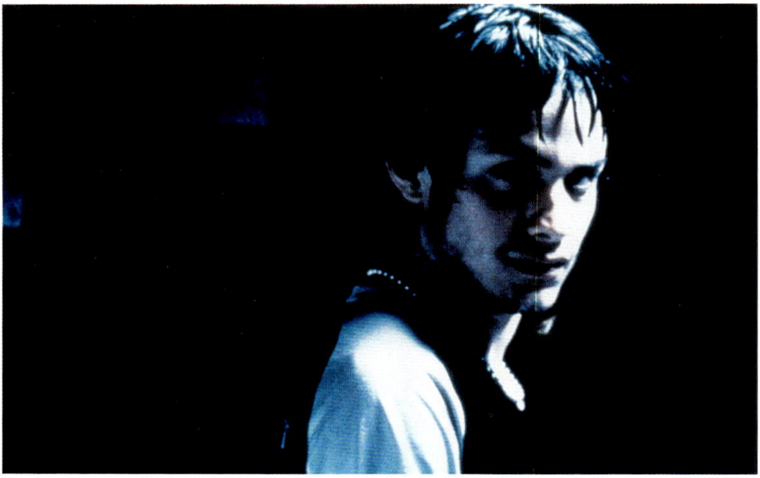

The look that launched Gael García Bernal's career in *Amores perros* (2000).

between Octavio (Gael García Bernal) and his brother, Ramiro (Marco Pérez), as by the gruesome and close-up dogfighting. Another feature of the culture depicted, which had direct implications for its future sales and was initially seen by the distributors as a risk, was its lack of inhibitions about using profanities. The dialogue between Octavio, Jorge (Humberto Busto), Ramiro and Jarocho (Gustavo Sánchez) is gritty and colourful. As soon became clear, the film's X-rating, far from denting circulation figures, led to exponential sales as a result of the creation of a new niche within the market (youth culture + action + experimental + X-rating), which was launched as a result of its success at Cannes.

The most striking narratological innovation inaugurated by *Amores perros* in Latin American film was the use of three, interconnected plots, which was a radical departure from a conventional, linear plot (even with flashbacks). In order to solve the problem of having three plots, González Iñárritu and the screenwriter Guillermo Arriaga came up with an ingenious filmic solution by creating an intersection – the car accident – at which the three life stories meet (or, indeed, collide), producing greater coherence by having the intersection viewed synoptically from different vantage points. Thus the car accident is first experienced by the viewer from within the truck which Octavio is driving (it concludes the establishing sequence of the film), it is then rerun at the conclusion of the first 'Octavio y Susana' segment, viewed from behind Valeria's car in the 'Daniel y Valeria' second segment and perceived over El Chivo's shoulder in the third 'El Chivo y Maru' segment of the film. One of the golden rules of conventional filmmaking – that a scene should not be portrayed twice because it may confuse the viewer – is broken in order to provide a solution which leads to greater coherence in the plot. This solution also opened up in one fell swoop new pathways within cinematic space.

Extras – such as the old man who is seen in segment one threatening a rival with a machete if he comes near his dogs, or the middle-aged man whose wallet Ramiro grabs in the bank robbery scene in segment three – double as protagonists; the old man is revealed to be El Chivo (Emilio Echeverría), the hitman, in segment three, and the middle-aged man in the bank is Leonardo, the fixer who organizes the hit for Gustavo Garfias (Rodrigo Murray), the corrupt businessman.[15]

This decision to provide new dimensions to extras – who conventionally simply function as stage-props allowing the action to follow the protagonists – related back to the hypothesis being tested in González Iñárritu's film, namely that reality is simply the end product of a complex combination of events in which individuals meet other individuals by chance. This uncertainty in the plot is suggested by the conclusion of the film. El Chivo places the gun midway between the two half-brothers, Gustavo Garfias and Luis Miranda Solares (Jorge Salinas), and

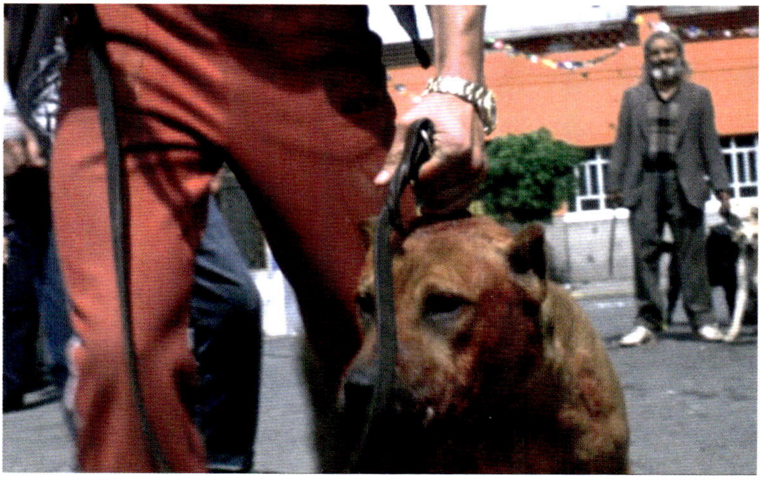

The 'chance' encounter between Jarocho and El Chivo in *Amores perros.*

lets them fight it out to the death; we do not see what happens next. Whereas in the original screenplay two 'shots' are heard to ring out as Chivito leaves the house,[16] the issue is deliberately left hanging in the air in the final cut version of the film.

Amores perros depicts a gritty reality in which brothers fight each other for women (Octavio and Ramiro fight over Susana (Vanessa Bauche) in segment one), or for power and money (the struggle between the two half-brothers in segment three, called Cain and Abel at one point by El Chivo), and dogs bite the throats out of other dogs, which is as raw as any found in the classics of Nuevo Cine Latinoamericano in the 1960s. One thinks of the torture scenes in Glauber Rocha's *Deus e o diabo na terra do sol* (1964) and the vicious murder of children in Miguel Littín's *El chacal de Nahueltoro* (1968). But the difference between *Amores perros* and the Nuevo Cine Latinoamericano is that it combined a depiction of a gritty reality with virtuoso cinematography and editing which might appear to undermine the political rawness of that reality. The dynamic, edgy portrayal of the car crash, for example, which has so impressed viewers, was achieved by a new technique pioneered by the director of photography, Rodrigo Prieto, who used skip bleach in post-production in order to enhance the contrast of colour and tone within the frame. As he explained in an interview:

> The contrast in general is enhanced with skip bleach, but so is the contrast of the grain. [The process] desaturates certain lines and colours, such as skin tones, but the reds and blues [are] even enhanced . . . We wanted the film to feel realistic, but with an edge. We were after the power of imperfection [and wanted to] use 'mistakes' to enhance the urgency and impredictability of life in a place like Mexico City.[17]

By making the whites in the frame that much whiter, Prieto was, in effect, producing a quasi-hallucinogenic effect, dazzling the viewer, thereby inducing a more vivid visual sensation in the viewer's mind. Though Prieto used a pre-digital technique in that the photographer smeared bleach on the film reel, this was a compositional strategy more akin to the digital paradigm in which colour transpositions can be engineered with a mouse. *Amores perros* was in effect pushing the boundaries between 35mm and digital film – bringing into being a new hybrid reality in which the slickness of digital editing was integrated into the universe of 35mm film. This slick grit, combined with the use of non-professional actors, was a winning formula which would prove to be distinctive for Latin American cinema, and it was not surprising that *Amores perros* (2000) went on to win the best film prize at a number of international film festivals (BAFTA, Cannes, Flanders, Chicago, Bogotá, Valdivia, São Paulo, Tokyo).

Nueve reinas ('Nine Queens', 2000), by the Argentine film director Fabián Bielinsky, is a heist thriller which manages to keep you on the edge of your seat. It won a string of awards, although these were, predictably, confined mainly to Latin American film festivals. It won the Silver Condor from the Argentine Film Critics Association (2001), the Audience award at the Bogotá Film Festival (2001) and the Elcine First Prize at the Lima Latin American Film Festival (2001), although it did win the prize of best actor for Ricardo Darín and Gaston Pauls at the Biarritz International Festival of Latin American Cinema (2001). Just as the two main characters, the old trickster, Marcos (Ricardo Darín) and the young trickster, Juan (Gaston Pauls), are trying to work out the other's next move, so the viewer also becomes involved in trying to work out who is double-crossing whom. In many ways, it is the viewer who is finally double-crossed when, as we discover in the final sequence, the younger trickster is the one who held the final trump card. While we are being gradually persuaded that the young man is mad to invest his money in the sale of the set of antique stamps – the *Nine Queens* of the title – and to see his father's words 'You won't survive' as the prediction of what will happen to him, in the final scene he goes back to the warehouse and we see all his accomplices, from the Spanish businessman, Vidal Gandolfo (Ignasi Abadal) to the old man, Sandler (Oscar Núñez), to the aunt who sells the stamps (played by Pochi Ducasse), to the stamp expert (Leo Dyzen), sitting round playing cards, looking like actors relaxing after the 'show'. Then we see – the film's final twist – that he is in fact the lover of Marcos's sister, Valeria (Leticia Brédice). For in a sense it has been a show, mainly for the old trickster, but also for us, the viewers, who have also been taken in by the young trickster's team. So we have been deceived twice, once as film viewers who suspend our disbelief in order to enjoy the filmic spectacle unfolding before our eyes, but also as 'naive' detectives who 'miss' the true, implicit trickster by focusing on the obvious, explicit trickster. And all is revealed in the last minute of the film.

Nueve reinas is part of a new dynamic in Latin American film in that the social metaphor is there – we can read this film as a story about national malaise, the bankruptcy of the Argentine economy after the decade of pegging the peso to the U.S. dollar, along with the moral bankruptcy of the Argentine president who presided over this demise. There are two scenes in particular where this social metaphor appears: in the first we hear Marcos – almost like the voice-over in a documentary film – telling us about the innumerable ways in which everyone is getting ripped off in the streets of Buenos Aires; in the second we see the crowds struggling to get into the national bank, and we realize that the cheque is useless. The social metaphor, therefore, is evident – the film appears to suggest that the politicians who sold the country down the river are as much the criminals of the piece as the petty thieves and heist criminals (including the two protagonists of the film, Marcos and Juan) who populate the streets of Buenos Aires. But notice that these two scenes are not the gravitational centre of the film, as perhaps they would have been had this been a film of the 1990s like *El viaje* which – in an explicit way – draws attention to the problems associated with debt. Here the film is on the *petite histoire* of two tricksters rather than the *grande histoire* of Argentina's bankruptcy. And this is where the paradigm shift enunciated by this film resides. *Nueve reinas* is a clever, fast-moving film and the viewer

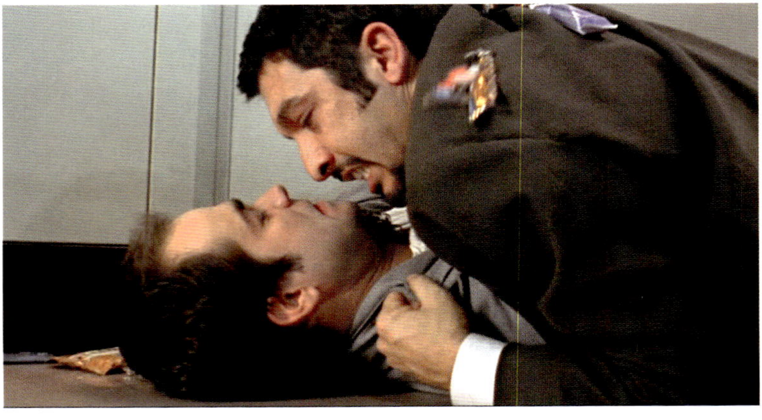

Marcos attacks Juan in the grocery shop when his dodgy deal is about to be discovered in Fabian Bielinsky's *Nueve reinas* (2000).

is always being tested as to whether what is seen is spontaneous or staged. And this changes as the film develops so that the viewer is 'taken in' by the first scene in the grocery shop when Marcos 'saves' Juan from being arrested – only to reveal it was a set-up – but is likely to 'get' the scene towards the end of the film when Marcos is attacked by an older man who wants to steal the briefcase and see it as 'staged'. So the viewer begins to 'discover' the first level of duplicity (Marcos's disguise) while remaining oblivious to the second level of duplicity (Juan's disguise), thereby making the final recognition-scene all the more aesthetically effective. *Nueve reinas* is, indeed, as much about the multi-layered nature of art as it is about the story of a younger trickster fooling an older trickster out of love for the older trickster's sister.

It is also an excellent litmus test of the relationship between Latin American (or perhaps Argentine) film and Hollywood film. It is the only Latin American film to be privileged with a remake by the Hollywood studios. *Criminal* (2004), directed by Gregory Jacobs, with John C. Reilly as Richard Gaddis (Marcos), Diego Luna as Rodrigo (Juan) and Maggie Gyllenhaal as Valerie (Valeria), follows the original plot of Bielinski's film closely but, as Carla Meyer points out, the 'inferior American version strips the menace and texture from the original without offering any big stars to compensate'.[18] *Nueve reinas* and *Amores perros* demonstrated in different ways the news of 'New' New Latin American Cinema of the twenty-first century.[19]

In 2001 the Mexican Guillermo del Toro released *El espinazo del diablo* ('The Devil's Backbone'), a gothic horror film set in 1939 during the final stages of the Spanish Civil War. Dr Casares (Federico Luppi) and Carmen (Marisa Paredes) run an orphanage which looks after the children of Republican soldiers who have died in the war. The title of the film provides the most grotesque stage prop, a dead foetus with an enlarged and deformed backbone which is kept in a large jar for scientific purposes. Carlos (Fernando Tielve), who epitomizes the innocence that del Toro always places at the centre of his horror films, arrives at the orphanage and soon discovers that it is haunted by the ghost of one of the orphans, Santi (Junio Valverde) who was murdered by Jacinto, the caretaker (Eduardo Noriega) who incarnates conscience-free evil. The crime was witnessed by the local bully, Jaime (Íñigo Garcés) but he was too afraid to tell anyone. When asked in an interview why he set his ghost story in the Spanish Civil War, Guillermo del Toro made the following comment:

> The best ghost stories are set against wars, because they leave plenty of ghosts behind. Coming from the outside to the Spanish civil war, it felt very black and white to me. It took place within the family – you could have a fascist father, a fascist son and a republican son and they would argue passionately, and even be capable of taking each other to the firing squad. I tried to make the orphanage in the film a microcosm of the war. I wanted to create a situation where the republican figures in the movie allowed for this fascist creature to grow and nurture, and ultimately take over. The republican government represents the best possible leftist government that has ever taken place on earth – women were emancipated, education was very experimental, culture was booming – and yet it all went to hell.[20]

Carlos's courage, however, emboldens Jaime, and when it appears that all the children will be murdered by Jacinto, they gang up on him, thrusting sharpened stakes into him (in a gesture reminiscent of the vampire motif of del Toro's previous film, *Cronos*), causing him to fall into the very pool in which he drowned Santi. With a touch of poetic justice, he is weighed down by the stolen gold he has stuffed into his clothes. A ghoulish detail is that Santi is waiting for him at the bottom of the pool and 'hugs' him. Though to some degree a traditional horror movie – Santi with his white make-up looks like a younger, Mexican version of Frankenstein's monster – *El espinazo del diablo* has some of del Toro's signature devices, ranging from black humour (Dr Casares offers Carlos a drink from the jar in which the foetus with the deformed backbone is contained; the beautiful Carmen, who has only one leg, is forced into having sex with Jacinto because of her husband's impotence) to absurdity (the bomb which lands in the courtyard without exploding but is somehow 'alive') to the focus on blood and gore as leading to redemption (Dr Casares's ghost gives the final speech of the film, suggesting that Jacinto's evil has been destroyed). In some ways *El espinazo del diablo* could be seen as a dry run for the film del Toro would make five years later, *El laberinto del fauno*, which was also set in the Spanish Civil War.

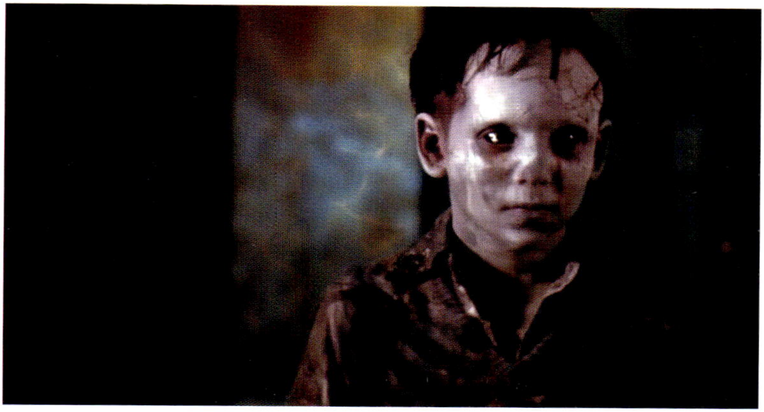

The ghost, Santi, in Guillermo del Toro's *El espinazo del diablo* (200).

Following the trend set by *Amores perros*, *Y tu mamá también* ('And Your Mother Too', 2001), directed by the Mexican film director Alfonso Cuarón and co-written with his brother Carlos, was privately financed, ironically enough by a nutritional supplements corporation.[21] Winning first prize for the film (the Marcello Mastroianni Award), as well as awards for the screenplay and for the two lead male actors at the 2001 Venice Film Festival – though it failed to gain an Academy Award after nomination in the category of Writing (original screenplay) at the 2002 Hollywood ceremony – Cuarón's film appears at first to focus unremittingly on the psychology of men. As Alfonso Cuarón explained in an interview:

> The story wasn't autobiographical, but there are elements from when Carlos and I were growing up. The nanny in the film is played by our nanny in real life, and one of the destinations the trio go through is her town in real life; Carlos and I went to a wedding in the same place where you see the wedding in the film, and the President of the time was present and everyone was more interested in the President than the newlyweds. We also had a car like the one in the film and there is a town the trio visit that is also the name of the street where we grew up. The character of Diego 'Saba' Madero, the friend of Julio and Tenoch, is a character that we know. Of course, we both also had trips to the beach and the incident with the pigs in the tent happened to my cinematographer, Emmanuel Lubezki.[22]

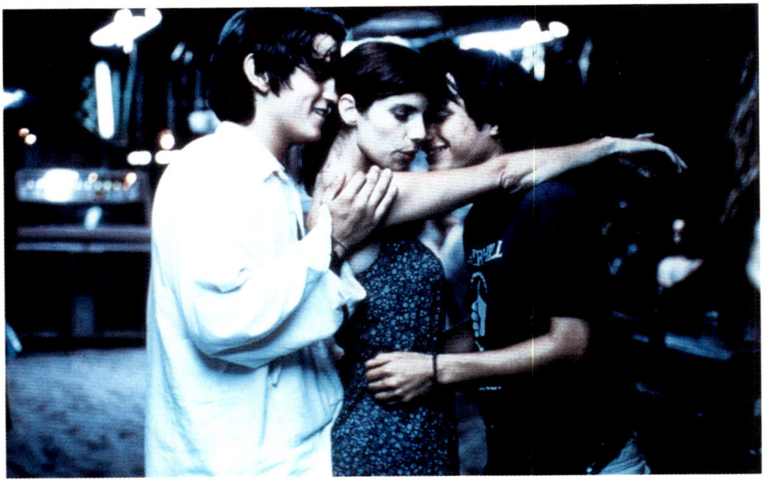

The threesome in *Y tu mamá también* (2001).

What makes Julio and Tenoch tick, as *Y tu mamá también* suggests, is sex, but also the power over others that having sex with somebody gives the individual. Thus it is no coincidence that Julio tells Tenoch he has been sleeping with the latter's girlfriend in order to get his own back on Tenoch after he sees him sleeping with Luisa, the Spanish wife of Tenoch's cousin. A brinkmanship ensues, until Julio plays his trump card and tells Tenoch that he has also slept with Tenoch's mother. Soon afterwards the final bombshell explodes: the two young men kiss like lovers. The fact that *Y tu mamá también* is not only a road movie but also introduces the sub-theme of male bonding suggests that Cuarón is quoting the work of Wim Wenders (in whose films, particularly *Kings of the Road*, *The American Friend*, *Paris, Texas* and *Wings of Desire*, these two themes are central).[23]

Y tu mamá también is thus not only a film about the sexual mores in operation in modern Mexico, but it also makes some probing comments about the sexual interplay between generations, a practice that culture terms and defines as taboo. The film in a sense re-enacts a journey which pushes the envelope of the taboo gradually further and further from conventional, 'straight' normative sexuality. It begins with pre-marital sex (Julio and Cecilia), evokes the practice of 'swapping' sexual partners (Julio and Ana), probes the taboo involved in stealing another man's woman (Julio steals Luisa), as well as stealing a woman with whom there is a family connection (Tenoch steals his cousin's wife). If that were not enough, the film then proceeds to break the taboo of two men sharing one sexual partner (Julio and Tenoch share Luisa), before graduating to the devastating revelation that a man will also sleep with his best friend's mother (Julio has slept with Tenoch's mother), before concluding on the final taboo of gay love between two men. The successive stages of this process of gradually breaking down social taboos is carefully choreographed, and demonstrates that this film is as much about the psychology of sex as about the 'liaisons dangereuses' that define human relationships. *Y tu mamá también* is also a specifically Mexican reading of Laclos's insight into the destructiveness of sexual relationships, for it evokes Octavio Paz's sense of the Mexican subject as '*hijo de la chingada*' (son of the whore) expressed in his classic essay *El laberinto de la soledad* ('The Labyrinth of Solitude', 1950). By having two Mexican men sexually exploit a Spanish woman, we might argue that this film attempts to 'reverse' the trauma of Conquest by exchanging the nationalities of the two parties involved in the primal scene.

There are other motifs within the film which suggest that Cuarón is playing with this notion. Chroniclers of Mexican history have often interpreted the growth of Mexican nationhood in terms of the Fall, the idea being that the Eden of the New World was somehow corrupted by the arrival of the Europeans. In *Y tu mamá también* there are a number of coy references to heaven, beginning with the sense of the search for Eden, and the (tongue-in-cheek) name of the beach they are searching for – Boca del Cielo (Heaven's Mouth). It is thus clear that Luisa, Julio and Tenoch are, in their own ways, searching for a sexual heaven. During the journey, we learn that Julio goes through the region once inhabited by his maid before she came to live in Mexico City, and this indicates that the journey may also be construed as a voyage back in time. The journey is thus multi-layered, evoking not only the sense of a personal journey backwards in time for certain individuals but also a tracking backwards into the history of a culture; in this case we are being drawn back to what might be called the 'dawn of Mexican time'.

This dawn also, paradoxically enough, functions as an image of the death to which Luisa is gradually drawing near, though only she knows this. Her husband's nickname, Jano, is a reference to the Latin god, Janus, who could tell the past and the future. The water which appears obsessively throughout the film is, indeed, symbolic of the death to which all the characters are drawn, especially Luisa. So while Luisa is running away from her husband Jano, she is being drawn towards the god Janus, who sits at the entrance to Hades.

The most distinctive characteristic of Cuarón's film, however, is its exploratory investigation of the language of film. In a presentation given at the Bloomsbury Theatre at University College, London, in November 2009, Cuarón mentioned that he believed that a plot is always a poison, and *Y tu mamá también* in many ways illustrates this notion. The voice-over is used in disarming ways. While used in a conventional manner to provide 'objective' information about the characters – for instance at the beginning of the film it emphasizes what happened in the past – as the film develops it also begins to predict what will happen in the future, an example being what will happen to the pigs that attacked the tent Julio, Tenoch and Luisa stayed in on the beach, right down to the most specific details of how many there were (twenty-three), how many would be sacrificed the following spring (fourteen) and how many would spread a disease (three). This endows the narrative with an eerie sensation of prolepsis. At other times it appears as if the voice-over has a mind of its own, and is interested in events which are not necessarily within the 'camera-mind', as it were. At the conclusion of the wedding party sequence, for example, the voice-over – as if bored with Julio and Tenoch's antics as they attempt to seduce Luisa – provides information about what the president did later that day and, indeed, the next day, when he attended a conference on globalization. The peripatetic nature of the voice-over is echoed by the roving eye of the camera. In the scene in which we hear about the president's actions, the camera – as if it had a mind of its own – leaves Julio and Tenoch behind and follows the waitress carrying the food out to the drivers who are waiting outside the party. The camera-eye is more interested – it appears – in their lives than those of the wedding guests. The innovation of *Y tu mamá también* is that it absorbed the peripatetic nature of the road movie formula and applied it not only to the main action of the film but also to the personae of the voice-over and camera. Cuarón's film thereby tracks this splitting of the filmic personality into different instantiations.

The Argentine film director Lisandro Alonso's *La libertad* ('Freedom', 2001), the most experimental film released that year in Latin America, was screened in the 'Un Certain Regard' section at the 2001 Cannes Film Festival. It focuses on the everyday life of Misael Saavedra, a woodcutter, grafting documentary into the discourse of a feature film (for some viewers it should have been a short), to produce a film with a strange beauty. The shoot took ten days with a twelve-person crew, and it 'studies its subject with a thoroughness of detail and a lentitude of pace that create the effect of events occurring in real time'.[24] Thus we see Misael chopping down wood, counting it, loading it on his truck, going to the toilet and – in a striking final sequence – eating an armadillo, 'staring directly at us as if daring us to question or challenge the integrity of his way of life'.[25] Since it focuses on the drudgery of manual labour *La libertad* forces the audience to think about the nature of human liberty.[26]

Ônibus 174 ('Bus 174'), a Brazilian documentary film directed by José Padilha and released in 2002, is a beautifully crafted piece of work which weaves live film footage of a bungled hold-up of Bus 174 in Rio de Janeiro by Sandro do Nascimento into an absorbing set of interviews with members of the police force who dealt with the event, along with members of Nascimento's family. It won over 23 awards worldwide and its (extraordinary) 99 per cent rating on the Rotten Tomatoes website, with an audience rating of 89 per cent, showed it to be the critics' choice.[27]

Cidade de Deus ('City of God', 2002), by the Brazilian director Fernando Meirelles, is arguably the most significant Latin American film of the twenty-first century so far. The film is based on the novel of the same name by Paulo Lins (*Cidade de Deus: Romance*, 1997), a true story of the life of a number of gang members living in the City of God, a violent shanty town in western Rio de Janeiro, in the 1960s, '70s and '80s. The characters – who include Busca-Pé, Barbantino, Acerola, Inferninho, Tutuca, Martelo, Carlinho, Pretinho, Pelé, Pará and Manguinha – are, as Lins has pointed out, 'based on real-life people' who 'had already gained public visibility in the Brazilian press by the time the researched facts surfaced'.[28] While the novel is a series of vignettes of the everyday lives of a cross-selection of hoodlums, the film focused on the interlocking lives of a set of people, including the narrator, Buscapé ('Rocket', Alexandre Rodrigues), his older brother, Marreco ('Goose', Renato de Souza), and his two gangster friends, Alicate ('Clipper', Jefechander Suplino) and Cabeleira ('Shaggy', Jonathan Haagensen), Dadinho ('Li'l Dice', Douglas Silva) who, at eighteen, takes on the name of Zé Pequeno ('Li'l Zé', Leandro Firmino da Hora), his accomplice, Bené ('Benny', Phellipe Haagensen) and his girlfriend, Angélica (Alice Braga), and their enemies, Cenoura ('Carrot', Matheus Nachtergaele) and Mané Galinha ('Knockout Ned', Seu Jorge). The film, like the book, was based on a true story of people in a real place and to keep this documentary feel Meirelles and his co-director, Kátia Lund, decided to use non-professional actors:

> I wanted the audience to look at Li'l Ze and actually see the real Li'l Ze, and not an actor playing a role. The idea was to have these unknown actors in order to eliminate the filter, to let the spectator have a direct relationship with the character. All this, I thought, would bring out the truth I wanted to have in the film. Middle-class actors would not know how to interpret those characters.[29]

Once the casting was done, the actors, many of whom were gangsters from Cidade de Deus, were trained by Fátima Toledo and Kátia Lund for a year.[30] Though this had the effect of launching the acting careers of a number of those who starred in the film, it allowed *Cidade de Deus* to retain a gritty, documentary feel. A documentary realism is also enhanced by the inclusion of a news clip of an interview with the actual man on whom Mané Galinha is based during the concluding credits.

The film also mimicked the *cinéma vérité* mood by using a hand-held digital camera which, with its mobility and jerkiness, had the effect of being a consciousness accompanying the development of the action rather than simply recording the events. The hand-held is, indeed, used for virtuoso effects, such as when in the opening scene it appears to be on the chicken's shoulder as it is making a run for it.[31] Often when the characters are talking to each other the camera pans rapidly between them, and the speed of the pan causes a loss of focus, which adds a documentary-type spontaneity. The cinematography has a mobile feel about it, using a number of camera angles such as a tilt frame when the gangsters jump down in their pursuit of the chicken in the opening sequence, an aerial shot when two of the Tendership Trio are up the tree listening to the policemen discussing what to do next, directly below them, and – most spectacular of all – the swivel, 360-degree shot at the beginning and conclusion of

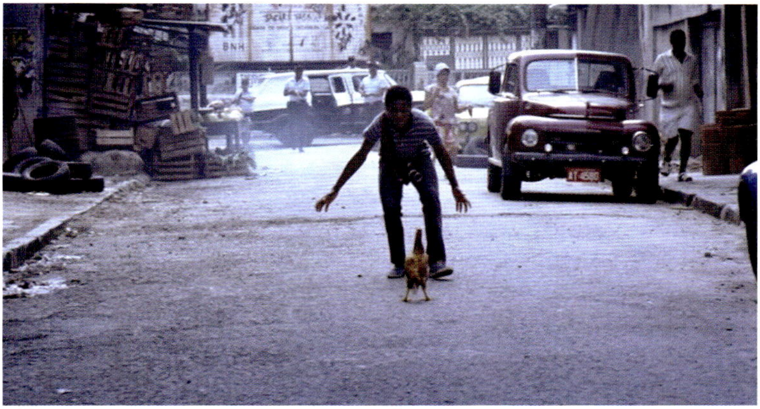

Buscapé trying to catch the runaway chicken in Fernando Meirelles's *City of God* (2002).

the film which follows Buscapé's head as he surveys the police on one side and Pequeno Zé's gang on the other. This last take is digitally created in that the colours change while the camera swivels, from the blues and greys of the present to the brown and golden tones of the childhood sequence in the City of God.

The film can be seen as a symphony of colours, with the blue-greys of the 1980s contrasting with the earth tones of the 1960s and the pinks and blues of the disco era of the 1970s.[32] The editing in the film explores a variety of effects, including fade and double-exposure in the sequence recounting the history of the Zadia apartment,[33] the use of a passing blue car to create the bridge between the 1960s and '70s as Buscapé walks down the street to school after seeing the body of Cabeleira who has been gunned down by the police, as well as slow motion, fast motion, split screen and shallow focus. In an interview César Charlone explained how he experimented with filming in 35mm and 16mm combined with digital post-production:

> Fernando invited me to film the short, and suggested I do it as a rehearsal for what we would later do in *City of God*. And so, in the four days we filmed *Palace II* (Golden Gate), I tested our 'format'. I tried out 8 types of camera film, 35 and 16 mm, different types of lighting, different types of filming styles, more marked or with more improvisations. Some scenes more planned out and others in sequence. Changes in speed . . . All in all we

> turned *Palace II* (Golden Gate) into a laboratory short. And the last major experiment was technological. To shoot using film, do all the post-production in video and put it back into film, using all the benefits proportioned by electronics (to shoot in other speeds, change them while editing, change the lighting, the continuity and the framing on the telecine, use 35 and 16 indistinctly, etc., etc.) . . . We believed that a small loss of technical quality was unimportant if compared to the advantages that the process furnished us in relation to our 'actors'.[34]

The filming took place on 35mm or 16mm during the day and was then digitized in the evening after the shoot, and Charlone would work on it during the night, and convert it back into 35mm or 16mm film before presenting it to Fernando the following day.[35] This shuttling between film and digital video was innovative at the time, and expanded the visual potential of the frame in an unprecedented way.

The plot in *Cidade de Deus* is kept firmly under control by the voice-over which explains what is going on and which often uses a camera-click effect to signal the beginning of a new narrative, for instance the life of a new protagonist, such as Mané Galinha. The overall structure of the film – though a linear plot can be created – is like a spiralling vortex in that it loops back into the past at certain key junctures. Thus the opening sequence of the film is revealed to be the 'beginning of the end' of the film once we approach the conclusion, and this technique also allows for some events to be perceived from a different point of view later on. When we learn about how Zé Pequeno took over his first drug den our first perspective is that of Blacky and Buscapé as they hear the hammering on the door and our second perspective is an off-the-shoulder point of view of Zé Pequeno's gang as they enter the apartment. This filtering of the plot means that certain events are only revealed to the viewer later on – it is only when we follow Zé Pequeno's narrative that we realize that he not only killed all the people in the motel but also Buscapé's brother, Marreco.

Cidade de Deus attacks not only the drug culture which ruins people's lives in Brazil, but also the way in which the authorities react. The police allow the killing in the City of God to carry on as long as it does not escalate out of control and affect their 'clients', the middle classes. It is, ironically enough, only as a result of Zé Pequeno's refusal to pay for his guns that the police decide to act – because they have been providing him with the guns in the first place. The media are also shown to be important players within the dynamics of drug culture; as a result of his ability to take photographs – that is, produce images which are appetising to the middle-class press – Rocket escapes his roots in the City of God. It is a world which, as he says at the beginning of the film, if you fight it, you will never survive, and which, if you run from it, 'you'll never escape'; but Buscapé has, in effect, proved that you *can* escape, since he becomes – as the closing sequence of the film makes clear – a professional photographer. No longer Rocket, he is 'Nelson Rodrigues, *fotógrafo*'. *Cidade de Deus* is a masterpiece of a film which managed to combine the grittiness of a documentary-type slice of life created with non-professional actors and slick virtuoso digital editing. It was a dynamic mixture which was destined to have a significant impact on the future evolution of Latin American film. It won 55 awards and had 29 nominations, including an Academy Award nomination for best director (Meirelles), best adapted screenplay (Bráulio Mantovani), best cinematography (César Charlone) and best film editing (Daniel Rezende).

Because of the film's enormous success, a TV spin-off of *Cidade de Deus* was created: *Cidade dos homens* ('City of Men'), with some episodes

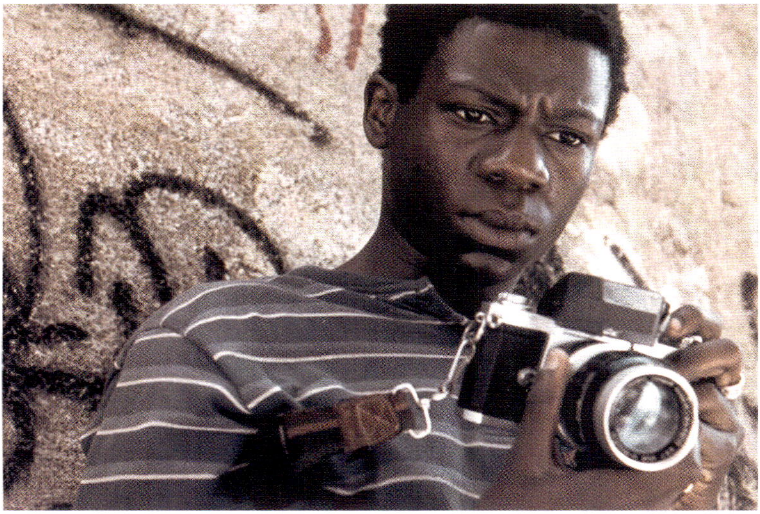

City of God: Buscapé is now a photographer.

directed by Kátia Lund and Fernando Meirelles. The TV series went back to the original novel written by Paulo Lins and focused on two teenagers, Luis Claudío, aka Acerola (played by Douglas Silva, who played Dadinho in *Cidade de Deus*), and his friend Uolace, aka Laranjinha (Darlan Cunha). The first season was produced in 2002, airing on Globo TV between 4 and 18 October 2002 and released on DVD in February 2003. The episodes focus on the characters' everyday life, including going to school, surviving in the favela, dealing with the drug culture and its power struggles, going to the beach and trying to seduce young girls. The first episode in the series, *A Coroa do Imperador* ('The Emperor's Crown') pursues an intriguing connection between the Napoleonic Wars of the early nineteenth century and the gang warfare in Cidade de Deus in the twenty-first, while drawing some parallels between the life of a playboy and the life of the poor in the favela. *Dois para Brasília* ('Two Tickets to Brasilia') follows Acerola as he goes with his girlfriend to visit her grandfather in prison in Brasilia, sparking up some insight into prison life in Brazil, while *Buraco Quente* ('Hot Spot') follows Laranjina's cousin, Espeto, a drug dealer, who is shot by the police, which leads to a re-evaluation by him as well as by Laranjina and Acerola as to the pros and cons of the life of a drug baron. The TV series, unlike the film, is episodic, and the mood is more light-hearted than *Cidade de Deus* but the filming and editing – particularly the use of the rapidly moving hand-held camera and the voice-over – possesses the recognizable Meirelles-cum-Lund filmic signature.[36]

González Iñárritu's *21 Grams* was the big film of 2003, winning an Academy Award nomination for Benicio del Toro in the category of Actor in a Supporting Role and for Naomi Watts for Actress in a Leading Role. *21 Grams* is similar to González Iñárritu's previous film, *Amores perros*, in that it is a story built around the tragedy caused by a car crash. It is also, like, the previous film, non-linear and shuttles between the past, present and future of the various protagonists in disarming ways. But it is different in that it is filmed in an English-language environment and includes famous actors such as Sean Penn, Naomi Watts and Benicio del Toro. This was a significant paradigm shift for Latin American film in the early 2000s and led to the creation of what might be called a new genre – the English-language Latin American film. This paradigm shift was significant for the evolution of Latin American film in that it was the

Acerola dreaming of making it big in *City of Men* (2007).

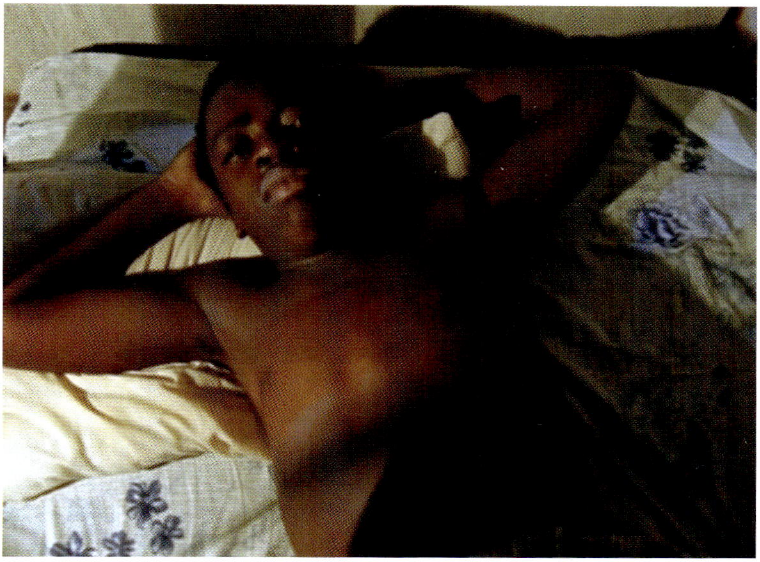

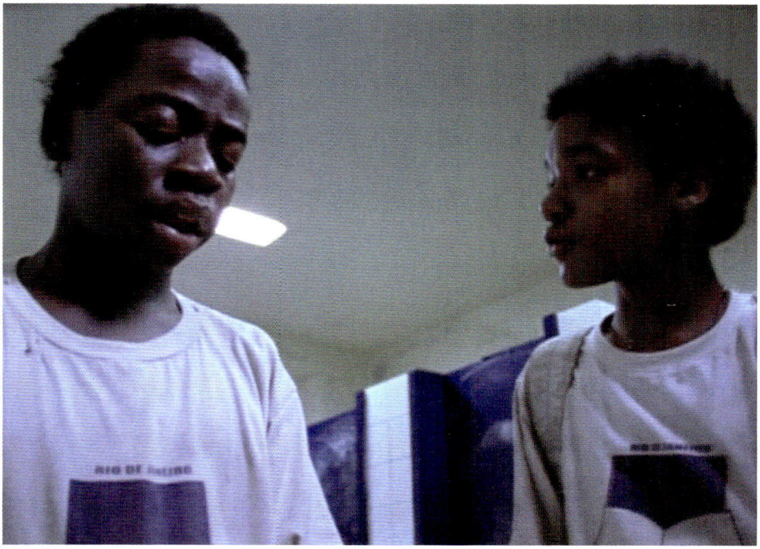

The favela youth discuss social power in *City of Men*.

symptom of a linguistic and cultural osmosis. Unlike the osmosis of the first half of the twentieth century, when Latin America was 'invaded' by foreign film directors eager to tell its story, this osmosis was going in the opposite direction. Latin American directors were 'invading' Hollywood.

21 Grams opens with vignettes from the lives of Paul Rivers (Sean Penn), a mathematics professor whose heart is failing, his wife Jane (Charlotte Gainsbourg) who is desperate to have his child, Jack Jordan (Benicio del Toro), a former convict who desperately immerses himself in Christianity in order to mend his ways, and Cristina Peck (Naomi Watts), whose life is destroyed when she hears the news that her husband and two young daughters have been killed in a hit-and-run accident. We never see the accident. (In a powerful piece of cinematography it happens off screen to the left of the camera space occupied by the gardener with whom Jane's husband, accompanied by his two daughters, has just been talking. We see the gardener blowing the leaves as Jack's truck whizzes past. Then we hear a skid and the gardener, realizing what has happened, runs to the scene to the left of the camera field. We are left looking at the abandoned leaf-blower until the sequence concludes.) But it is the unseen lynchpin which binds the lives of the characters together. It is at the point that the heart of Cristina's husband is transferred to Paul that the tragedy – or better the tragedy of the tragedy – begins to unfold. Inhabited by his heart, Paul appears to take on Cristina's husband's character and, abetted by Cristina, seeks revenge for the death of 'his' daughters. The plot at this point echoes the animistic mindset of the sacrificial ceremony of the pre-Columbian Aztecs whereby the life of an individual, contained within his heart, is removed from the body of the sacrificial victim and used to sustain the lives of others.

The disarming shuttling between the lives of the different characters – which is synchronic – combined with the movement back and forth from past to future to present – which is diachronic – is initially confusing for the viewer but it is purposeful in that it underlines the random synchronicity which binds human beings together as well as the human experience of time as a past–present–future continuum in which the three temporal dimensions are experienced simultaneously (in the sense that the future – as its Latin root suggests – is an 'about-to-happen' present while the past only exists in terms of its being experienced in the present). The combination of the synchronic and diachronic shuttling

The truck speeds past the gardener just before the crash in *21 Grams* (2003).

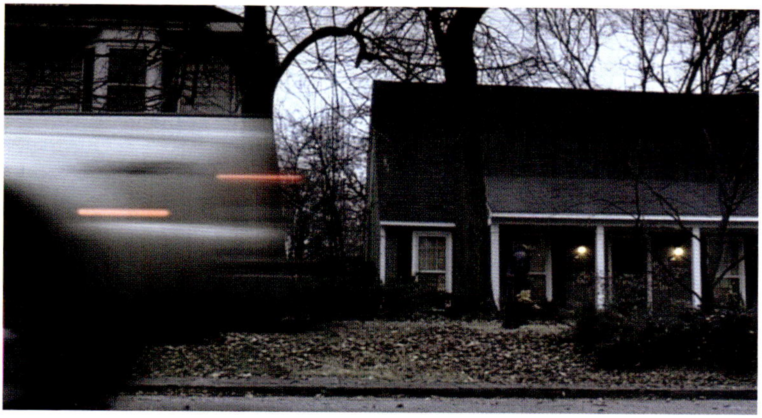

in the film's narrative is predicated on its digital structure of feeling. Digital editing allows for the combination of different filmed sequences as well as the re-coding of the cinematography of a given shot or scene at the touch of a mouse and this digital structure of feeling underlies the expressiveness of *21 Grams*. It would make no sense, after all, to shoot and edit a film which articulates a reflection of the randomness of the events which radically change human lives in a linear way. It would be like writing an essay about the absurdity of human life in balanced prose accompanied by edifying logic. *21 Grams* is thus as much a film about the desire for revenge as it is a reflection on how time and space come together in our lives. Digital cinematography allows for new types of event-association to be assembled. When Cristina goes to the place where the car accident took place the sequence is filmed by a hand-held digital camera which follows her and performs a 360-degree panning shot around her head. This sequence breaks the 180-degree rule but it does not do so gratuitously because the aim of this new hallmark shot of digital cinematography is to capture the character completely. We now know her pain completely.

There are other ways in which digital cinematography can bring new avenues of revelation into the viewer's field of vision. The sequence, for example, in which Paul is told by his doctor that he must check himself into the hospital because his heart transplant is not working, to which he responds 'I'd rather die outside', is followed by the sequence in which Jack is being driven away from prison by his friend and wife, suggesting that Paul and Jack are joined in some way that is unknown to them, but known to the 'camera-consciousness'. Their destinies are linked even though they appear at this point in time to be heading in different directions. Both have begun a new journey towards the 'outside', and it is a journey in which their destinies will be 'crossed' (by misfortune). As we find out later on, Paul will plan to take revenge on Jack for what he has done but he – rather than Jack – will die in the process. (Paul will lie in wait close to Jack's apartment, see him leave, force him to walk to a secluded spot, and threaten to shoot him; Paul does not shoot him, as we first think, instead shooting at the ground. Jack returns later on, tries to persuade Paul to shoot him, and then – perhaps in order to escape the painful effects of asphyxia caused by his ailing heart – Paul shoots himself.) This synoptic cut, characteristic of digital cinematography but different from traditional cross-cutting which is based on temporal linearity, convergence and cause-and-effect mechanics, allows for new synergies of association between random events to be constructed.

The digital *Weltanschauung* also allows for the strategy of partial disclosure of the filmed space. Thus in the first sequence, when the viewer 'sees' Paul ambushing Jack, taking him off to enact his revenge, we hear and therefore 'see' Paul shooting Jack. González Iñárritu thereby plays with the viewer's expectations: if we see one man leading another off to a secluded place while brandishing a gun, shouting at him, insulting him, ordering him to kneel at his feet, and then when we see the gun pointed at the victim's head and hear the gunshots we 'know' he has been shot and 'believe' that the director simply spared us the sight of the death. These signals – the brandishing of the gun, the anger in the murderer's face, the pointing of the gun at the victim's head – are the grammar of film which we as viewers have learned and which film directors also learn (normally at film school). They are the techniques which are 'in the book', as it were, used by directors in order to build their visual message to the viewer. The digital *Weltanschauung*, however, allows for new ways of seeing reality to emerge. It is not that these did not exist before the advent of digital film, but digital film allowed them to emerge more forcefully, widening the vocabulary of what is cinematographically thinkable. For almost 29 minutes, therefore, the viewer will believe that Paul has shot Jack, but it will transpire that Paul discharged

Jack believes Paul is going to shoot him, and so do we, in *21 Grams*.

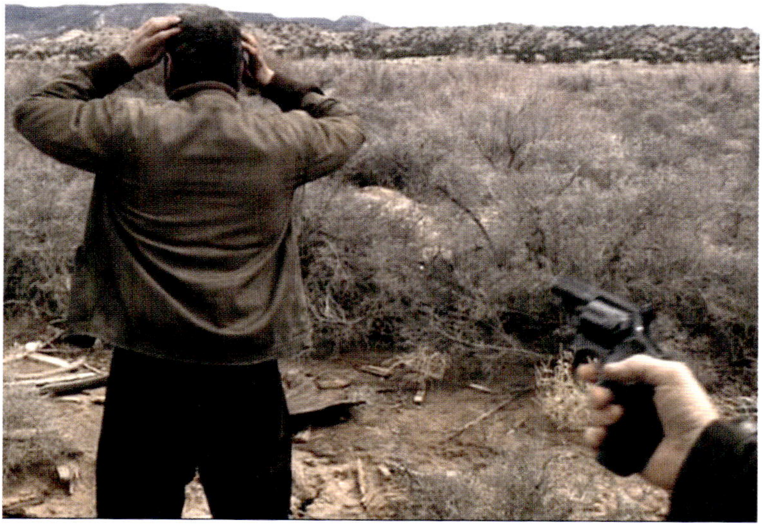

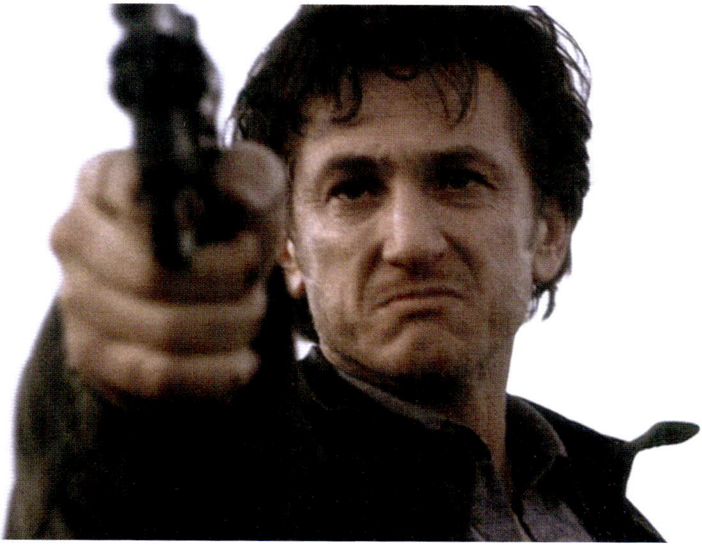

Paul points the gun and shoots, in *21 Grams*.

his bullets into the ground and then lied to Cristina, telling her he had killed Jack.

There are other ways in which the digital mindset explores the potentiality of film. For a director working in 35mm, film stock was so expensive that re-filming was associated with bad filming, with not getting it right in the first take. The digital *Weltanschauung*, however, allows the director to explore the once forbidden territory of the re-filmed event. González Iñárritu does this in an inventive way and articulates the unknown aspects of everyday life. We see the abbreviated first and the fuller version 29 minutes later, and the perspective as well as the shooting of the bullets changes. The abbreviated version is filmed with frontal or off-the-shoulder shots while the extended, later version also includes a camera-left shot. By deconstructing the grammar of 35mm film language in this way Gonzélez Iñárritu adds uncertainty combined with suspense to his drama.

Digital cinematography also allows for other types of event combination to occur. It allows sequences to be interpreted at different junctures of the film as either the past or the future. An example of this occurs towards the beginning of the film where we see Cristina in a bathroom snorting cocaine. Because the scene follows closely on from the scene in which Cristina is in a therapy group explaining the problems she had in the past with her drug addiction, we assume that the bathroom cocaine snorting scene is a recreation of her past habits. But we discover towards the end of the film that it is part of her future. This scene opens the sequence in which Cristina emerges from the motel room to ask Paul if he has shot Jack. It is not that the scene is misconstrued by the viewer as a flashback to Cristina's past, which is then shown 'actually' to be a fast-forward to her future life; it is more the case that González Iñárritu is deliberately playing with the viewer's expectations in order to show how the past can be osmotic with the future. The past and the future are, in a sense, merged when Cristina pushes open the door of the room she is in.

This shuttling between past, present and future allows for a new understanding of time to emerge. In the traditional 35mm universe the present of the film is firmly anchored as a reality which has access to the past via flashbacks (often indicated by a dissolve) but not to the future except in the sense that the development of the plot allows the future gradually to be turned into the present. González Iñárritu's more fluid understanding of the reversibility of the past, present and future is catalysed by the flexibility offered by the digital format of film. In a sense the digital merging of different time dimensions allows the film to express the notion that Cristina's mindset in the past – when she took drugs and presumably had less control over her emotions – has 'erupted' into the present and persuaded her to seek revenge. Digital film allowed for new mind-event associations to take place, and González Iñárritu has shown himself to be very keen to explore the new connections that digital film offers.

Enrique Colina's *Entre ciclones* ('Hurricanes', 2003, chosen as Latin America's representative for the Cannes Critics Week, tells the story of a young man, Tomás (Mijail Mulkay), a trainee working for a national telecommunications company who loses his home when the roof caves in after a hurricane. But worse than natural hurricanes are the cyclones created by the disasters of everyday life. Tomás finds his job difficult because of his bad-tempered boss, nicknamed 'El Conde' ('The Count', Mario Balmaseda), and his personal life is complicated in that he finds it difficult to choose between three women, a sexy mestiza, Mónica (Indira Valdés), a rich but older Spanish woman, Adriana (Klara Badiola), and a wild young girl, Elisa (Yahima Torres), with a passion for tattoos and stripping naked, and who happens to be his boss's daughter. The arrival

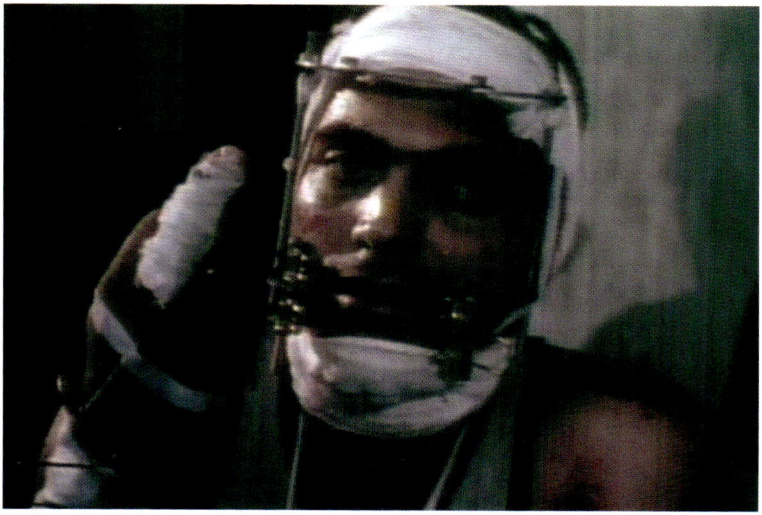

The protagonist gives the finger to the audience at the end of Enrique Colina's *Entre ciclones* (2003).

on the scene of his friend Miguel (Renny Arozarena), who has just come out of prison, eventually leads to Tomás's downfall (literally, in that he is arrested as Miguel's accomplice is ransacking Adriana's apartment, attacked by some rival thugs and thrown off the roof of a ten-storey building). The final scene of the film in which Tomás – now in a wheelchair, with multiple fractures, is advised to take up Zen Buddhism by a friend, at which point he gives the finger to the camera – articulates the black humour at the centre of *Entre ciclones*; Cuba is a place where hurricanes smash your home to pieces, the black market is rife, your boss is psychotic, your lover uses black magic to ensnare you and the only way to survive is to laugh at your bad luck.[37] As Colina suggests, the film 'uses the idea of a fall without any hope of survival as a metaphor [of Cuba's plight]'.[38]

Machuca (2004), directed by Andrés Wood and winner of the Most Popular International Film at the 2004 Vancouver International Film Festival, is Chile's version of *La historia oficial* (1984). An emotionally drenched reaction from a child's perspective to the horrors of civil war, it sold 700,000 tickets and was the 'third most successful Chilean film ever'.[39] Gonzalo Infante (Matías Quer) is a rich, bright and sensitive kid at an exclusive boys' school in Santiago, and the film picks up pace when five boys from the other side of the tracks are introduced as new students. Despite the local bully's attempts to ostracize them, Gonzalo develops a friendship with Pedro Machuca (Ariel Mateluna). They visit each other's homes and Machuca is as impressed by Gonzalo's wealth (his Adidas trainers) as Gonzalo is appalled by Machuca's living conditions (he lives in a shanty town with an open-sewer latrine). Gonzalo has his first kiss with Machuca's cousin, Silvana (Manuela Martelli), who lives in the same shanty town as Machuca, and he and Machuca subsequently share concentrated-milk-fuelled snogging sessions with her. The idyll is broken when cracks begin to emerge in the society: there are food shortages; the dogs are stolen; the pigs are burned; a meeting at the school ends in bitter recriminations between the upper-middle-class and the working-class parents, the latter accused of being Communists; and finally Augusto Pinochet's coup occurs, and the three-year social experiment engineered by Salvador Allende (1970–73) is obliterated. The headmaster of the school, Father McEnroe, is dramatically removed by troops and a new headmaster, a member of the military, is installed.

The devastation of this world is experienced by Gonzalo when he witnesses Silvana being murdered by troops who are attacking the shanty town; the scenes are vividly portrayed with a jerky hand-held camera in shallow focus with desaturated colour tones and a hint of dark sepia. The final separation between the two boys occurs when Gonzalo proves that he does not belong to the shanty town by showing a solider his Adidas trainers. The last sequence of the film, in which we see Gonzalo's family moving into a new luxurious home, suggests that his family has done well out of the coup. The strength of the film lies in its use of the child as a witness to the social events; his innocent perspective underlines the brutality of the coup.

Like *Machuca*, *Días de Santiago* ('Santiago's Days', 2004), directed by the Peruvian Josué Méndez, focuses on the aftermath of war, but in this case it is the civil war between the *terrucos* and the Peruvian military that provides the (never visualized) back-story. A Peruvian re-vamping of Martin Scorsese's *Taxi Driver* (1976), *Días de Santiago* tells the story of a 23-year-old man, Santiago (Pietro Sibille), who served in the Peruvian Navy and who now works as a taxi driver. One of his veteran friends has committed suicide, others are planning a bank job, but Santiago desperately wants to find order and purpose in his life. His inability, though, to adjust to the tasks of everyday life – he loses his temper when buying a fridge, he attacks a drug pusher in a local disco, he knocks out his girlfriend when she playfully tries to touch his revolver – leads to the final

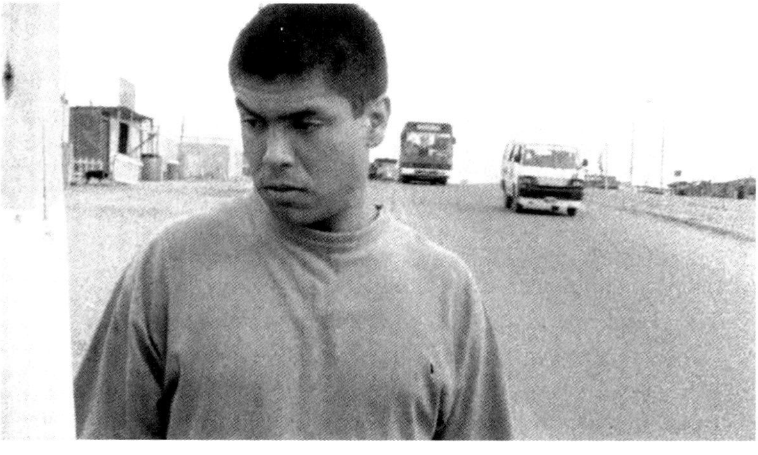

Santiago waiting in black and white for his girlfriend in *Días de Santiago* (2004).

desperate scene when he tries to kidnap his sister-in-law who is being bullied by his brother, breaks down a door to find his father raping his sister, and then in a game of Russian roulette attempts suicide; the gun clicks three times and then the screen goes black. Santiago's disorientation is powerfully expressed by a rapidly zigzagging narrative propulsion, a tense, jerky hand-held camera and a (seemingly random) switching from colour to black-and-white during the course of the film. Like a number of other Latin American films of the early 2000s, *Días de Santiago* deconstructs the protagonist-as-national-representative trope common in the previous two decades, and re-focuses national destiny from the perspective provided by youth culture.

Diarios de motocicleta ('The Motorcycle Diaries', 2004), directed by the Brazilian Walter Salles, recreates the story of Ernesto 'Che' Guevara's trip from the southern tip of the subcontinent to its northern tip with his friend Alberto Granado in 1952. Salles's film shows us a Che whose eyes are gradually opened to injustice in Latin America, although the politics is presented obliquely rather than frontally (neither Marx nor Marxism are mentioned, and the word 'Communist' is used only once, when the mineworkers they meet on their way through Chile describe themselves thus). *Diarios de motocicleta* can be described as a road movie, as a coming-of-age movie, even as an elegy to the awesome beauty of the Latin American landscape, but its most distinctive feature is its blend of the fiction film with the documentary. It starts as a fiction film – with the lavish, detail-perfect sets of 1950s Buenos Aires providing the establishing scenes when Che Guevara (Gael García Bernal) and Alberto Granado (Rodrigo de la Serna) set off on their journey, along with the parties in Miramar, the first stop on their journey – and gradually turns into a documentary – or perhaps better, a 'featurementary', combining aspects of a feature film with those of a documentary. The conversations with the market vendors in Valdivia, Chile, with the guide in Cuzco, the women in the street in Cuzco who talk about their everyday problems, the man who talks about how he was ejected from his land – these are all micro-narratives, punctuating the flow of the film and providing it with an extemporaneous, real-life quality. This journey towards the documentary-real culminates in the final sequence of the film in which we see the face of an 82-year-old Alberto Granado in Cuba watching a plane take off, echoing the immediately preceding (fictional) sequence

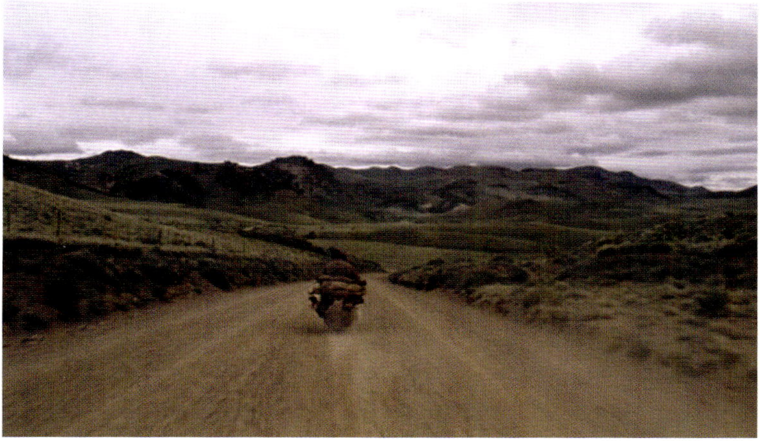

Che Guevara and Alberto Granado arrive in Chile, in Walter Salles's *The Motorcycle Diaries* (2004).

in which Granado bids farewell to Che. The sense of the documentary-real is also provided by the dates which are provided on screen to indicate the stages of the two young men's journey. The reality bedrock is additionally suggested through the black-and-white 'moving' stills occurring at various junctures of the film, often to indicate the political injustice of how people live – such as when the people crowded in the boat following the steamer are suddenly seen in black-and-white, or in the final sequence when we see a succession of images of people that Che Guevara has seen on his journey through the subcontinent. These photographs are in the style of the Peruvian ethnographic photographer Martín Chambi, whose most important work dates from the 1930s, and have a subliminal political message of injustice.

Diarios de motocicleta is more a coming-to-consciousness drama than a political film. Politics is reduced to an undercurrent that emerges when Guevara throws a stone at the Anaconda Mining Company truck; when he rejects Granado's proposal to establish an Indo-American society based on Tupac Amaru's rebellion because it would be a bloodless revolution ('*Una revolución sin tiros?*' – 'A revolution without bullets?', he asks Alberto incredulously); in his birthday speech in which he calls for an end to the division between nations in Latin America; and gives a concrete example of ending division between peoples by swimming across the Amazon river to the south side of the leper colony in San Pablo. The film drops a broad hint about the politicization which is about to occur by having Che say, almost at the conclusion, '*todo ese tiempo que pasamos en la ruta sucedió algo. Algo que tengo que pensar por mucho tiempo. ¡Cuánta injusticia!*' (While we were going on our journey something did happen. Something I have to think about for a long time. So much injustice!) but, interestingly enough, it does not depict that politicization directly. Salles combines the feature-film format with a documentary edge to produce a film about Che Guevara's famous journey from Argentina to Colombia which is partly sentimental and partly political; it won an Academy Award nomination in the category of Best Writing (Adapted Screenplay).

Another road movie was released in 2004: *Familia rodante* ('Rolling Family'), directed by the Argentine Pablo Trapero. It tells the story of a large Argentine family who take a very long trip northwards in their camper van from Buenos Aires to Misiones province in order to attend a wedding. This comedy-drama traces a deliberate departure from the 'nation-image' dramas of the 1990s (such as *El viaje* and *La frontera*) in which the protagonists represent a national consciousness. Here it is the small story that counts: there is no mention of politics or work or ambition, and the film focuses on the everyday narrative of their lives – at home, as it were. We see them eating, drinking, talking, smoking, looking at the countryside, brushing their teeth, going to the toilet, swimming in a river when the camper van breaks down, laughing, gossiping, arguing, fighting, crying, flirting, seducing and falling in love. They make up

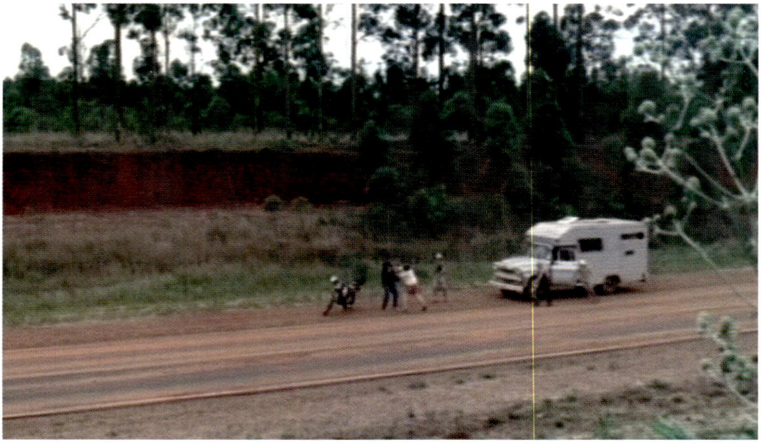

Oscar jumps off the van and punches Claudio, his daughter's druggie boyfriend, in *Familia rodante* (2004).

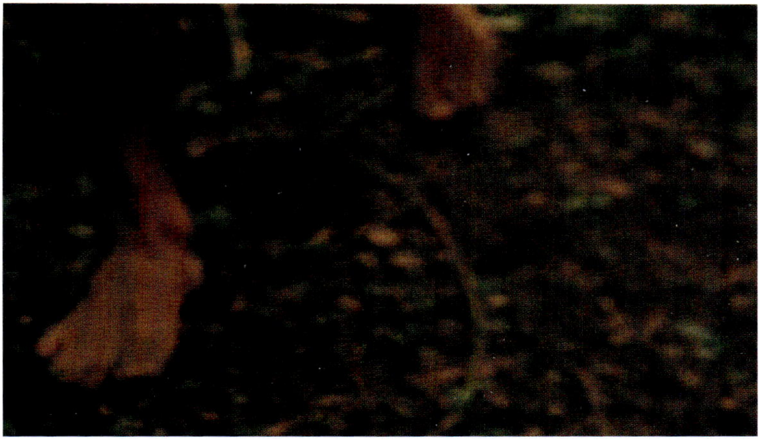

The feet of a mysterious unidentified individual walk past the camera in Lisandro Alonso's *Los muertos* (2004).

their new narratives as they go along – Yanina (Marianela Pedano) tries to seduce her cousin Gustavo (Raúl Viñoles), Ernesto (Carlos Resta) tries to seduce Marta (Liliana Capurro) and is thrown off the camper van when her husband, the driver, Oscar (Bernardo Forteza) finds out. The documentary feel of the film is underlined not only by the hand-held camera, which imbues the film with the spontaneous-cum-casual look of a home movie, and the non-professional actors who were employed in the film by the director when he arrived in different towns, but by the fact that the star of the film, the grandmother and matriarch of the family, Emilia, is played by Pablo Trapero's actual grandmother, Graciana Chironi. A picaresque film, *Familia rodante* deliberately eschews any broader significance, either of a political or a philosophical nature, focusing on the drama of the everyday.

Lisandro Alonso's *Los muertos* ('The Dead', 2004), like *Familia rodante*, uses the motif of travel but deconstructs it in order to produce a haunting film about death. The film opens with some lush jungle photography which is upended when the camera comes across two dead bodies, face down on the jungle floor. We then cut to the everyday life of Argentino Vargas, a convict who is coming to the end of his prison sentence for killing his two brothers (whose bodies, we assume, are those we see in the film's opening sequence). He is released, has sex with a prostitute, travels in a boat, kills a goat, visits his sister and he is portrayed throughout in long, reflective takes which – like the protagonist – studiously avoid depth. We never find out why Vargas killed his brothers; when the boatman asks, he says he has forgotten. At the centre of the film, as Gonzalo Aguilar suggests, is the 'absence of experience as transmissibility and legacy';[40] *Los muertos* is a horror film which combines the horror of murder with the horror of never knowing why.

Lucrecia Martel's *La niña santa* ('The Holy Girl', 2004), as the director suggests,

> isn't strictly autobiographical, but what I put in it is my personal experience in life, my memories. When I was in my teens, I was a very religious person. I thought I had a special relationship with God, or anything that was up there. Now, I don't believe in miracles, but I do believe in the emotion you feel in front of a miracle – the emotion of something unexpected revealed to you.[41]

The film is set in a dilapidated hotel, the Termas, during a medical conference, and it focuses on the burgeoning sensuality-cum-spirituality of the 'holy girl' of the title, Amalia (María Alche). The plot, if it can be described as such, springs from one of the doctors attending the conference, Dr Jano (Carlos Belloso), who rubs himself sexually against Amalia. Far from rebuffing him, Amalia first attempts to grab his hand and then – bizarrely – proceeds to stalk him. The acting and the dialogue are awkward (deliberately so), the cinematography is typically just off-centre (in that we might see a character through a half-open door or their figure is never quite in the middle of the frame), and the transition from sequences is abrupt and occasionally puzzling. Martel's vision is of a world in which people live on top of each other and rub up against each other, with unforeseen consequences. She also shows how aspects of our work, school, home and love lives collide with one another in unexpected ways. As Philip French suggests, *La niña santa* is 'a curiously muffled, dreamy film that simultaneously engages and distances us'.[42] The film seems to be heading towards an explosive denouement when Amalia's best friend, Josefina (Julieta Zylberberg), who has been caught in bed with her cousin, blurts out that Amalia has been molested by one of the doctors but, predictably, the film ends before the denouement occurs. It is as if the camera forgot to complete the script. And the viewer becomes 'the voyeur of the voyeur'.[43]

One film that proved successful at film festivals as well as at the box office (where it made U.S.$12,594,630) was *María, llena eres de gracia* ('Maria Full of Grace', 2004), an HBO co-production directed by Joshua Marston which won the Dramatic Audience Award at the 2004 Sundance Film Festival. It tells the larger narrative of drug-running in contemporary Colombia through the eyes of a young girl, María Alvarez, who quits her job in a rose factory in order to become a 'mule', carrying pellets of cocaine in her stomach from Bogotá to New York for $5,000. María is miraculously 'saved' from detection when she is stopped at immigration because she is pregnant with her boyfriend's child and thereby avoids being X-rayed. While María is saved by 'grace', her fellow mule, Lucy (Guilied Lopez), is not so lucky; one of the pellets breaks in her stomach causing her to become drowsy when they are picked up by the gang members in New York. The horror of the film is not so much the drugs as the murder of Lucy by the gang members: in order to retrieve their drugs haul they cut her open and abandon the body, as Don Fernando informs María. The film is shot and edited in a conventional way, as suggested by the continuity editing, the eye-line match and the use of suspense – on the aeroplane when Lucy becomes gradually more and more ill, and especially when Don Fernando (Orlando Tobón) calls Lucy's sister Carla (Patricia Rae), while María is in the kitchen, to tell her that Lucy has been found dead. This cinematographic conventionality is counterbalanced by the use of an unknown actress, Catalina Sandino Moreno, who had no previous professional acting experience. She was referred by the Rubén Di Pietro acting school in Bogotá to a casting audition (attended by 900 competitors) where she won the leading role. The main reason Sandino Moreno won the part was because of her naturalness; she was in effect following in the footsteps of actors such as Gael García Bernal and Alexandre Rodrigues who were 'unknowns' launched by the blockbusters *Amores perros* and *Cidade de Deus*. Sandino Moreno was subsequently named Best Actress at the Berlin Film Festival and nominated as Best Actress in the 77th Academy Awards (the first Colombian actor to be recognized in this way). Latin American film at this time was experimenting with nonprofessional actors and achieved such impact with this strategy that it came to be known as one of the defining characteristics of the 'new' new Latin American cinema.[44]

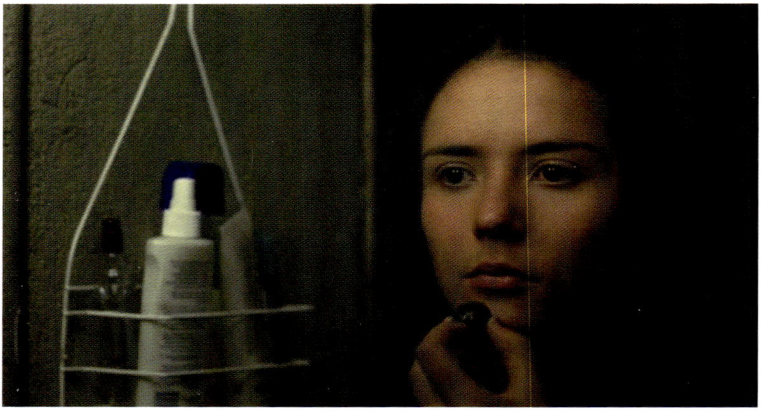

María gets the hang of her new job as a mule in *María, llena eres de gracia* (2004).

A Venezuelan film released a year later, *Secuestro express* (2005), directed by Jonathan Jakubowicz, has a number of ingredients in common with *María, llena eres de gracia* – the main similarity being the Latin America–poverty–crime syllogism. Martin (Jean Paul Leroux) and Carla (Mia Maestro) are a young couple enjoying a night out when they are kidnapped in Venezuela by Trece (Carlos Julio Molina), Budu (Pedro Perez) and Niga (Carlos Madera). They are taken off to a penthouse owned by Marcelo, a gay drug dealer, who persuades them to leave Martin with him as part of the drug deal. In an odd twist, Martin happens to be one of Marcelo's acquaintances, as we later discover. Trece, Budu and Niga leave with Carla only to discover that their car has been stolen; they return to the apartment to find Martin and Marcelo having sex, which shocks Carla. Martin later escapes and is unconcerned about leaving Carla behind ('*mátala*', 'kill her', he tells one of the gang). He is later picked up by a taxi driver who happens to know the gang, and delivers him back to them. They kill him in the boot of a car in a game of Russian roulette (one of the strongest scenes of the film). Meanwhile, Carla's father Sergio (Rubén Blades) hands over $25,000 to her kidnappers and they discuss whether they should release her or rape and murder her. Trece pays his share to the others to let her go unharmed, and Carla is released, only to be picked up by another set of kidnappers. The moral of the story clearly is that the underworld is wide and deep and that the best advice is never to trust anyone: 'You can either kill the beast or invite him to dinner', as the voice-over informs us towards the end of the film. Trece returns to the scene, kills Carla's new kidnappers and sets her free. The conclusion is thus not irredeemably bleak in that there is the suggestion that there are 'good' baddies like Trece who balance out the 'bad' baddies. As Peter Bradshaw says, 'Claims to seriousness on the film's behalf are, certainly, undermined by the way it gloatingly fetishises and sexualises the tokens of poverty in the slums of Caracas: the tattoos, the drugs, and of course the weaponry.'[45] The fast-forward editing along with the use of drug-related slang and popular, earthy speech suggests that this film is essentially a Venezuelan remake of the Brazilian *Cidade de Deus*, explaining its audience impact (it was the hit of the decade in Venezuela with 932,530 viewers[46]) but, apart from the feisty performance by Mia Maestro, the acting rarely convinces.

Madeinusa (2005), directed by Claudia Llosa, tells the story of a young woman living in a small Quechua-speaking town in the Andes, Manayaycuna (meaning 'the town no one can enter' in Quechua) who is determined to get on in life at any cost – as we discover at the film's conclusion. The protagonist Madeinusa (Magaly Solier) and her sister Chale (Yiliana Chong) both desperately want to be chosen as the town's Virgin for the procession of Holy Week which is about to take place. Madeinusa is chosen, much to her sister's disgruntlement, although it becomes clear that this has occurred because she is favoured by her father, Don Cayo (Juan Ubaldo Huamán) who also happens to be the mayor of the town. The town has a peculiar custom during Holy Week. Immediately after the ceremony to mark Christ's crucifixion on Good Friday they put a blindfold on his statue in the local church. Easter Saturday – when Christ is supposedly dead – is known as *tiempo santo* (holy time) and is seen as a time when any sins may be committed because God is unable to see them. The period of *tiempo santo* is measured by an old man in the main square, counting down the seconds until it begins, and then until it ends. Don Cayo has decided that he will take the opportunity of committing incest with Madeinusa during *tiempo santo*. This bizarre state of affairs is further complicated by the fact that just as the ceremony is about to begin a foreigner, Salvador (Carlos de la Torre), arrives in town from Lima, having been brought by a driver called El Murdo. In order to avoid problems with this 'gringo', Don Cayo simply decides to lock Salvador up in his house while *tiempo santo* is going on. Madeinusa is attracted to Salvador because of his light-coloured

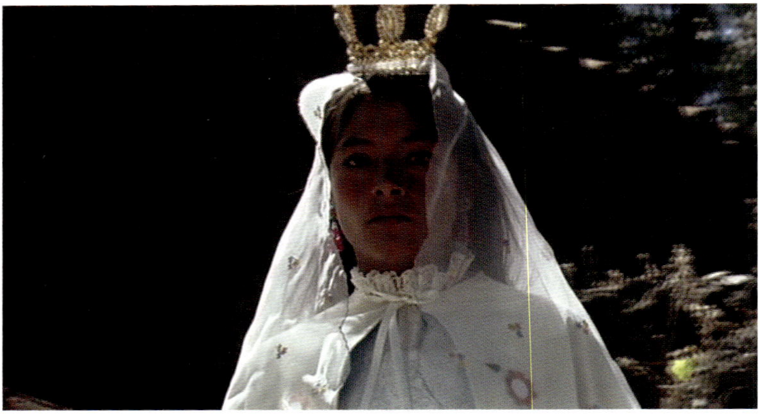

Madeinusa is the festival queen in Claudia Llosa's *Madeinusa* (2005).

eyes, and during *tiempo santo* she offers herself to him. Her father later has sex with her but becomes furious that he has been beaten to it by Salvador, and he destroys her earrings, of which she is very fond. Madeinusa persuades Salvador to take her off to Lima with him; when she goes to retrieve her earrings from her father she discovers that he has ripped them to pieces and so she decides to take a terrible vengeance by putting rat poison in his chicken broth. Don Cayo begins to vomit after drinking the broth and soon dies. When Chale returns home she realizes her sister has poisoned her father but chooses instead to blame the 'gringo', screaming out her accusation for all to hear. In a bizarre twist, Madeinusa also decides to blame the gringo, running out into the street and chanting '*El gringo ha envenenado a mi padre!*' (The gringo has poisoned my father!). In the final scene we see Madeinusa in the truck with El Murdo, and it is clear that she has taken Salvador's place, who we presume is now rotting in the town prison. The film is striking in that it follows a well-worn formula, that of using non-professional actors, and it works with the notion of magical realism, such that the dividing line between the real and the magical becomes blurred. There are some experimental shots – two featuring close-ups of some poisoned rats at the beginning of the film, and one a reflection shot of the 'time-machine' used to count down *tiempo santo* – but the cinematography is otherwise conventional and focuses on providing visual solutions to the plot.

Carlos Reygadas's *Batalla en el cielo* ('Battle in Heaven', 2005) was the most innovative film of the year, an experimental piece that pushes

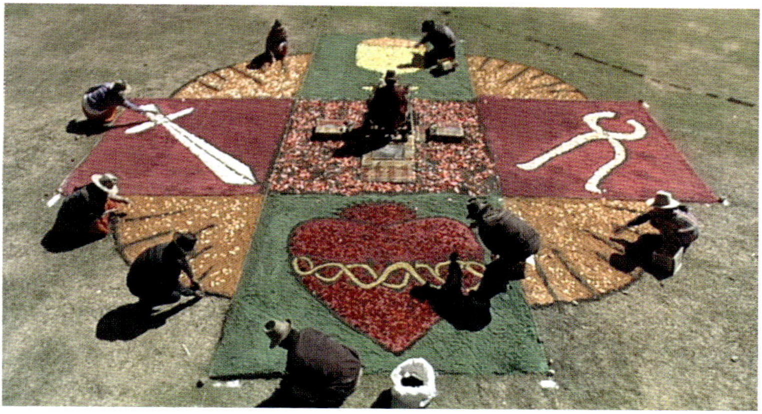

The time machine in *Madeinusa* (2005).

up against the boundaries of human and filmic experience. The human experience of the main characters has gaps which the film never completely explains. We learn that Marcos (Marcos Hernández), a private security guard, and his (unnamed) wife (Bertha Ruiz) have kidnapped a baby which on the morning the film opens has died, but we never find out how the child died nor the couple's motive for the kidnapping. When we see the child's mother, Viki (Rosalinda Ramirez), it becomes apparent that she is hardly well-heeled, so it would be difficult to imagine that she could pay a handsome ransom. Early on in the film Marcos kneels on the floor when he is on the metro and a woman says '*gracias*' when he gets up, but it is difficult to work out exactly what happened and why a woman should be smiling at him from the next carriage later on. We learn that the daughter of Marcos's boss, Ana (Anapola Mushkadiz) works in a sex boutique but we never find out why; since she is rich (as well as beautiful) her motives are enigmatic. We see Marcos stab Ana to death but his motive for doing so is obscure, especially when one considers that he loves her. These gaps in the plot are echoed by the distance of the characters from their emotions. The early establishing scene when Marcos and his wife, as we eventually discover, are standing behind their stall in the metro shows us two, expressionless people in hieratical pose, while an alarm sounds to which they are oblivious: Marcos turns his head slowly from left to right to ask his wife a question. Even when they discuss the death of the child they have kidnapped the couple's faces do not reveal any emotion. In their voluminousness they seem like

Botero models; in their distance from their emotions like characters in a Brechtian play; and their stiff hieratic pose – when they stare at the camera – is reminiscent of Ancient Egyptian sculpture.[47] These three traits flow naturally from the actors who appear, as Philip French suggests, 'from their general discomfort, to be non-professional'.[48] Reygadas clearly thrives on this 'discomfort'. As he noted in an interview:

> What I don't like about the theatre is the fact that the actors are representing roles. I don't understand; I get very bored and I find it a little ridiculous. I even feel sorry for the people acting. Theatre is interesting as a catharsis for actors because it's the only way you can be idiotic and get away with it. I really, really don't like theatre and I feel so far from it.[49]

The title of the film, '*Batalla en el cielo*', echoes the notion of the war in heaven according to the Book of Revelation:

> Now war arose in heaven, Michael and his angels fighting against the dragon. And the dragon and his angels fought back, but he was defeated and there was no longer any place for them in heaven. And the great dragon was thrown down, that ancient serpent, who is called the devil and Satan, the deceiver of the whole world – he was thrown down to the earth, and his angels were thrown down with him. (Revelation 12:7–9)

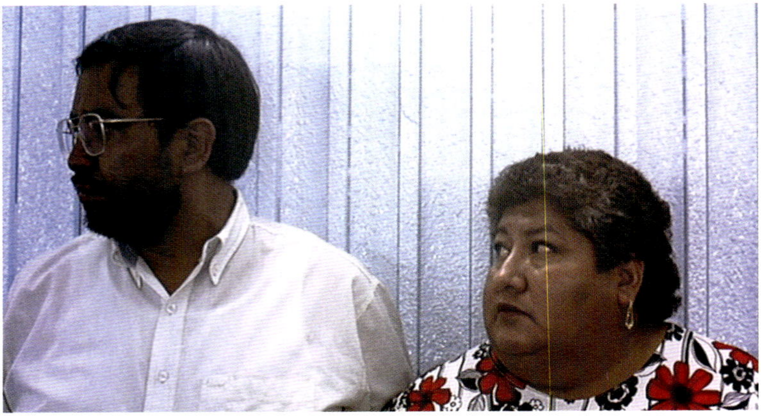

Marcos and his wife stand motionless and emotionless in the metro, in Carlos Reygadas's *Batalla en el cielo* (2005).

The film appears to dramatize its own version of the 'war in heaven' and it does so through the struggle of the main character, Marcos. Though our first glimpse of Marcos in the metro is of a character who is distanced not only from his emotions but also from ethics (in that he seems unconcerned that the child he kidnapped has died), he appears to embark on a path of 'redemption' – as a result of Ana telling him he should give himself in to the police and his wife encouraging him to participate in the pilgrimage to the basilica of Santa María de Guadalupe. So, according to an allegorical reading of the film, Marcos cleanses himself by walking through a shallow pool of water, repents of his sins (as signalled by covering his face with his hands), expresses contrition by approaching the basilica on his knees, covered by a blue hood, and pays for his sins by dying in the basilica itself.

But this allegorical reading is made problematic by a number of factors, such as his (unexplained) murder of Ana just before he begins the pilgrimage and the inclusion of fellatio at the beginning and end of the film, as if to suggest the heaven of sex rather than the heaven described in the Book of Revelation. It is noteworthy, too, that the final scene of the film shows Marcos smiling. This is the only time he is seen smiling – as if to suggest that he and Ana are finally in paradise. Or are they? As Jon Romney points out, 'It's finally hard to know whether Reygadas takes his transcendental, religious theme seriously, or is deriding it outright – or even deriding us for taking it seriously.'[50] The most striking part of the film is its cinematography, not only in terms of its use of awkward though curiously moving shots of the main characters in mute, hieratic poses, but also the travelling, circular panning shot of the ambient buildingscape when Marcos and Ana make love, followed by the tilt-panning horizontal to vertical shot of Marcos and Ana lying next to each other on the bed. Sound is also part of Reygadas's experimental repertoire. There is some curiously insistent emphasis on the simple fact of breathing, and an ironic deflation of the convention of extradiegetic music when one of the characters in the garage asks: '*Qué música es ésta, hijo?*' (What music is that, son?), and the viewer has a double-take as he realises that the music is, in fact, intradiegetic (part of the scene rather than external to it). *Batalla en el cielo* focuses enigmatically on the interplay between sex and religion and its cinematography highlights rather than smooths over the gaps in our understanding of both.

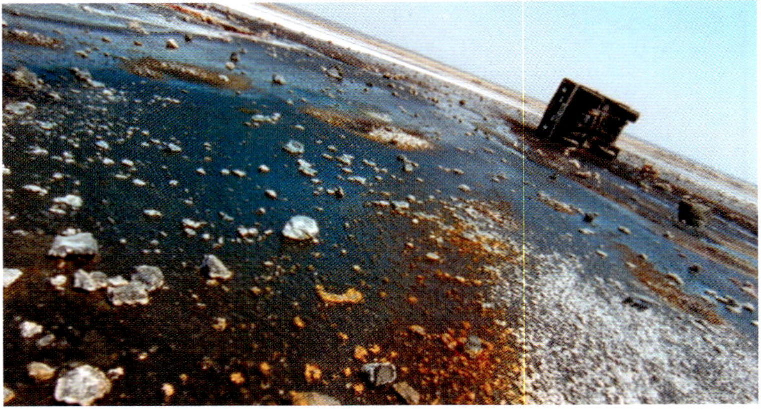

Tilt shot of the vehicle in which Tessa's dead body is found in Meirelles' *The Constant Gardener* (2005).

Alongside this experimentalism, a new direction began to emerge in Latin American film in the mid-2000s. Firstly a number of Latin American film directors, probably taking a leaf out of González Iñárritu's book in *21 Grams*, began to film in English. Fernando Meirelles, for example, released *The Constant Gardener* in 2005. The second characteristic was that Latin American film directors began to use famous actors. The two trends are likely to have been concomitant. So Meirelles had a starry cast in *The Constant Gardener*: Ralph Fiennes (Justin) and Rachel Weisz (Tessa), who received an Academy Award in the category of Actress in a Supporting Role for her performance. Based on John le Carré's novel of the same title, it tells the story of the search by a diplomat for the killer of his wife which leads to his discovery of the corruption of medical companies working in Africa and a treacherous conspiracy which will destroy the lives of millions of innocent people. The story is told in a loop-like way, beginning with Justin's farewell to Tessa as she leaves with Arnold on what will be her last journey, then we cut to soldiers taking a body in a black bag from a vehicle, then to the British High Commission where Justin's superior, Sandy, has to tell Justin that his wife has been murdered, cut to the beginning of their love affair when Tessa interrupts Justin's presentation, and then back to the defining moment of the film – Justin identifies his wife's dead body, along with Sandy, who vomits. And thus the film begins with Justin's reconstruction of what his wife had discovered about a pharmaceutical company, the corruption based on clinical trials in which the British government is embroiled.

Though the dialogue is English, the language of the film is Brazilian. There are the hallmarks of Meirelles's cinematic fingerprints – the edgy use of the hand-held camera, especially when the protagonists are walking among the crowds of Africa, the camera eye which is positioned about 18 inches (45 cm) off the ground and follows the protagonists as if it were a loyal dog, the off-the-back-shoulder shot, the aesthetically striking contrasts in colour between the grey of London (no one has filmed the greyness of London quite like Meirelles – it takes a Brazilian to see it for what it is) and the reds and oranges and yellows of Africa. All these techniques hark back to the cinematography of *Cidade de Deus*, produced expertly between the cameraman, César Charlone again, and the director, Meirelles. The viewer follows Justin's search and, rather like Tessa, he ignores the 'sensible' advice a number of people offer him to return to Britain. And in a sense Justin 'becomes' Tessa because he flies in the face of convention by offering the pilot $800 to fly a young girl away from the danger zone to safety, just as Tessa had attempted to persuade him to drive some patients at the hospital 30 miles (50 km) to get them home. The film ends on a note of magical realism: when returning to the place where Tessa died Justin 'sees' her face, and she comes to him in the form of a swirling wind which hovers near the car. While the film sticks closely to le Carré's novel – thus the denouement is triumphantly expressed when Tessa's cousin, Arthur Hammond, is able to read out the secret letter that Bernard Pellegrin had sent Sandy some months earlier, telling him to silence Tessa and her report – the film is more about a tragic love affair than anything else, and is indeed more powerful as a result of this directorial decision.[51]

2006 was perhaps the 'year of experiment' for Latin American film. Lisandro Alonso's *Fantasma* ('Phantom', 2006) is true to Alonso's tried-and-tested filmic formula in that it explores the links between documentary and fiction and relies on long takes and sparse dialogue. But *Fantasma* adds the new ingredient of self-reflexivity to the mix. So we see – separately – the non-professional 'stars' of Alonso's two previous films, Misael Saavedra from *La libertad* (2001) and Argentino Vargas from *Los muertos* (2004), wandering about in the Teatro San Martín in Buenos Aires looking for the premiere of *Los muertos*. As Jens Andermann suggests, *Fantasma*

> transforms film-watching into a performative act, which becomes uncomfortably conscious of itself as the intradiegetic ambient

noise (sounds from the street and from other parts of the theatre perforating the showroom) turns indistinguishable from the one entering the (same) showroom during projections.[52]

As the film develops its (plotless) plot, *Fantasma* becomes a commentary on the staged nature of film and – by implication – the theatricality of reality itself. The 'phantom' of the title is the ghost in the machine of life which the viewers – with Alonso's help – are searching for.

In *Children of Men* (2006), which received three Academy Award nominations, in the categories of Cinematography, Film Editing and Writing (Adapted Screenplay), Alfonso Cuarón created a gripping sci-fi movie, based loosely on P. D. James's novel of the same title, which allegorized the problems of the modern world in the face of infertility. Civilization is on the brink of destruction as a result of a seventeen-year dearth of new human births and Britain, the only country with a semblance of government, has become a police state. Despite the grimness of the opening scenes of the film in which refugees are being herded into concentration camps in order to keep law and order, the film eventually emerges as a modern version of the nativity story in that Kee (Clare-Hope Ashitey) gives birth to a baby girl. The visual design of the film is striking; it combines the chunky visuality of video games during the battle sequences with long takes that provide an extraordinary elegance to the narrative. As J. Hoberman points out:

> Although cinematographer Emmanuel Lubezki insisted on shooting the movie's climactic seven-and-a-half minute tracking shot – Clive Owen cradling a newborn born in a mad dash from a nightmare prison camp through an urban free-fire zone – in a single take, other apparent instances of virtuoso choreographed continuous motion were actually series of short shots digitally combined.[53]

Cuarón demonstrated with *Children of Men* that he was pursuing a new language for Latin American film, one which combined the filmic language of sci-fi movies with an auteurist experimentalism.

Babel (2006), directed by Alejandro González Iñárritu and written by Guillermo Arriaga, is a film about the differences that divide people, countries and cultures, which often produce misunderstandings and sometimes lead to deportation, depression or death. Like *Amores perros* and *21 Grams* before it – which it completes as the third part of a trilogy about death – Babel cross-cuts between different storylines, thereby creating a suspense which is filmic rather than existential. There are three main narratives: Richard Jones (Brad Pitt) and his wife Susan (Cate Blanchett) are an American couple holidaying in Morocco in an attempt to patch up their marriage, when Susan is shot in the neck by a stray bullet from a gun fired by a young Moroccan, Yussef (Boubker Ait El Caid) who is out hunting for jackals with his brother, Ahmed (Said Tarchani). Yussef, Ahmed and their father, Abdullah, are later hunted down by the police and Ahmed is shot and killed. A helicopter is sent and Susan is transported to Casablanca, operated on and survives. The second narrative occurs on the border between the United States and Mexico. Richard and Susan's two children, Mike and Debbie, are being looked after by their nanny, Amelia (Adriana Barraza, who won an Academy Award nomination in the category of Actress in a Supporting Role) in San Diego, when she takes them over the border – with her nephew, Santiago (Gael García Bernal) – so she can attend her son's wedding in Mexico. On their return to the United States Santiago panics at the border, drives the car off and abandons Amelia and the children in the

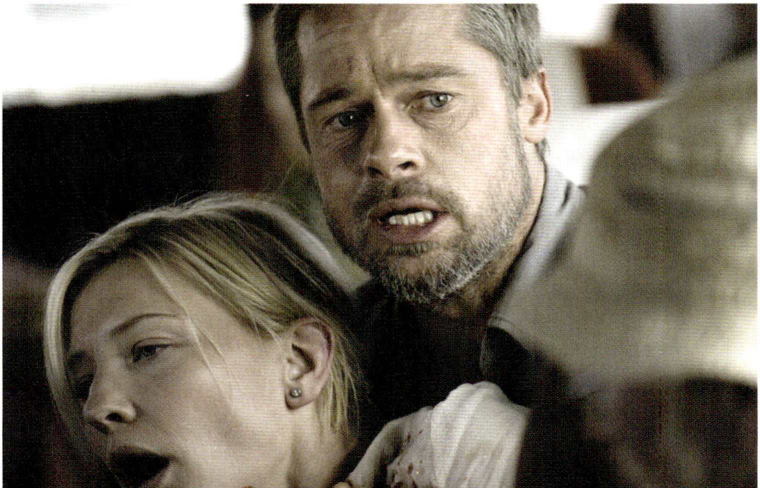

Susan (Cate Blanchett) with her husband (Brad Pitt) just after she has been shot in the neck in *Babel* (2006).

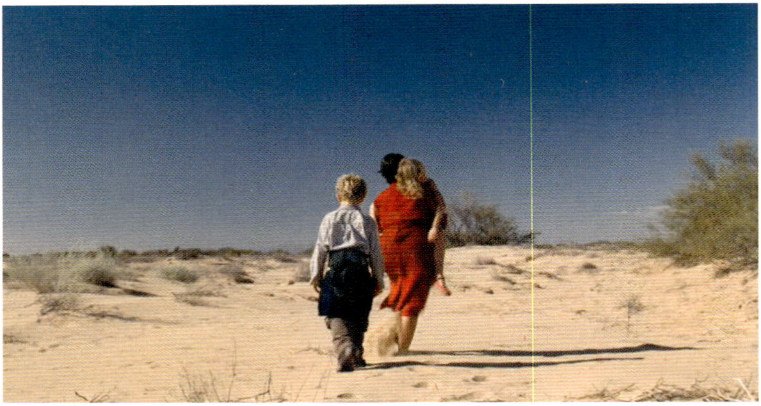

Amelia lost in the desert with the two children in *Babel*.

desert. Amelia goes off to find help when it gets light; as a result of her actions – she is accused of kidnapping the children – Amelia is deported with immediate effect to Mexico. The first and the second narratives are connected by a phone call which is heard from Amelia's perspective near the beginning of the film and from Richard's close to the conclusion.

The third narrative has a tenuous connection to the first two, even if it is ultimately more intriguing and thought-provoking. It tells the story of a beautiful, deaf young Japanese girl, Chieko Wataya (Rinko Kikuchi, who also won an Academy Award nomination in the category of Actress in a Supporting Role), who attempts to seduce a teenage boy (by taking off her knickers and flashing him in a café), her dentist (by forcing him to put his hand up her skirt) and a detective, Kenji Mamiya (Satoshi Nikaido) (by taking all her clothes off). The connection with the other two stories is that her father, Yasujiro Wataya (Koji Yakusho) had years earlier in Morocco given his gun to his hunting guide, Hassan Ibrahim, as he later explains to a detective. Hassan had subsequently sold the gun to Abdullah, as seen in the opening sequence of the film. In this way *Babel* echoes a theme explored in *Amores perros*, namely, the irony of how chance occurrences lead to events with life-changing consequences for certain individuals. *Babel* explores the so-called 'butterfly effect', in that it depicts the links between people on far-flung continents rather than in one city (as in *Amores perros*). An example of this type of tenuous connection between different parts of the world is suggested when the story of the shooting of Susan appears on the news in Japan;

Chieko sees it but does not realize its implicit significance for her life. Some reviewers were not impressed by the tenuousness of these connections. Ed Gonzalez, for example, argued:

> Though there is value to *Babel*, the filmmakers are careless about it. Commentaries rise to the surface only to dissipate in a cloud of connect-the-dot-isms. Just when you begin to appreciate the film's political perspectives, the filmmakers allow nuance to evaporate as they thrill in showing us how action in one part of the globe resonates in such a way that it affects someone's life thousands of miles away.[54]

And Peter Bradshaw was also unimpressed. He accused *Babel* of being

> the exasperatingly conceited new film from Alejandro González Iñárritu. It is well acted and handsomely photographed, but still extraordinarily overpraised and overblown, a middlebrow piece of near-nonsense: the kind of self-conscious arthouse cinema that is custom-tailored and machine-tooled for the dinner-party demographic. The script is contrived, shallow, unconvincing and rendered absurd and almost meaningless by a plot naivety that is impossible to ignore once its full magnitude dawns on you.[55]

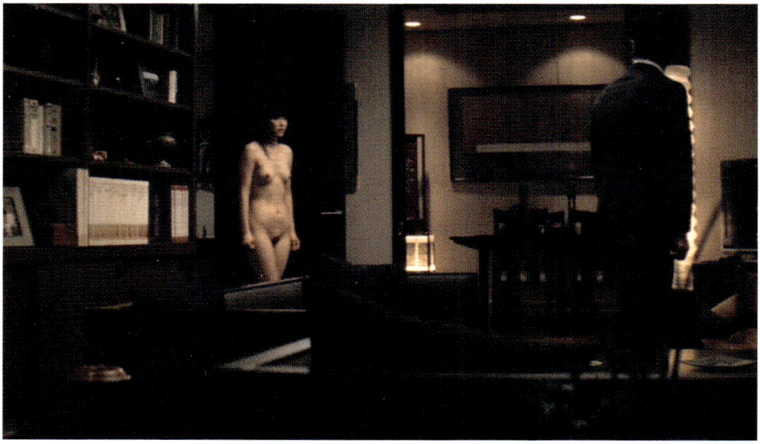

The enigmatic young Japanese girl, Chieko, in *Babel*.

But – *pace* Gonzalez and Bradshaw – there may well be a good reason why González Iñárritu devises such a globally stretched plot. If one compares the fate which is meted out to the representatives of the different nations portrayed in *Babel*, it is noticeable that some nations pull the short straw whereas others have disaster heaped upon them. Philip French makes an important point in this respect:

> While the movie seems to be sending out an ecumenically bland message about us all being part of mankind, and not sending to ask for whom the bell tolls, it is evident that some men's deaths are more significant than others, and indeed that America is the bell-ringer. The immediate assumption is that the bullet has been fired by a terrorist, and the European tourists panic and flee. A crisis is created, worldwide interest aroused. But whereas, partly by nature, partly by social deference, the authorities are courteous and helpful in their treatment of middle-class citizens, the peasants in Morocco are brutally ill-treated by their own police, and the Mexicans at the U.S. border are viewed with contempt and suspicion.[56]

While Amelia's life is in effect over at the end of the film – she has been deported summarily back to Mexico and will have to build her life again from scratch – and Ahmed's life is literally over, it is striking that the American family emerges relatively unscathed from its 'disaster'. Susan will recover from her operation and her two children have, somewhat miraculously, survived their experience in the desert. This idea is reinforced by the newsreader's comment towards the end of the film: 'The American people finally have a happy ending, after five days of frantic phone calls and hand wringing.' It is as if the film is hinting that Moroccans and Mexicans pay the price whereas Americans survive to live another day, and the Japanese find themselves in a curious limbo region somewhere in between (in the sense that Chieko Wataya is severely depressed and frustrated while her father, Yasujiro Wataya, will not be charged for any role in Susan's shooting).

There are some cinematic signals in *Babel* that indicate González Iñárritu's signature. When we see the tourist bus winding its way along the road, we know it will be shot at, and thus we experience the same dread we felt when watching the repeated car crash in *Amores perros*. The soundtrack (plaintive guitar interspersed with brooding organ music) and the use of silence – for instance, obliteration of the tourists' speech – gives a sense of distance, as if we as the viewers are helplessly watching people who are about to be struck down by tragedy.

The novelty of the film, though, lies in its exploration of the Babelian motif. The problem with communication underlies a number of episodes, including the slightly odd bilingual conversation Amelia the nanny has with the children (she speaks in Spanish and they reply in English), the argument between Richard and Susan based on their inability or unwillingness to reach out to each other, the awkward attempts by the Japanese youth to communicate with Chieko and her friend, both of whom are deaf; and the diplomatic stand-off between Morocco and the United States which leads to a delay in the arrival of the helicopter. Finally the film focuses on the deliberate non-communication between director and viewer – *Babel*, after all, ends with an enigma buried within the third narrative. Chieko writes a note for the detective and the contents of the letter are deliberately left to remain a mystery to the viewer.

It is ironic, of course, given that *Babel* is about communication problems, that while making the film González Iñárritu and Arriaga fell out. As Jo Tuckman points out:

> But whatever the truth about the end of one of the most successful writer-director teams of recent times, Arriaga was clearly less involved in making *Babel* than he had been in the previous films. This has some critics busy identifying hints as to González Iñárritu's future direction. He has never made a full-length feature without Arriaga, coming late to the industry after a successful career as a radio DJ and a maker of TV commercials. Fernanda Solórzano, critic for the Mexican culture magazine *Letras Libres*, sees evidence of Iñárritu beginning to shake off the shackles of Arriaga's obsession with interweaving, fragmented plot structures and solemn moral messages. As a result, *Babel* is filled with loose ends and a touch of moral ambiguity, she says, but also with a freer exploration of character.[57]

This question was in a sense answered when, four years later, González Iñárritu brought out his next film, *Biutiful*, which has a less complicated plot and is more character-focused.

Despite its initial acclaim, *Babel* did not obtain as many awards as expected (it won the Golden Globe for Best Motion Picture and, despite seven Academy Award nominations including two nominations for best supporting actress, it only won an Academy Award for Best Original Score).[58] This is surprising given the expert crafting of the cinematography.[59] The cross-cutting, for example, allowed for some thought-provoking connections between unlinked events. Occasionally González Iñárritu will use visual rhyme, as when Ahmed and Yussef running off after Yussef's bullet has hit the bus leads immediately to the running of a young boy in the next sequence with close to identical framing. Often the switch between the narratives leads to an emotional as well as graphic overlay of one event onto another. The throttling of the hen at the wedding feast in Mexico is followed immediately by the sequence in Morocco where Susan is losing large amounts of blood from the bullet wound. Though Mike is focusing on the blood spurting from the hen's decapitated throat, his horrified look merges emotionally with the horrified look of the tourists on the bus as they see blood pouring from Susan's neck. By fusing the two sequences through adroit editing González Iñárritu allows the second sequence to infiltrate the first – though looking at a hen, Mike is also (metaphorically) watching the tortured body of his blood-covered mother.[60] It should be noted that González Iñárritu's cross-cutting is not traditional in the sense of being the shuttling between two spatially separated actions occurring simultaneously, according to Griffith's time-honoured formula. In *Babel* Mike's horrified gaze at the severed chicken's neck occurs *after* the shooting of his mother since, as we know from the early telephone conversation between Richard and Amelia, she was already in hospital by the time Michael travelled to Mexico. But the emotional overlay between the two scenes is just as effective. Pointing in a similar direction, the tense episode in which Susan is forced to have her neck sewn without anaesthetic and ends with her blood-curdling scream is followed by a seventeen-second silence as we focus on Chieko's face quizzically watching the conversation between the receptionist and one of the patients in the dentist's waiting room. The silence operates as much as the traumatized after-effect of Susan's pain as an expression of Chieko's puzzled consciousness.

Babel uses the hand-held camera deftly, encouraging it to become another 'real-life breathing' witness to the events, especially during tense action takes, such as when Richard is desperate for Susan to get medical help and he jumps off the bus in order to persuade the driver of a passing truck to take his wife to hospital. When the police arrive to question Ibrahim about the gun, the camera moves fluidly, even nervously, turning from Ibrahim to the officers and back again. One of the most exhilarating hand-held takes in the film is the 'floating camera' sequence in which Chieko and her friends meet some boys who offer them drugs; they play in the water fountain, and then go to a disco. When Chieko sees that no one wants to dance with her, she leaves and her depressed self-absorption is expressed through an adroit use of shallow focus combined with bokeh (out-of-focus light sources) and the obliteration of sound at various points. There is some creative use of the bokeh effect for the lights in the background later on in the film when the detective asks Chieko if she actually saw her mother jump from the balcony. Bokeh is used effectively to signal an element of the plot outside the viewer's field of vision. This version of events is vehemently rejected by Yasujiro Wataya, who tells the detective that his wife shot herself in the head and, furthermore, that Chieko was the first to find her, and that he has explained this many times to the police already. Given that this version of events directly contradicts what Chieko has just told the detective it is not surprising that he looks confused. The detective goes to a restaurant to read the message written for him by Chieko; he takes it out and reads it, and the expression on his face is one of deep sorrow, suggesting that it is a significant statement. Since the viewer will never discover what the letter says the film concludes on an enigmatic note.

El laberinto del fauno ('Pan's Labyrinth', 2006) was the most successful Latin American film of 2006 in terms of awards as well as at the box office. It received Academy Awards for Make-up, Cinematography and Art Direction, and was further nominated for Writing (Original Screenplay), Original Score and Foreign Language Film. The main genre to which *El laberinto del fauno* belongs is fantasy film in the style of C. S. Lewis's *The Chronicles of Narnia* (original novels published 1950–56; latest film version in 2010) with which it shares a number of characteristics, including the notion of a land of mythical creatures and talking animals to which children (unlike adults) have special access through the imagination. In *El laberinto del fauno* a young girl, Ofelia (Ivana Baquero), stumbles into the faun's labyrinth and is told that she is actually Princess Moanna and that she has three tasks to perform. Whereas Lewis's novel is set in England and access to the fantasy world is found at the back of the wardrobe, del Toro's film is set in Spain in 1944, five years after the conclusion of the Spanish Civil War with General Franco in power. *El laberinto del fauno*, unlike the English genotype, thereby takes on a political dimension in that the real world is a world of pain and death, epitomized by Captain Vidal (Sergi López i Ayats), a Franco-like figure who ruthlessly hunts down the Republicans who are hiding in the forested hill above the Nationalist camp. He brutally murders two rabbit-poachers, suspecting them of being Republican spies, and sadistically tortures one of the Republicans – who happens to have a stutter – who is captured after an ambush. The magical world upon which his new step-daughter, Ofelia, stumbles, the faun's labyrinth (the labyrinth here an obvious allusion to Jorge Luis Borges's work) is a world scorned by Captain Vidal. When he finds a mandrake in a bowl of milk under the bed of his wife – the faun's cure for Carmen's (Ariadna Gil) illness – he explodes with anger and blames Carmen for filling Ofelia's head with fairy tales. It is in this sense that Guillermo del Toro builds a specifically Latin American version of the fantasy film in that a clear association is made between totalitarianism and the rejection of imagination and creativity.

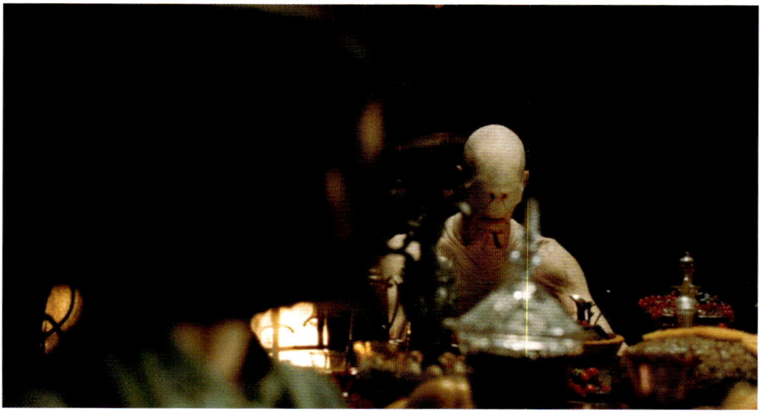

The eyeless monster awakes when Ofelia steals a grape in Guillermo del Toro's *Pan's Labyrinth* (2006)

Carmen becomes, as it were, the mediator between these two polarized attitudes towards life and, at this point in the film, she sides with her husband and tells her daughter that life is cruel and full of pain. And that '*la magia no existe*' (magic doesn't exist). As a result – perhaps not surprisingly, it's a fantasy film after all – Carmen is 'punished' for her words. As soon as she puts the mandrake on the fire it begins to burn and scream (with the aid of some highly impressive animatronics); Carmen loses its protection and promptly dies in childbirth.[61]

Though starting as a fantasy film and gradually morphing into political allegory, *El laberinto del fauno* is transformed into a thriller, especially in its final third when Captain Vidal is determined to take his revenge on any Republican who comes his way, culminating in the dramatic struggle with the maid, Mercedes (Maribel Verdú), who is discovered to be a spy. High tension is created when Captain Vidal gets his instruments ready to torture Mercedes, and the viewer is drawn powerfully into the film when Mercedes attacks the captain, cutting the left side of his mouth open to avenge the torture of the stuttering Republican. Harmony is restored when the Republicans attack the Nationalist stronghold and shoot the captain, although they are too late to save Ofelia, who has been shot by Captain Vidal. The most striking feature about *El laberinto del fauno* is that it demonstrated how seemingly effortlessly a Mexican film director could capture the adoration of the mainstream film market, which for many years had remained the jealous preserve of the English-speaking world. It made over $83 million at the box office and won numerous prizes, including three Academy Awards, and scooped many other awards including three BAFTAS (Costume Design, Make-up and Hair, and Film Not in the English language) and – in Spain – Goyas for Best Cinematography, Editing, Make-up and Hairstyling, New Actress for Ivana Baquero, Original Screenplay, Sound and Special Effects. *El laberinto del fauno* demonstrated that Latin American film was a force to be reckoned with on the world stage.

The outstanding film of 2007 was *Blindness* (2007), directed by the Brazilian Fernando Meirelles. It recreates José Saramago's novel *Ensaio da cegueira* ('Essay on Blindness', 1995), published in English as *Blindness* (1997), and is a powerful film that continues Meirelles's English-language filmmaking trajectory. It extends his interest in exploring a plot- and character-driven formula, in contrast to the digital flamboyance of the Portuguese-language *Cidade de Deus*. Saramago's story is in some respects a what-if thought experiment drawing on a lineage of disaster narratives ranging from *Lord of the Flies* to *Day of the Triffids*, setting out to answer the question: what would happen if an epidemic of blindness broke out across the world? Saramago's answer is bleak in that he sees democracy as the first casualty, totalitarianism as the government solution – food shortages produce a survival of the fittest mentality, leading to oppression, violence, rape, war and anarchy. Meirelles's filmic version of Saramago's *Weltanschauung* produces imaginative solutions to the dilemma that Peter Bradshaw has identified: 'Cinema is a visual medium, so no film version of *Blindness* could entirely reproduce its buried literary conceit of the "blind" reader having to imagine what the narrator is describing.'[62] The event which inaugurates the plot – involving a Japanese driver (Yusuke Iseya) who suddenly can't drive because he is blind – is presented via a series of directorial shots (the drivers stuck in the traffic jam, sounding their horns and getting agitated) rather than POV shots, so that it takes a while for us to work out what is going on; all we see is car after car whizzing past, interrupted by a shot of traffic lights turning red to green and an aerial establishing shot of a busy traffic junction. Then we hear the driver's exclamation as his car brakes abruptly, leading to the discovery that he is blind. The whiteness of this blindness only envelops the screen as a POV shot just before the Japanese driver describes his symptoms – 'like light shining through a sea of white; it feels like I'm swimming in milk'. From this point onwards the film has a steady forward momentum with plot as the centre of gravity; the driver's blindness infects the doctor he goes to see and the latter infects one of his patients, a call girl who wears dark glasses (Alice Braga), and the eventual result is mass-blindness and the government's decision to quarantine the sufferers in an attempt to curb its spread. The centre of gravity of the plot gradually swerves towards the doctor (Mark Ruffalo) and his wife (Julianne Moore) who become the leaders of this new vulnerable group.

The film, like the novel, is not only an allegory of human exploitation in the abstract; it becomes almost a case study of how scarcity and want lead to the powerful exploiting the vulnerable. The King of Ward 3 (Gael García Bernal) takes control of the food supply and first demands valuables from Wards 1 and 2 and then demands their women. One woman is raped and beaten to death and subsequently the doctor's wife

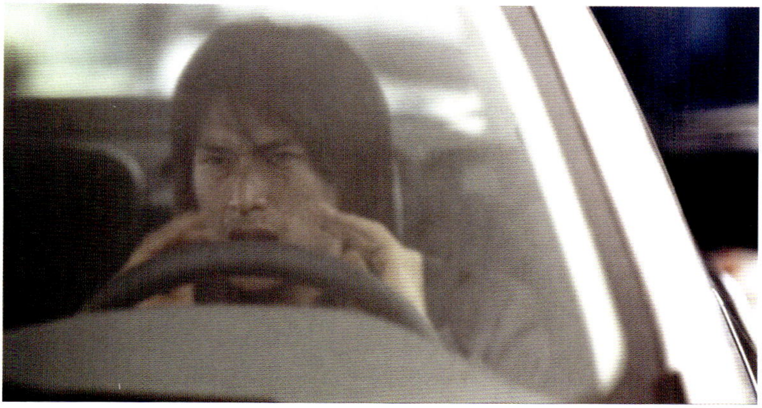

A Japanese driver realizes he is blind in *Blindness* (2008).

takes her revenge by killing the King of Ward 3, stabbing him in the neck. Mayhem follows, fire breaks out, and the doctor and his wife lead their group out to safety. Despite some of the negative reviews of the film, which have seen it as unremittingly bleak,[63] *Blindness* ends on a positive note in that the Japanese driver regains his sight, leading to the hope that the others too will regain theirs.

One of the main difficulties of the film, as Meirelles suggested in an interview, was the depiction of blindness itself:

> The big difficulty was the fact that the characters were blind. First of all, to establish relationships between characters – well, relationships are really all based on eye contact. When you're flirting or angry with someone, it's all done through eye contact. And in this film, the characters couldn't have any eye contact. Also, because they don't see, it was difficult to work out where to put the camera, because when you're cutting a film, you go to a camera and show what a character's seeing. In this film nobody sees except Julianne Moore, so I couldn't cut the film in the normal way. So we tried to make the image less trustworthy. Sometimes the image is very washed-out and you don't see much, *or* it's out of focus, *or* you look at something and think it's the image, but you realise it's just the reflection. I didn't want you to trust your eyes.[64]

It is clear that Meirelles and César Charlone, the film's cinematographer, thought of various cinematic solutions to this underlying problem. As a result we find in the film some delicately choreographed digital photography to suggest visual disorientation, ranging from the use of white-out shots as described above, when the call girl with sunglasses (Alice Braga) goes blind, when the doctor loses his sight (the profile of foreground and background is oddly merged as if to suggest that the doctor no longer inhabits his wife's space) and when a new group arrives in the hospital. There is innovative use of blurred images combined with the shrill sound of car horns, screeching of tyres and revving engines when the Japanese driver steps out of his car near his apartment, and moral darkness, as, for example, when the screen becomes saturated with black and green tones when the (unnamed) thief who steals the Japanese driver's car is forced to get out of it, and the sequence of the delivery of the women of Ward 1 to satisfy the sexual needs of Ward 3, during which the preponderance of black to near-black tones almost completely obscures visibility. At times it is difficult to trust your eyes because of the use of mirrors. When the thief takes the Japanese driver home the shot of the mirror to the right of the frame disorients the viewer, and in the shot of the call girl and her client on the bed, the mirror which this time is to the left of the frame likewise makes it at first difficult to distinguish image from body. All of these filmic techniques are combined in order to create a sensation in the viewer's mind of 'agnosia', which the doctor defines, in his conversation with his wife early on in the film, as 'an

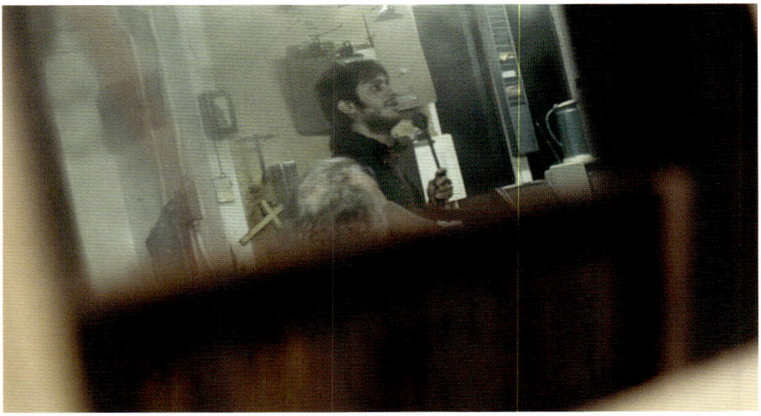

King of Ward 3 uses the public address system to gain control in a shot which emphasizes his duplicity in *Blindness* (2008).

inability to recognize familiar objects'. *Blindness* is a harrowing film in which strong acting performances from Moore and García Bernal are complemented by a sophisticated, digital cinematography which express the horror of a postmodern world in an arresting way.

Tropa de Elite ('Elite Squad', 2007), directed by the Brazilian José Padilha, is a semi-fictional hard-hitting action film based on the operations of the Special Police Operations Squad of Rio de Janeiro, the Batalhão de Operações Policiais Especiais (BOPE). While the terrain – drug lords in the favelas and the armed struggle with the police in Rio de Janeiro – is similar to that covered in Meirelles's *Cidade de Deus* released five years earlier, Padilha's film presents the action from the perspective of the police. As Padilha pointed out in an interview:

> *Elite Squad* is like being a cop in an environment as violent as Rio, and what the cop thinks/how he sees the world. I chose a first-person perspective here because it's the right one. Nascimento, like Henry in *Goodfellas*, is full of facts and he tortures people, but you bond with him. It's also why the film became polemic.[65]

This has led some to interpret the film as having a fascist ideology; it was an enormous box-office success (making U.S.$14,660,695) and it won a Golden Bear at the Berlin International Film Festival in 2008.[66]

Luz silenciosa ('Silent Light', 2007), directed by Carlos Reygadas, filmed in Cuauhtémoc, Chihuahua, in northern Mexico, tells the story of Johan (Cornelio Wall), who struggles to choose between his family – Esther (Miriam Toews) and their five children – and his lover, Marianne (Maria Pankratz). The film is set in a Mennonite community and the dialogue is mainly in Plautdietsch, the language spoken by the low-German Mennonites, though there is some Spanish. As is commonly the case in Reygadas's work, all the actors are non-professional and were chosen from the Mennonite community. Some aspects of the plot of *Luz silenciosa* are based on the film *Ordet* (1955) by Danish filmmaker Carl Theodor Dreyer, in which the main character's wife dies apparently out of grief as a result of her husband's impiety, only then to be resurrected mysteriously, as well as some of the cinematic motifs (clocks ticking, long takes of the landscape, the wheat and wind blowing in the trees).[67] But Reygadas's work uses Dreyer's film as a prop on which to construct his meditations about film. The deliberate and paused acting of the non-professional actors is used in order to suggest that people are awkward about the roles that have been thrust upon them in their lives, as if they do not understand what will happen next. Johan's first 50-second crying sequence, for example, is tearless and awkwardly natural. When he goes to see his friend Zacarías (Jacobo Klassen) at the garage, the conversation between Zacarías and the other mechanic has overtones of Harold Pinter in that, while they are talking about the machine parts that need to be fixed ('timing belt, crankshaft, and redo the valves'), the second mechanic moves screen-right in order to have Johan framed in a background piggy-in-the-middle shot to contrast his existential pain with their mundaneness. To further underline the ordinariness of the conversation, Zacarías even farts. Anti-staginess (which Reygadas has always sought in his films) is preserved by having the third mechanic enter the frame from screen-right and blurt out his lines too quickly, thereby talking over the second mechanic's lines. We find out what Johan's problem is when Zacarías says, 'I thought you stopped seeing her'. The pain of his experience is illustrated in his remark, 'Just talking about it feels like lead being poured into my guts.' Johan then admits that 'It's true that Marianne is a better woman for me', at which point Zacarías's rejoinder, 'And that may be founded in something sacred, even if we don't understand it', encapsulates the dilemma faced by Johan, and around which the whole film revolves. At this juncture in the film his decision appears to have been made for him by the lyrics of a popular Mexican song, 'No volveré' (I'm Not Coming Back), which are heard in the background and which Johan begins to sing along to. The lyrics express the desire to end a relationship – '*Te lo juro que no volveré / aunque me hagas pedazos la vida / si una vez con locura te amé / y de mi alma estarás depedida*' ('I swear I'm not coming back / even if you smash my life to pieces / If I loved you madly once / You're saying goodbye to my soul'). Johan gets into his truck, ready to drive off, it seems, into his lover's arms. But before he leaves he drives in a circle three times around Zacarías, breaking the expectations of a conventional plot and, in the process, breaking the 180-degree rule since the hand-held camera follows him, and he sings the lyrics of the song before driving off into the distance – a bold cinematic technique.

Immediately afterwards, Johan goes to meet Marianne in the countryside and they kiss. To express the ecstasy of the experience the photographer uses bokeh for the orange and yellow points of light resting on their heads. Produced by a shallow depth of field, Reygadas's use of bokeh is unusual in this scene since the effect is positioned in the foreground of the image rather than the background, which is the convention. The out-of-focus region of the image is thus the space between the camera and the protagonists. Reygadas is suggesting that the love experienced echoes what Zacarías had mentioned earlier – that it is 'sacred' and something we do not understand. He depicts that love as a light coming from a place that is beyond our understanding which, in cinematic terms, is the out-of-focus region of the image. But Reygadas is also drawing the viewer into the concept of love as deriving from an unknown source by situating the space between the camera and the protagonists – which is the space within the filmed frame that viewers are invited to inhabit. Reygadas's playfulness with regard to cinematic conventions also emerges when Johan goes to see his father (Peter Wall) to discuss what he should do. He says that he does not want his mother to know, to which his father replies, 'Don't worry. This is only between us.' Moments later Johan's father winks at the camera, drawing attention to the scene as a filmed reality.

The film comes to its emotional climax during a car journey in which Johan tells his wife that, despite his best efforts, he has seen Marianne again. Esther who, up until this point, had seemed impassive, almost removed from her emotions, is for once overwhelmed and calls Marianne a 'damn whore!' Soon afterwards she asks Johan to stop the car and shelters from the rain under a tree, crying her heart out. Wondering

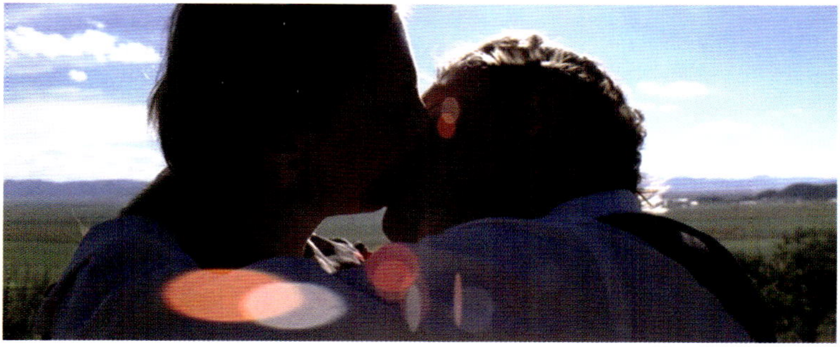

Johan and Marianne kiss with bokeh effect in the foreground in Carlos Reygadas's *Luz silenciosa* (2007).

what has happened, Johan goes to look for her, comes across her inert body and shouts out in pain. A passing truck driver takes them to the hospital where Johan is told that Esther has died of a massive heart attack. Esther's death, which appears to have been caused by Johan's revelation, and her subsequent resurrection as a result of Marianne's kiss at her wake (we first hear a sharp intake of breath and then we hear her breathing and see her eyes opening) are faithful to Dreyer's script for *Ordet*. However, the use of light as the main structuring technique (in the beginning and final sequences of dawn and dusk, as well as when Marianne visits Esther's body and the room is saturated with white light emanating from the window behind her), is part of Reygadas's filmic signature.

The bokeh orange and yellow points of light, which first appear when Johan and Marianne kiss, reappear after Esther's resurrection. An experimental film with some visually arresting cinematography, particularly in terms of the use of light and the use of bokeh to portray the sacred space of love, *Luz silenciosa* broke new ground in Latin American cinema's search for new ways of portraying the 'unseen'.

La mujer sin cabeza ('The Headless Woman', 2008), directed by the Argentine Lucrecia Martel, is a film about a middle-class dentist, Verónica (María Onetto), the 'headless' woman of the title. Early in the film, Verónica is driving along in her car when suddenly she hits something and comes to a halt; the camera focuses on the right side of Verónica's face (as if positioned in the front passenger seat of the car) and there are no establishing, frontal, aerial or directorial shots to counterbalance this lateral camera shot. In effect the viewer sees less than the protagonist and much of the 'drama' of the film springs from this blind spot. After the crash, in the side mirror the viewer sees a dead dog in the road and our assumption is that Verónica sees the same thing, but we cannot be sure. She is then seen having her head X-rayed to check for injuries and the camera angle is what might be called the 'headless shot', a medium shot showing the torso and legs without the head. This particular shot becomes more insistent as the film develops. The plot is overwhelmed by odd, unexplained events. Verónica goes to a hotel room and has sex with a man who, as we find out later, is married to her cousin. She suddenly becomes carless but it is not explained where her car has gone. She begins to insist that she has run over and killed someone but is persuaded by her family that she has imagined this due to the shock of running over a dog. This seems reasonable in that the viewer saw a dead dog in the road – that is, until there is a report of the discovery of a young man's body in the canal that runs alongside the road where the accident took place. When Verónica visits her aunt, her aunt refers to some 'ghosts' which live in the house, and we see – in very shallow depth of field – a person leaving the room they are in. This turns out to be the cook's son. Or is it?

The film abounds with mysteries such as these.[68] The film could be read as a story about a woman who ran over a dog but there are too many gaps in the narrative. The cleaners keep asking if they can clean her car; Verónica's friends and family seem anxious – indeed overanxious – to tell her that nothing happened, that it was only a dog. As Joanna Page suggests, Martel's cinema 'intensifies the destabilizing forces that are already at work in the social systems she depicts, heightening the power of becoming that is inherent in the unexplained accidents, popular beliefs, apocryphal texts and forbidden desires of her films'.[69] The disorientation is enhanced by the deliberate use of extremely shallow focus, so that the viewer often cannot make out the background, as well as disorientating camera angles – the main character is very rarely centre-frame and there are a number of headless shots – and apparently inane conversations about hair colour, hairstyles and flower pots. To cap it all, the film ends abruptly. The fact that we never find out whether Verónica did kill a young man or, indeed, see the body, makes this film an allegory of the guilt of the middle classes about the disappeared bodies of the Dirty War (1976–83). The film theatricalizes the middle classes' collusion in the plight of the *desaparecidos*, whose bodies were – for them – deliberately blurred figments of their imagination. This film is an ironic send-up of their imagination.

Lisandro Alonso's *Liverpool* (2008), co-written by Salvador Roselli, tells the story of the journey home by Farrel (Juan Fernández) to Tierra del Fuego. As so often in Alonso's work the landscape – which in *Liverpool* is as much the sea glimpsed from the freighter on which Farrel travels as the remote and stunningly beautiful snow-capped mountains of Tierra del Fuego – takes on a protagonist's role. As Alonso suggested in an interview about the film, 'For me, there is always the place where I want to shoot, before the story and the characters. Once I decide where to shoot, I travel there and I start investigating what happens with the people who live there.'[70] *Liverpool* contains some of the signature motifs of Alonso's work – the taciturn protagonist, the reflective, long takes and the mixture of documentary and fiction. The title is explained in the last scene when we see Farrel's daughter Analia (Giselle Irrazabal) holding a trinket bearing the name of Liverpool, a gift from her father. Whereas *Los muertos* concluded on a note of mystery – we do not know what happened when Argentino Vargas got home – in *Liverpool* Alonso concludes with a sense of the importance of a gift from father to daughter.

Perro come perro ('Dog Eat Dog', 2008), directed by Carlos Moreno and Colombia's official nomination for the Academy Award, is in one sense a standard Colombian *vicario* revenge-murder-and-gore movie. It tells the story of a powerful businessman, El Orejón (Blas Jaramillo), intent on avenging the murder of his godson, William Medina, and getting his money back from 'El Mellizo' (The Twin). The two *vicarios* sent to retrieve his cash, Víctor Peñaranda (Marlon Moreno) and Eusebio 'El Negro' Benítez (Óscar Borda), accidentally kill one of the twins during their interrogation, but Víctor finds the money and hides it while he plans his escape. Every single character in the film double-crosses someone else (even the laughing doorman takes a pop at Víctor late in the film) and at the conclusion not one of the male characters is left standing. So far, so standard. But the film has two twists. The first is the black magic which the witch, Iris, casts on Eusebio at El Orejón's instigation, leading to his hand rotting away and hellish black water flooding mysteriously out of the shower drain and the toilet. The second twist is that while the *vicarios* are waiting in the hotel an unidentified man keeps on ringing up asking to speak to his girlfriend, Adela. He is told to get lost with some choice Colombian insults. But at the end of the film he suddenly appears and attacks Víctor with a metal bar, asking what he has done with Adela and killing him. The supernatural quality of *Perro come perro* – which sits uneasily with the depiction of raw violence (the worst of which occurs when one of the twins is sawn in half with a chainsaw) and the black humour of Adela's forlorn and persistent boyfriend – is revealed in the final scene when Eusebio dies and is led away, walking past his own dead body, by William Medina's ghost. While certainly not a financial success – it made a grand total of $80 in box-office takings in the United States – *Perro come perro* offers an intriguing take on the Latin American gangster movie genre.[71]

Alamar (2009), directed by the Mexican Pedro González-Rubio, is a film about the relationship between a five-year-old boy, Natan, and his father, Jorge. The film is bookended in Italy – it begins with Natan and his mother speaking Italian in Rome, and the main story emerges using a sequence of fishing trips in the stunningly beautiful Chinchorro reef off the eastern coast of Mexico. Father and son fish together, talk together, the boy learns from his father and also from his grandfather, and the film becomes a beautifully shot elegy in a minor key to the relationship between father and son. The film has something of a documentary feel about it – showing how the fish is caught, how it is de-scaled – redolent in a tangential way of Grierson's documentary *The Drifters*. And yet *Alamar* is clearly a feature film – or, more precisely, a hybrid genre in which the conventions of the documentary film and the feature film merge, a featurementary.

An unnerving film, both thematically and cinematically, *Agua fría del mar* ('Cold Water of the Sea', 2009), directed by the Costa Rican film director Paz Fábrega, expresses the force and power of Nature. This is done in the sense of the unnervingly beautiful pans of the Costa Rican seascape, the snakes writhing in the mud as if in some horribly synchronic dance, but it is also about the power, perhaps sinister, of women, expressed simultaneously in the protagonist as well as the young girl she finds on the beach. In a Q&A session at the Odeon Panton Street cinema in London in November 2009, the director mentioned the connection between them, as if the young girl were the symptom of the older girl's malaise, one of the enigmatic elements of the film. The film is also open-ended in the sense that it does not conclude; it ends with the young girl stepping out of her father's truck and walking down to the beach, without any clear sense of what will happen next. *Agua fría del mar* is an intriguing debut film and also a landmark of contemporary Costa Rican cinema.

La teta asustada ('The Milk of Sorrow', 2009), directed by the Peruvian Claudia Llosa, is a poetic and atmospheric portrayal of the trauma experienced by a daughter, Fausta, on hearing about her mother's rape in a remote Andean village in the 1980s, when the Sendero Luminoso and the military were involved in a vicious and violent war. The film opens with the song of the mother's despair, which turns out to be her last will and testament, in Quechua, describing her pain. It is at this point that the film takes a bizarre turn. It describes Fausta's resistance to having her mother cremated in the back yard; instead she wants to take the body back home to the Andes, and will not allow the burial to take place until this can happen. Fausta accepts some menial work in the local household of a rich and famous female musician in order to scrape some money together to take her mother 'home'. The musician gradually becomes more and more interested in the young girl's songs of sorrow, and indeed ends up stealing one of them – a story about a mermaid – in order to present it to Lima's elite, to great acclaim. A subsequent visit to the doctor leads to the discovery that Fausta has a potato in her womb, whose presence is a mystery until she explains that it is her way of protecting herself from rape. The magical realism, so evident in Llosa's first film, *Madeinusa*, is also present here in that the potato is actually growing in Fausta's womb and – although we do not see this – she has to cut out the sprouts which are growing within her vagina.

The magical realism is not only unusual, it also has a gendered focus in that it involves a magic formula designed to thwart the violence that men visit on women's bodies. There is also a political, even class-based edge, in that it shows how the aristocracy, as epitomized by the 'criollo' concert pianist, exploits mercilessly the indigenous population. Aída offers Fausta pearls if she will sing – this is enticing for the young girl since she needs the money in order to afford a decent burial for her mother – but then Aída refuses to honour her side of the bargain. But the tables are turned when the young girl has an operation and is able to bury her mother near the sea. The film is cinematographically strong, and has

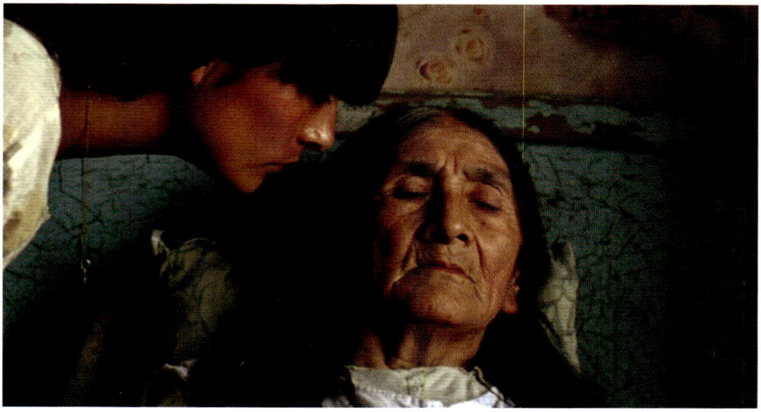

Mother and daughter in *La teta asustada* (2009).

Aida offers Fausta pearls if she sings for her in *La teta asustada*.

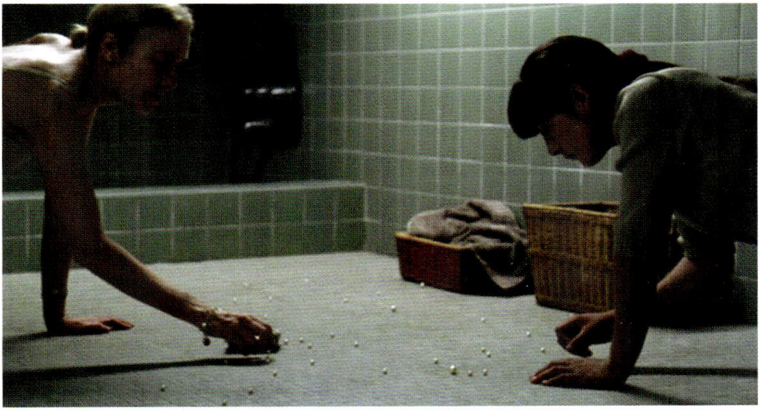

long, intensely emotive shots of Fausta's face, allowing us to 'enter' her pain, which is also expressed in the sad songs she sings. The tragedy is laced with humour, such as the various staged courtship scenes and the episode when a driver is shot because he cannot get his truck carrying a boat through a tunnel in the Andes. This beautifully shot film won its director a Golden Bear at the Berlin Film Festival in 2009, and was a nominee for an Academy Award in the best Foreign Language Film category, suggesting that Claudia Llosa is one of Latin America's most important female directors.

One of the most successful Latin American films of 2009 was *El secreto de sus ojos* ('The Secret in their Eyes', 2009), directed by the Argentine director Juan José Campanella, which won an Academy Award for Best Foreign Language Film. *El secreto de sus ojos* is a crime thriller based on Sacheri's novel *La pregunta de sus ojos* ('The Question in their Eyes'), which mixes politics and passion. It focuses on the buried romance of a now-retired criminal court investigator, Benjamín Espósito (Ricardo Darín), and Judge Irene Menéndez-Hastings (Soledad Villareal) who had worked together in 1974 on a still-as-yet-unresolved rape case, as silhouetted against the murkily corrupt and violent world of the Guerra Sucia in Argentina (1976–83). Campanella's film is, as Peter Bradshaw states, 'a supremely watchable, well-made and well-acted movie with a dark, sinewy sense of history: a tremendously slick thriller'.[72] Shot and edited digitally, it won the Goya Award for Best Spanish Language Foreign Film and the Academy Award for Best Foreign Language Film at the 82nd Academy Awards. *El secreto de sus ojos* manages to combine a number of genres. As Geoffrey McNab points out, it 'deliberately blurs genre lines and storytelling styles. This is a murder mystery. It is also a love story, a drama about memory and bad faith and even, in an oblique way, a political allegory about 1970s Argentina.'[73] Unlike films such as *La historia oficial* (1984) or *Garage Olimpo* (1999), which narrates the Dirty War as if it were a story of the present, *El secreto de sus ojos* alludes to it in the past tense and is more concerned with seeing the fin-de-siècle – the film is set in 1999 – as an echo chamber of those events. The preterite feeling is engineered through having the protagonist write a novel about those years, a device which was not to the taste of all reviewers. Tim Robey, for example, was unimpressed: 'Already notorious as the one that beat *A Prophet* and *The White Ribbon* to the Best Foreign Film Academy Award, this flashback-legal-procedural-whodunit from Argentina was in every way the safe choice: handsome, fitfully absorbing, fundamentally trite.'[74] But, *pace* Robey, what allows this film to rise above triteness is its chilling vision of what might be described as 'murderous office politics' as embodied in the rivalry between Espósito and Romano (Mariano Argento). Things begin to turn nasty in the prosecutor's office when Espósito, who in Ricardo Darín's performance, as Jonathan Romney suggests, 'faintly recalls Al Pacino with a quizzical, impish streak',[75] accuses Romano of obtaining by violent coercion two false confessions in the case of the rape and murder of a beautiful 23-year-old girl, Liliana Coloto (Carla Quevedo). The film is structured around a succession of false hypotheses, and the first of these is Romano's solution to the whodunit. This is disproved once Espósito's accusation is upheld and Romano loses his job and is transferred elsewhere. Espósito, with the help of his sidekick, Pablo Sandoval (Guillermo Francella), then goes to visit Liliana's widowed husband, Ricardo Morales (Pablo Rago), who vows to make the murderer pay for his actions. While flicking through some family albums, Espósito notices that in many of the photographs Liliana's cousin, Isidoro Gómez (Javier Godino), appears to be looking at her. This second hypothesis – that Gómez was the rapist – at first leads nowhere since Gómez has in the meantime disappeared without trace. Breaking into Gómez's mother's house allows some letters written by Gómez to be retrieved but these at first provide no clues as to his current whereabouts. Eventually the code of the letters is broken to reveal that he is a fan of a local football team, Racing Club, and the need to attend a football match provides a perfect alibi for some virtuoso cinematography. It begins with a beautiful aerial shot of Racing Stadium, followed by a sweep over the game; we see a player hit the bar and we fly into the crowd, ending up at Espósito's side; we then follow him and Sandoval as they push through the crowd looking for Gómez until they clap their hands on the shoulder of the wrong man. But the free-floating digital camera really comes into its own when Espósito suddenly recognizes the real Gómez and returns to confront him at the exact moment when a goal is scored. The camera sways and swerves with the crowd's emotion, and Gómez is seen running off into the tunnel. This is followed by a cinematically thrilling chase through the tunnels at the back of the stands in which the camera runs on the shoulder of Espósito and Sandoval like a third participant in the chase. They hurtle down stairs, check the toilets and run after Gómez as he drops over a wall and runs onto the pitch. Here he is punched by one of the players as he is running into the penalty area. This sequence is a virtuoso performance, demonstrating how the digital camera took even further the original promise of the hand-held camera, which produces an experience of a living, 'breathing' camera participating actively in the world around it. Gómez is taken off to be questioned and, at this point, the second resolution of the film is provided by Irene Menéndez-Hastings who uses some reverse psychology to make Gómez confess to the rape and murder by insulting his manhood.

At this juncture in the film a number of new unexpected twists emerge. The second resolution is 'undone' when justice is overturned by Espósito's rival, Romano, who gets Isidoro Gómez released so he can assist him in his undercover work fighting against 'subversives', thereby getting his revenge on Espósito. Espósito and Irene go to see Romano who explains that they can do nothing about it. The thriller becomes more thrilling when Espósito and Irene are leaving Romano's offices and, just as the lift door is closing, a hand is seen forcing it open and Gómez steps in. The tension is visible, especially in Irene's face, when Gómez takes out his automatic and readies the cartridge. Sandoval is subsequently found shot dead in Espósito's apartment in what was clearly a case of mistaken identity. Aware that Espósito's life is now in danger, Irene arranges for him to work in a lawyer's office in a remote region in the north, Jujuy. At the station, she says to him, '*no podemos hacer nada*' ('we can't

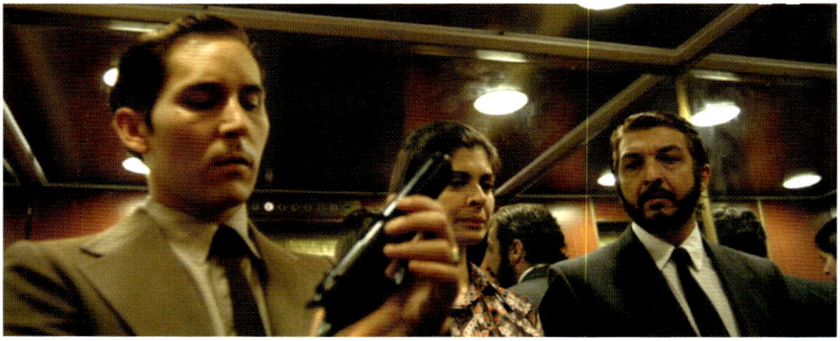

Gómez checks to see if his gun is working, standing in the lift next to Irene and Espósito in *El secreto de sus ojos* (2009).

do anything'), and this sentence has a personal as well as a political meaning: they cannot fight against the fascists, nor can they embark on a love affair. As Espósito leaves for Jujuy the film appears to reach a new plateau which is, in effect, the third resolution. At this point the film fast-forwards to the present and Espósito and Irene discuss – as a result of reading the latest draft of Espósito's novel – what might have been at that earlier juncture of their lives.

The film has two more twists before its final resolution. Espósito decides to search for Morales, eventually finding him in a remote part of Buenos Aires province, where he asks him to read the novel. Rather unexpectedly, Morales becomes annoyed with Espósito's continued fascination with the murder of his wife 25 years earlier but he softens when Espósito explains his own desire for revenge on Gómez – because he was also responsible for Sandoval's murder. Morales confesses to Espósito that – many years before, in 1975 – he lay in wait for Gómez, kidnapped him and shot him in the boot of his car before disposing of the body, a sequence of events that is reconstructed visually. This is in effect the fourth resolution of the film. It is only when he is driving back and rerunning the different events in his head that it dawns on Espósito that Morales's version of the events does not add up. He decides to walk back in order to spy on the house. At nightfall he sees Morales walking towards an outhouse on his property and, following him, discovers the fifth and final level of truth. Morales had captured Gómez and kept him locked up on his property for 25 years, in what is in effect a reversal of the reversal of justice performed by Romano when he originally released Gómez – people's justice in the face of government injustice created by the Guerra Sucia. After 25 years of imprisonment Gómez cuts a pathetic figure, saying to Espósito, '*Por favor pídale que aunque sea me hable*' ('Please ask him to just talk to me'). This final act of people power liberates Espósito from the burdens of the past; he leaves flowers at Sandoval's niche and also declares his love to Irene, turning the '*temo*' (I fear) written on a piece of paper at the beginning of the film into '*te amo*' (I love), thereby correcting the typewriter's delinquency (the Olivetti was unable to type out the letter 'a'). The political resolution to the nightmare of the past is echoed by the flowering of love between Espósito and Irene. Rather surprisingly, *El secreto de sus ojos* becomes a thriller with a happy ending.[76]

Biutiful (2010), directed by Alejandro González Iñárritu, is redolent of his earlier work in its fascination with death – such that we see life through a thanatocentric lens – and it is different in that it has a linear plot. *Amores perros*, *21 Grams* and *Babel* all sacrificed linearity in favour of a kaleidoscope effect, but in *Biutiful* the only non-linear element is the opening sequence in which, as we realize at the end of the film, Uxmal (Javier Bardem) has just died and is speaking to his father in a snowy dreamscape. In an interview González Iñárritu said that he wanted the plot to be centred around the main character in *Biutiful*: 'The first three films that I did were more plot-driven films and the events were what was moving the story forward. In this case, I wanted it to be a character-driven film.'[77] That central role is played by Javier Bardem in a haunting performance (for which he won an Academy Award nomination for Actor in a Leading Role) of a man who is dying from cancer (he has only a few months to live). He earns his living from shady deals with illegal African and Chinese immigrants, as well as a corrupt local cop, and has a sometimes separated and sometimes traumatic relationship with his wife, Marambra (Maricel Álvarez), a bipolar, drug-taking prostitute who likes to sleep with Uxmal's brother, Tito. Uxmal seems, indeed, to have the Pluto touch in that everything he touches turns to death – he has recently sold his family plot in the local cemetery in order to raise some funds (and in the process meets his grandfather's dead body) and when he attempts to provide extra heat for some Chinese immigrants he buys some heaters which turn out to be faulty and kills all 25 of them. He is also psychic and can see the spirits of the dead after they have recently departed and he moonlights by relaying their final messages to grieving (and perhaps gullible) relatives.

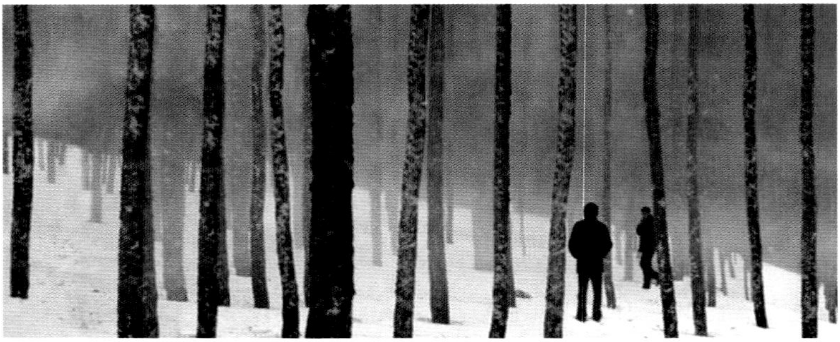

Uxmal meets his dead father in a snowy dreamscape in González Iñárritu's *Biutiful* (2010).

Yet, even though the film seems unremitting in its bleakness – the working conditions of the immigrants are dire, the Barcelona police are either corrupt or brutal or both, Uxmal's flat is unhygienic and cramped, his wife commits incest, his grandfather's tomb is opened up and we see the embalmed body, and the visions Uxmal has of the dead are spooky – a dignity emerges from Uxmal's struggle to survive and his desire to provide for his children after his (physical) death.

Just before his death Uxmal manages to give some onyx stone to each of his children, Ana and Mateo. He arranges for Ige, a Senegalese illegal immigrant whom he has taken care of after her husband's deportation, to look after his children, giving her his life savings. Immediately before his death, he gives his daughter a family heirloom – the ring his mother had given to his father when he escaped to Mexico from Spain.

The pace of the film allows for moments of philosophical reflection – as experienced through Uxmal's eyes when, for example, he learns that his cancer is so far advanced that he has only months to live. As González Iñárritu suggested in an interview, *Biutiful*, unlike his earlier films, 'was more lyrical. I didn't adhere to any clockwork rules for plot. This was more like a fluid current that was taking me to different events and things that this guy was going through.'[78] The cinematography and sound mixing characterizing the sequence after the point at which Uxmal realizes he has killed 25 Chinese immigrants contrive to produce a powerful expression of a mind which through extreme pain and guilt becomes disconnected from its empirical environment. The sight and sound of everyday life becomes blurred, discordant, confusing. The musical score used for the soundtrack, engineered by Gustavo Santaolalla as in González Iñárritu's previous films, is haunting and delicately choreographed, allowing *Biutiful* – which won an Academy Award nomination for Best Foreign Language Film – to realize its potential as a melancholic and poetic disquisition on human failure, death and the afterlife.

A sequel to José Padilha's *Tropa de Elite* was released in 2010: *Tropa de Elite 2 – O Inimigo Agora é Outro* ('Elite Squad: The Enemy Within'), with the same protagonist, Roberto Nascimento (Wagner Moura), involved in his personal war against crime, corruption and evil. In the sequel Padilha decided to integrate Nascimento's private life into the drama; Nascimento is divorced from his wife, Rosane, who has married his rival, Fraga, and he therefore loses contact with his son. As Padilha suggested in an interview:

> I decided that, yes, it's going to be a political thriller. My character is going to go through a sort of adventure in this political/police world. But this family is going to be part of this. It's going to affect their son. It's going to have to do with his relationship with his former wife. So I decided to come up with a plot that will be complete, in this way.[79]

Elite Squad 2 was even more successful at the box office than the original, making U.S.$63,024,876.

Preludio (2010), directed by the Mexican Eduardo Lucatero, shot on a roof garden in Mexico City, depicts in an engaging way the gradual growth of a love affair between an (unnamed) aspiring rock star and a chef who has returned from Acapulco to Mexico City. The two individuals start up a conversation before the party which they are both attending; the small talk gradually turns into 'big talk' in that we see a relationship growing between them. The film, as the director explained in a discussion at the Odeon Panton Street in London on 19 November 2010, was prepared over the course of a year and was filmed in one day (the previous day was the rehearsal). There were two takes and the director chose the second (in the first take, a beer bottle had been knocked over, which he thought was a distraction). He was also impressed by the energy and the momentum of the closing stages of the film – something magical occurred that had not happened in previous performances. *Preludio* is an example of one-take, long-take cinema. It is the prelude in the sense that the film appears to indicate the time preceding the growth of a love affair. It starts small (discussion of food, spying on neighbours), and gradually the frame is opened up to hint that for these two people this may be the most important meeting of their lives.[80]

No films from Latin America were selected for the Palme d'Or competition at the Cannes Film Festival in 2011 but the year certainly had some highlights, including Nicolás Goldbart's *Fase 7*, an Argentine science fiction film, Andrés Wood's *Violeta se fue a los cielos* ('Violeta Went to Heaven'), about the charismatic left-wing folklore singer, Violeta de la Parra, and Everardo Gout's 'brutal Mexican thriller', *Días de gracia* ('Days of Grace'), about the grace period that exists in Mexico when the gangsters and the cops take time off to watch the World Cup.[81]

Pablo Larraín's *No* (2012), chosen for the Directors' Fortnight at Cannes, tells the story of the 'No' campaign in Chile in 1988 in the lead-up to the referendum on whether Augusto Pinochet should remain in power for a further eight years. Each side was given a fifteen-minute evening slot on television in the run-up to the election in order to put their case across, and the Resistance Movement, rather than resorting to political ideology, decided to use the language of advertising. The strategy paid off and, against all the odds, the 'No' vote won and Pinochet was obliged to accept a humiliating stand-down; he conceded the referendum and resigned his position as President of Chile (even though he remained as Head of the Armed Forces for another ten years). Larraín's film focuses on the trials and tribulations behind the scenes of the 'No' campaign. Its central character is a skateboarding adman, René Saavedra (Gael García Bernal), who masterminds the campaign. *No* was shot with rebuilt U-matic video cameras, giving the film a smeary 1980s look, making it easier to switch between the fiction of *No* and the documentary sections when excerpts of the 'real' ads from the 1988 campaign are spliced in. As Larraín suggested in an interview, 'You could make really, really a thousand movies, there are so many stories, it's absolutely endless . . . There's a huge mystery about those days.'[82] By avoiding the Left versus Right parameters of the Pinochet story and allowing the narrative to grow obliquely, Larraín manages to explore the mystery of that period in a powerful way.

Post tenebras lux (2012; Latin for 'light after darkness'), directed by Carlos Reygadas, is a highly experimental film loosely based on the director's experience of building his home in Morelos, a city to the south of Mexico City as Reygadas points out:

> For example, this last film, *Post tenebras lux*, I had just finished my previous film; then, I had children and started building my house in the countryside. Of course, a lot of ideas and feelings developed. I tried to put all of those together in a form – that, in this case, certainly seems to be a strange form – but actually it has its own logic.[83]

The film opens with a young girl (Rut, Reygadas's daughter) who is wandering around a waterlogged football pitch at dusk, surrounded by dogs, cows and horses. This opening sequence sets the tone for the rest of the film, which has the appearance of a home movie of a famous film director. But this documentary feel is spliced with a number of other fantastic events. In the second sequence, for example, we see a red devil – with a suspicious similarity to the Pink Panther – snooping around a house, carrying a workman's toolbox and sporting large, dangling genitalia. The film revolves around a family, Juan (Adolfo Jiménez Castro), his wife Natalia (Nathalia Acevedo) and their two children, Rut and her older brother, Eleazar, and since we later hear Natalia talking to Rut about her dream with animals, this suggests that the opening sequence was the dream rather than a depiction of her actions. In an early sequence Juan is depicted hitting one of the dogs savagely (the blows rain down off-screen), an event which appears to be behind a later conversation when Juan tells Natalia that the vet did not believe him (presumably when he explained how the dog got hurt). Juan and Natalia do not appear to fit into the local community and, at a local event, Juan is asked if he is Mexican. One of the members of the community, Siete (Willebaldo Torres) appears to be involved in some shady deals involving tree-logging. Siete introduces Juan to the local people and later on tells him that he has taken drugs and been an alcoholic, a situation not helped when he stumbled in on his father having sex with his fifteen-year-old sister. Siete is later seen having a conversation with Guante in which the latter offers to pay Siete to fell a tree for him, since – he says – he wants revenge on his sister. The film also contains a rather bizarre sequence in a swingers' bath spa in France in which the rooms are named after intellectuals and artists such as Hegel and Duchamp. Juan and Natalia go to the Hegel room and Natalia has sex with a man while she is caressed by another man and a large-breasted woman, and her husband watches.

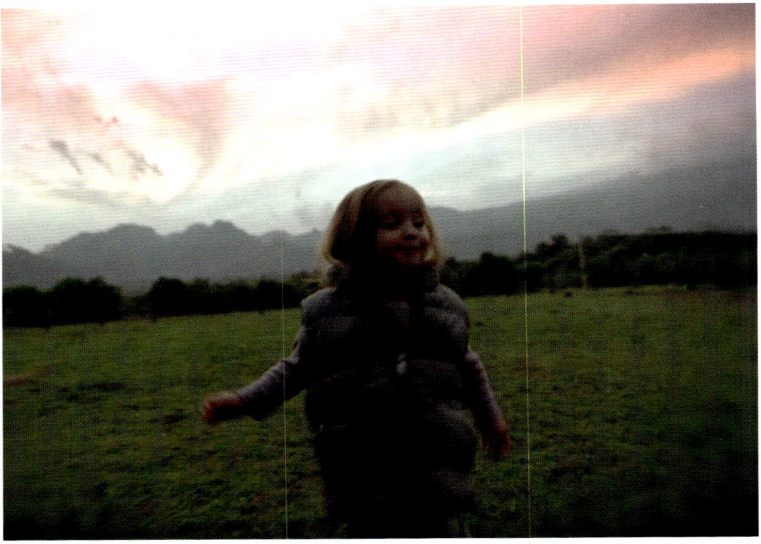

Rut, Carlos Reygadas's daughter, in a field in *Post tenebras lux* (2012).

The fulcrum of the drama occurs when Juan returns to the house to pick up the buggy that Natalia has forgotten, only to find Siete and an accomplice robbing his home. Juan challenges them but Siete becomes aggressive, draws a gun, follows Juan up the stairs and shoots him. Juan is later discovered by his friend, Jarro.

Juan is subsequently seen, ill and bedridden, and he ignores Natalia's plea to go to the police. Samanta, Siete's wife, tells Siete that someone came looking for him on Juan's behalf, and Siete returns to Juan's house where he finds the children playing on their own. Eleazar tells him that his father has died and this inauspicious event seems confirmed by the devil who enters one of the rooms on his second visit to the house. Siete returns home to find that his wife and children have disappeared and, as a result of his guilt at murdering Juan – after seeing a tree fall to the ground, symbolizing his own demise – Siete commits suicide by pulling his own head off.

This climactic suicide is followed by the final part of a rugby sequence; after going down by one try the losing team forms a scrum, refusing to accept defeat with the words, 'they've got individuals, we've got a team' (which is the concluding leitmotif of the film). In an interview Reygadas states that he ended the film on this note because it was a message of defiance in the contemporary world, uniting against bankers. *Post tenebras lux* is a highly experimental film built around a series of autobiographical vignettes interspersed with dream sequences which are deliberately enigmatic but have an oblique referentiality to the rest of the film.

The confusion which Reygadas's films often produces in the viewer – *Post tenebras lux* was booed by some viewers at the 2012 Cannes Film Festival – is there for a reason.[84] As he explained in an interview:

> Very often, the way we experience life, we really don't know what's going on in the present tense. And it doesn't always make sense in the future either. If you walk out of your house and you see a corpse in the middle of the countryside, you just see a corpse. You don't know where it comes from, why it's there, who this man was. Then maybe you talk to your neighbors, there's something in the newspapers, and eventually everything makes sense. Or maybe it doesn't. But in cinema and television, we want things to be explained immediately and for everything to make sense. But in reality, I think life is much closer to the way I make films than to what most films are like.[85]

Reygadas uses a blur-edged digital kaleido-cam along with the Academy ratio throughout the film in order to echo this sense of unknowing about the events that occur in our lives. This means that the whole film is made with a very clear central circular zone with objects having blurred edges – as if they have had double exposure – in the area surrounding the central in-focus area. As Reygadas explained:

> I really wanted something that gave great definition in the center, but I didn't want to have something that gave full definition all over the place, because that made me think of this kind of digital image we're looking at now [Skype video call]. These digital images are so defined it's like the curvy aspect of vision has been completely withdrawn, so I wanted something that would be blurred on the sides. When we were mounting the lens on the camera, we found by accident there would be this double image, like a bevel, at the edge. I just realized that it was a reinterpretation of images. If you want to see how things look really, you can

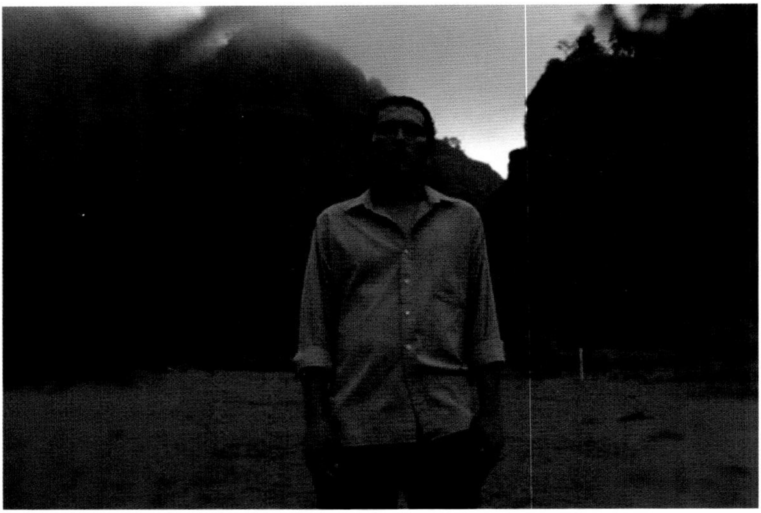

Siete shortly before he commits suicide in *Post tenebras lux*.

> look at them with your own eyes, but if you're ready to see a film or a painting – or to paint something or film something – you might as well reinterpret those images to make them more relative, to make them convey something different than that which we're so used to associating them with. This will always remind us that things aren't necessarily as they seem.[86]

Though not to everyone's taste, Reygadas's *Post tenebras lux* was the major Latin American film of 2012.[87]

The following year, 2013, produced some thoughtful takes on the theme of dispossession in Latin American film. Diego Quemada-Díez's *La jaula de oro* ('The Golden Dream', 2013) tells the story of Juan (Brandon López) and Sara (Karen Martínez) who want to escape from the poverty of Guatemala and ride northwards on the trains. On their way they meet up with a non-Spanish-speaking Indian boy, Chauk (Rodolfo Domínguez). Quemada-Diez worked as a camera assistant with Ken Loach on *Carla's Song* and some of the grittiness of Loach's style has found its way into *La jaula de oro* which combines fiction with documentary. The film, as the director pointed out in a Q&A at the London Film Festival on 15 October 2013, was based on an amalgamation of 600 stories of refugees who sought a better life in the United States.

The documentary feel of the film is enhanced by the quasi-improvised non-professional acting of the three main actors and its appeal to the travelogue genre – the structure is episodic and built around a series of train journeys, with long, beautiful takes of the Latin American countryside. The reality depicted is stark; despite taping her breasts to avoid detection, Sara's gender is discovered by some kidjackers and she is kidnapped, never to be seen again. People who offer to help are simply leading the protagonists to their next dance with death.[88] Chauk is suddenly shot dead by a bullet which comes out of nowhere when he and Juan are walking through some fields, just after they have crossed the border.[89] The final sequence of the film shows Juan now working in a meat-packing factory in the States, the lifeless bodies of the slaughtered animals on the conveyor belt providing a powerful visual symbol of the refugees who died en route, rounded off with Juan looking up at the snow which operates throughout the film as an image of the elusive ideal of the 'golden cage'.[90]

Alejo Moguillansky's *El loro y el cisne* ('The Parrot and the Swan', 2013) is a romance-cum-comedy about a hapless sound recordist, Loro (Rodrigo Sánchez Mariño), who is working on a documentary about classical ballet – called the Grupo Krapp – for an (amusingly gauche)

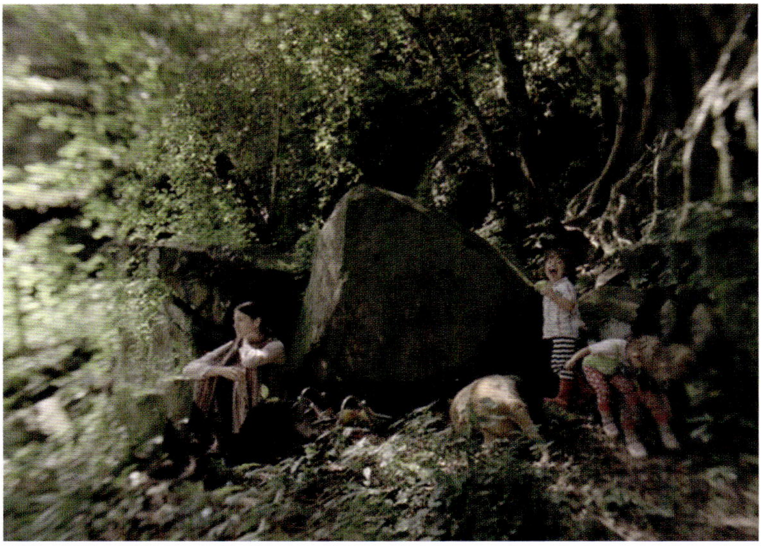

The bevel effect in *Post tenebras lux*.

American producer. Loro begins to fall for one of the ballet dancers, Luciana (Luciana Acuña), who turns out to be pregnant, though we never discover the identity of the father. When Luciana decides to leave and go home to San Francisco, Córdoba, Loro also abandons the set and goes looking for her. The comical dimensions of the *mise-en-abyme* technique (Loro and his swan, Luciana, are 'acting out' the clichés of the plot of a classical ballet) are exploited to their maximum when Loro begins to record the conversations between Luciana's father and his actor friend in their back garden in San Francisco, Córdoba. The beginning and end of the film exploit to humorous effect the awkwardness of subtitles, covering the filmed scene with words. *El loro y el cisne* reveals its romantic credentials by ending with Loro and Luciana's first kiss.

Perhaps the most distinctive trait of 2013 is that it proved to be the year in which Latin American film directors were lionized by Hollywood, and invited to take on big-budget mainstream action features. Following his success with *Hellboy* (2004), Guillermo del Toro was invited to direct *Pacific Rim* (2013), a science fiction film with a budget of $190 million. It is set in the 2020s when the world is being attacked by monsters, called Kaijus, which have emerged from the floor of the Pacific Ocean. The human race pulls together and constructs gigantic humanoid robots called Jaegers to fight the Kaijus. By 2025 the Kaiju attacks have become more frequent and the world government decides to build some enormous wall fortifications along the coast while the four remaining Jaegers are sent to Hong Kong to defend the unfortified coastline there.

Stacker Pentecost (Idris Elba) asks a retired pilot, Raleigh Becket (Charlie Hunnam), to help him destroy the Kaijus by dropping a nuclear bomb through the Kaiju portal at the bottom of the Pacific Ocean. Raleigh teams up with Mako Mori (Rinko Kikuchi) in a hi-tech Jaeger, Gipsy Danger, though this nearly ends in disaster when, during a test-run, Mako relives the moment her parents were killed in a Kaiju attack and almost fires weapons while the robot is still in the hangar. A scientist studying the Kaiju, Newton Geiszler (Charlie Day), establishes a link with part of the brain of a Kaiju and learns that the portal on the ocean bed of the Pacific Ocean will only open for a Kaiju. After a series of violent struggles with the beasts of the deep Raleigh and Mako eventually gain entrance to the Kaiju kingdom, and blow it up with a nuclear warhead, thereby saving the human race from extinction. Though a science fiction film –

and therefore tied to some of the stock ingredients of that genre – *Pacific Rim* demonstrates some features which are recognizably part of del Toro's repertoire, including the use of ethics-free monsters (from the wicked nephew in *Cronos* to the evil captain in *El laberinto del fauno*) as well as angelic innocence symbolized by a young girl (Aurora in *Cronos* and Mako as a young girl in *Pacific Rim*). There is also some continuity in terms of the cast in that one of del Toro's favourite actors, Ron Perlman, who was Angel de la Guardia in *Cronos*, takes on the role of Hannibal Chau in *Pacific Rim*, who is involved in the trafficking of Kaiju body organs (and so is a character we love to hate) and, in a rather amusing scene typical of del Toro's black humour, he is swallowed by a recently born Kaiju (during the end credits he cuts his way out with a pocket knife). Del Toro drew inspiration from Francisco Goya's famous painting of *The Colossus* in order to depict the modernized battle of the titans between the Kaijus and the Jaegers in Hong Kong harbour, and the special effects used – especially given that the film is in 3-D – produce a sense of grandeur.

Pacific Rim is also recognizably part of del Toro's trajectory in that it revamps a number of Christian symbolic motifs: the captain, Pentecost, rallies his troops with the words that they will 'cancel out the Apocalypse', and the killing of the Kaijus by the Gipsy Danger wielding a sword is highly reminiscent of stock images of the Archangel Michael triumphing over the Devil. When del Toro was asked about the Catholic elements in an earlier film, *El laberinto del fauno*, he responded, 'once a Catholic,

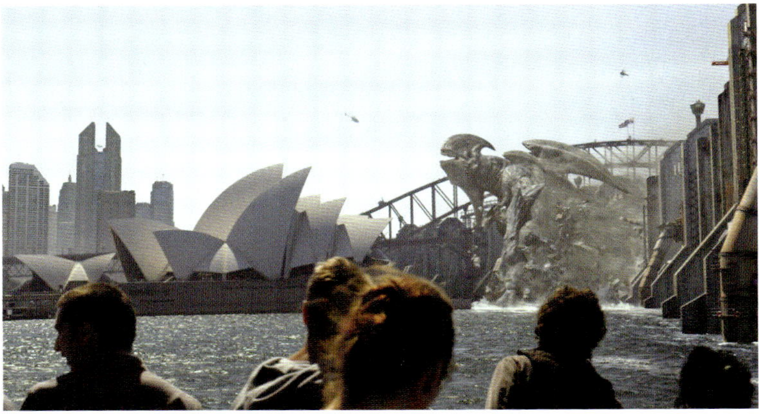

The attack of the Kaiju in Guillermo del Toro's *Pacific Rim* (2013).

always a Catholic'.[91] The same might be said of *Pacific Rim*. Apart from its extraordinary box office success (over $400 million in worldwide earnings to date), *Pacific Rim* is a ringing endorsement of the cinematic versatility of a Latin American film director who now finds himself lionized by the Hollywood film industry, something which an earlier generation of Latin American film directors could only have dreamed of.

Guillermo del Toro is not the only Latin American film director who has ventured into mainstream Hollywood. Alfonso Cuarón's latest film, a science fiction thriller, *Gravity*, which opened the 70th Venice International Film Festival in August 2013, had no fewer than ten Academy Award nominations, the most for any Latin American film.[92] It went on to win in seven categories – Cinematography, Film Editing, Original Score, Sound Editing, Sound Mixing, Visual Effects and, most importantly, Best Director. *Gravity* tells the story of two astronauts, Dr Ryan Stone (Sandra Bullock) and Matt Kowalsky (George Clooney), who are on a mission to repair the Hubble Space Telescope, 327 miles above earth. Both characters are surrounded by cosmic emptiness – in space there is no oxygen, no water and no atmosphere – but they are also living with an inner emptiness. As Robbie Collin suggests:

> Stone is a medical engineer who has recently lost her young daughter, and for her, the all-pervasive silence of space comes as a comfort blanket. Kowalsky, the pilot, is also suffering as a result of separation: during an earlier mission, his wife absconded with another man.[93]

The opening scene, in which the two astronauts are repairing the telescope is breathtaking, not only because of the stunning shots of the earth but because of the combination of the hand-held 'floating' camera, the 3-D effects and long takes.

The first long take of the film is more than fifteen minutes long. Disaster strikes when the astronauts are suddenly hit by the shrapnel from a Russian satellite, at which point the special effects suck the viewer into the filmic space. As Alex Ramon says:

> The visuals are beyond praise: cinematographer Emmanuel Lubezki creates images that are at once dreamy, nightmarish and

hyper-real. The use of 3-D is vital and expressive here, sending the protagonists hurtling and twirling, colliding and gliding through space, in a thrilling ballet that puts us right there with them.[94]

Unlike *Avatar*, in which 3-D was used to create a more haptically enhanced film experience, in *Gravity* the 3-D effects are intrinsic to the meaning of the film, which expresses the anguish of modern mankind's dilemma: we are lost in space. There is even a touch of magical realism when Matt Kowalsky – although we know he is already dead – appears to force open the door to the spacecraft, get in and encourage Dr Stone to carry on her mission. The scene seems almost too real to be a dream but, we tell ourselves, it must have been. The coincidence that two of Latin America's most prominent film directors have taken on the 'cosmic' challenge of a sci-fi movie in the same year – del Toro with *Pacific Rim* and Cuarón with *Gravity* – suggests how far Latin American film has travelled since even the early years of the new millennium.

From the early days of images in movement as captured in Guillermo and Manuel Trujillo Durán's *Un célebre especialista sacando muelas en el Gran Hotel Europa* (1897) to the movement-images of the early Mexican gangster silent movie, *El automóvil gris* (1919), the time-image in films such as Tomás Gutiérrez Alea's *Memorias del subdesarrollo* and the digital-image which subtended the films of the new millennium, such as *Cidade de Deus* (2002) and *Gravity* (2013), Latin American cinema has traced a journey combining tough human stories with extraordinary visual

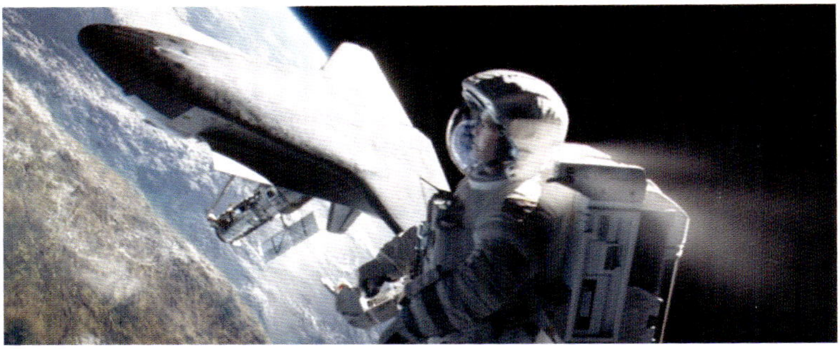

Matt Kowalsky is floating in space in Alfonso Cuarón's *Gravity* (2013).

richness. In each of the phases of Latin American film we have witnessed a striking openness to otherness. In the 1950s, film directors such as Julio García Espinosa and Tomás Gutiérrez Alea were open to the otherness of European avant-garde film (Italian neo-Realism, especially) and in the early years of the new millennium to the otherness of the English language; thus a group of films such as *21 Grams* (2003), *The Constant Gardener* (2005) *Children of Men* (2006) and *Blindness* (2007) appeared to create a new genre of the Latin American English-language film. *Pacific Rim* (2013) and *Gravity* (2013) suggest that Latin American film has finally taken a new step, into 'outer space'.

REFERENCES

Introduction

1 Quoted in Frank Tomasulo, 'Theory to Practice: Integrating Cinema, Theory and Film Production', *Cinema Journal*, XXXVI/3 (Spring 1997), p. 113.
2 Anonymous, 'Mexican Wave Rides High in the Film World', BBC News, 22 February 2007; see www.bbc.co.uk/news.
3 In an interview by the author with Fernando Birri held at the Bloomsbury Hotel, London, 1 November 2007.
4 This is a brief selection of the major works; for more information on the secondary literature see the Select Bibliography.
5 Laura Mulvey, 'Then and Now: Cinema as History in the Light of New Media and New Technologies', in *The New Brazilian Cinema*, ed. Lúcia Nagib (London, 2003), p. 269.
6 Ibid.
7 Donald F. Stevens, ed., *Based on a True Story: Latin American History at the Movies* (Wilmington, DE, 1997); Randal Johnson, *The Film Industry in Brazil: Culture and the State* (Pittsburgh, PA, 1987); Stephanie Dennison, ed., *Contemporary Hispanic Cinema: Interrogating the Transnational in Spanish and Latin American Film* (Woodbridge, 2013); Jethro Soutar, *Gael García Bernal and the Latin American New Wave: The Story of a Cinematic Movement and its Leading Man* (London, 2008).
8 For a good treatment of the funding of Latin American cinema see Stephanie Dennison, ed., *Contemporary Hispanic Cinema: Interrogating the Transnational in Spanish and Latin American Film* (Woodbridge, 2013).

1 Inauspicious Beginnings (1895–1950)

1 Paola Marrati, *Gilles Deleuze: Cinema and Philosophy* (Baltimore, MD, 2008), p. 24.
2 Randal Johnson and Robert Stam, *Brazilian Cinema* (East Brunswick, NJ,

1982), p. 19; Guy Hennebelle and Alfonso Gumucio-Dagrón, *Les cinémas de l'Amérique Latine* (Paris, 1981), p. 94.

3 Hennebelle and Gumucio-Dagrón, *Les cinémas de l'Amérique Latine*, p. 84; Carl J. Mora, *Mexican Cinema: Reflections of a Society, 1896–1980* (Berkeley, CA, 1982), p. 6.

4 Cynthia Tompkins, *Experimental Latin American Cinema: History and Aesthetics* (Austin, TX, 2013), p. 3.

5 John King, *Magical Reels: A History of Cinema in Latin America* (London, 1990), pp. 15–17.

6 Marrati, *Gilles Deleuze*, p. 24.

7 D. W. Griffith, whose *The Birth of a Nation* (1915) is one of the classics of Hollywood film, is seen as the 'father of film technique'. An obsessive experimentalist, he exploited the dynamic combination of the three standard film shots – long shot, medium shot and close-up – and he devised a new concept – parallel editing – as well as inventing the tracking shot.

8 Gilles Deleuze, *Cinema 2: The Time-Image*, trans. Hugh Tomlinson and Robert Galeta (London, 1989), p. 4.

9 Ibid., p. 3.

10 Ibid., p. 5.

11 Marie Seton, *Sergei M. Eisenstein* (London, 1978), p. 231.

12 Jan Leyda, *Kino: A History of the Russian and Soviet Cinema*, 3rd edn (Princeton, NJ, 1983), p. 302.

13 Laura Podalsky, 'Patterns of the Primitive: Sergei Eisenstein's *¡Que viva México!*', in *Mediating Two Worlds: Cinematic Encounters in the Americas*, ed. John King, Ana M. Lopez and Manuel Alvarado (London, 1993), p. 27.

14 Jacques Aumont, et al., *Aesthetics of Film* (Austin, TX, 1992), pp. 34 and 131.

15 Quoted in Seton, *Sergei M. Eisenstein*, p. 197.

16 Quoted ibid., p. 205.

17 Mora, *Mexican Cinema*, pp. 28–88.

18 Johnson and Stam, *Brazilian Cinema*, p. 27.

19 Ana López, 'Celluloid Tears: Melodrama in the "Old" Mexican Cinema', *Iris*, 13 (Summer 1991), pp. 29–51.

20 Hennebelle and Gumucio-Dagrón, *Les cinémas de l'Amérique Latine*, pp. 130–31.

21 Ibid., pp. 156–7. See also Stephanie Dennison, 'Sex and the Generals: Reading Brazilian Pornochanchada as Sexploitation', in *Latsploitation, Exploitation Cinemas, and Latin America*, ed. Victoria Ruétalo and Dolores Tierney (New York, 2009), pp. 230–44.

22 Octavio Paz says that the blind beggar is familiar from the Spanish picaresque tales: *Fundación y disidencia* (Mexico City, 1994), p. 224.

23 Luis Buñuel, *My Last Sigh: The Autobiography of Luis Buñuel*, trans. Abigail Israel (New York, 1983), p. 200.

24 'Restrenan en pantalla grande *Los olvidados*, con final inédito', *La Jornada* (8 July 2005).

25 Paz, *Fundación y disidencia*, p. 223.
26 Carlos Monsiváis, 'Mythologies', in *Mexican Cinema*, ed. P. A. Paranaguá, trans. Ana López (London, 1995), p. 121.
27 Peter Evans, *The Films of Luis Buñuel: Subjectivity and Desire* (Oxford, 1995), p. 86.
28 Buñuel, *My Last Sigh*, p. 199.
29 Gilles Deleuze, *Cinema 1: The Movement-Image*, trans. Hugh Tomlinson and Barbara Habberjam (London, 1992), p. 133.
30 Geoffrey Nowell-Smith, 'Cities: Real and Imagined', in *Cinema and the City: Film and Urban Societies in a Global Context*, ed. Mark Shiel and Tony Fitzmaurice (Oxford, 2001), p. 102.
31 Michael Wood, 'Buñuel in Mexico', in *Mediating Two Worlds: Cinematic Encounters in the Americas*, ed. John King, Ana M. López and Manuel Alvarado (London, 1993), pp. 49–50.
32 Quoted in Evans, *The Films of Luis Buñuel*, p. 85.
33 For further discussion of this film, see Stephen Hart, 'Buñuel's Box of Subaltern Tricks: Technique in *Los olvidados*', in *Luis Buñuel: New Readings*, ed. Peter William Evans and Isabel Santaolalla (London, 2004), pp. 65–79.
34 Hennebelle and Gumucio-Dagrón, *Les cinémas de l'Amérique Latine*, p. 381.

2 Nuevo Cine Latinoamericano and the 'Time-image' (1951–1975)

1 Susan Hayward, *Key Concepts in Cinema Studies* (London, 1996), pp. 192–3.
2 Roy Armes, *French Cinema* (London, 1985), pp. 175–82.
3 Mirtha Ibarra, *Tomás Gutiérrez Alea: volver sobre mis pasos* (Madrid, 2007), pp. 31–2.
4 For more information on the film, see the documentary *Chiaroscuro: The Making of El Mégano*, included in Stephen Hart, *Chiaroscuro: The Life and Work of Julio García-Espinosa* (London, 2011).
5 Víctor Fowler Calzada, *Conversaciones con un cineasta incómodo: Julio García-Espinosa* (Havana, 2004), p. 42.
6 Ibid., p. 43.
7 Régis Debray, *Revolution in the Revolution? Armed Struggle and Political Struggle in Latin America*, trans. Bobbye Ortiz (New York, 1967).
8 Robert Young, *Postcolonialism: An Historical Introduction* (Oxford, 2003), p. 209.
9 David Deutschman, ed., *Che Guevara and the Cuban Revolution: Writings and Speeches of Ernesto Che Guevara* (Sydney, 1987), p. 194.
10 Octavio Cortázar, email to author, 3 January 2004.
11 Chris Payne, 'A Vatican for Film-makers', *The Guardian* (28 November 2003), p. 10.
12 Ibid.

13 Titón had, indeed, produced a documentary on agrarian reform called *Esta tierra nuestra* ('This Land of Ours') as part of the same cultural programme in 1959.
14 The intertitle at the beginning of *Cuba baila* sets the scene for its revolutionary message; 'La trama pudo suceder en cualquier periodo de nuestra pasada vida republicana. Hoy la clase media despierta y la politiquería agoniza'; *Cuba baila, guión* (Havana, 1961), p. 6A.
15 Guy Hennebelle and Alfonso Gumucio-Dagrón, *Les cinémas de l'Amérique Latine* (Paris, 1981), p. 145.
16 Quoted in Randal Johnson and Robert Stam, *Brazilian Cinema* (East Brunswick, NJ, 1982), p. 33.
17 Glauber Rocha, 'The Aesthetics of Hunger', in *Twenty-five Years of the New Latin American Cinema*, ed. Michael Chanan (London, 1983), pp. 13–14.
18 See Lúcia Nagib, *Brazil on Screen: Cinema novo, New Cinema, Utopia* (London, 2007), pp. 3–30. For a discussion of Rocha's later films see Karlo Posso, '"Brazyl Unyversal": The Aesthetics and Ethics of Glauber Rocha's Late Films', *Hispanic Research Journal*, XIV/1 (2013), pp. 9–32.
19 See Vicente Ferraz (dir.), *Soy Cuba: O Mamute Siberiano* (2005).
20 As pointed out to me in an interview with the scriptwriter of *Soy Cuba*, Enrique Pineda Barnet, in London on 28 November 2005.
21 Authors' emphasis; Fernando Solanas and Octavio Getino, 'Towards a Third Cinema', in *Twenty-five Years of the New Latin American Cinema*, p. 18.
22 Julio García Espinosa, 'For an Imperfect Cinema', in *Twenty-five Years of the New Latin American Cinema*, p. 33.
23 Jorge Sanjinés, 'Problems of Form and Content in Revolutionary Cinema', in *Twenty-five Years of the New Latin American Cinema*, p. 34.
24 Fernando Birri, 'Cinema and Underdevelopment', in *Twenty-five Years of the New Latin American Cinema*, p. 12.
25 Ibid.
26 Rocha, 'The Aesthetics of Hunger', p. 13.
27 Gilles Deleuze, *Cinema 1: The Movement-Image*, trans. Hugh Tomlinson and Barbara Habberjam (London, 1992), p. 210.
28 Gilles Deleuze, *Cinema 2: The Time-Image*, trans. Hugh Tomlinson and Robert Galeta (London, 1989), pp. 2–3.
29 Ibid., p. 3.
30 Ibid., p. 4.
31 Ibid., p. 6.
32 Hennebelle and Gumucio-Dagrón, *Les cinémas de l'Amérique Latine*, p. 80.
33 Stephen Hart, interview with Jorge Sanjinés, La Paz, Bolivia, 21 July 2001.
34 José Sánchez-H., *The Art and Politics of Bolivian Cinema* (Lanham, MD, 1999), pp. 83–4. Given this, it is ironic that the musical score was performed by a symphony orchestra whose director, Gerald Brown, was a member of the Peace Corps at the time; Alberto Villalpando, as he has explained in an interview, enlisted the latter's help since he was a personal contact; see Sánchez-H., pp. 157–8.

35 Jorge Sanjinés, 'Problems of Form and Content in Revolutionary Cinema', in *Twenty-five Years of the New Latin American Cinema*, p. 35.
36 Ibid.
37 Jorge Ruffinelli, *Patricio Guzmán* (Madrid, 2001), p. 134.
38 Warren Buckland, *Film Studies* (London, 1998), pp. 111–15.
39 Quoted in John King, *Magical Reels: A History of Cinema in Latin America* (London, 1990), p. 179.
40 Ruffinelli, *Patricio Guzmán*, pp. 146–7.
41 An important film of this period, especially in terms of its portrayal of gender issues, is *De cierta manera* (1974–8), directed by the Cuban filmmaker Sara Gómez; see Guy Baron, 'The Illusion of Equality: *Machismo* and Cuban Cinema of the Revolution', *Bulletin of Latin American Research*, XXIX/3 (2010), pp. 354–66 (esp. pp. 355–7).

3 Nation-image (1976–1999)

1 Beatriz Sarlo, 'Cultural Studies and Literary Criticism at the Cross-Roads of Value', in *Contemporary Latin American Cultural Studies*, ed. Stephen Hart and Richard Young (London, 2003), p. 33.
2 'The Official Academy Awards Database' [Academy of Motion Picture Arts and Sciences, Hollywood], http://awardsdatabase.oscars.org, accessed 6 January 2014.
3 Quoted in John Mraz, 'Recasting Cuban Slavery: *The Other Francisco* and *The Last Supper*', in *Based on a True Story: Latin American History at the Movies*, ed. Donald F. Stevens (Wilmington, DE, 1997), pp. 112–13.
4 Quoted in José Antonio Evora, *Tomás Gutiérrez Alea* (Madrid, 1996), p. 40; my translation.
5 Tomás Gutiérrez Alea, 'Rapture and Rupture: Eisenstein and Brecht', in *The Viewer's Dialectic* (Havana, 1988), pp. 52–66.
6 Dennis West, 'Strawberry and Chocolate, Ice Cream and Tolerance: Interviews with Tomás Gutiérrez Alea and Juan Carlos Tabío', *Cineaste*, XXI/1–2 (1995), p. 18.
7 Evora, *Tomás Gutiérrez Alea*, p. 42.
8 Jerome Branche, 'Barbarism and Civilisation: Taking on History in *The Last Supper*', *The Afro-Latino Forum*, I/1 (1997), p. 3.
9 Susan Ryan, 'Pixote, a lei do Mais Fraco', in *South American Cinema: A Critical Filmography, 1915–1994*, ed. Timothy Barnard and Peter Rist (Austin, TX, 1996), p. 195.
10 Randal Johnson, 'The *Romance-Reportagem* and the Cinema: Babenco's *Lúcio Flavio* and *Pixote*', *Luso-Brazilian Review*, XXIV/2 (1987), p. 38.
11 Marc Lauria, 'Pixote', www.sensesofcinema.com, accessed 1 February 2014.
12 Johnson, 'The *Romance-Reportagem*', p. 43.
13 Robert M. Levine, 'Fiction and Reality in Brazilian Life', in *Based on a True Story*, p. 203.

14 Quoted in Deborah Shaw, *Contemporary Cinema of Latin America: Ten Key Films* (London, 2003), p. 147.
15 Ibid.
16 Lauria, 'Pixote'.
17 Robert M. Levine, 'Fiction and Reality in Brazilian Life', in *Based on a True Story*, pp. 208–11.
18 An important documentary of the early 1980s was Pedro Chaskel's *Una foto recorre el mundo* (1981), which focused on how the images of Che Guevara changed the world. Other important films which came out that year were Adolfo Aristarain, *Tiempo de revancha* (1981) and *Sólo con tu pareja* (1981), directed by the up-and-coming Alfonso Cuarón. Román Chalbaud's *La gata borracha* (1983) is a Venezuelan film about a man who is bored with his marriage, sleeps with a prostitute and when his wife finds out there are fireworks.
19 Donald F. Stevens, 'Passion and Patriarchy in Nineteenth-century Argentina: María Luisa Bemberg's *Camila*', in *Based on a True Story*, p. 87.
20 Caleb Bach, 'María Luisa Bemberg tells the untold', *Américas*, XLV/2 (March–April 1994), p. 23.
21 Sheila Whitaker, 'Pride and Prejudice: María Luisa Bemberg', *Monthly Film Bulletin* (October 1987), p. 293.
22 Warren Buckland, *Film Studies* (London, 1998), pp. 82–6.
23 Ruby Rich, 'An/Other View of New Latin American Cinema', in *New Latin American Cinema: Volume One: Theory, Practices and Transcontinental Articulations*, ed. Michael T. Martin (Detroit, MI, 1997), p. 286.
24 Miguel Torres, 'Camila', *Cine Cubano*, 113 (1985), p. 78.
25 John King, *Magical Reels: A History of Cinema in Latin America* (London, 1990), p. 96.
26 Andrew Graham-Yooll, 'María Luisa Bemberg', *The Independent* (24 May 1995), p. 16.
27 Bach, 'María Luisa Bemberg Tells the Untold', p. 22.
28 Anonymous review in the *Daily Telegraph* (9 June 1995).
29 Lita Stantic, 'Working with María Luisa Bemberg', in *An Argentine Passion: María Luisa Bemberg and her Films*, ed. John King, Sheila Whitaker and Rosa Bosch (London, 2000), p. 33.
30 Jorge Ruffinelli, 'De una *Camila* a otra: historia, literature y cine', in *Estudios Iberoamérica y el cine*, ed. Francisco Lasarte and Guido Podestá (Amsterdam, 1996), p. 11.
31 María Luisa Bemberg, 'Being an Artist in Latin America', in *An Argentine Passion*, p. 222.
32 For further discussion of the film see Stephen M. Hart, 'Bemberg's Winks and Camila's Sighs: Melodramatic Encryption in *Camila*', *Revista Canadiense de Estudios Hispánicos*, XXVII/1 (2002), pp. 75–85.
33 Javier Tolentino, *Julieta en el País de las Maravillas: una conversación con Norma Aleandro* (Madrid, 2004), pp. 32–5.

34 For more on snares in films, see Peter Lehman and William Luhr, *Thinking about Movies: Watching, Questioning, Enjoying* (Oxford, 2003), pp. 37–8.
35 Ibid., pp. 65–6.
36 Other important films of the second half of the 1980s are Paul Leduc's *Frida* (1986), an experimental film about Frida Kahlo, and Miguel Littín's documentary, *Acta general de Chile* (1986).
37 For further discussion of Lombardi's films see my article, '"Slick Grit": Auteurship Versus Mimicry in Three Films by Francisco Lombardi', *New Cinemas*, III/3 (2005), pp. 159–67.
38 Segre, '"La desnacionalización de la pantalla": Mexican Cinema in the 1990s', in *Changing Reels: Latin American Cinema Against the Odds*, ed. Rob Rix and Roberto Rodríguez-Saona (Leeds, 1997), p. 33.
39 Shaw, *Contemporary Cinema of Latin America*, p. 161.
40 Segre, '"La desnacionalización de la pantalla"', p. 43.
41 Shaw, *Contemporary Cinema of Latin America*, p. 39.
42 Quoted in Sergio de la Mora, 'A Career in Perspective: An Interview with Arturo Ripstein', *Film Quarterly*, LII/4 (Summer 1999), p. 2.
43 María Luisa Bemberg, 'Being an Artist in Latin America', manuscript notes of a lecture given at the University of Warwick in 1992, supplied by Professor Jason Wilson.
44 Emilie Bergmann, 'Abjection and Ambiguity: Lesbian Desire in Bemberg's *Yo, la peor de todas*', in *Hispanisms and Homosexualities*, ed. Sylvia Molloy and Robert McKee Irwin (Durham, NC, 1998), p. 232.
45 Rosa Sarabia, 'Sor Juana o las trampas de la restitución', *Revista Canadiense de Estudios Hispánicos*, XXVII/1 (2002), p. 125.
46 María Luisa Bemberg, 'Somos la mitad del mundo', *Cine cubano*, 132 (July–August 1991), p. 17.
47 Ibid., p. 15.
48 Antonio de la Campa and Raquel Chang-Rodríguez, *Poesía hispanoamericana colonial: antología* (Madrid, 1985), p. 260.
49 Octavio Paz, *Sor Juana o las trampas de la fe* (Mexico City, 1984).
50 Susan E. Ramírez, '*I, the Worst of All*: The Literary Life of Sor Juana Inés de la Cruz', in *Based on a True Story*, pp. 47–62.
51 King, Whitaker and Bosch, *An Argentine Passion*, p. 48.
52 'Maria Luisa Bemberg', Strictly Film School, www.filmref.com, accessed 9 October 2014.
53 Silvio Caiozzi's *La luna en el espejo* (1990) is a Chilean film about an old man, Don Arnaldo, who lives in a fantasy world peopled by mirrors. He seeks to have control over the world but it is an illusory control. It is similar to a number of other Chilean films of this period which express disillusionment at the castrating effects of Pinochet's dictatorship using a displaced metaphor. It is similar in some respects to *La frontera* of the following year (discussed below). Other important films are Alex Cox's *El patrullero* (1991) and María Novaro's *Danzón* (1991).

54 Ismail Xavier argues that *El viaje* attempts to 'reach encompassing views of contemporary experience or of politics in certain regions through overt allegorical strategies' in 'Historical Allegory', in *A Companion to Film Theory*, ed. Toby Miller and Robert Stam (Malden, MA, 1999), p. 350.
55 Philip Strick, 'El viaje', *Sight and Sound* (September 1993), p. 54.
56 As suggested to me in a conversation with former head of IMCINE, Ignacio Durán Loera, in London on 13 November 2009.
57 Adolfo Aristarain's *Un lugar en el mundo* (1992) is like other films of this period in that it enunciates a new political space for Latin America.
58 'Feature Commentary with Director Guillermo del Toro', chapter Five, extra feature on the Special DVD Edition of *Cronos* (StudioCanal, 2006).
59 Ibid., chapter Seven.
60 'Extended Interview with Director Guillermo del Toro', extra feature on the Special DVD edition of *Cronos.*
61 Del Toro mentions in an interview that he always believed that Catholicism, alchemy and vampirism are linked. 'Feature commentary with director Guillermo del Toro', chapter One.
62 'Extended Interview with Director Guillermo del Toro'.
63 'Feature Commentary with Director Guillermo del Toro', chapter Four.
64 Ibid., chapter Four. Pointing in a similar direction the main character goes through the main processes of alchemy – water, fire, earth, air; ibid., chapter Five.
65 Ibid., chapter Six.
66 'Extended Interview with Director Guillermo del Toro'.
67 'Feature Commentary with Director Guillermo del Toro', chapter Five.
68 'Extended Interview with Director Guillermo del Toro'; my translation.
69 'Feature Commentary with Director Guillermo del Toro', chapter One.
70 Ibid., chapter Two.
71 Shaw, *Contemporary Cinema of Latin America*, p. 37.
72 Barbara A. Tenenbaum, 'Why Tita Didn't Marry the Doctor, or Mexican History in *Like Water for Chocolate*', in *Based on a True Story*, p. 157.
73 See figures in www.boxofficemojo.com/movies, accessed 1 November 2013; I remember the great excitement with which this film was greeted by U.S. audiences when I saw it in Lexington, Kentucky, in the spring of 1993.
74 Joan Smith, 'Love and Other Illegal Acts', www.salon.com, 4 October 1996.
75 As Tenenbaum points out, like water for chocolate 'in Mexican slang . . . often implies the height of as-yet-unfulfilled sexual longing, particularly in women'; see 'Why Tita Didn't Marry the Doctor', p. 158.
76 Quoted in Harmony W. Wu, 'Consuming Tacos and Enchiladas: Gender and the Nation in *Como agua para chocolate*', in *Visible Nations: Latin American Cinema and Video*, ed. Chon A. Noriega (Minneapolis, MN, 2000), p. 184.
77 John Kraniauskas, 'Como agua para chocolate', *Sight and Sound*, II/10 (1993), p. 42.

78 For a discussion of magical realist motifs in *Como agua para chocolate*, see Nathanial Gardner, *Como agua para chocolate, The Novel and Film Version* (London, 2009), pp. 72–80; Sergio Cabrera's *La estrategia del caracol* (1993) is a Colombian film about the antics of a number of people searching for a place to live; it ends up becoming a metaphor of modern man trapped by his environment.

79 Catherine Davies, 'Recent Cuban Fiction Films: Identification, Interpretation, Disorder', *Bulletin of Latin American Research*, xv/2 (1996), p. 177.

80 Michael Chanan, 'Cuban Cinema in the 1990s', in *Changing Reels*, pp. 9–11.

81 Paul A. Schroeder, *Tomás Gutiérrez Alea: The Dialectics of a Filmmaker* (London, 2002), p. 109.

82 Paul Julian Smith, '*Fresa y chocolate*: Cinema as Guided Tour', in his *Vision Machines* (London, 1996), p. 88.

83 Quoted ibid., p. 81.

84 Dennis West, 'Strawberry and Chocolate, Ice Cream and Tolerance', p. 19.

85 Stephen Wilkinson, 'Homosexuality and the Repression of Intellectuals in *Fresa y chocolate* and *Máscaras*', *Bulletin of Latin American Research*, xviii/1 (1999), p. 22.

86 *Tomás Gutiérrez Alea: volver sobre mis pasos; una selección epistolar de Mirtha Ibarra* (Madrid, 2007), pp. 219 and 221; my translation.

87 Quoted in Evora, *Tomás Gutiérrez Alea*, p. 53; my translation.

88 On 10 November 2009 Mirtha Ibarra also told me that Gutiérrez Alea had never been gay.

89 For further discussion of the interplay between politics and art in Gutiérrez Alea's work, see David Wood, 'Tomás Gutiérrez Alea and the Art of Revolutionary Cinema', *Bulletin of Latin American Research*, xxviii/4 (2009), pp. 512–26.

90 'I have always been very interested in making low-budget films. In the mid-1990s Cuba found itself with very low petrol reserves and so I decided to use the locale where Reina actually lives, which is a house opposite my house. In that way we avoided having to use transport. It is something which is very close to my heart, that is, harmonize aesthetics with modest budgets, and vice-versa. Nevertheless I should point out to you that I do not choose the style, the style chooses me' (email from García Espinosa to author, 15 July 2005; my translation); 'Actually it is an homage to Italian Neo-Realism after a period of thirty years, but there is also a conscious decision to not allow any of the constituent parts (the acting, the photography, the soundtrack, etc.) to become more important than the story itself. You need to bear in mind that the 1990s in Cuba were similar to the immediate post-war years in Italy. To such an extent that, given the number of bicycles which were being used at that time in Havana, I thought that it would be possible to make a Part II of Bicycle Thieves' (email from Espinosa to author, 15 July 2005; my translation).

91 Sandra Brennan's review for the *New York Times* is available at http://movies2.nytimes.com, accessed 15 March 2006. See also Lisa Nesselson, 'Queen and King', *Variety*, CCCLVII/5 (28 November 1994), p. 97. Strangely, neither of these reviews refers to Part II of the movie, focusing exclusively on Part I, perhaps for political reasons. In Part II, Carmen returns from Miami to Havana to 'reclaim' her home back from her servant, Reina.

92 It was not the director's intention, however, to make any reference to the gas chambers of the Second World War. As Espinosa has pointed out: 'In fact you can see it as an allegory of the 1990s but the gas chamber has nothing to do with the Nazis' gas chambers; or at least that was not my aim when I made the film' (email to the author, 15 July 2005; my translation).

93 Email from García Espinosa to the author, 15 July 2005.

94 For further discussion of *Moebius* see Geoffrey Kantaris, 'Buenos Aires 2010: Memory Machines and Cybercities in Two Argentine Science Fiction Films', in *Memory Culture and the Contemporary City*, ed. Uta Staiger, Henriette Steiner and Andrew Webber (New York, 2009), pp. 191–207. Other important films of this period were Arturo Ripstein's *Profundo carmesí* (1996), which is about one woman's obsession with a man leading her to commit blood-curdling crimes, and Tata Amaral's *Um Céu de Estrelas* (1996), in which a young girl's desire to fulfil her dreams ends in violence; for discussion of the latter film see Charlotte Cleghorne, 'The Dystopian City: Gendered Interpretations of the Urban in *Um Céu de Estrelas / A Starry Sky* (Tata Amaral, 1996) and *Vagón fumador / Smokers Only* (Verónica Chen, 2001)', in *New Trends in Argentine and Brazilian Film*, ed. Cecilda Rêgo and Carolina Rocha (Bristol, 2011), pp. 225–42. The following year Enrique Gabriel's *En la puta calle* (1997), as its title suggests, offered a worm's-eye view of the world, while Adolfo Aristarain's *Martín (hache)* (1997) provided a psychological study of the mind of a deluded man. An important documentary of this period was Carlos Marcovich's *Quién diablos es Juliette?* (1997); see Geoffrey Kantaris, 'Dereferencing the Real: Documentary Mediascapes in the Films of Carlos Marcovich (*Quién diablos es Juliette?* and *Cuatro labios*)', in *Visual Synergies in Fiction and Documentary Film from Latin America*, ed. Miriam Haddu and Joanna Page (New York, 2009), pp. 219–36.

95 Ismail Xavier argues that in Brazilian films of the 1990s, 'the child is the only universal left'; 'Brazilian Cinema in the 1990s', in *The New Brazilian Cinema*, ed. Lúcia Nagib (London, 2003), p. 62.

96 Geoff Andrew, 'Walter Salles', *The Guardian* (26 August 2004).

97 Ibid.

98 Ibid.

99 Ibid.

100 1998 was a good year for Latin American film: Fernando Solanas's *La nube*, Alejandro Agresti's *El viento se llevó lo que*, Víctor Gaviria's *La vendedora de rosas*, Sergio Castilla's *Gringuito* and Fernando Spiner's *La sonámbula* all

came out that year; for discussion of the last film, see Joanna Page, 'Retrofuturism and Reflexivity in Argentine Science Fiction Film: The Construction of Cinematic Time', *Arizona Journal of Hispanic Cultural Studies*, XVI (2012), pp. 227–43. The millennium was rounded off by two powerful Argentine films, Marco Bechis's *Garage Olimpo* (1999), based on a tale of torture from the Dirty War, and Juan José Campanella's *El mismo amor, la misma lluvia* (1999).

4 The Slick Grit of Contemporary Latin American Cinema (2000–2014)

1 Gilles Deleuze, *Cinema 2: The Time-Image*, trans. Hugh Tomlinson and Robert Galeta (London, 1989), p. 7.
2 This was by Steven Sassoon, an engineer at Eastman Kodak.
3 *The Idiots*, directed by the Danish director, Lars von Trier, and released in 1998, was filmed on a Sony DCR-VX000, and can therefore be seen as the first movie filmed on digital video.
4 *Avatar* (2009) is no. 1 in the list of highest-grossing films to date, making $2,782,275,172.
5 Patricia Pisters, *The Neuro-Image: Deleuzian Film-philosophy of Digital Screen Culture* (Stanford, CA, 2012), p. 8.
6 William Brown, *Film-Philosophy for the Digital Age: Supercinema* (New York, 2013), pp. 1–2.
7 Ibid., p. 2.
8 Ibid.
9 Deleuze, *Cinema 2: The Time-Image*, p. 5.
10 Bernardo Pérez Soler, 'Pup fiction', *Sight and Sound* (May 2001), p. 29.
11 Paul Julian Smith, *Amores perros* (London, 2002), pp. 11–12.
12 John Patterson, 'Aztec Cameras', *The Guardian* (18 May 2000), p. 11.
13 A similar sense of the metropolis at the turn of the twenty-first century is evident in a number of Brazilian films which were set in São Paulo and released in the early years of the new millennium, creating, as Lúcia Sá has argued, 'a shared feeling of nostalgia for a city that no longer exists'; the films discussed are *Urbânia* (2001) by Flávio Frederico, *O Principe* ('The Prince', 2002) by Ugo Giorgetti, and *O Invasor* ('The Trespasser', 2002) by Beto Brant; see 'Flânerie and Invasion in the Monstrous City: São Paulo in Recent Cinema', *Journal of Latin American Cultural Studies: Travesia*, XX/1 (2011), p. 36.
14 Although Gael García Bernal is now one of Latin America's most famous actors, he was virtually unknown when he starred in *Amores perros*; the film launched his career.
15 The role of an extra consists in being an inconspicuous part of the stagecraft of a given film in order not to deflect attention away from the protagonist, something I learned when working as an extra in Hugh Hudson's *Chariots*

of Fire in the Great Court run, which was filmed in Eton College in July 1980.

16 Smith, *Amores perros*, p. 74.

17 Jean Oppenheimer, 'A Dog's Life: Interview with Rodrigo Prieto', *American Cinematographer*, LXXXII/4 (April 2001), p. 23.

18 Carla Meyer, '*Nine Queens* remake misses original's intensity', *San Francisco Chronicle* (10 September 2004).

19 A number of other films released in 2000 showed that Latin America had finally turned the corner. These include Marcelo Piñeyro's *Plata quemada* (2000), based on the novel of the same title by Ricardo Piglia, a film about fraud and double-crossing, and Juan Carlos Tabío's *Lista de espera* (2000), a film about solidarity in Cuba.

20 David Archibald, 'Insects and Violence', *The Guardian* (28 November 2001).

21 Smith, *Amores perros*, pp. 85–6.

22 Jason Wood, *The Faber Book of Mexican Cinema* (London, 2006), p. 98.

23 Warren Buckland, *Film Studies* (London, 1998), pp. 69–70.

24 Michael Guillen, 'At the edge of the World: Lisandro Alonso on *La libertad*', www.twitchfilm.com (26 November 2009); Joanna Page, *Crisis and Capitalism in Contemporary Argentine Cinema* (Durham, NC, 2009), p. 63.

25 Ed Gonzalez, 'La Libertad', *Slant*, www.slantmagazine.com (1 October 2001).

26 A number of other significant films released in 2001, such as Lucrecia Martel's *La ciénaga* (2001) and Juan José Campanella's *El hijo de la novia* (2001) are not discussed here for reasons of space.

27 See *Ônibus 174* on www.rottentomatoes.com, accessed 1 December 2013.

28 Paulo Lins, 'Cities of God and Social Mobilisation', in *City of God in Several Voices: Brazilian Social Cinema as Action*, ed. Else R. P. Vieira (Nottingham, 2005), p. 129.

29 Fernando Meirelles, 'Writing the Script, Finding and Preparing the Actors', in *City of God in Several Voices*, p. 15.

30 Leandro Firmino da Hora who plays Zé Pequeno as a hoodlum – and he is convincing – told me in an interview in November 2010 that he knew a number of gangsters in Cidade de Deu, having grown up with them, but he had followed his mother's advice and studied hard at school, thereby escaping a life of crime.

31 In an interview with César Charlone, the cinematographer of *Cidade de Deus*, in London on 27 November 2004, I asked him how he had engineered that particular shot and he told me he had simply run with the camera behind the chicken at about a foot from the ground.

32 In his presentation given at the Institute of Contemporary Arts, London, on 27 November 2004, César Charlone demonstrated how he used the flexibility of digital editing to produce a colour coding for each of the three decades.

33 There is a good discussion of the apartment sequence in Stephanie Muir, *Studying 'City of God'* (Leighton Buzzard, 2008), pp. 95–7.

34 César Charlone, 'The Writing Studio: The Art of Writing and Making Films', www.writingstudio.co.za, accessed 1 November 2013.

35 In his presentation given at the Institute of Contemporary Arts, London, on 27 November 2004, César Charlone explained how he mixed 16mm and 35mm film with digital post-production.

36 There were other important films released in 2002, including Carlos Carrera's *El crimen del padre Amaro*, Carlos Sorín's delicately done *Historias mínimas*, Carlos Reygadas's *Japón* and Adrián Caetano's *Un oso rojo*; for discussion of the latter film, see James Scorer, 'Once upon a time in Buenos Aires: Vengeance, Community and the Urban Western', *Journal of Latin American Cultural Studies: Travesia*, XIX/2 (2010), pp. 141–59.

37 Dan Fainaru suggests that, despite the irony, there is little in *Entre ciclones* 'to make the Havana authorities squirm in their seats, pull out their scissors or suspect it of dissident tendencies'; 'Hurricanes (Entre ciclones)', *Screen Daily* (9 June 2003); see www.buscacine.com/cinealdia.

38 In an email from Enrique Colina to the author on 5 September 2013. Other significant films released in 2003, which cannot be discussed here for reasons of space, include Albertina Carri's *Los rubios* and Fernando Pérez's *Suite Habana*.

39 Demetrious Matheou, *The Faber Book of New South American Cinema* (London, 2010), pp. 343–4.

40 Gonzalo Aguilar, *New Argentine Film: Other Worlds*, trans. Sarah Ann Wells (New York, 2008), p. 69.

41 S. F. Said, 'Sex and the Saintly', *The Telegraph* (25 January 2005).

42 Philip French, 'La niña santa', *The Observer* (6 February 2005).

43 Isabel Maurer Queipo, ed., *Directory of World Cinema, Latin America* (Bristol, 2013), p. 207.

44 There were a number of other important films released in 2004, including Fernando Solanas's *Memoria del saqueo*, Sebastián Cordero's *Crónicas*, Daniel Burman's *El abrazo partido*, Carlos Sorín's *Bombón: el perro*, Juan José Campanella's *Luna de Avellaneda*, Fernando Eimbcke's *Temporada de patos*, and Nicolás López's *Promedio rojo* which cannot be discussed here for reasons of space.

45 Peter Bradshaw, 'Secuestro Express', *The Guardian* (9 June 2006).

46 Audun Solli, *The Power of Film in Venezuela and Mexico, 1980–2010: Contesting and Supporting State Power* (Oslo, 2014), p. 221.

47 Peter Bradshaw, in 'Battle in Heaven', *The Guardian* (28 October 2005), says of the actors, 'They all have faces like Easter Island statues.' See, for example, also when Marcos and Ana, after greeting a man in a wheelchair with his nurse in the street outside Ana's house, look – without moving and without speaking – at the camera in a choreographically similar shot.

48 Philip French, 'Battle in Heaven', *The Observer* (30 October 2005). As far as Marco Hernández, Bertha Ruiz and Anapola Mushkadiz are concerned, it is the case that they are non-professional actors.

49 Charlotte Higgins, 'I am the Only Normal Director', *The Guardian* (22 August 2005).
50 Jon Romney, 'Review: Battle in Heaven', *Independent on Sunday* (30 October 2005).
51 A number of other significant films were released in 2005, including Fabián Bielinsky's *El aura*, Alex Bowen's *Mi mejor enemigo* and Marcelo Gomes's *Cinema, aspirinas e urubus*. For discussion of the latter film, see Stephanie Dennison, 'The Brazilian Sertão as Post-national Landscape in the Work of Marcelo Gomes', *New Cinemas: Journal of Contemporary Film*, xx/1 (2012), pp. 3–15. Amat Escalante's striking feature *Sangre* ('Blood') was selected for Un Certain Regard at the 2005 Cannes Film Festival.
52 Jens Andersmann, *New Argentine Cinema* (London, 2012), p. 91.
53 J. Hoberman, *Film After Film; or, What Became of 21st Century Film?* (London, 2012), p. 21.
54 Ed Gonzalez, 'Babel', *Slant*, www.slantmagazine.com (9 October 2006).
55 Peter Bradshaw, 'Babel', *The Guardian* (19 January 2007).
56 Philip French, 'Babel', *The Observer* (21 January 2007).
57 Jo Tuckman, 'Who really made *Babel*?', *The Guardian* (9 February 2007).
58 *Babel* formed part of the record sixteen nominations for Mexican films in 2007; see Diego Cevallos, 'Film: Oscar Nominations – for Mexicans or Mexican Filmmaking', IPS News (22 February 2007); see www.ipsnews.net.
59 Some critics reacted in a hostile manner to González Iñárritu's experimentalism. Deborah Shaw, for example, argues that *Babel* 'creates an implied world cinema gaze that is central to the construction of a world cinema auteur, and for the marketing of a film'. As she goes on to say: 'Nevertheless, the gaze is flawed, as it can work through a universalist and melodramatic take on "the human condition". Esperanto failed as an international language as it lacked cultural and national roots, and *Babel* cannot provide a model for a new cinematic language for the same reason'; *The Three Amigos: The Transnational Filmmaking of Guillermo del Toro, Alejandro González Iñárritu and Alfonso Cuarón* (Manchester, 2013), p. 154.
60 González Iñárritu is, of course, employing a standard technique used in Film School exercises, the Kuleshov effect, whereby editing two sequences together allows the emotional reaction provoked by the first to spill over into the second.
61 Perhaps the best example, though, of the animatronics in the film is the eyeless monster who chases after Ofelia in her second task and who uses his hands to 'see'.
62 Peter Bradshaw, 'Meirelles Scores with *Blindness*'s Vision of Horror', *The Guardian* (14 May 2008).
63 Roger Ebert, for example, has argued the following: '*Blindness* is one of the most unpleasant, not to say unendurable, films I've ever seen. It is an allegory about a group of people who survive under great stress, but frankly I would rather have seen them perish than sit through the final three-quarters

of the film. Not only is it despairing and sickening, it's ugly. Denatured, sometimes overexposed, sometimes too shadowy to see, it is an experiment to determine how much you can fool with a print before ending up with mud, intercut with brightly lit milk', www.rogerebert.com (2 October 2008).

64 Robert Hull, 'Interview: Blindness', www.screenjabber.com, accessed 15 November 2013.

65 Gary Kramer, 'Interview: José Padilha', *Slant*, www.slantmagazine.com (7 November 2011).

66 A number of striking films were released in 2007, including Ricardo Darín's *La señal*, Rodrigo Plá's *La zona*, Nicolás Prividera's *M*, a documentary, Vivien Lesnik Weisman's *El hombre de las dos Habanas* and Patricia Riggen's *La misma luna*. Manuel Pérez Paredes released a documentary, *Che Guevara donde nunca jamás se lo imaginan* ('Che Guevara as You have Never Seen Him Before'), which contained some new footage of an interview with his father as well as an informative interview with his companion, Alberto Granado, while Luis Ospina released a hilarious send-up of the documentary genre, *Un tigre de papel* ('A Paper Tiger'), about the father of collage in Colombia, Pedro Manrique Figueroa; his life in the arts and in politics is meticulously traced from 1934 until his mysterious disappearance in 1981.

67 For a discussion of the reworking of Dreyer's film in *Luz silenciosa*, see Cynthia Tompkins, *Experimental Latin American Cinema: History and Aesthetics* (Austin, TX, 2013), pp. 180–81.

68 For an excellent discussion of these ghostly presences in the film see Deborah Martin, 'Childhood, Youth, and the In-between: The Ethics and Aesthetics of Lucrecia Martel's *La mujer sin cabeza*', *Hispanic Research Journal*, XIV/2 (2013), pp. 144–58.

69 Joanna Page, 'Folktales and Fabulation in Lucrecia Martel's Films', in *Latin American Popular Culture: Politics, Media, Affect*, ed. Geoffrey Kantaris and Rory O'Bryen (Woodbridge, 2013), p. 85.

70 Violeta Kovacsics and Adam Nayman, 'Interviews / Shore Leave: Lisandro Alonso's Liverpool', *Cinemascope*, http://cinema-scope.com, accessed 1 December 2013.

71 There were a number of other significant films released in 2008, including Andrés Wood's *La buena vida*, José Pedro Ficopovicu's *El círculo*, a documentary, José Mojica Marin's *A encarnacão do demônio*, Christian Poveda's *La vida loca*, Pablo Larraín's *Tony Manero* and Carlos Sorín's *La ventana*, which for reasons of space cannot be discussed here.

72 Peter Bradshaw, 'Film Review: The Secret in their Eyes', *The Guardian* (10 August 2010).

73 Geoffrey MacNab, 'The Secret in their Eyes', *The Independent* (13 August 2010).

74 Tim Robey, 'The Secret in their Eyes, review', *The Telegraph* (10 August 2010).

75 Jonathan Romney, 'The Secret in their Eyes' review, *Uncut* (August 2010).

76 Other significant films of 2009 were Sebastián Silva's *La nana*, Ciro

Guerra's *Los viajes del viento*, Adrián Biniez's *Gigante*, Cary Fukunaga's *Sin nombre* (2009), and Lucía Puenzo's *El niño pez* (2009).

77 Christina Radish, 'Director Alejandro González Iñárritu Interview Biutiful', www.collider.com, accessed 15 December 2013.

78 Ibid.

79 Bill Graham, 'Director José Padilha talks *Elite Squad: The Enemy Within*', www.collider.com, accessed 1 December 2013.

80 A number of significant films were released in 2010 demonstrating Latin America's cinematic maturity, including Pablo Trapero's *Carancho* and Miguel Cohan's *Sin retorno*. Indigenous film gained impact during this decade, including works such as *Eréndira ikikunari* (2006) and *Aukinime* (2010); see Charlotte Cleghorne, 'Revisioning the Colonial Record: *La relación de Michoacán* and Contemporary Mexican Indigenous Film', *Interventions: International Journal of Postcolonial Studies*, xv/2 (2013), pp. 224–38.

81 Peter Bradshaw, 'Days of Grace – Review', *The Guardian* (25 July 2013).

82 Manohla Dargis, 'Cannes Festival: From Chile, Pablo Larraín's *No*', *New York Times* (22 May 2012).

83 Andrew Alexander, 'Interview with Filmmaker Carlos Reygadas: Mexican Auteur Brings *Post Tenebras Lux* to Atlanta', http://burnaway.org (19 April 2013).

84 Dennis Lim, 'Cannes Film Festival: Loud Boos Don't Faze Carlos Reygadas', *New York Times* (27 May 2012).

85 Alexander, 'Interview with Filmmaker Carlos Reygadas'.

86 Ibid.

87 A landmark Brazilian film of 2012 was *O Som ao Redor* ('Neighbouring Sounds'), directed by Kleber Mendonça Filho, which was Brazil's official Academy Award nomination; Shalini Dore, 'Brazil Sends *Neighboring Sounds* to Oscars', *Variety* (20 September 2013).

88 Peter Bradshaw argues that Quemada-Díez, unlike directors such as Andrea Arnold and Clio Barnard, who have used Loach's work as inspiration to create 'beautifully realized and photographed dramas of naturalism', is 'closer to the gritty, grainy original' of Loach's style; 'Cannes 2013: *The Golden Cage*', *The Guardian* (23 May 2013). Ken Loach, who attended the LFF screening, said he was impressed by the film.

89 The shock of the event was enhanced, no doubt, by the director's clever decision not to tell the actor that his character would be 'shot' until the morning of the take; as Quemada-Díez pointed out in a Q&A at the London Film Festival on 15 October 2013.

90 Other notable films released in 2013 which are not discussed here for reasons of space are Santiago Loza's *La Paz*, an atmospheric film about a young man from the upper classes, Liso (Lisandro Rodríguez), who is unable to reconnect after a spell in a psychiatric hospital, and Amat Escalante's *Heli*, which won the Best Director award at the 2013 Cannes Film Festival, and contains a grim and graphic torture scene.

91 As Guillermo del Toro remembered: 'When I showed *Pan's Labyrinth* to my friend Alejandro González Iñárritu, he said: "That's a truly Catholic film." And there was me thinking that it was a truly profane film, a layman's riff on Catholic dogma. It's true what they say: once a Catholic, always a Catholic'; quoted in 'Pan's People', *The Guardian* (17 November 2006).

92 The Academy Award nominations for *Gravity* were in the following categories: Actress in a Leading Role, Cinematography, Directing, Film Editing, Music (Original Score), Best Picture, Production Design, Sound Editing, Sound Mixing and Visual Effects. It won seven Oscars: Best Director, Best Cinematography, Best Visual Effects, Best Original Score, Best Sound Mixing, Best Sound Editing and Best Editing – a record for a Latin American film; see Catherine Sheard and Andrew Pulver, 'Oscars 2014: *Gravity* dominates, but *12 Years a Slave* wins Best Film', *The Guardian* (3 March 2014).

93 Robbie Collin, '*Gravity*, Venice Film Festival 2013, Review', *The Telegraph* (28 August 2013).

94 Alex Ramon, TIFF 2013; *Gravity* (dir. Alfonso Cuarón); see www.popmatters.com, accessed 15 January 2014.

SELECT DIRECTORS' BIOGRAPHIES

Alonso, Lisandro (*b.* 1975), Argentine film director who has directed four features, *La libertad* ('Freedom', 2001), *Los muertos* ('The Dead', 2004), *Fantasma* ('Phantom', 2006) and *Liverpool* (2008). Known for his experimentalism.

Babenco, Héctor (*b.* 1946), Brazilian film director who has directed a number of films, including *Pixote: a lei do mais fraco* ('Pixote: The Survival of the Weakest', 1980) (normally considered his masterpiece), *Kiss of the Spider Woman* (1985) and *Carandiru* (2003).

Bemberg, María Luisa (1922–1995), Argentine director known for her portrayal of strong female protagonists, directed films such as *Camila* (1984, nominated for an Academy Award), *Miss Mary* (1986), *Yo, la peor de todas* ('I, the Worst of All', 1990) and *De eso no se habla* ('I Don't Want to Talk About It', 1993).

Birri, Fernando (*b.* 1925), Argentine documentarist who is considered to be the father of Nuevo Cine Latinoamericano. His works include *Tire dié* ('Throw us a Dime', 1960) and *Los inundados* ('The Flooded', 1961). He co-founded the Escuela Internacional de Cine y Televisión (International School of Film and Television) with Julio García Espinosa, Gabriel García Márquez and Tomás Gutiérrez Alea, in San Antonio de los Baños, Cuba, in 1986, and produced a film based on one of García Márquez's short stories, *Un señor muy viejo con unas alas enormes* ('A Very Old Man with Enormous Wings', 1988).

Campanella, Juan José (*b.* 1959), Argentine director whose work includes *El mismo mar, la misma lluvia* ('The Same Sea, the Same Rain', 1999), *El hijo de la novia* ('The Girlfriend's Son', 2001), *Luna de Avellaneda* ('Avellaneda's Moon', 2004), *El secreto de sus ojos* ('The Secret in their Eyes', 2009), which won an Academy Award for Best Foreign Language Film, and *Metegol* (2012).

Colina, Enrique (*b.* 1944), Cuban film-maker and TV personality, who was well-known in Cuba as the host of a television programme about cinema called *24 × Segundo* ('24 Times a Second'). His films include *Estética* ('Aesthetics', 1984), *Vecinos* ('Neighbours', 1985), and *Entre ciclones* ('Hurricanes', 2003), which was invited to the Cannes Film Festival as Latin America's representative for the Critics' Week.

Cuarón, Alfonso (*b.* 1961), Mexican film director who is best known for *A Little Princess* (1995), *Y tu mamá también* ('And Your Mother Too', 2001), *Harry Potter and the Prisoner of Azkaban* (2004), *Children of Men* (2006) and *Gravity* (2013). The latter film received seven Academy Awards, including Best Director, the most a Latin American director has ever won. Known as one of the Three Amigos who have transformed Mexican cinema, the other two being Guillermo del Toro and Alejandro González Iñárritu.

del Toro, Guillermo (*b.* 1964), Mexican film director. As at home in Hollywood, where he has made films such as *Blade II* (2002), *Hellboy* (2004), *Hellboy II: The Golden Army* (2008) and *Pacific Rim* (2013), as with his Spanish-language Gothic horror films such as *The Devil's Backbone* (2001) and *Pan's Labyrinth* (2006). The latter – generally seen as his masterpiece – won three Academy Awards, for Best Art Direction, Best Cinematography and Best Makeup.

García Espinosa, Julio (*b.* 1926), Cuban film director who studied with Tomás Gutiérrez Alea in Italy in the early 1950s, returning to Cuba in order to make the documentary *El Mégano* (1955). He helped found the Instituto Cubano del Arte y la Industria Cinematográficos (ICAIC) soon after the Revolution and went on to be its director for a number of years. He directed a number of feature films, including *Las aventuras de Juan Quin Quin* ('The Adventures of Juan Quin Quin', 1967) and *Reina y Rey* ('Queen and King', 1994). He co-founded the Escuela Internacional de Cine y Television in 1986.

González Iñárritu, Alejandro (*b.* 1963), Mexican director of four acclaimed features: *Amores perros* ('Love's a Bitch', 2000), *21 Grams* (2003), *Babel* (2006) and *Biutiful* (2010). *Babel* won the Golden Globe Award for Best Motion Picture and received seven Academy Award nominations, including two nominations for Best Supporting Actress.

Gutiérrez Alea, Tomás (1928–1996), Cuban film director (often known by his nickname, Titón) who studied neo-Realism in Italy in the 1950s and, after the Revolution, helped found the ICAIC and was closely associated with the development of Nuevo Cine Latinoamericano. He subsequently made a number of films which launched Cuban cinema, including *Memorias del subdesarrollo* ('Memories of Underdevelopment', 1968), *La última cena* ('The Last Supper', 1977) and *Fresa y chocolate* ('Strawberry and Chocolate', 1993).

Guzmán, Patricio (*b.* 1941), Chilean documentarist who achieved fame with his documentary about the Chilean coup d'état, *La batalla de Chile* ('The Battle of Chile', 1975). His most recent documentary, *Nostalgia for the Light* (2010), uses a more 'poetic' approach to express the trauma of Chile's disappeared.

Llosa, Claudia (*b.* 1976), Peruvian director whose films include *Madeinusa* (2006) and *La teta asustada* ('The Milk of Sorrow', 2010), which was nominated for an Academy Award in the Best Foreign Film Category. Her most recent film, a short entitled *Loxoro* (2012), won the award for Best Short Film at the Berlin International Film Festival.

Lombardi, Francisco José (*b.* 1947), Peruvian director of a number of feature films, including *La ciudad y los perros* ('The Time of the Hero', 1985), based on the novel by Mario Vargas Llosa, *La boca del lobo* ('The Lion's Den', 1988), *Pantaleón y las visitadoras* ('Captain Pantoja and the Special Services', 2000), again based on one of Vargas Llosa's novels, *Tinta roja* ('Red Ink', 2000) and *La mariposa negra* ('Black Butterfly', 2006).

Martel, Lucrecia (*b.* 1966), Argentine film director and founder member of the New Argentine Cinema movement. Her main features are *La ciénaga* ('The Swamp', 2001), *La niña santa* ('The Holy Girl', 2004) and *La mujer sin cabeza* ('The Headless Woman', 2008).

Meirelles, Fernando (*b.* 1955), Brazilian film director who established his reputation with *Cidade de Deus* ('City of God', 2002), for which he was nominated for an Academy Award for Best Director, *The Constant Gardener* (2005), for which Rachel Weisz won an Academy Award for Best Supporting Actress (2006), and *Blindness* (2008), which is based on José Samarago's novel.

Padilha, José (*b.* 1967), Brazilian film director who began his career with the highly successful documentary *Ônibus 174* ('Bus 174', 2002), followed by *Tropa de Elite* ('Elite Squad', 2007) and its sequel *Tropa de Elite 2 – O Inimigo Agora é Outro* ('Elite Squad: The Enemy Within', 2010), both of which were highly successful commercially and received numerous awards.

Reygadas, Carlos (*b.* 1971), Mexican film director whose four features – *Japón* ('Japan', 2002), *Batalla en el cielo* ('Battle in Heaven', 2005), *Luz silenciosa* ('Silent Light', 2007) and *Post tenebras lux* (2012) – are experimental, thought-provoking and occasionally pornographic.

Rocha, Glauber (1939–1981), Brazilian film director closely associated with the Cinema Novo movement. His films include *Deus e o diabo na terra do sol* ('Black God, White Devil', 1964), *Terra em transe* ('Land in Trauma', 1967) and *Antonio das Mortes* (1969). He is also famous for his theory of the 'aesthetics of hunger'.

Salles, Walter (*b.* 1956), Brazilian director whose films include *Central do Brasil* ('Central Station', 1998), *Abril Despedaçado* ('Behind the Sun', 2001), *Diarios de motocicleta* ('The Motorcycle Diaries', 2004) – his most successful film, about Che Guevara's travels across the subcontinent on a motorcycle, *Linha de Passe* (2008) and *On the Road* (2012), based on Jack Kerouac's masterpiece.

Sanjinés, Jorge (*b.* 1936), Bolivian director who founded the Grupo Ukamau and established himself as an important voice within the Nuevo Cine Latinoamericano movement in the 1960s. His films include *Ukamau* ('And So It Is', 1966), *Yawar Mallku* ('The Blood of the Condor', 1969), *El coraje del pueblo* ('The People's Courage', 1971), *La nación clandestina* ('The Secret Nation', 1989), *Para recibir el canto de los pájaros* ('To Receive the Bird's Song', 1995) and *Insurgentes* ('Insurgents', 2012).

Trapero, Pablo (*b.* 1971), Argentine director whose most significant feature films are *El Bonaerense* ('The Man from Buenos Aires', 2002), *Familia rodante* ('Rolling Family', 2004), *Carancho* (2010) and *White Elephant* (2012). Typically, the focus of his films is everyday life.

SELECT BIBLIOGRAPHY

Aguilar, Gonzalo, *New Argentine Film: Other Worlds* (New York, 2008)
Amaya, Héctor, *Screening Cuba: Film Criticism as Political Performance during the Cold War* (Urbana-Champaign, IL, 2010)
Armes, Roy, *French Cinema* (London, 1985)
Aumont, Jacques, et al., *Aesthetics of Film* (Austin, TX, 1992)
Barnard, Timothy, and Peter Rist, eds, *South American Cinema: A Critical Filmography, 1915–1994* (Austin, TX, 1996)
Bermúdez Barrios, Nayibe, *Latin American Cinema: Local Views and Transnational Connections* (Calgary, 2011)
Brown, William, *Film-Philosophy for the Digital Age: Supercinema* (New York, 2013)
Buchsbaum, Jonathan, *Cinema and the Sandinistas: Filmmaking in Revolutionary Nicaragua* (Austin, TX, 2003)
Buckland, Warren, *Film Studies* (London, 1998)
Buñuel, Luis, *My Last Sigh: The Autobiography of Luis Buñuel* (New York, 1983)
Burton, Julianne, *Cinema and Social Change in Latin America: Conversations with Filmmakers* (Austin, TX, 1986)
—, ed., *The Social Documentary in Latin America* (Pittsburgh, PA, 1990)
Chanan, Michael, *The Cuban Image* (London, 1985)
—, ed., *Twenty-five Years of the New Latin American Cinema* (London, 1983)
Daicich, Osvaldo, *Apuntes sobre el Nuevo cine latinoamericano* (Córdoba, 2004)
Deleuze, Gilles, *Cinema 1: The Movement-Image*, trans. Hugh Tomlinson and Barbara Habberjam (London, 1992)
—, *Cinema 2: The Time-Image*, trans. Hugh Tomlinson and Robert Galeta (London, 1989)
Dennison, Stephanie, ed., *Contemporary Hispanic Cinema: Interrogating the Transnational in Spanish and Latin American Film* (Woodbridge, 2013)
—, and Lisa Shaw, eds, *Popular Cinema in Brazil, 1930–2001* (Manchester, 2004)
Deutschman, David, ed., *Che Guevara and the Cuban Revolution: Writings and Speeches of Ernesto Che Guevara* (Sydney, 1987)

Elena, Alberto, and Marina Diaz Lopez, *The Cinema of Latin America* (London, 2003)
Evans, Peter, *The Films of Luis Buñuel: Subjectivity and Desire* (Oxford, 1995)
—, and Isabel Santaolalla, eds, *Luis Buñuel: New Readings* (London, 2004)
Evora, José Antonio, *Tomás Gutiérrez Alea* (Madrid, 1996)
Falicov, Tamara Leah, *The Cinematic Tango: Contemporary Argentine Film* (London, 2007)
Foster, David William, *Contemporary Argentine Cinema* (Columbia, MI, 1992)
—, *Queer Issues in Contemporary Latin American Cinema* (Austin, TX, 2003)
Fowler Calzada, Víctor, *Conversaciones con un cineasta incómodo: Julio García Espinosa* (Havana, 2004)
Gardner, Nathanial, *Como agua para chocolate: The Novel and Film Version* (London, 2009)
Haddu, Miriam, and Joanna Page, eds, *Visual Synergies in Fiction and Documentary Film from Latin America* (New York, 2009)
Hart, Stephen, *A Companion to Latin American Cinema* (Woodbridge, 2004)
—, *Chiaroscuro: The Life and Work of Julio García Espinosa* (London, 2011)
Hayward, Susan, *Key Concepts in Cinema Studies* (London, 1996)
Hennebelle, Guy, and Alfonso Gumucio-Dagrón, *Les cinémas de l'Amérique Latine* (Paris, 1981)
Hershfield, Joanne, *Mexican Cinema: Mexican Women, 1940–1950* (Tucson, AZ, 1996)
Ibarra, Mirtha, *Tomás Gutiérrez Alea: volver sobre mis pasos* (Madrid, 2007)
Johnson, Randal, *The Film Industry in Brazil: Culture and the State* (Pittsburgh, PA, 1987)
—, and Robert Stam, *Brazilian Cinema* (East Brunswick, NJ, 1982)
Kantaris, Geoffrey, and Rory O'Bryen, eds, *Latin American Popular Culture: Politics, Media, Affect* (Woodbridge, 2013)
King, John, *Magical Reels: A History of Cinema in Latin America* (London, 1990)
—, Sheila Whitaker and Rosa Bosch, eds, *An Argentine Passion: María Luisa Bemberg and her Films* (London, 2000)
—, Ana López and Manuel Alvarado, eds, *Mediating Two Worlds: Cinematic Encounters in the Americas* (London, 1993)
Lasarte, Francisco, and Guido Podestá, eds, *Estudios Iberoamérica y el cine* (Amsterdam, 1996)
Lehman, Peter, and William Luhr, *Thinking about Movies: Watching, Questioning, Enjoying* (Oxford, 2003)
Leyda, Jan, *Kino: A History of the Russian and Soviet Cinema*, 3rd edn (Princeton, NJ, 1983)
Marrati, Paola, *Gilles Deleuze: Cinema and Philosophy* (Baltimore, MD, 2008)
Martin, Michael T., ed., *New Latin American Cinema, Volume One: Theory, Practices and Transcontinental Articulations* (Detroit, MI, 1997)
Matheou, Demetrios, *The Faber Book of New South American Cinema* (London, 2010)

Maurer Queipo, Isabel, ed., *Directory of World Cinema: Latin America* (Bristol, 2013)
Middents, Jeffrey, *Writing National Cinema: Film Journals and Film Culture in Peru* (Dartmouth, NH, 2009)
Miller, Toby, and Robert Stam, *A Companion to Film Theory* (Malden, MA, 1999)
Mora, Carl. J., *Mexican Cinema: Reflections of a Society, 1896–1980* (Berkeley, CA, 1982)
Nagib, Lúcia, ed., *The New Brazilian Cinema* (London, 2003)
—, *Brazil on Screen: Cinema novo, New Cinema, Utopia* (London, 2007)
Noriega, Chon A., ed., *Visible Nations: Latin American Cinema and Video* (Minneapolis, MN, 2000)
Page, Joanna, *Crisis and Capitalism in Contemporary Argentine Cinema* (Durham, NC, 2009)
Paranaguá, P. A., ed., *Mexican Cinema*, trans. Ana López (London, 1995)
Pick, Zuzana, *The New Latin American Cinema: A Continental Project* (Austin, TX, 1993)
Pisters, Patricia, *The Neuro-image: Deleuzian Film-philosophy of Digital Screen Culture* (Stanford, CA, 2012)
Podalsky, Laura, *The Politics of Affect and Emotion in Contemporary Latin American Cinema: Argentina, Brazil, Cuba and Mexico* (New York, 2011)
Ramírez Berg, Charles, *Cinema of Solitude: A Critical Study of Mexican Film, 1967–1983* (Austin, TX, 1992)
Richards, Keith John, *Themes in Latin American Cinema: A Critical Survey* (Jefferson, NC, 2010)
Rix, Rob, and Roberto Rodríguez-Saona, eds, *Changing Reels: Latin American Cinema Against the Odds* (Leeds, 1997)
Ruétalo, Victoria, and Dolores Tierney, eds, *Latsploitation, Exploitation Cinemas, and Latin America* (New York, 2009)
Ruffinelli, Jorge, *Patricio Guzmán* (Madrid, 2001)
Russo, Eduardo Angel, ed., *The Film Edge: Contemporary Filmmaking in Latin America* (Buenos Aires, 2010)
Sánchez-H., José, *The Art and Politics of Bolivian Cinema* (Lanham, MD, 1999)
Schaefer, Claudia, *Bored to Distraction: Cinema of Excess in End-of-century Mexico and Spain* (Albany, NY, 2003)
Schroeder, Paul A., *Tomás Gutiérrez Alea: The Dialectics of a Filmmaker* (London, 2002)
Seton, Marie, *Sergei M. Eisenstein* (London, 1978)
Shaw, Deborah, *Contemporary Cinema of Latin America: Ten Key Films* (London, 2003)
—, ed., *Contemporary Latin American Cinema: Breaking into the Global Market* (Lanham, MD, 2007)
—, *The Three Amigos: The Transnational Films of Guillermo del Toro, Alejandro González Iñárritu and Alfonso Cuarón* (Manchester, 2013)
Shaw, Lisa, and Stephanie Dennison, *Latin American Cinema: Essays on*

Modernity, Gender and National Identity (Jefferson, NC, 2005)
Shiel, Mark, and Tony Fitzmaurice, eds, *Cinema and the City: Film and Urban Societies in a Global Context* (Oxford, 2001)
Smith, Paul Julian, *Vision Machines* (London, 1996)
—, *Amores perros* (London, 2002)
Solli, Audun, *The Power of Film in Venezuela and Mexico, 1980–2010: Contesting and Supporting State Power* (Oslo, 2014)
Soutar, Jethro, *Gael García Bernal and the Latin American New Wave: The Story of a Cinematic Movement and its Leading Man* (London, 2008)
Stam, Robert, *Film Theory: An Introduction* (Malden, MA, 2000)
Stevens, Donald F., ed., *Based on a True Story: Latin American History at the Movies* (Wilmington, DE, 1997)
Stock, Anne Marie, *Framing Latin American Cinema: Contemporary Critical Perspectives* (Minneapolis, MN, 1997)
Tierney, Dolores, *Contemporary Latin American Cinema: New Transnationalisms* (Edinburgh, 2013)
Tolentino, Javier, *Julieta en el País de las Maravillas: una conversación con Norma Aleandro* (Madrid, 2004)
Tompkins, Cynthia, *Experimental Latin American Cinema: History and Aesthetics* (Austin, TX, 2013)
Vieira, Else R. P., ed., *City of God in Several Voices: Brazilian Social Cinema as Action* (Nottingham, 2005)
Wood, Jason, *The Faber Book of Mexican Cinema* (London, 2006)
Young, Robert, *Postcolonialism: An Historical Introduction* (Oxford, 2003)

ACKNOWLEDGEMENTS

My thanks for help of various kinds are due as follows: I express my gratitude to the directors, scriptwriters, producers, cinematographers, writers and actors who gave up time to discuss their work with me, including Fernando Birri, Lola Calviño, Michael Chanan, César Charlone, Enrique Colina, Octavio Cortázar, Alfonso Cuarón, Edmundo Desnoes, Ignacio Durán Loera, Vicente Ferraz, Leandro Firmino da Hora, Julio García Espinosa, Gabriel García Márquez, Ernesto Granados, Mirtha Ibarra, Ken Loach, Germán Martínez Martínez, Carlos Moreno, Laura Mulvey, Luis Ospina, Beatriz Palacios, Enrique Pineda Barnet, Jorge Sanjinés and Humberto Solás. I express my thanks to the Escuela Internacional de Cine y Televisión in San Antonio de los Baños, Cuba, especially to Aymara Mainet, Rafael Rosal and Héctor Veitía, whose support of the annual documentary film-making summer school, held there since 2006, has allowed me to think in new ways about digital film, as well as to all the *talleristas* I have worked with at the EICTV; a special vote of thanks for Owen Williams, who has been a rock over the years.

I express my appreciation for the support provided by the Faculty of Arts and Humanities at University College London, specifically the two terms of research leave which allowed me to complete this monograph. My special thanks to the UCL School of European Languages, Culture and Society, and to its director Dr Dilwyn Knox in particular, for the subvention which supported the reproduction costs of the colour illustrations. I am grateful to the British Film Institute for providing a number of the original stills and to Julio and Lola for some of the original photographs reproduced in the book. Thank you to Dany, Natasha, Matthew, Christian and Jordan for your patience. Last but not least, I express my deep thanks to Vivian Constantinopoulos and Aimee Selby at Reaktion Books for their sage advice and dexterity in guiding this book through.

PHOTO ACKNOWLEDGEMENTS

The author and publishers wish to express their thanks to the following sources of illustrative material and/or permission to reproduce it:

Courtesy of the BFI, London: pp. 75, 80, 88, 93, 96, 110, 118, 125; courtesy of Dolores (Lola) Calviño: pp. 52–3; courtesy of Enrique Colina: p. 133; courtesy of Julio García Espinosa: pp. 33–4, 40 and 78; courtesy of Jorge Sanjinés: pp. 59, 64.

INDEX

MW01714372

爱 就 是 在 一 起， 吃 好 多 好 多 顿 饭

TABLE SETTING : A TIME FOR LOVE

曾淼冰 著

中信出版社 · CHINACITICPRESS · 北京 ·

图书在版编目 (CIP) 数据

爱就是在一起，吃好多好多顿饭 / 曾焱冰著．— 北京：中信出版社，2014.10
ISBN 978-7-5086-4729-6
Ⅰ．爱… Ⅱ．曾… Ⅲ．宴会—设计 Ⅳ．TS972.32
中国版本图书馆 CIP 数据核字 (2014) 第 182703 号

爱就是在一起，吃好多好多顿饭

著　　者：曾焱冰
策划推广：中信出版社（China CITIC Press）
出版发行：中信出版集团股份有限公司
（北京市朝阳区惠新东街甲 4 号富盛大厦 2 座 邮编 100029）
（CITIC Publishing Group）
承 印 者：北京盛通印刷股份有限公司

开　　本：787mm×1092mm 1/16　　印　　张：12.5　　字　　数：110 千字
版　　次：2014 年 10 月第 1 版　　印　　次：2015 年 3 月第 6 次印刷
广告经营许可证：京朝工商广字第 8087 号
书　　号：ISBN978-7-5086-4729-6/G・1152
定　　价：49.80 元

服务热线：010-84849555　　传　　真：010-84849000
投稿邮箱：author@citicpub.com

推荐语　RECOMMEND LANGUAGE

演员
刘涛

我一直相信，若有热情，做什么都是美好的。这本书里美轮美奂的餐桌布置让人看到生活中最真实的美好，能感受到一餐一饭中爱意的表达。作为演员也作为母亲，我也时常要面对权衡双重角色兼顾的难题，这本书里对待生活的热情和智慧，给了我无穷的启发。

演员
陆毅

我想这是一本我可以和太太一起看的书。里面关于“爱”有了更直接、生动的诠释——用心陪伴家人和朋友，做好每顿饭、布置好每张餐桌，好好享受、慢慢聊天，让在一起的时光美好而难忘。

在我心里，家庭永远是第一位的，因为我非常清楚地知道，家人是会陪伴我一辈子的，而演戏不是。所以我会用更多的时间与他们在一起，和家人一同吃饭、陪父母聊天、与孩子玩耍，这些都是生命中最重要的。就像这本书里所说的，这些用心的陪伴和爱会是一种储备能量，无论生活会有怎样的忧愁，都会让我们觉得并不孤单。

作家

庄雅婷

一个女人的生活应该是这样，用柔软和美，包裹着智慧，绵绵不断地在寻常日子里生发出热情与爱。那种让人更好的能量，由食物与爱组成。

就像气味是一种记忆，绕过理性直接通向感情；就像食物是一种能量，安抚身体还慰藉心情。这漫长的日子里，山川河海最后归于你和我围坐的餐桌。这繁复的生活里，最后还是爱，解释一切。

有幸成为爱的餐桌边围坐的一员，和她们一起谈论美好的事。有时阳光照在我们的脸上，有时抬头，看见满天星光。

作家

细毛

冰冰第一次下厨请我们吃饭，做了红烧肉。颜色略黑，味道不错。那时她单身，锅碗瓢勺不齐。新婚之后，在家请客，很费了一些心思。漂亮高大的塔吉锅焖排骨，实在是壮观。然后有了小叶子，请朋友吃饭的时候，大人孩子各有照顾。餐桌餐盘鲜花桌布随意一摆就是美。一切都变得游刃有余起来。岂止是在餐桌上，生活里工作中，冰冰都踏踏实实地蜕变成长，而这种美好也感染着身边每一个朋友。她说：“我不希望小叶子给我争气，我要做一个自己争气的妈妈。”虽然对自己小狠，但是做最好的自己，小孩子自然错不了。冰冰这一本书，在怀孕之前就开始写作拍摄，所以比小叶子年龄大，可以算是给小叶子的礼物，也可以是给所有女人的礼物吧……

目录 CONTENTS

生 活 的 智 慧 和 乐 趣

THE WISDOM AND PLEASURE OF LIFE

P R E F A C E　　推 荐 序

当冰冰告诉我她打算出一本书的时候，我惊讶极了。因为我没法想象，应对一份忙碌的全职工作，照顾一个不到三岁的小孩，总能给家人做出漂亮美味的饭菜，并时常安排家庭旅行外出，怎么能够还有精力写书？

和我一起工作近八年，冰冰几乎每天都是最早到办公室的几个员工之一，而且打扮精致，永远没有蓬头垢面或衣着邋遢随意的时刻。似乎也没有见她在工作和生活中遇到过什么化解不开的让她焦躁的麻烦。偶尔在微博或朋友圈看到她做的美轮美奂的家宴、插花、烘焙和餐桌布置的照片，我会问她，你那么忙，怎么有时间做这些？她说这也并不是每天的生活，但有空的时候，就要抓紧时间，让陪伴家人的时间质量更高。她会早起、晚睡，不看电视，减少上网，或者通过巧妙安排提高效率——有固定的人给她送鲜花，在有机食品网上预订食材，安排得力的清洁人员打扫卫生、做家务，研究快速烹饪的技巧……这些看似微不足道的事情，恰恰是生活中的智慧，正是这些才让一个繁忙的现代职业女性的生活变得充满乐趣。就像她书里所言："女人都可以是天生的指挥家，让不同的音调汇集在同一个节奏上，眼观六路，从容周全。"

在这本书里，分享的正是围绕餐桌展开的一些生活中的感悟，包括和孩子、家人、朋友之间的情感故事，当然还有很多她日常餐桌布置的心得。看到她用心研究，把生活中的乐趣集合成作品，非常替她感到高兴，就像我们《VOGUE》杂志所赞赏的女性，事业、家庭、孩子、生活，什么都要做得出色，这需要的是能力和头脑。她的生活态度对我甚至都是一种感染——尽情享受和家人朋友相聚的每一分钟，让自己的生活更加完美！

Angelica

《VOGUE》中国版编辑总监　张宇

美丽餐桌上的故事

STORIES ON A BEAUTIFUL DINNER TABLE

P R E F A C E　　自序

头发雪白的玛蒂娜在她一长溜五花八门的茶叶盒旁巡视，从中抽出一个说，试试我的阿萨姆红茶吧，这是秋天的茶，味道香浓，能帮你改善时差带来的失眠。

接着，她又指挥她的女儿在偌大的茶具柜里挑选茶杯，那里排列着一套套精美无比的茶具，她是在为我挑选一个合适的杯子，不是 Old Country Rose（老镇玫瑰），而是 Polka Rose（波尔卡玫瑰），因为它适合我的年龄。

这是 1999 年冬天的一个下午，在德国的波恩。玛蒂娜是我认识的一位当地报刊女主编的母亲，已经 85 岁了，这是我第一次在欧洲人的家里享用下午茶。

看着玛蒂娜在杯子上架上银茶漏，将茶水缓缓地倒入茶杯中，随着升腾的热气，麦芽香和蜂蜜、玫瑰的气息瞬间充溢在空气中。雕刻着花纹的银茶漏、带着蕾丝的茶巾以及盘子里每一样精致的点心，仿佛把我带到了一个美丽而神秘的世界。那一次欧洲之行之后，五光十色的记忆渐渐被更多更新的信息取代，但那个下午的每个细节却越发闪亮，因为在那一刻它让我的心“突”地动了一下，留下了一个标记，在后来无数漫长而黯淡的日子里，像一个闪亮的音符，时常浮现。

再一次有这样心被“突”地击中的感觉是几年之后。在我好友细毛夫妇的家宴上。细毛是一位设计师兼作家，她丈夫尹齐是一位画家。他们在巴黎和北京两地生活，那一次是为庆祝他们迁入北京的新居。大到近乎空旷的客厅，中心是一张大大的餐桌，角落里，一盏20世纪70年代的欧洲古董落地灯发出橘色柔和的光线，桌上烛光摇曳，花影微动。那些美丽的餐盘、餐巾与精致的烛台和花朵让每个进入房间的人赞叹着迷，随后端出的一道道女主人亲手烹饪的菜品更是色味俱佳，而且都与盛装它们的容器配合得完美无瑕——桃红色的小水萝卜被切成极薄的薄片与蔬菜一起被装在翠绿的琉璃沙拉碗中，卷成花朵一样的节瓜片盛开在小小的地中海式迷你陶碗里，还有盛放清蒸鱼的家传的古典银盘、装甜品的西班牙彩陶小碗……我在时装杂志工作多年，见过无数奢华与精美的晚宴场面，或许餐具用品和桌面装饰精致昂贵超过这儿很多倍，但我却从来不曾有过像那一刻心里的感动。因为这不是商务宴请，而只是招待朋友，是每一天自自然然地发生在生活中的。这让我又想起多年前的那个下午，那个有着雪白头发的老太太，她的茶杯、她的点心、她银色的茶漏，还有她缓缓冲泡出的艳红色的茶汤与她一举一动中的悠闲和享受……

如果说玛蒂娜的下午茶是多年前在我心里留下的一串模糊的音符，那么细毛家的宴请则是串联起这些细小音符的指挥棒，就是从那一刻起，我的心被打开了一扇窗，就像那些年繁忙而漠然的生活忽然照进了一束暖暖的光，照出了新的乐趣。

也是从那一刻起，我开始尝试改变自己的生活，去留意那些会打动我的美丽的盘盘碗碗、烛台花器，为家人朋友精心地准备日常的餐饭，布置美丽的餐桌，这样一顿顿饭下来，丰富的不仅仅是我餐具的库存，更是整个生活，所有的一切都不一样了。生活原本就是不断枯燥地重复，没有轰轰烈烈，唯有这些美好的细节让生活越品越有滋味。

后来，朋友说，你把平时的美图和方法创意都集合起来出本书吧。这确实是个让我兴奋的建议。最初，我觉得这是一本关于如何布置餐桌的书。对很多中国家庭来说，如何让饭菜更美味，甚至让厨艺更接近于专业厨师的水平都不在话下，但如何让一张餐桌美丽迷人，却是未曾思考过的领域。我想以我的经验告诉大家怎么去给一顿饭定下一个有趣的基调，怎么像杂志上的大片那样摆放餐具，还有鲜花。于是我开始以“专业”的态度去学习布置餐桌、摆放餐具、插花、拍摄，一丝不苟，力求完美。但当我拥有了很多“符合标准”的图片、很多“信达雅”的如教科书一般的文字时，我却忽然发觉，这些怎么反而不如我平时随便用手机拍摄的图片生动诱人？不如我胡乱写在帖子里的段落更有趣？会有人捧着这样一本书去按部就班地学习吗？我又凭什么让别人向我学习？生活并不是一门功课，我也没有资格做教师，我们需要的其实是爱、分享和乐趣，难道不是吗？

有趣的是，在意识到这些并开始反思的时候，我发现自己怀孕了。于是这本书的进程被暂停了整整三年，在这期间，我依然做饭，从给一个未见面的小胎儿做饭，到给一个婴儿、一个小女孩做饭。我还是喜欢呼朋唤友地在家里大摆家宴，和朋友一起聊天、喝下午茶，这个时候，女儿小叶子就在旁边，从躺着到坐着，从睁大眼睛看着到能伸出小手开心地摆弄餐桌上的花草、餐具。在这个过程中，我再没有去想过任何书本上教授的规则，也不再苛刻地要求自己做到完美——积木玩具可以上桌做装饰吗？为什么一定用鲜花而不是蔬菜？要照顾小孩，时间紧迫用自助的方式招待客人不是更好吗？从有条有理到毫无章法，我忽略了“对错”这个观念。一个早晨，我把一条羊毛大披肩铺在了桌上当桌布，摆上了并不配套但符合我当时心情的各种类型的花花草草图案的盘碟，食物有西式的面包、果酱、火腿，也有中式的八宝粥和摊小蛋饼，刚刚两岁的小叶子坐在她的儿童椅里，看着我忙忙碌碌地端盘摆碗，忽然喃喃自语地说：“妈妈弄得真漂亮！”

我想我真的是被感动了。连后来她撒娇不要自己吃饭都表示顺从。那顿早餐之后，我打开电脑上久违的文件夹，把之前写了一半的文字全部放弃。那些冷冰冰的餐桌礼仪，摆盘、插花的方法被一一放弃。我终于想明白了，我要和大家谈的不是简单的一张张美丽而空洞的餐桌，而是关于餐桌上欢乐的时光；不是一顿顿餐饭，而是一次次美丽的相聚；不是奢华晚宴的长桌上一丝不苟的花饰，而是清晨花园里采集来的带着露水的植物；更不是那些商务宴请上正襟危坐的绅士淑女，而是边聊天边烹饪，其乐融融的午后时光。这不是什么了不起的事，也不属于艺术范畴，更不是让人高不可攀的对昂贵餐具的炫耀，而是爱和给予，是一个个欢乐的餐桌故事。而用心布置这些餐桌，只是一个可以让我的朋友和家人快乐的方式，还有我自己。

对，就是这样。

2014 年 3 月 20 日

PART 1

不仅关于餐桌和美食，还关于爱

IT'S NOT ONLY ABOUT A DINING TABLE AND FOOD, IT'S ALSO ABOUT LOVE

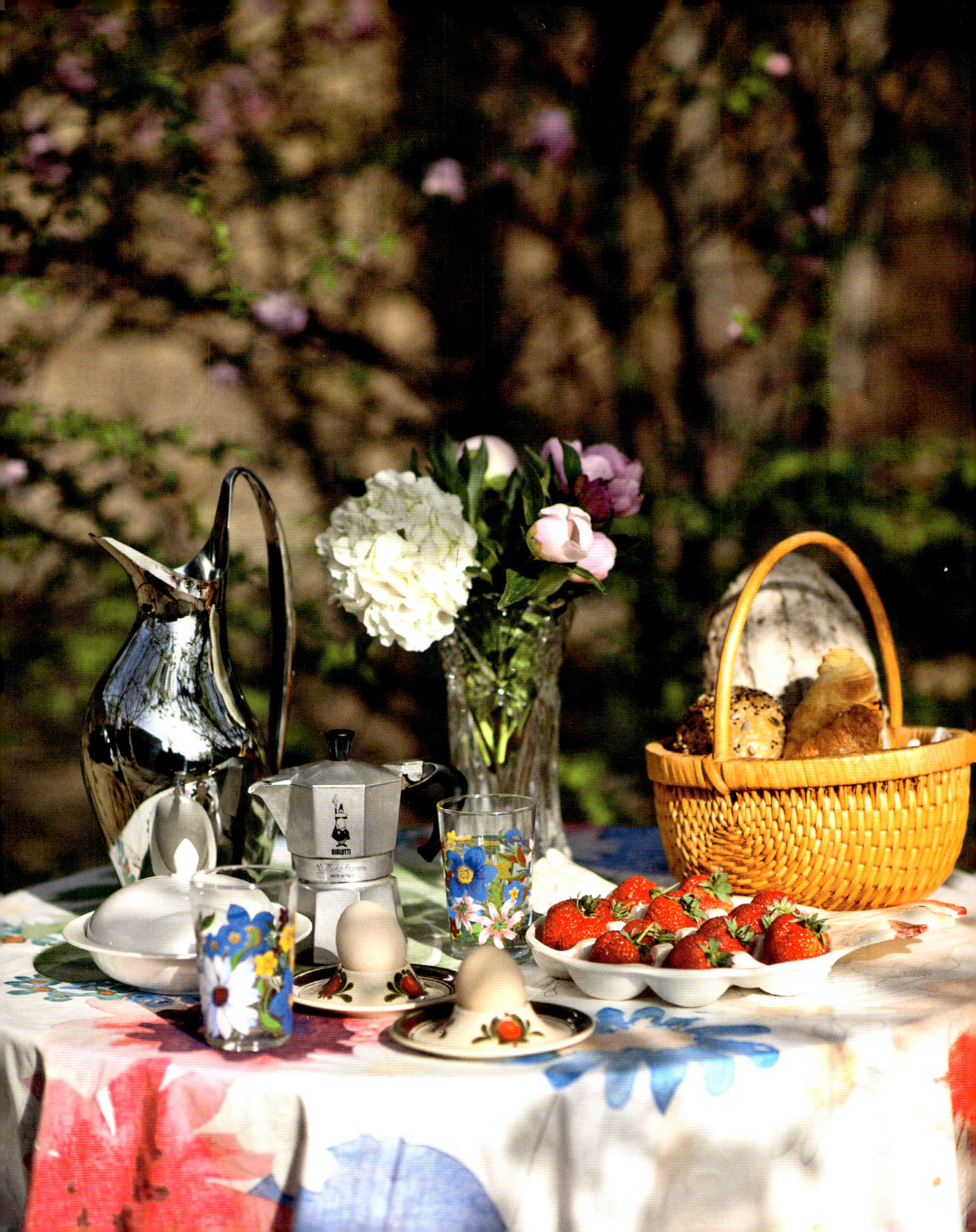
BIALETTI

多　出　来　的　清　晨

EARLY MORNING BLESSINGS

生活中的这些美好的细节和片段，都会久久地留在她的记忆深处，作为一种储备能量，在未来的某些岁月中，帮她抵御现实生活可能遇到的忧愁。

从花盆里剪下了两枝含苞待放的艳粉色芍药，搭配了一枝素色的绣球，插在水晶花瓶里，每片花瓣都吸附着清晨的阳光，美艳艳的、娇滴滴的，仿佛还沾着露珠儿。在这个乡下的小院里，正值春末天气。还有很多花——白玉兰的花瓣落了满地，雪一样；紫玉兰还在绽放，还有粉色的樱桃花、榆叶梅；梨花的花枝被压得低低地垂下，走过时，会被碰到脸颊。

这个清晨是从六点钟开始的。别人会因为休息日而睡个懒觉，但当了妈妈后，懒觉被剥夺了，索性让一天开始得更早。迎着浅灰色的晨曦准备周末的早餐，把前一晚泡好的各种谷物放进锅里煮粥，选美丽的桌布，挑喜欢的餐具，插好花、洗好水果，摆在盘子里，这时候小叶子刚刚睡醒。

◀ 尽管把喜欢的餐具拿出来使用，古董的、现代的、时髦的、乡村的，只要它们彼此气场相合。

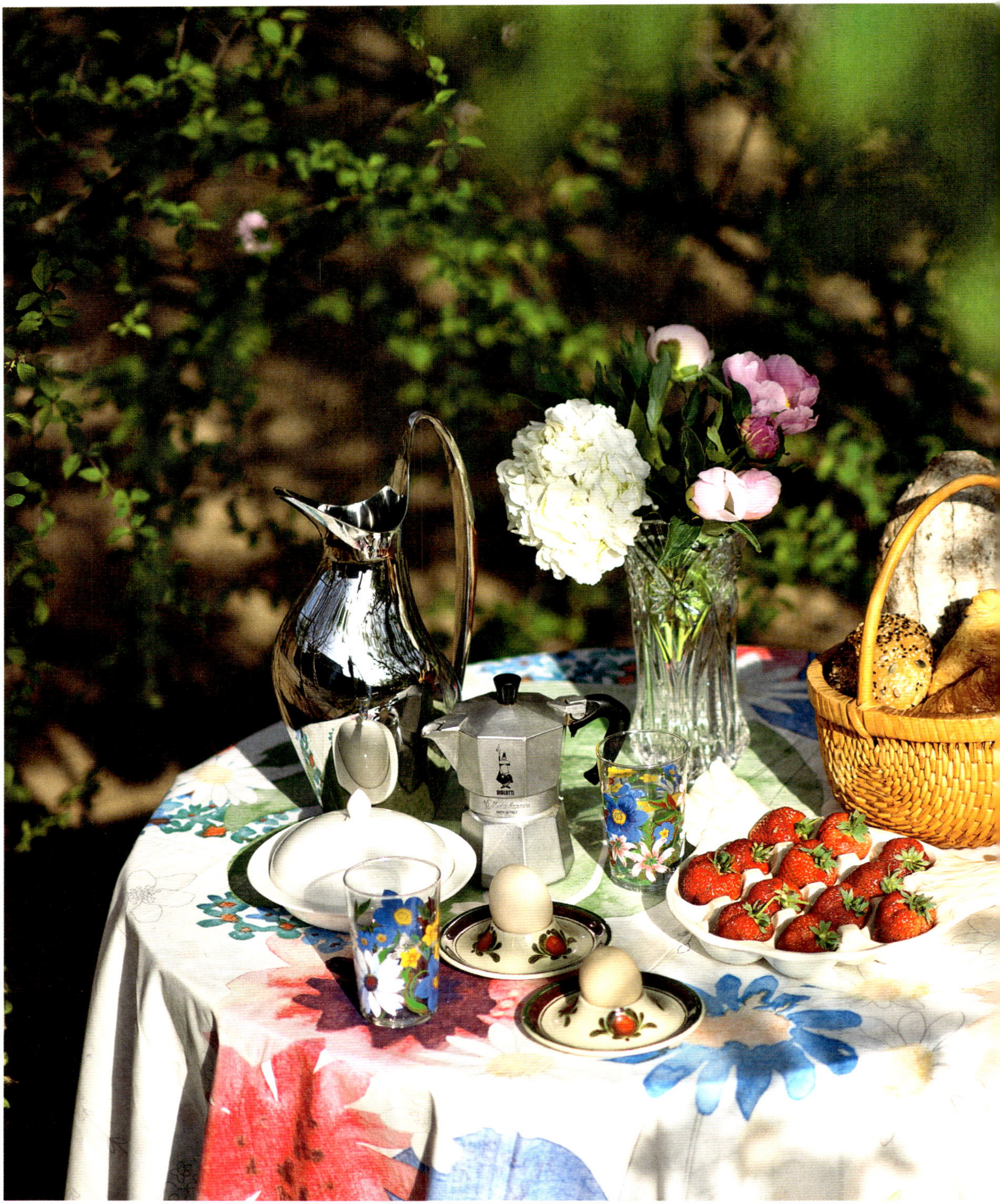

在乡下小院中的早餐桌，如水彩般流动的色彩自然融入花树间的氛围，在清晨带来愉悦的感受。

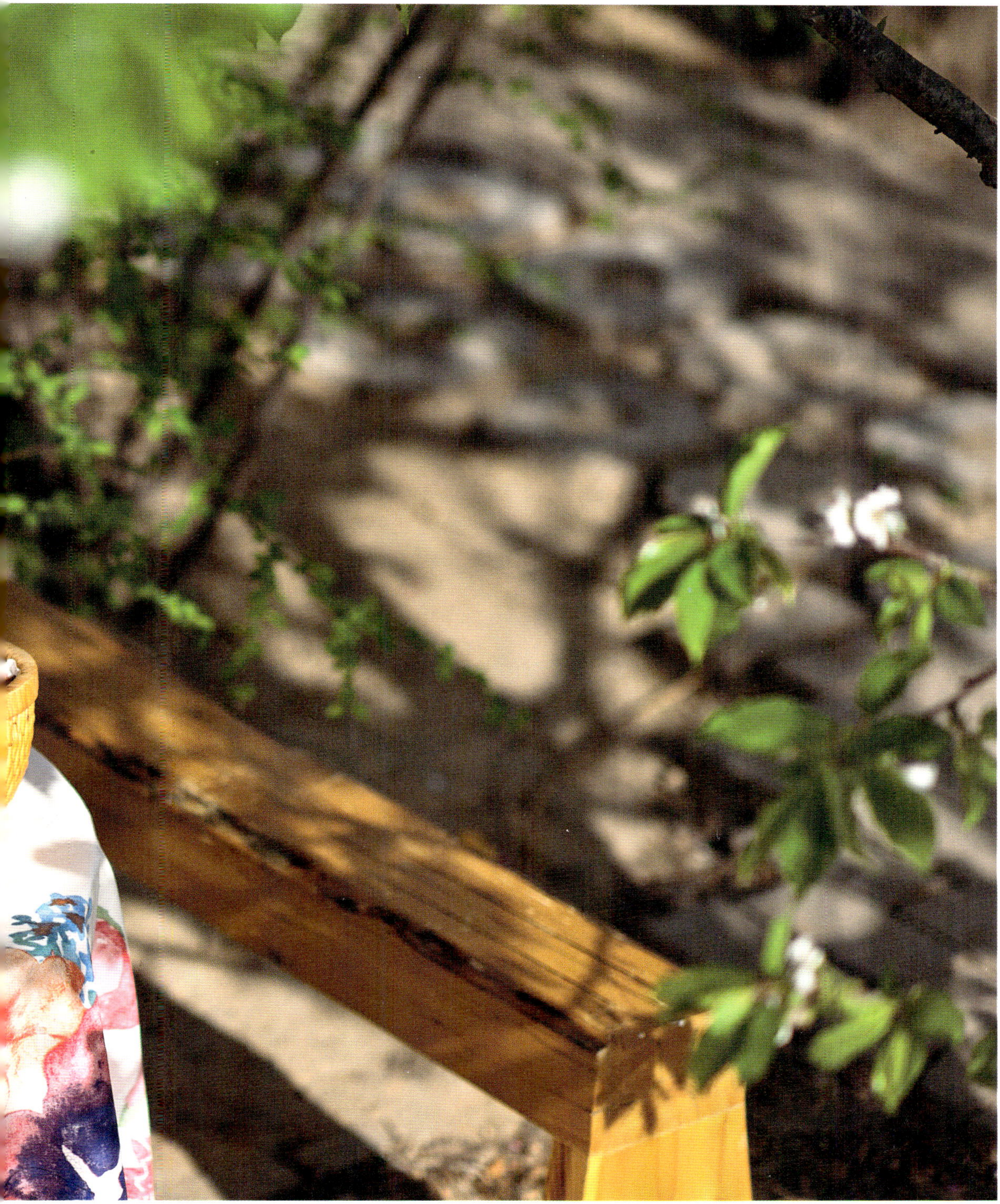

让两岁的小叶子起床变成越来越费时的事。她醒来，要吮着手指对你甜甜地笑，要咿咿呀呀地和你说说梦见了蚂蚁还是蜗牛，还要继续在床上打滚儿，要你躺下陪她，把小脚丫踢到天上，闪躲着和你玩耍，捉也捉不住。这样甜美的时光是赶着出门上班的日子所无法享受的。与她腻够了，慢慢起床，再去煎蛋、煮咖啡，把面包放进烤箱加热，或摊一摞松软的蛋饼，配上奶油和各种莓果。这时粥已经煮得糯糯的，飘出了香味，食物摆上餐桌，一家人的周末早餐正式开始。

女人都可以是天生的指挥家，让不同的音调汇集在同一个节奏上，眼观六路，从容周全。这也是像我们这样朝九晚没谱的职业女性被迫学会的“效率”，否则休假时光便只能混沌虚度了。在杂志上，我们总不厌其烦地追问那些成功女性，你是如何平衡生活和事业的?但实际上，真实的答案永远是顾此失彼。我们所能做到的最好的努力，就是让这一生的总账收支平衡，让孩子和家人的记忆中，存在有质量的陪伴和印象深刻的在一起的好时光。

而食物是最能留住记忆的。它总能轻易就把我带回到过去的岁月中——早餐中香喷喷的炒米饭配泡菜、白菜鸡蛋热汤面、一咬一口油的猪肉小笼包、脆得掉渣儿的油条。还有在厨房里，我站在妈妈腿旁，看着她把雪白的馒头切成片，裹上黄色蛋液，在锅里吱吱地炸出金灿灿的颜色。还有爸爸煮的豆浆，香味弥漫在空气中，他总是给我倒上热腾腾的一杯，看着我都喝下才安心……这些就像一扇门，只要一个熟悉的味道或相似的场景，就能解开密码，记忆立刻被打开，已经很遥远的昨天，就在这里。多年后，在我离开父母和我三个人组成的那个家庭后，无论是一个人生活，还是有了自己的家人，无论在什么样的房子里，是忧伤还是欢乐，窗外是阴雨还是艳阳，只要清晨可以坐在餐桌旁，喝一杯热热的豆浆或咖啡，吃一片面包或一颗水煮蛋，就觉得，一切都不会太糟。

在刚刚有女儿小叶子的时候，抱着那一团软软香香的小婴儿，不知为什么，脑子里也出现了一个早餐的画面——一家人围坐在桌前，玻璃瓶里有鲜榨的果汁，粗糙的陶瓷大扎壶里是牛奶，竹篮里有面包，彩陶大盘里有水果，那种充满明亮光线和爱意的画面，那种一家人在一起享受美味和清晨的感觉，就是我希望能给怀中的这个小女孩的。这其实和当年的我站在母亲腿边看她吱吱地炸着馒头片没有区别，我相信生活中的这些美好的细节和片段，都会久久地留在她的记忆深处，作为一种储备能量，在未来的某些岁月中，帮她抵御现实生活可能遇到的忧愁。

于是，每个周末，我都尽量“努力”地做早餐。所谓努力，并不是要在早餐桌上摆上如自助餐台那么丰盛的食物。在清晨，那些沾着露水的蔬果便是最美的。想象着果盘里将要摆出的颜色，红的、黄的、绿的，以及一个橙子被剥开时微妙的撕裂声和弥漫在空气里清香的味道，一颗鸡蛋在锅边被打破，摊在平底锅中渐渐凝固时发出的吱吱的声响，还有煮咖啡和烤面包的香气，若此时还有阳光，那便是完美。

就像此刻这个乡下小院里的清晨，空气中充满了花香，阳光透过树叶投下的影子，瞬息万变。坐在可爱的小桌旁，轻声地说着话儿，慢慢地吃着早餐，呷一口玻璃杯里冰凉的果汁，看着小叶子用小手灵巧地敲开她喜欢的水煮蛋。这时，太阳从云后出来了，牛油变得软软的，用刀刮上厚厚的一层，抹在微热的面包上。一只蜜蜂飞了过来，发出嗡嗡的声音。又一阵风吹过，满墙的花影都乱了。

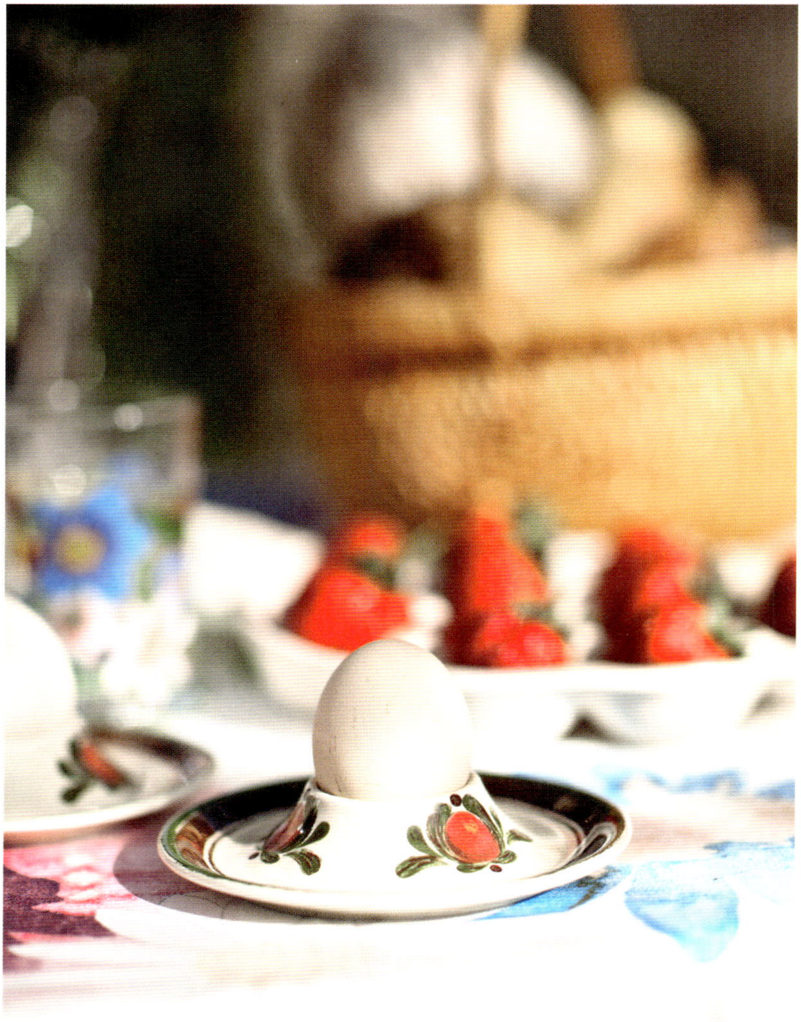

在旧货市场寻找一些好玩儿的东西，就像这对田园风格的德国老蛋托。

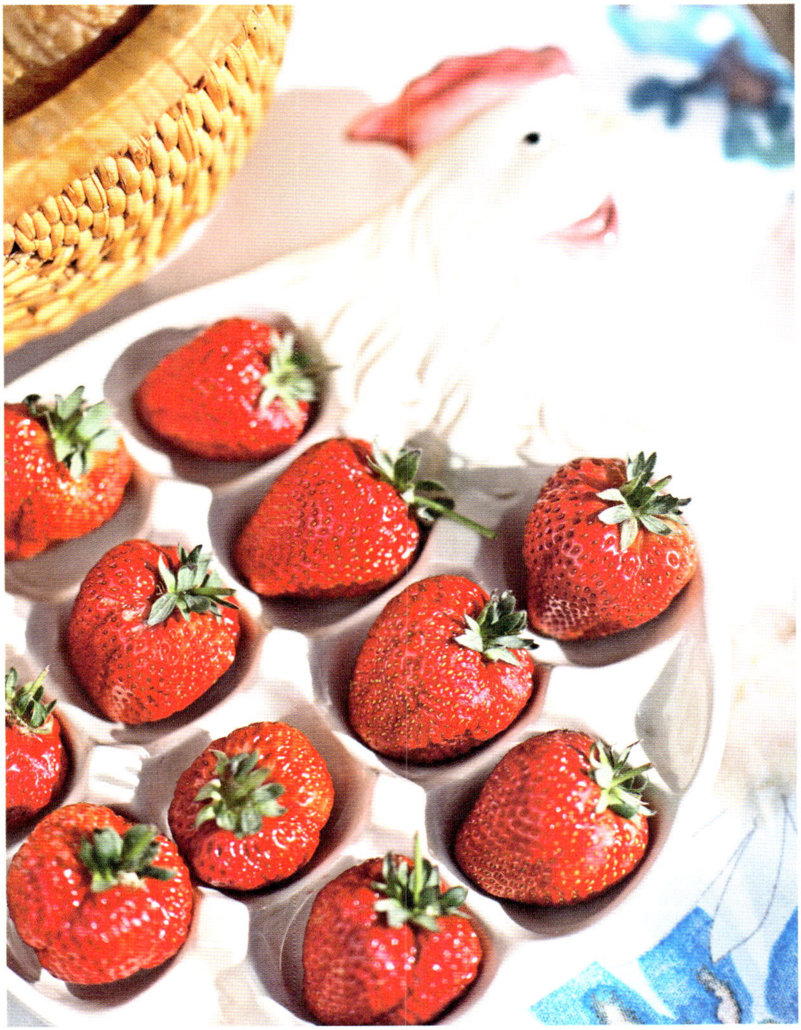

乡村氛围的点睛之笔，清晨听到公鸡叫……

花园里的早餐桌

BREAKFAST IN THE GARDEN

早餐桌的灵魂

对于早餐桌，桌布简直就是灵魂。你也许是简约派，只爱纯白，但这时不妨放宽一次原则，试试彩色的印花桌布，就像一个一生钟爱小黑裙的女人，也不妨碍她在清晨穿一袭印花丝缎的晨衣。特别要说的是，这里所说的桌布，不一定是真正的桌布，我曾用羊绒大披肩、旧的棉布格子床单以及钩花茶巾当过桌布，效果出奇的好。不必担心面料的色彩会抢了食物的风头，因为这时你的胃口绝对不会忽略食物的存在。或者，你可以像我一样，把印花面料反过来，用背面朦胧的色彩，也是一种不一样的味道。而餐巾的选择，要足够大，颜色尽量与桌布呈对比，这不光美观，还可以随时清理咖啡或茶渍以及面包屑。

轻松，还是要轻松

也许你从头一天晚上就开始准备布置餐桌了，为它花了很多时间和心思，但当家人揉着惺忪的睡眼走出卧室时，他的反应不应该是惶恐而手足无措地问你，家里是要来客人吗？最佳的反应是，发出欢快的轻呼，然后迅速跳到椅子旁坐下，用手去抓桌面上已经准备好的食物！

轻松、随意的美丽才是周末早餐的最佳氛围。把那些精致严谨、一丝不苟的风格留到晚宴去吧。选那些很田园的、自然的、柔软的装饰，让一切看上去漫不经心。你甚至可以把任何你喜欢的东西都摆出来，那些从跳蚤市场淘来的古老的瓷器杯盘、复古的搪瓷茶壶、旅行带回的陶瓷罐子、乡村的竹篮……当然，加入一些现代感的东西会显得更有细节。精致时髦的加上古老怀旧的，粗糙的加上细腻的，让它们在对比中和谐共处的关键是，保持所有物品的色调和质地呼应和统一，风格相融。

别嫌麻烦，多做一步

把买来的食物去掉那些讨厌的塑料包装，摆放在美丽的盘子中，把成包的麦片分装进玻璃杯，把果汁倒进精致的水罐，把果酱挤入玻璃小瓶，这些小动作并不多此一举，它能让一切看起来更像home made（自制），让普通的食物显得更精致美味，而且气氛更温馨。

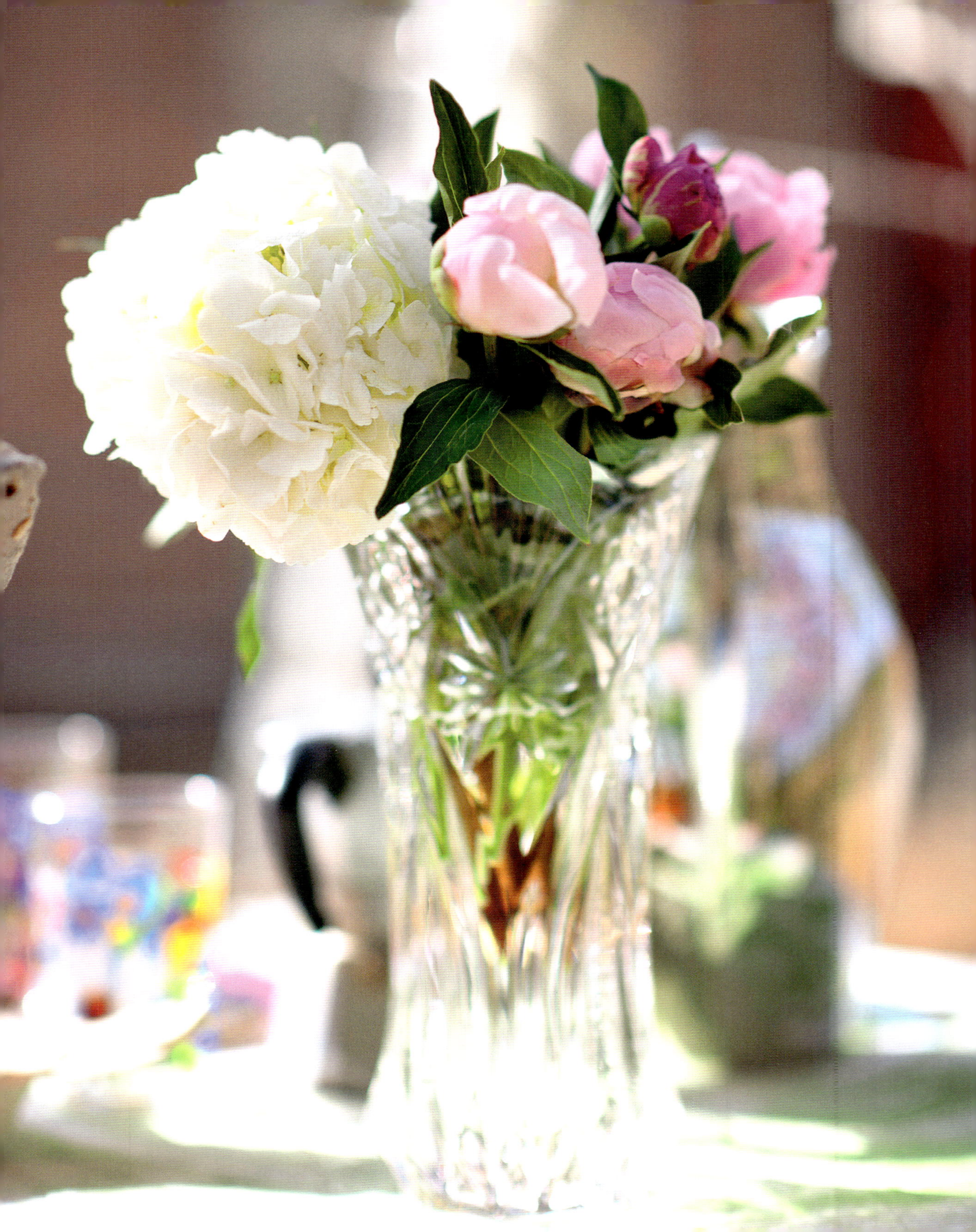

那一把清新的花束

随手从花园里采来的带着点滴晨露的花朵是布置早餐桌最好的选择。当然，清晨常有但花园不常有，不如去花市选一些简单的花朵吧，比如小雏菊，比如芍药和绣球。和其他花相比，这三种花更有清晨的感觉，非常清新，而且它们仿佛会吸附阳光，每片花瓣都跟着阳光的变化而变幻。与其相对，那些个性张扬的花朵不太适合出现在早餐桌上，同样，也不用费很多心思和时间去做插花，工艺过于精致的造型反而失去了早晨慵懒的感觉。

◀ 选择花卉不必追求名贵、奇特，新鲜娇艳的花朵最适合早餐桌。

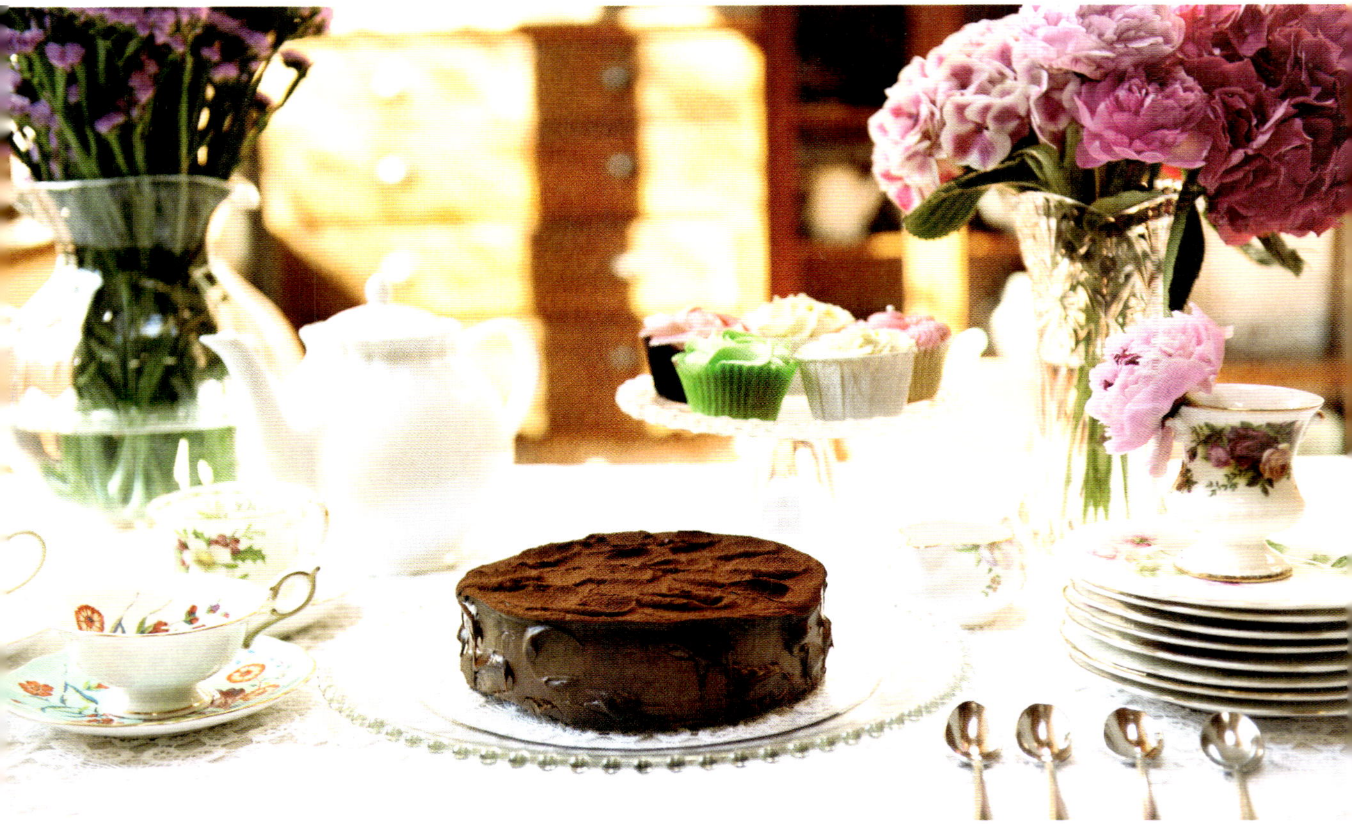

下午茶是和朋友聊天欢聚最便捷的形式。拿出你收藏的最漂亮的瓷器，摆放上美丽的花朵，还有精致的点心，还有什么能比这更轻松惬意呢？

那一场风花雪月的茶

A GLORIOUS AFTERNOON TEA

“一杯茶和一块点心，能解决所有的烦恼。”

影片《了不起的盖茨比》（*The Great Gatsby*, 2013）让人印象深刻的一个情节是，盖茨比为了和已为人妇的昔日情人黛西见面，搬运来了“全城的鲜花”，布置了花园般令人惊讶的环境。巨大而奢华的蛋糕，精致无比的银质茶具，屋外大雨倾盆，他紧张地等待着时钟的指针指向下午四点，每一秒都是一下重重的心跳，真的像那首英国老民谣所唱：“当下午钟敲四下，世上的一切瞬间为茶而停。”只是这里应该改成：“当下午钟敲四下，世上的一切瞬间为你而停。”所有极致夸张的形式感，往往是为了表达某种难以言说的情愫，这让他们多年后精心策划的邂逅充满了戏剧性和伤感的味道。而让我感到伤感的是，我一直想找到一个和影片里一样古典的银茶漏，有着精致的雕花和优雅圆润的弧线，但踏遍了各种店铺却久久求之不得。

说起如影片中这般经典的英式下午茶，要追溯到第七世贝德芙公爵夫人安娜。她会寄出手写的邀请函，请朋友和她一起享受下午在花园中的美好时光，用一些简单的甜点、蛋糕和涂了黄油的面包打发午餐到晚餐之间的空虚时光，由此揭开了风靡于世的下午茶的序幕。而真正推波助澜，让这种英伦下午茶变为集合礼仪、插花、品茶和茶点于一体的文化的，是维多利亚女王，她的热爱和推动，让 Afternoon Tea（下午茶）经过几十年的演变和丰富，进入了全盛时代。“二战”之后，随着人们生活方式的改变，下午茶的仪式被简化了，茶壶改成了茶杯，茶叶改成了袋泡茶。因而，茶漏和茶巾这样的物件，也渐渐变得不多见了。就连我牛津大学历史系毕业的同事都说，Paper Doily（茶巾，一般是蕾丝制成或钩成的装饰织物，用在下午茶的茶桌上）这个词已经不是出生于 20 世纪 80 年代的英国人所熟悉的了，是老奶奶时代的词语。而有趣的是，恰恰是在这一代年轻人中，下午茶的整套程序和仪式感又重新成为了时髦，这应该说是件好事，因为这是一种简单易得的幸福和娱乐。这样的形式也可以让忙碌的人们变得精致且慢节奏一点。

盖茨比紧盯着时钟的指针一点一点指向下午四点，黛西分秒不差地如约而至。这个时间是传统英式下午茶最正点的时间。开始得过早，会让人觉得你没吃饱，而过晚，又让人觉得你很饿了，这真是个微妙的节点，也是“下午茶”和“傍晚茶”这两件不同的事在时间上的一个重要区别。Afternoon Tea 也称为 Low Tea，其名字源于上流社会通常会将优雅的下午茶摆在花园的回廊里，用低矮的（Low）茶几摆放食物。像盖茨比所准备的那样，Afternoon Tea 会用银质茶壶泡茶，搭配甜品、司空、奶油和果酱，在去皮白面包或黑面包薄片上涂上黄油，里面夹着黄瓜片、鸡蛋或肝酱等。另外一种 High Tea（傍晚茶）则是指在较高的餐桌上进行的 Meat Tea（有肉食的茶点），它是三餐的一部分，源自英国北部的蓝领和劳工阶层。对他们而言，傍晚茶等于一天劳动后晚餐前的加餐，甚至等于晚餐，通常在下午五六点进行，食物包括肉类、土豆、面包、馅饼、奶酪、蔬菜、茶等等。这和我们所说的“下午茶”是两个完全不同的概念。

纯正主义者还会严格地认为，下午茶的茶应该仅限于印度茶或中国茶。点心也会谨慎地按照传统三层点心盘从上而下分别摆放水果挞和杯子蛋糕、司空、黄瓜三明治。就连配司空的奶油，也必须是德文郡奶油。不过，即使在英国，如此恪守传统的老派绅士和淑女也所剩无几了，现代人更喜欢随性发挥，给传统加入新鲜的元素，让下午茶变得更轻松有趣。我经常会在下午沏上两三种茶，伯爵红茶、中国绿茶、花草茶，或是自己用金橘、玫瑰、蜂蜜、薄荷等组合搭配出的有意思的私房茶。再准备上几种点心，除了传统的那些，也会有自己烤的巧克力布朗尼、黄油桃酥，或是咸味的橄榄油小番茄配很薄的面包片或脆饼，甚至中式的糕饼或茶点。当然还要摆上最应季的鲜花做装饰，用我钟爱的 Wedgwood（韦奇伍德）茶具，还有古董的手绘点心盘。哦，对了，必须提一下，后来我一个久居欧洲的朋友终于在一家古董店里遇到了一个和《了不起的盖茨比》里几乎一模一样的银茶漏，有着精致的雕花和优雅圆润的弧线，并有着一百多年的历史，这份难得而珍贵的礼物圆了我这个“不纯正”的人一个纯正的细节梦。

与此相仿的银茶漏，我还在一个叫玛蒂娜的德国老太太家见过。那是我第一次去欧洲，有幸到她家吃下午茶。玛蒂娜的头发雪白，穿着质地很好的灰绿色印花亚光丝绸连衣裙和奶油色开司米开衫，涂着精致完美的红色唇膏。她坐在茶桌前的木椅上，动作悠缓，指挥着她的女儿——一位五十多岁的杂志女主编，一一从她如宝藏一般的茶具柜里取出那一刻她心目中最合适的瓷器。“Royal Albert（皇家阿尔伯特），对，就是它，不，不要 Old Country Rose，它对这位姑娘来说太老气了，Polka Rose 才是她的。”她喃喃

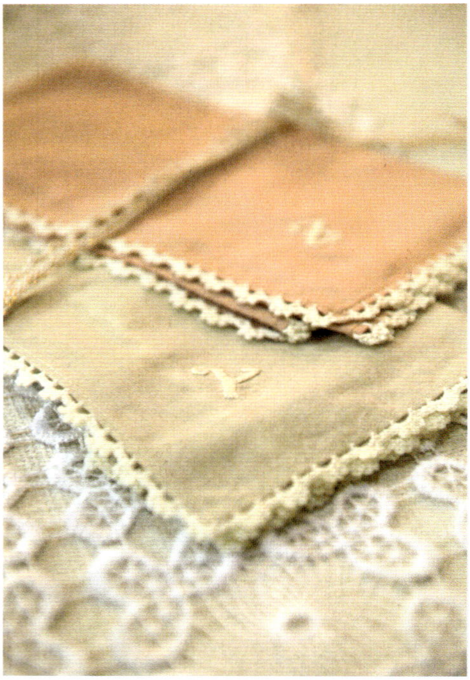

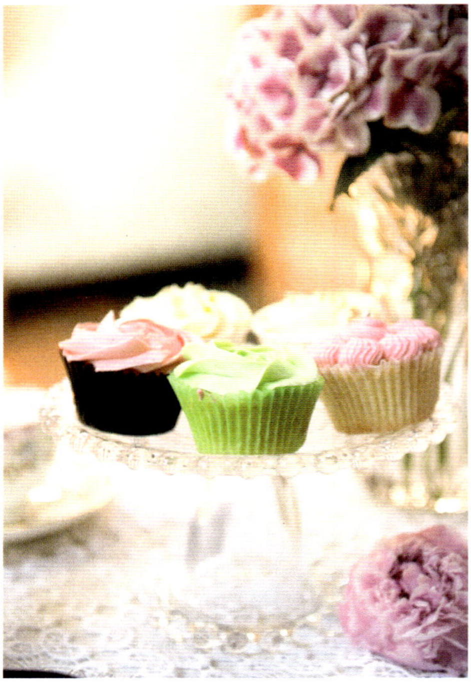

带蕾丝边的亚麻小餐巾可以对折使用，也可以叠成三角形。

大多数时候，下午茶用不着摆放三层点心盘那么隆重，各种漂亮的杯子蛋糕就足够营造气氛。

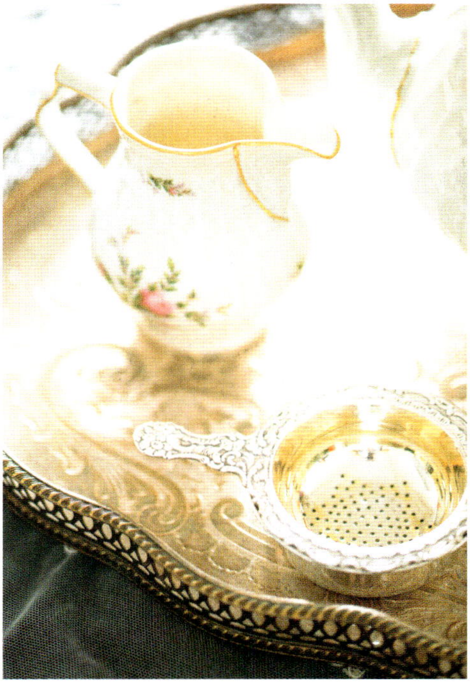

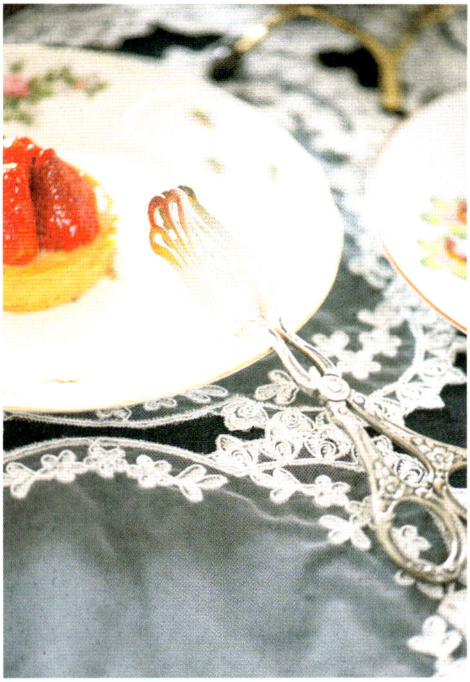

这个银茶盘来自英国，而茶漏来自北欧，不同历史背景的物件聚在一起，本身就是有趣的事情。

像这样从欧洲古董商店淘来的银质点心夹，非常能给下午茶的餐桌增添亮点。

地念叨，“你看，这餐巾上的蕾丝花边是从我母亲的一套大裙子上剪下来的，这是我为了纪念她特地做的，她最喜欢饮茶。”老太太津津乐道地给我讲她的每一样物品的典故，还有盘子里的点心——只有在三条街之外拐角那家法国人开的面包房卖的这种司空才最香甜、软硬适度。老太太泡上一壶阿萨姆红茶，在杯子上架上一个同样雕刻着花纹的古典的银茶漏，然后将茶水缓缓地倒入茶杯之中，麦芽香和蜂蜜、玫瑰的气息瞬间充溢在空气中。她往茶杯中加了牛奶和糖块，并示意我试试搭配奶酪会有最好的效果。“你太年轻了，可能还顾不上坐下喝茶。你想和任何人交谈，哪怕是女王，都可以从一杯茶开始……”老太太像是在和自己说话，“是的，一杯茶和一块点心，能解决所有的烦恼。”

▶ 我喜欢收集花卉图案的茶杯，并将不同品牌和年代的茶杯混合在一起使用。

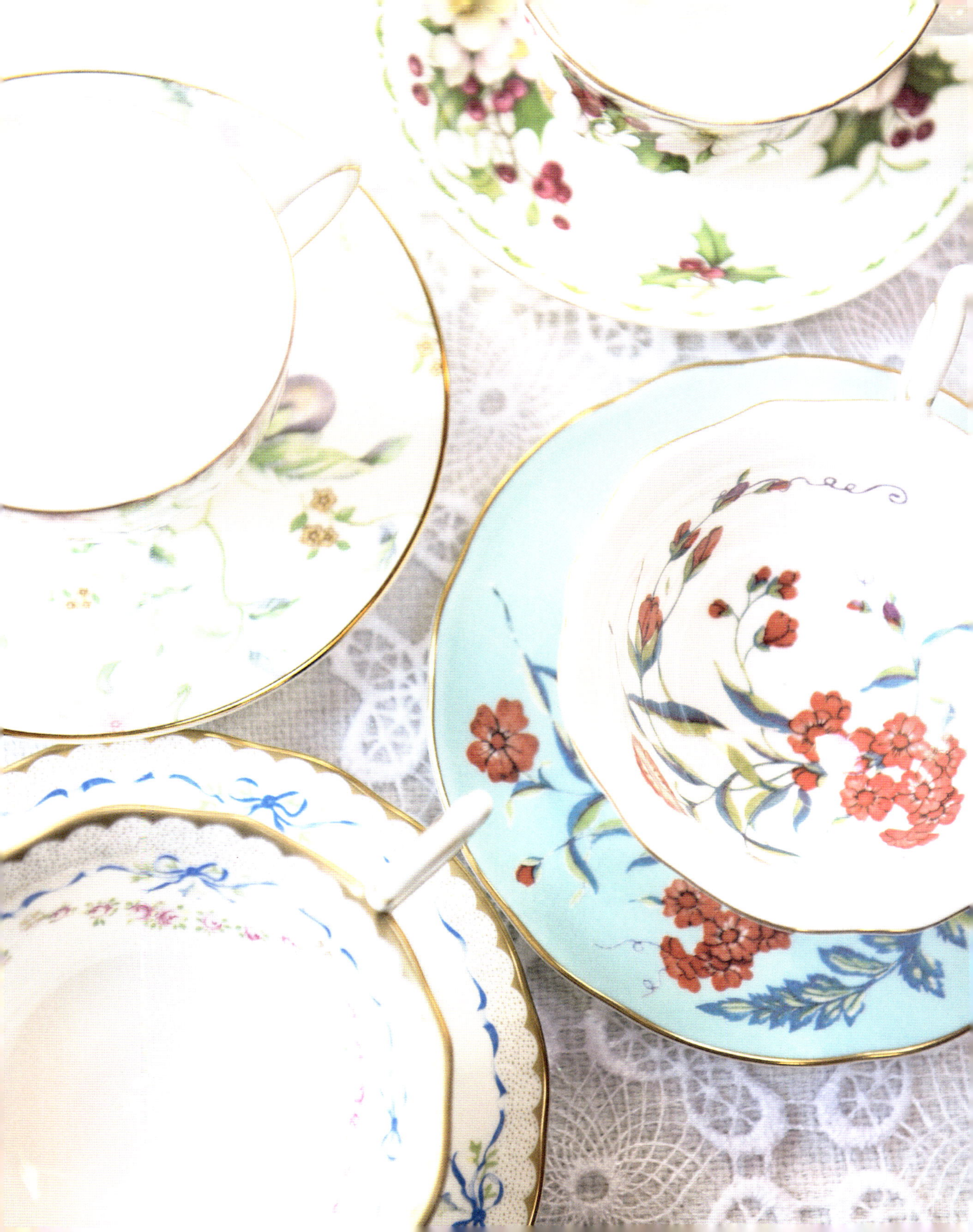

复古优雅的下午茶餐桌

HOW TO DECORATE A VINTAGE TEA TABLE

混搭的乐趣

一个复古的下午茶餐桌可以说是餐桌布置中最精致最有乐趣的部分。你可以有机会展示你所有美丽的收藏，包括精美的茶具、饰有蕾丝的餐巾、晶莹剔透的香槟杯、骨质或珊瑚镶嵌把柄的甜品刀叉等等。完美的布置可以让下午茶充满风花雪月的浪漫，也提供了一个让人们彼此敞开心扉认真交流的绝好时机。

复古的下午茶餐桌从不介意茶具是否成套。你可以从跳蚤市场上寻来漂亮的古董茶杯、瓷盘或细脚香槟杯，也可以在小店或国外的拍卖商店里寻来祖母时代的钩花茶布、银质点心叉或一把维多利亚式的茶壶，甚至可以DIY（自己动手做）饰有蕾丝的餐巾，并用喜欢的小花枝和丝带做装饰……你需要精心维护的只是各种物件之间统一的色调：柔美的粉色、褪色的丁香色、白色和奶油色是最受欢迎的下午茶“愉悦色调”。当你为客人斟上一杯香茶时，和大家细细分享这些宝贝得来的故事以及布置的巧思，也是打开话题的最佳方式。

▶ 有人说，如果下午茶用袋泡茶而不是茶叶，那是“假高级”，但如果用茶叶，记得一定要有一个茶漏配合。

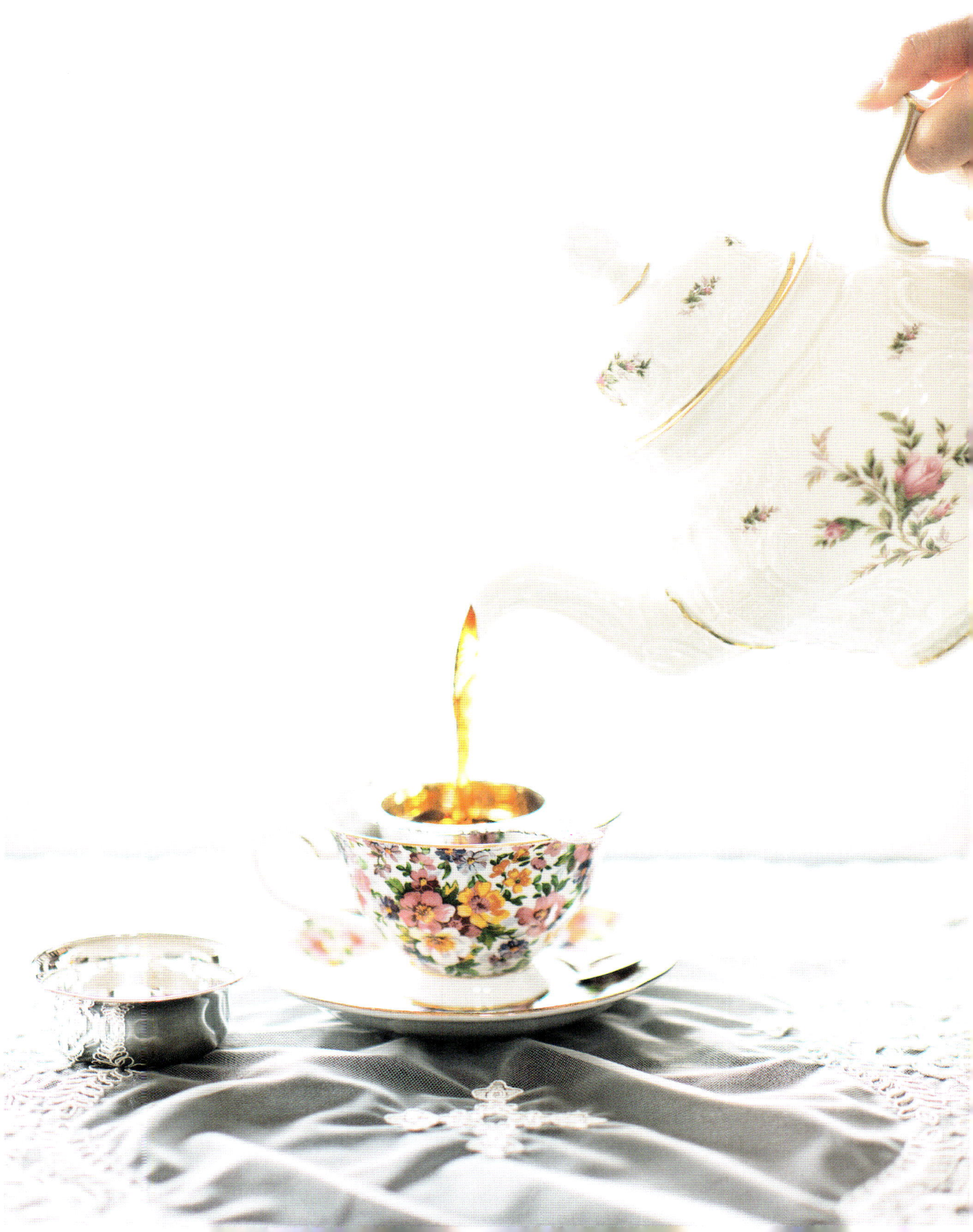

鲜花是主角

下午茶餐桌上可以没有洗手碗或三层点心盘，但绝不能缺少鲜花。无论是水晶玻璃花瓶还是陶瓷罐子或银质水壶，都是很好的花器。

花材就选市场上最应季的花朵吧，让人感受到时节本身就是一种时髦。在我心目中的“最适合白天的花朵”排行榜上，绣球一直名列第一。无论是在早餐桌上，还是有关下午茶的记忆里，都有绣球的身影，斜插一枝在水晶花瓶中，和精美的骨瓷杯碟相映成趣，让下午时光格外美好。

注意细节

虽然不必恪守百分之百的传统礼仪、程序和摆放规则，但有一些细节是如同“喝汤不能出声”一样，属于教养和礼貌的范畴，需要被了解和遵守。比如茶杯和茶托是一体的，别让它们分开；茶勺要放在茶托上，千万别用来一勺一勺舀着喝茶（或咖啡）；小巧的三明治应该用手直接取食，但记住用前三根手指吃东西，而不是用全部五根手指，更不要卖弄风情地翘起你的小指。如果想优雅地吃掉一个司空，首先用手将司空从中间一掰两半，然后用公用匙往托盘里舀一勺果酱和一勺奶油。掰下一口大小的司空，用你的个人茶点刀在上面涂抹一些果酱和奶油。吃的时候，茶点刀要放在盘子边缘。

另外，餐桌上可以有很多你喜欢用的瓷器物件，但基础的餐具标配你也需要了解一

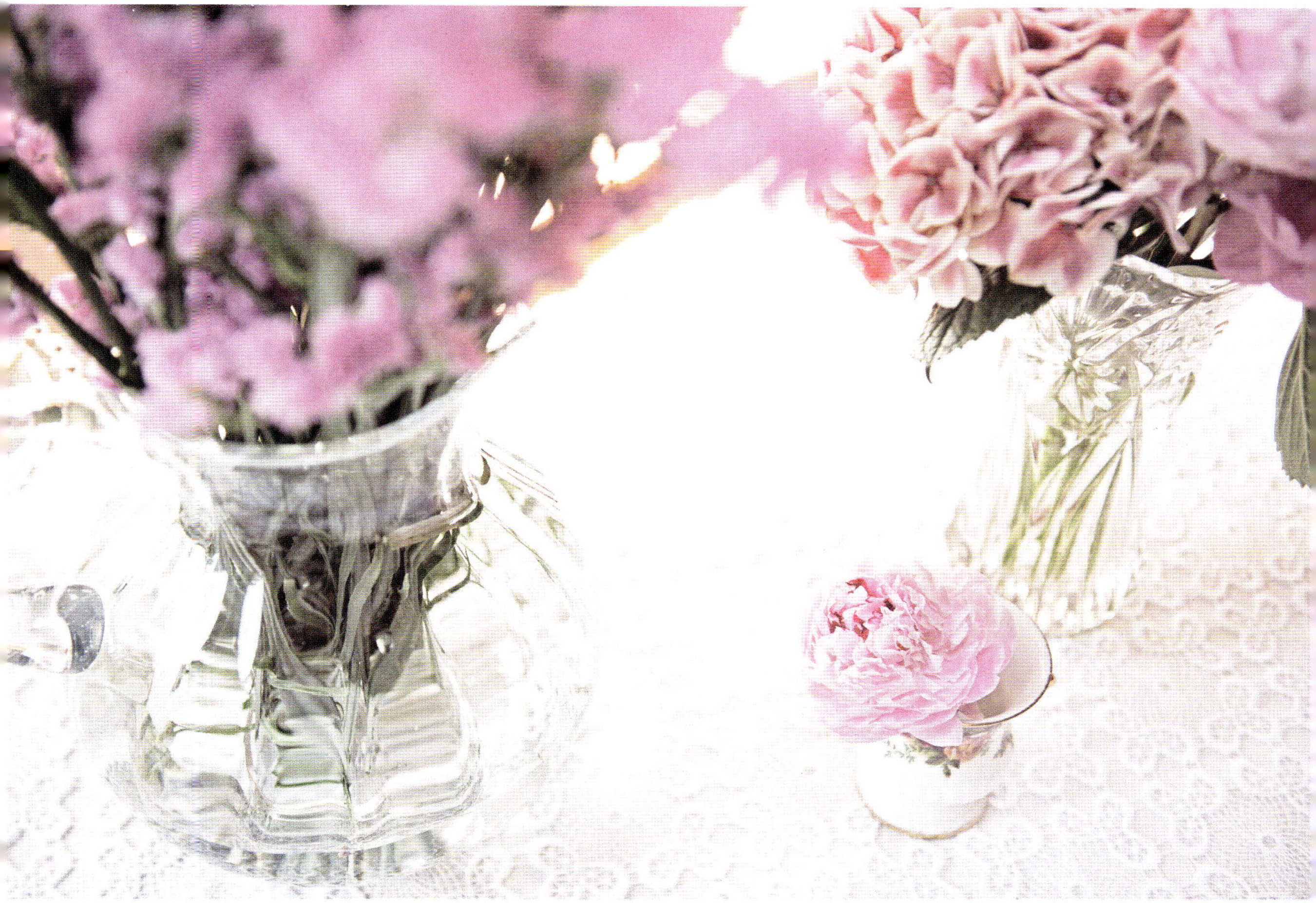

如果你拿不定主意选什么样的花来布置茶桌，就统统选粉色系的花朵，浅粉色、丁香色、白色，是下午茶桌上永远欢迎的颜色。

下：每个人面前有一个甜点盘、一套茶杯茶托、一把茶匙、一把糕点叉、一把用来切司空的茶点刀和一小块折成三角形的小餐巾（有蕾丝就更完美了）。茶具托盘中有茶壶、茶漏、茶叶、装着方糖的糖碗、糖钳、装着牛奶的牛奶壶、放置柠檬片的小容器以及用来取柠檬片的小叉子。这些都是在客人到来之前摆放在餐桌上的，而茶壶则是等客人就座之后，再端上餐桌的。

冲泡中国绿茶，讲究的是用 85℃左右的热水冲泡，而各种红茶则需要用滚开的沸水冲泡。过夜水和千沸水都会影响茶的口感。往茶里添加牛奶是英式传统，即茶杯中先倒入茶，再添加牛奶，这里的牛奶最好是全脂奶，才能带出红茶更香浓的味道。

女主人的魅力

即使你吃饭穿衣都有佣人伺候，但下午茶和性生活一样，需要你亲自参与打理。这里面有一个小典故，用中国茶招待客人在 17 世纪的英国绝对是炫富的重要表现。那时的英国名媛贵妇们都备有一把精致的小钥匙，用来开启茶叶箱，即使泡茶，也一定由女主人亲自主持，以防仆人偷走茶叶。这个传统流传下来，虽然茶叶不再金贵，但这却成了女主人显示其风范和对客人尊重的基本形式。

走吧，野餐去！

LET'S GO FOR A PICNIC!

藤编的篮子、格子花布，再装上满满的食物。
天气阴晴不定，也许会有阵雨。
阵雨就阵雨吧，正好躲到树下，听听雨丝敲
打树叶的声音。

我认识一对酷爱野餐的夫妇，他们会仅仅因为下午刚出炉的点心格外香甜，便兴奋地从冰箱里拿出奶酪，带上切好的蔬果，调好拌沙拉的酱汁装在小玻璃瓶里，冲出门去。在路过青龙桥三岔口的西贝莜面村时打包上一份《舌尖上的中国》里提到的传奇的黄馍馍和凉皮、酸奶，在颐和园五点停止售票前的临界点冲入北如意门，沿着西堤漫步，看昆明湖上的晚霞，在小山坡上野餐，直到闭园才离开，美美地享受清清静静的小时光。

野餐就是这样，无论是去海边、树林、河畔，还是只在家附近公园里的草地上，揽上藤篮，说走就走。没有要求，没有难度，只要有美味的食物和好心情、好天气，就足够了。

即便是在北京，在春天沙尘暴、夏日桑拿天，还有雾霾和污染的夹缝中，我们一样享有野餐的乐趣。确实，我们生活在不那么美好的环境中，但如果你不打算马上离开这

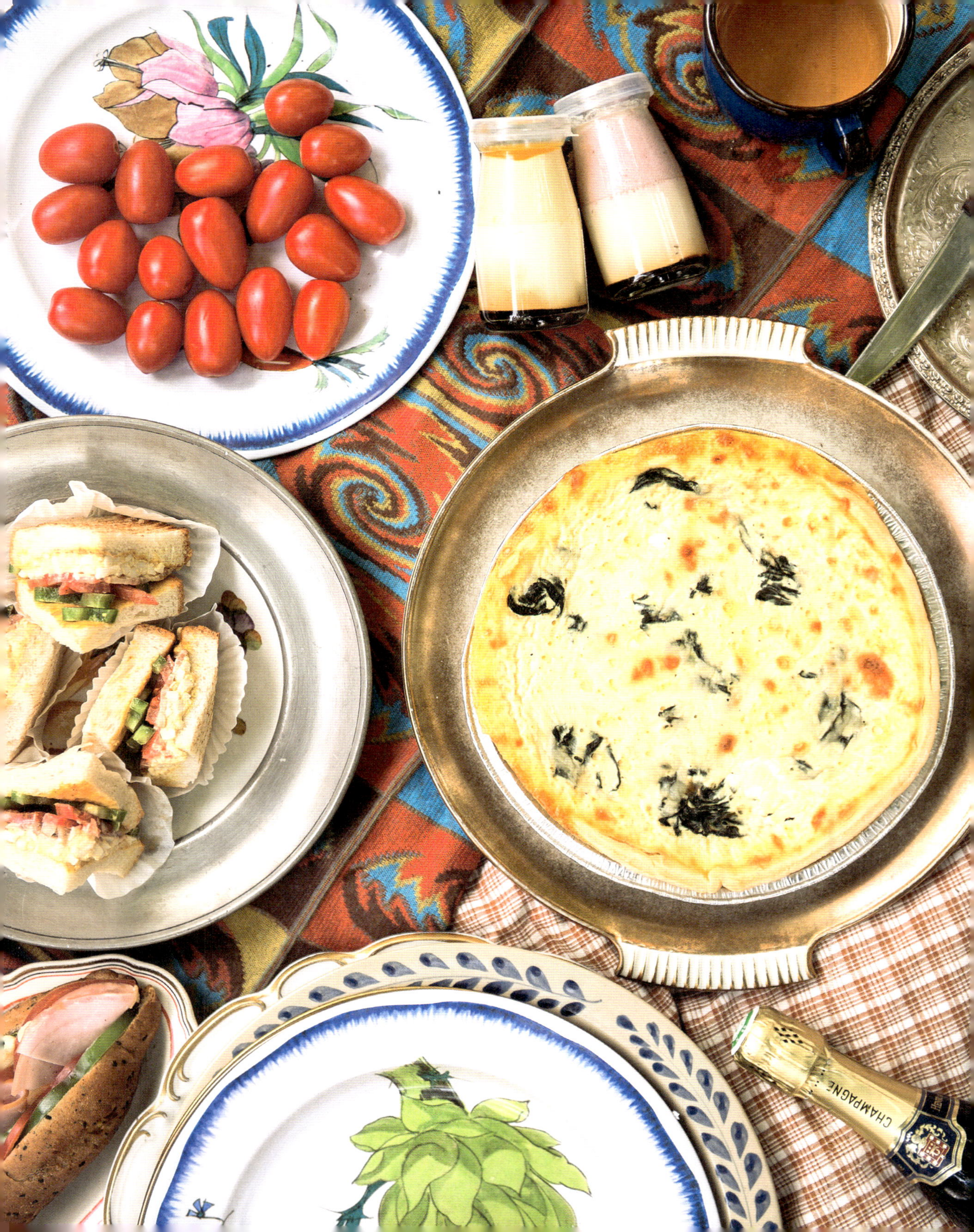
CHAMPAGNE

座城市，就必须找到它的可爱之处，否则，了无生趣。就像丰子恺先生所言：“你若爱，生活哪里都可爱。你若恨，生活哪里都可恨……既然无处可躲，不如傻乐。既然无处可逃，不如喜悦。”

颐和园便是这样一个让人喜悦的地方。三四月，柳条返青，草色渐绿。昆明湖的水波早就荡开了，满满一池，温柔沉静。此时，把野餐布铺在湖畔的大草地上，一边喝着去年冬天自家酿的玫瑰草莓小酒，一边吃着酱肉、烤鸡肉卷，还有用春天刚刚摘下的嫩菠菜苗、小黄瓜和圣女果做成的沙拉和糯糯的新豌豆做成的饭团子，一边体会着春日的颐和园——从“草色遥看近却无”到“嫩蕊商量细细开”，再到“满园深浅色，照在绿波中”，这些诗句会慢慢从心底忆起，就像那些含苞待放的花枝，等待着一个被开启的讯息。

到了六月的下旬，夏日气息浓烈到了极致。天长而夜短，暑气升腾。不过这也是荷花盛开的好季节。一定要早起，四五点出门一点不过分。趁着清晨的凉意，骑车到圆明园，无论是从绮春园宫门还是从长春园东门进入园内，都可以立即欣赏到满池的荷花。这次不一定提野餐篮了，可以用一个轻便的中式或日式印花布制成的小包裹，带上易泡杯和小茶碗，再带几样点心，稻香村的就不错，还有装着滚开热水的老式保温瓶。湖畔赏荷花，喝茶吃点心，在暑气和人潮上来前迅速离开，美好的一天都会留有那份挥之不去的清香。

北京最好的时候，是九月到十一月之间。天气也仿佛像这里人的性格，绝不拖泥带水，

◀ 用充满田园风格的陶瓷和搪瓷器皿盛放食物，可以使这些简单的食物带给人更丰富的愉悦享受。

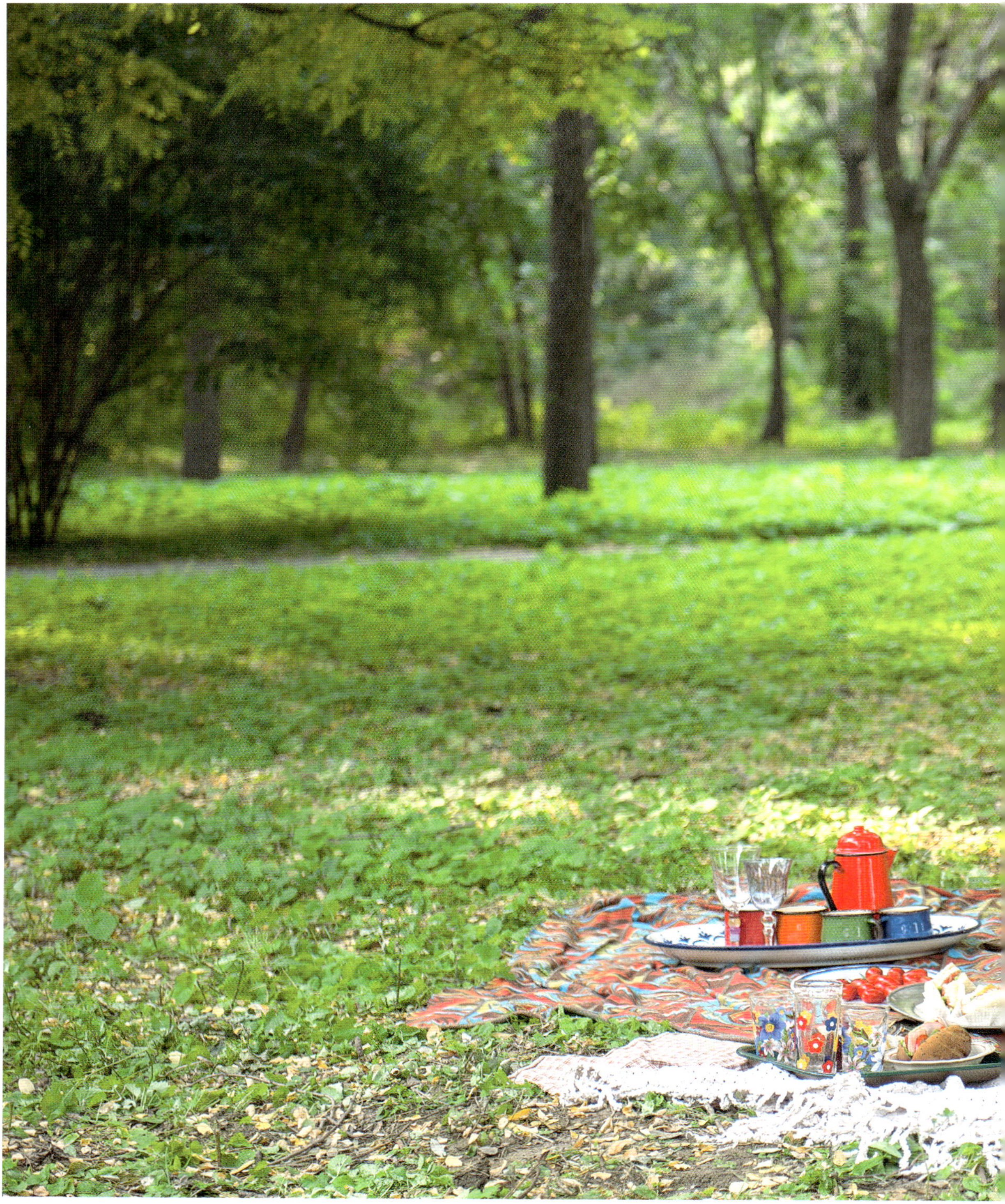

在铺满落叶的林间草地上野餐，选择的色调也是秋叶般的红褐色

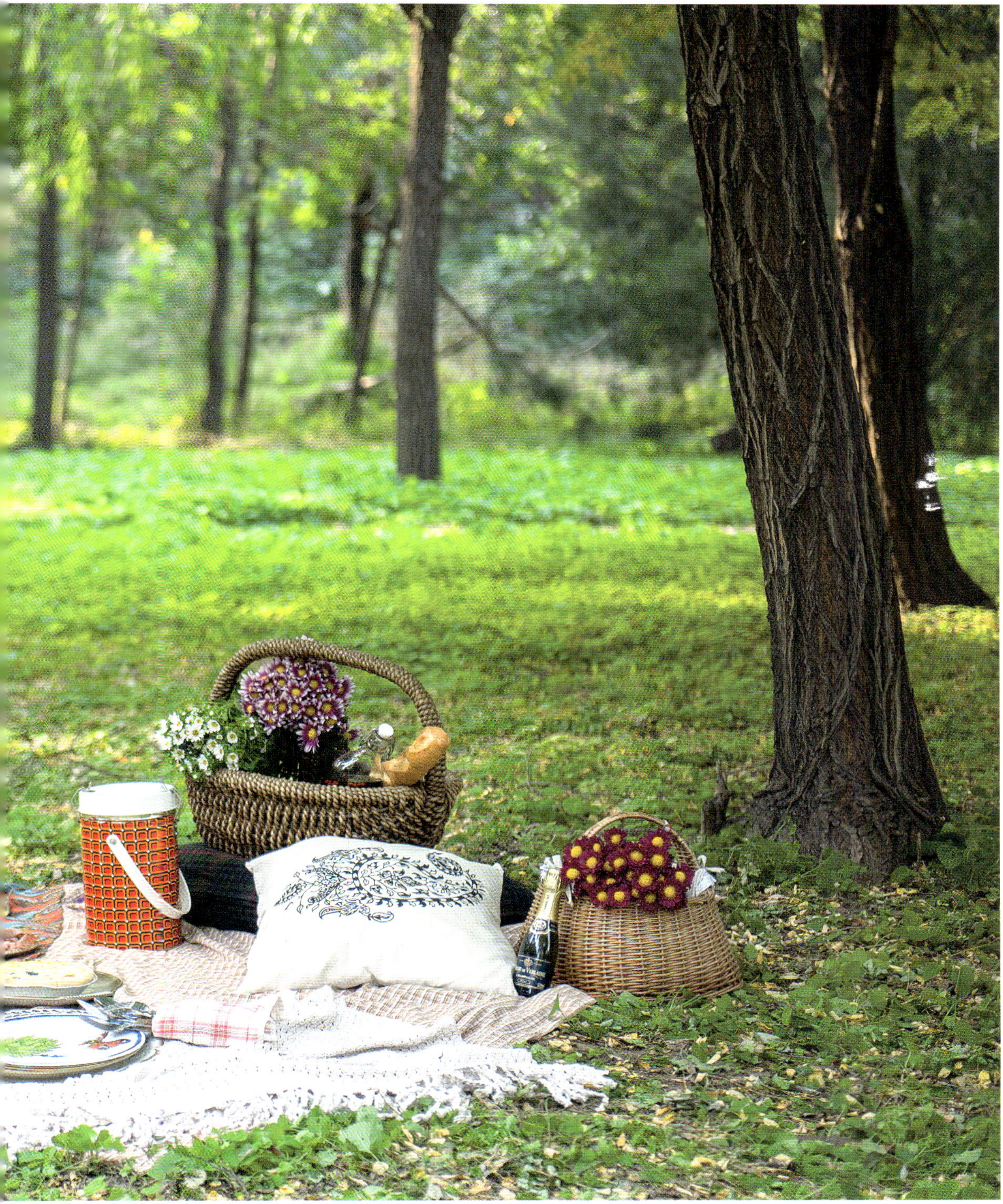

暑气说没就没了，又可以抓紧时间到户外去大肆野餐了，这一切完美得仿佛寒冷来临前的恩赐。到菜市场里挑一些这个季节特有的水果，像玫瑰香葡萄、柿子还有大枣，这些水果香甜得能让人直接回到童年。还有刚收获的南瓜、栗子、红薯，无论是煮一锅浓浓的奶油南瓜汤放进保温桶，还是来一款松软的栗子蛋糕或简单的烤红薯干儿，这些秋日的食物都会让人幸福感爆棚。另外，那些高热量的美味也名正言顺地拿出来“御寒”吧，香浓起司球、红糖香蕉玛芬、核桃酥、巧克力布朗尼，还有炸猪肉丸子、酱牛肉，或是一份鳗鱼饭，带着它们去金山岭或黄峪口登山赏叶，看被秋色遍染的树木、山坡和湖水，那份静美和绚烂让人如临画境。我曾去过黄花城那一段水长城，长城断壁苍凉，下面是水库的碧波，如果赶上雨水丰润，满满的水会漫过堤坝，轰然泄入千尺之下低洼的溪槽。可以赤足沿大坝走到长城下，攀岩而上，在农户搭起的凉棚里驻足，付几元钱租一张木桌、几把铁椅。将翠绿色印花桌布铺开的瞬间，立刻觉得野长城也不再荒凉。打开藤篮，里面要有一瓶香槟、几个长脚玻璃酒杯，湖面上有人荡起木舟，长城上草木间的虫鸣隐约可辨，夕阳渐暖，这样的野餐野酒别有一番滋味。

然后就到了漫长而寒冷的冬季。很少有人能想象，这个时候也可以出去“野”一下？但如果哪天你看到窗外冬日暖阳闪耀或忽然漫天飞雪，还真可以即兴去“撒点野”！

记得一个冬日的清晨，我拉开窗帘，被眼前突如其来的大雪震撼，于是迅速呼朋唤友，装上高度数的烈酒、带上川味麻辣牛肉干，还有切成片的火腿、用手捏着吃的绿葡萄干奶酪块儿、巧克力坚果意式脆饼和一壶滚烫的咖啡，最最重要的是，还要有一个电热的暖手炉，抱着它，站在辽阔的野鸭湖畔，整个冰湖被白雪覆盖，在阳光下闪闪发光。远处是燕山山脉灰色的剪影，岸旁是被雪花镶嵌的深深浅浅的草木枝丫。看着孩子们捡来了树枝，一人一根，在雪地上写写画画，然后又一起跑去堆雪人，用小铲子把雪扬上天空，仰着红彤彤的小脸，等着雪花落下。此时，喝下一口同样冰凉凛冽却会在身体里燃烧的伏特加酒，让白色的哈气在唇边蔓延……

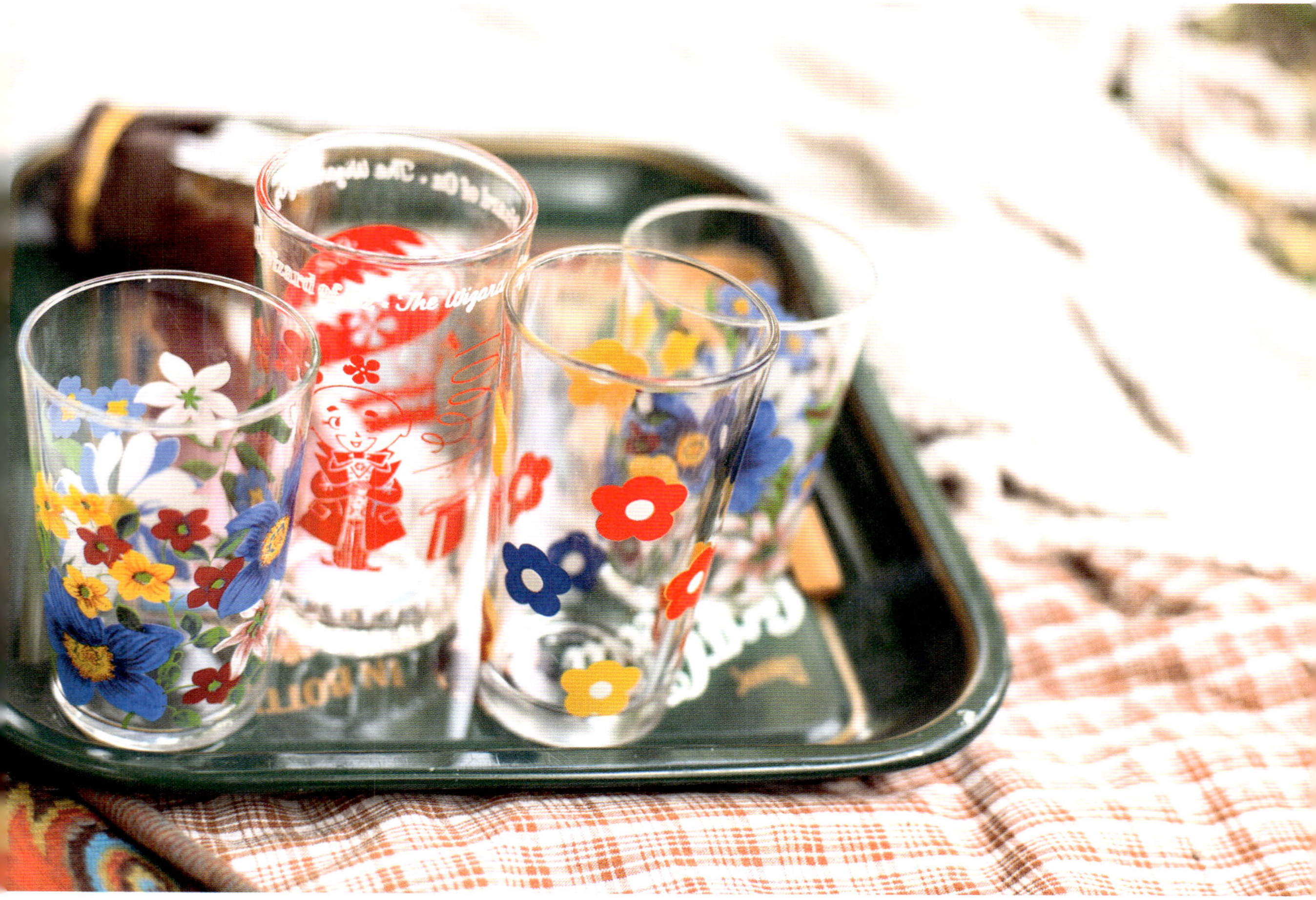

别再用一次性纸杯了，像这样不同花色的玻璃杯不仅美观，还方便大家辨识取用，并且环保。

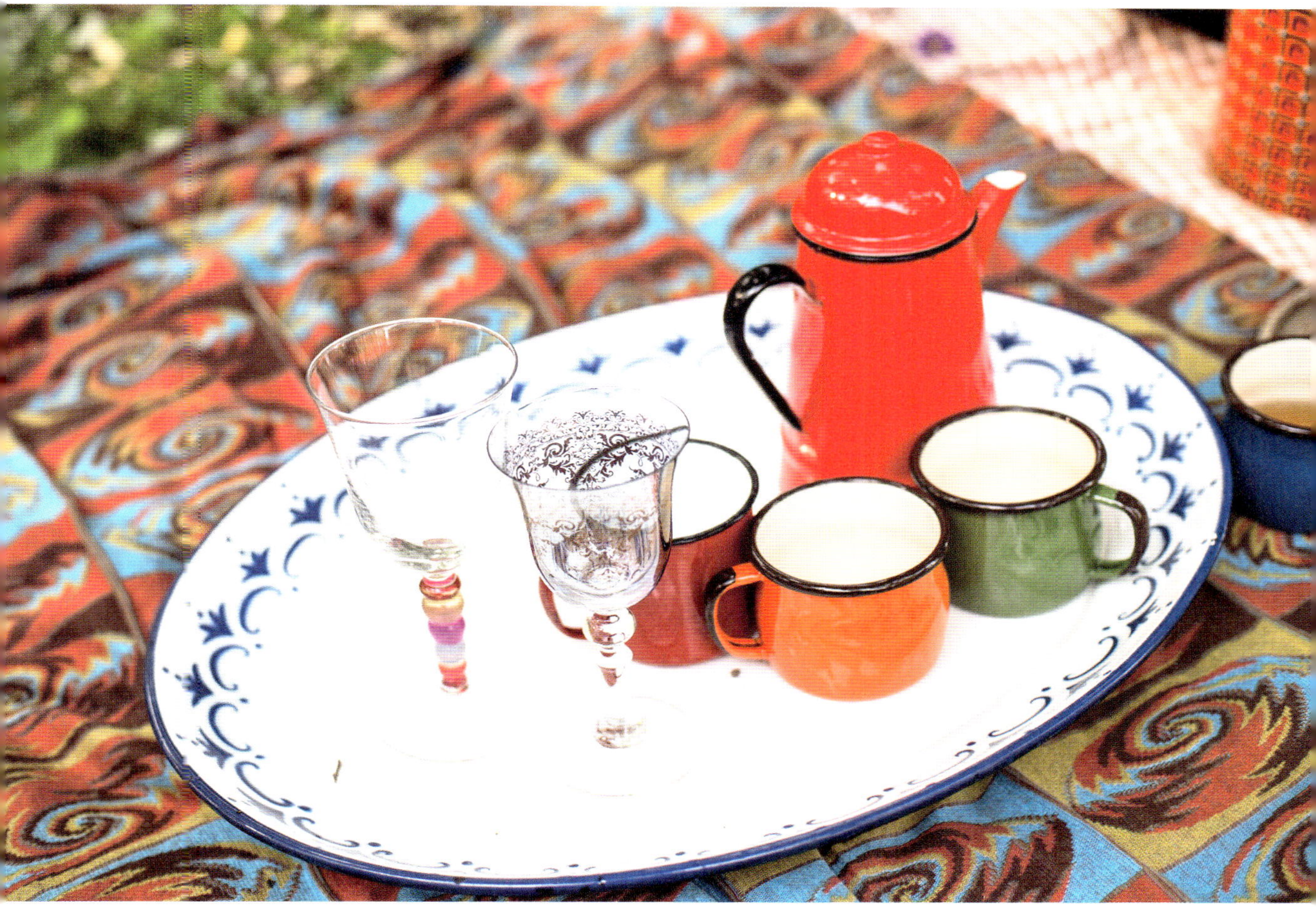

太昂贵精致的餐具违背了野餐轻松的初衷，反而是这样的搪瓷餐具和便宜且漂亮的酒杯更适合野餐氛围。

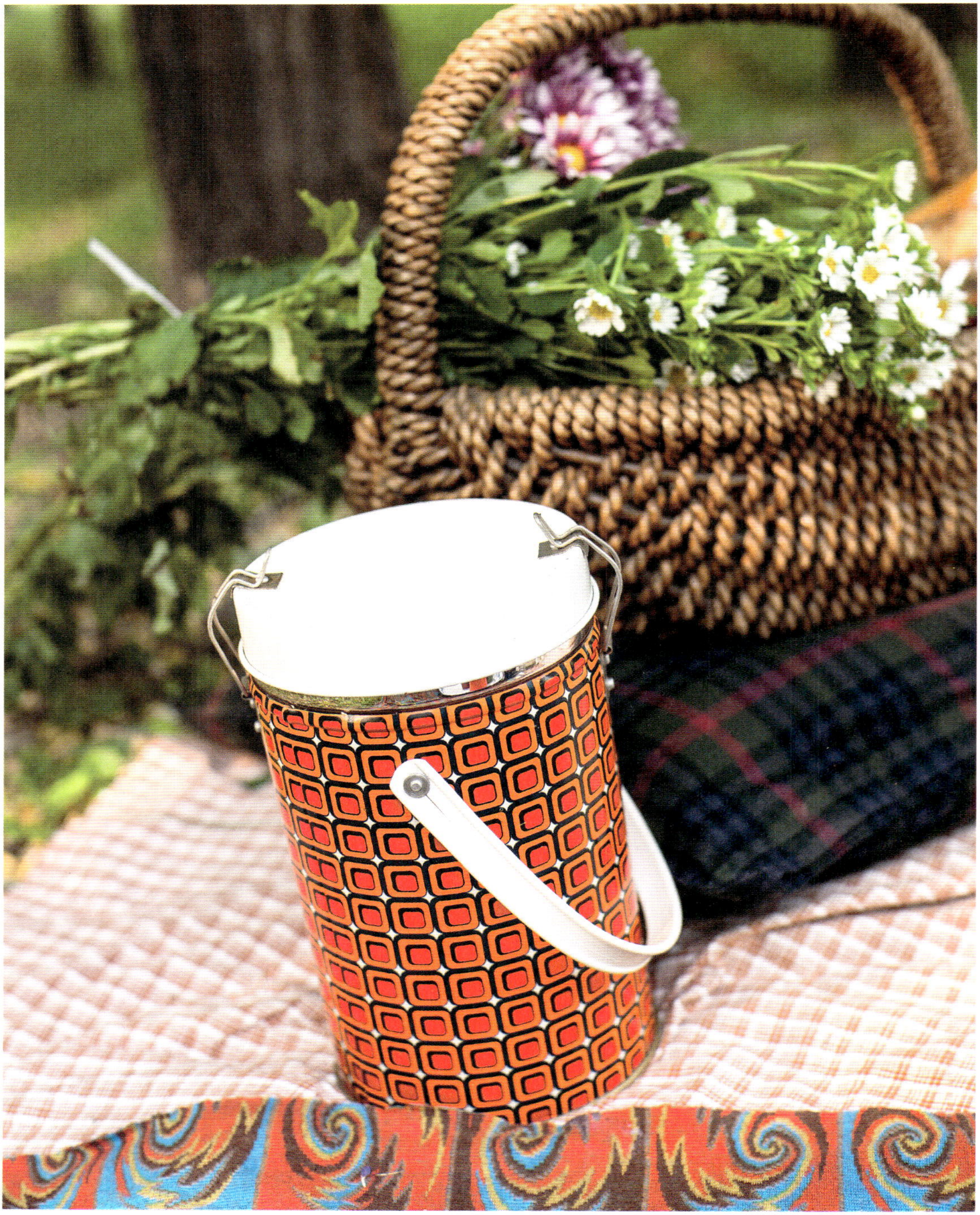

一个色调很有秋日气息的复古保温桶实用又颇具暖意。

草 地 上 的 野 餐

DRESSING UP YOUR PICNIC 'TABLE'

怎样布置一个野餐“餐桌”

在19世纪中期，马奈(Manet)和莫奈(Monet)一人画了一幅画，都叫“草地上的午餐”。这两幅画从题材和构图都如出一辙，区别是女主角是否穿了衣服，但我提到这两幅画，只想让你留意一下他们野餐布上的物品：与环境和人物着装色调和谐的野餐布、藤编的篮子、葡萄酒、酒杯，精致的盘碟里装着松软美味的蛋糕、面包……

虽然对现代人来说，轻巧和方便实用是野餐餐具的要点，但这不意味着你非要去用那些丑陋的一次性餐具、塑料桌布和盘碟。那不光让你看上去不够优雅有品位，也会被人指责不环保。当然，在没有男仆和马车的情况下，你也不必把最贵重的瓷器都搬到草地上来，总有些实用又好看的东西可以选择，比如复古的搪瓷餐具——轻便、不易破损，而且好看。另外，一些来自宜家或花卉市场货架上的便宜且轻巧的玻璃酒杯、瓶子之类的都非常方便，就算不小心坏了也不会太心疼。当然，木质、椰壳或竹子这样天然材质的餐具也是非常好的选择。

所有的这些东西凑在一起，难免看上去杂乱无章。这就需要你用布置餐桌的审美和技巧去对付这块野餐布了。先确定一个主题，那可以是某一种色调或风格。根据这个主题选定野餐布，其他的餐具则从野餐布里挑选能呼应的色彩。如果是海洋风，就主打蓝色和白色这样的地中海色调；如果玩 20 世纪七八十年代的复古风，则可以用一块偏暖色调的格子餐布，然后配上搪瓷杯子、金属饭盒和保温水壶来装食物；若像上文中那样秋日的野餐，就多用些暖暖的橘红点缀，用同样大地色调的针织野餐毯来营造暖意，另外，一小束雏菊也会让人立刻融入氛围。总之，不管你有多少创意，只要记住，抓住一个“亮点”就不会凌乱。

舒适很重要

对于一场成功的野餐，舒适性是非常非常重要的。野餐的营地要选在有遮挡的树荫下，或者干脆支一个帐篷或简易的凉棚。低矮的小树枝或简单的支架和一大块轻柔的薄纱布就能做到，一点也不难。另外，地面不要太潮湿，野餐布尽量有防潮功能，但如果你偏爱轻柔织物带来的古典感觉，那就准备一块防水布悄悄垫在最下面。

当然，如果你车的后备厢还有空间，带几个柔软的靠垫也很有必要，或坐或卧，在树荫下看看书，会让人觉得舒适至极。如果有年纪大的人一起野餐，那别怕沉，带一把折叠椅或板凳给他们吧。

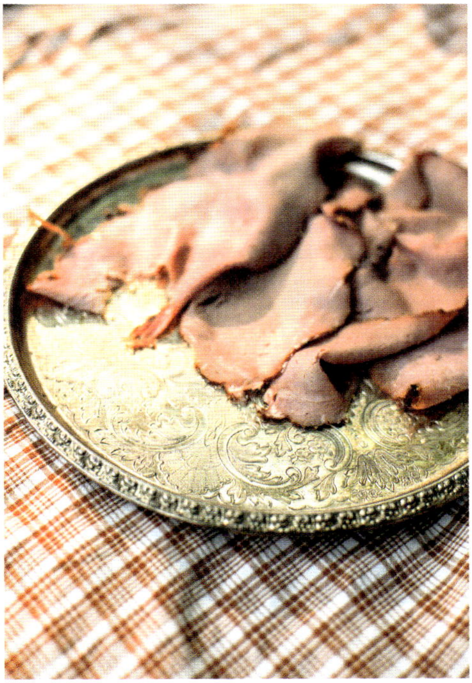

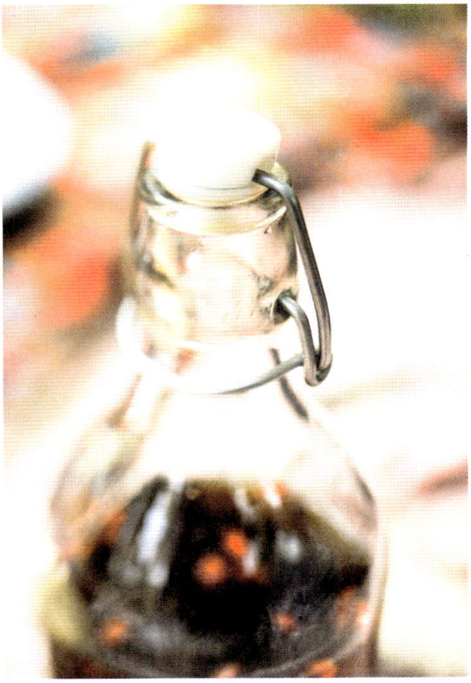

来自英国的老银盘让野餐变得具有质感。

无论装酒还是饮料，密封瓶在野餐中都非常好用。

野餐吃什么

野餐的餐单其实相当不设限，可以走西式路线——鸡蛋火腿三明治、烤吐司、德国香肠、意大利火腿，还有杯装的提拉米苏和各式各样新鲜的水果，制作简单、方便携带，摆出来又好看。你也可以尝试东瀛风，寿司、鱼生是野餐中最受欢迎的食物之一，因为它的美味恰恰非常适合冷食。

带中式的食物去野餐，以往总让人觉得有一点难度。汤汤汁汁容易洒漏，食物变冷又影响风味。但其实这也是偏见。小时候春游时，妈妈总会塞到我们书包里的五香茶叶蛋、卤味豆腐干、酱牛肉都让人念念不忘。上一次去野餐，我的一位医生朋友居然带了一大份朝鲜冷面！她把调好的汤汁装进大瓶子，将切好的苹果片、梨片用盐水浸过后装盒，还有酱牛肉片、黄瓜丝、辣椒酱、香菜碎、辣白菜、煮熟切好的鸡蛋，这些被她以医生井井有条的姿态分别装在一个个小巧的便当盒中，毫无意外，她的冷面成了当日最受欢迎的食物，被一抢而光，一滴汤都没有剩下。

带几个瓶子

瓶子在野餐中的功能性和装饰性都非常强。它可以用来分装每人份饮料、酸奶，这比杯子更方便，还不会洒漏出来。也可以用来装自酿美酒或红酒、香槟，就像安徒生童话《瓶颈》（*The Bottle-Neck*）里装着最上等的香槟，与火腿、干酪和香肠一起被放进野餐篮子里的那支神奇的瓶子，陪伴着美丽的森林、阳光，还有正在相恋的年轻而美貌的男女。

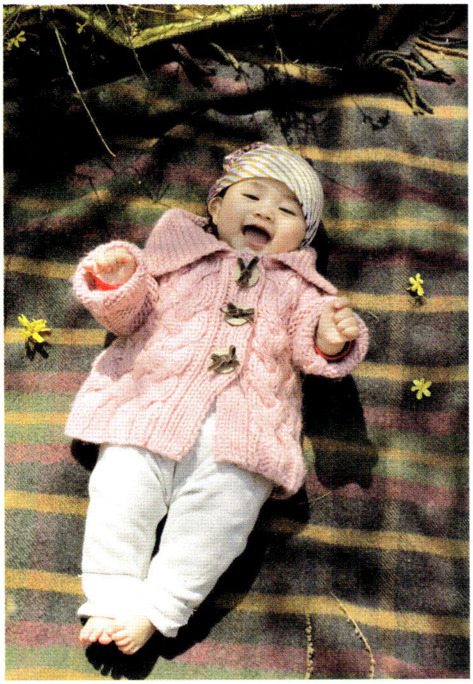

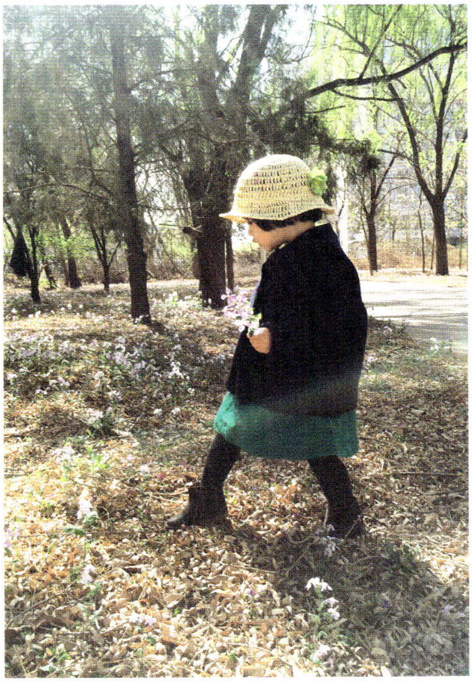

在家附近的公园里野餐，从小叶子四个月躺在毯子上玩耍，到她两岁多奔跑于林间，她爱极了这里的阳光、树叶和土地上奇妙的花花草草。（摄影：黄鹭）

两 个 人 的 餐 桌

T A B L E F O R T W O

两个人的最好时光，就应该是香艳的、奢靡的。所有精心制作的美食和巧思布置的装饰，都是点燃爱火的前奏。

在读伊莎贝尔·阿连德（Isabel Allende）的《阿佛洛狄特：感官回忆录》（*Afrodita: Guentos,Recetas y Otros Afrodisiacos*）的时候，我就一直在想，她笔下那些有着强大催情效果的“迷魂苹果”、“修女的青春”、生的或熟的贝类、野禽、好时光菲力牛排或是芦笋鱼子酱拌面，到底是在什么样的餐桌上享用的？装着它们的，是怎样诱惑的器皿？花瓶里会有什么样妖艳的鲜花？摇曳的烛光下，是否是一个鎏金的烛台？覆盖桌面的，是精美的蕾丝还是华贵的丝绒？而那把用来将无花果和糖、胡桃、白兰地、豆蔻混合在一起制成的催情可丽馅饼送到唇边的餐叉，有没有温润性感的牙白色骨把？

掺杂着这些幻想，那活色生香的场面愈发生动。两个人的最好时光，就应该是香艳的、

▶ 将M小姐的餐桌改变一些细节，翻版成白天约会版——充满暧昧、暖意和华美细节的餐桌，是两个人约会所应该有的风格。

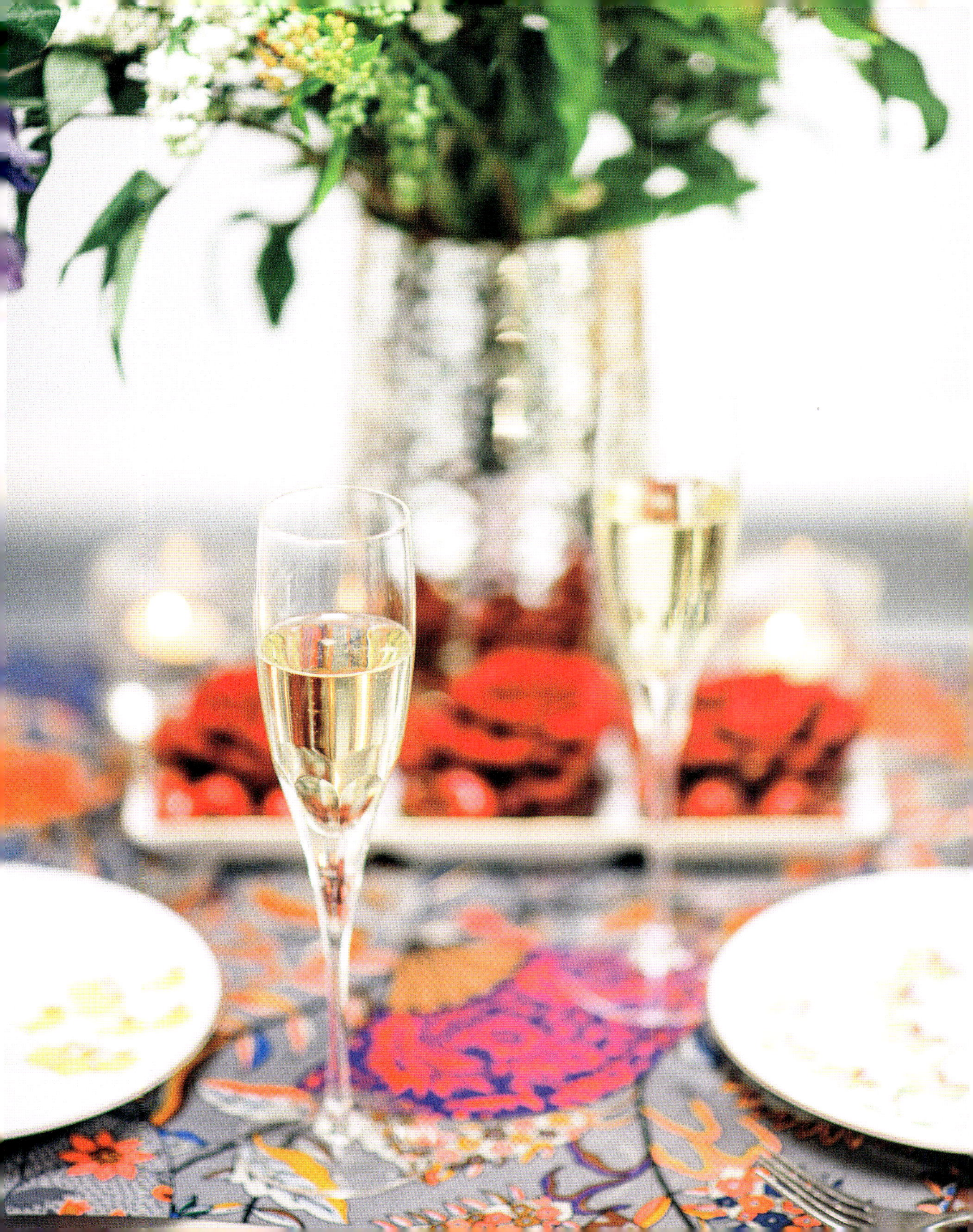

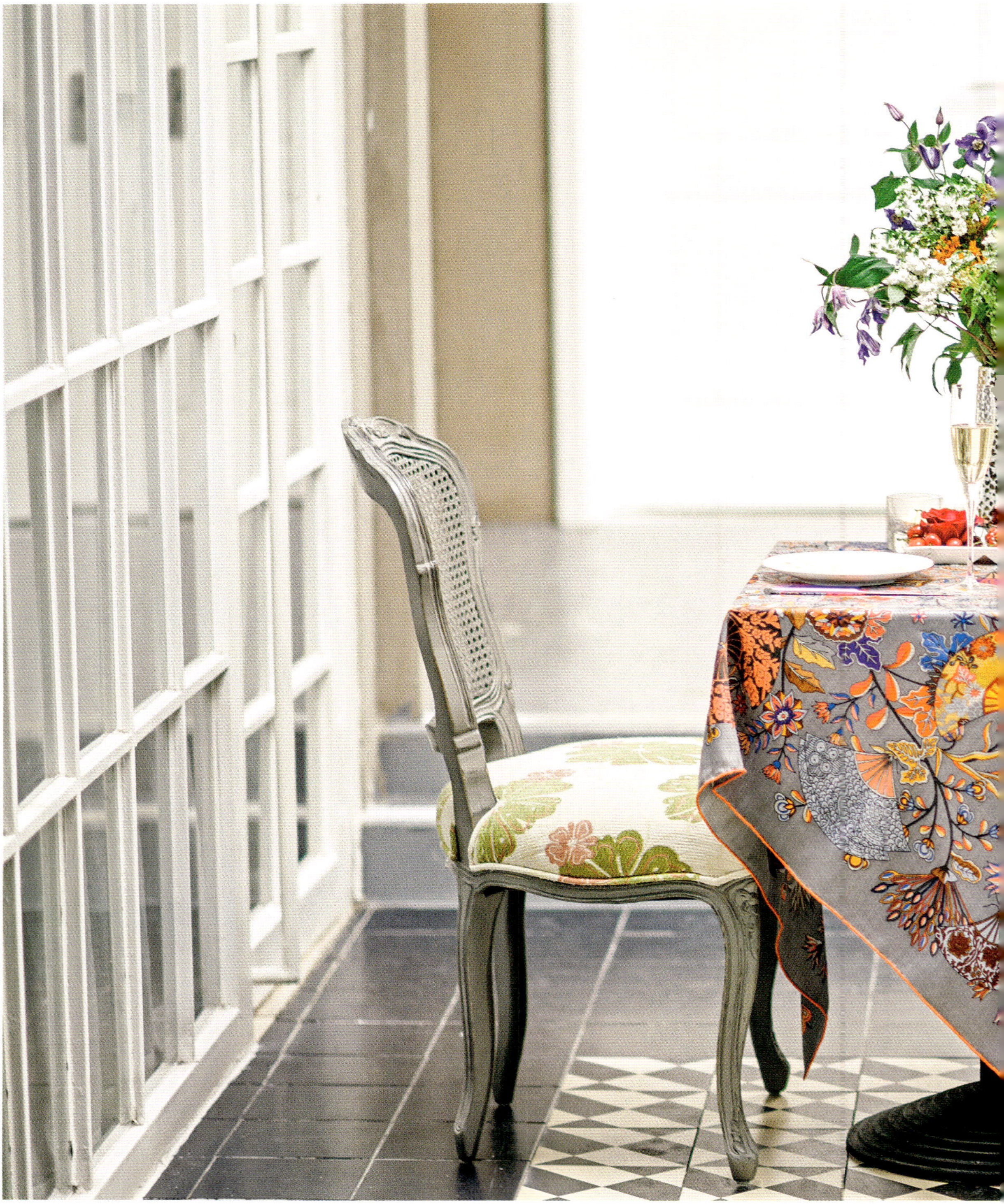

即使非常奢靡艳丽的桌面摆设，也要保持整体风格的清爽和随意，这样才不会做作和让人因“用力过猛”而难为情。

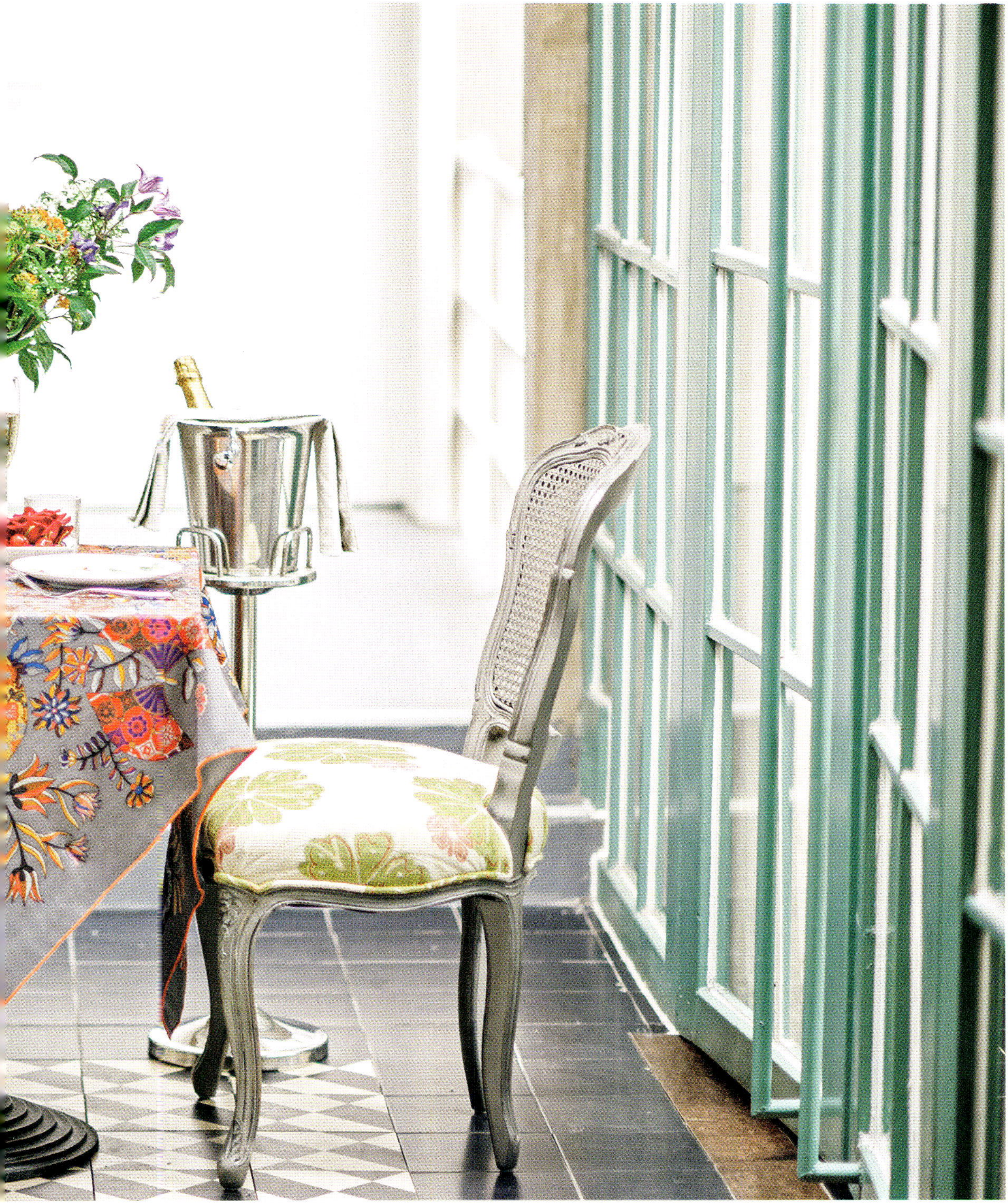

奢靡的。所有精心制作的美食和巧思布置的装饰，都是点燃爱火的前奏。就算肉麻点儿、夸张点儿也可以被原谅，毕竟，体内多巴胺分泌旺盛的时刻，在人的一生中全部加起来也不会比发愁的时间多。但我那个正准备布下甜蜜陷阱网住心动男人的闺密 M 小姐还是忧愁地说，可我并不擅长烹饪啊，更不懂如何布置餐桌……但这又如何呢？千万别把自己弄成一个油头满面的“煮妇”，就算男人贪吃，也不会想和一个用围裙抹着油手的女厨子做爱，除非是一个扮成厨娘的性感女郎。这其中的差别就像看《八方食圣》和《露西亚的情人》（*Lucía y el sexo*）。况且，就连阿连德也坦言自己是个不善于下厨的女人，而这并不妨碍制作春膳——没人让你去寻找无尾熊的爪子、蝾螈的眼睛和童子尿，更不需要把餐桌摆出英国皇室范儿或爱丽舍宫国宴标准。省点儿力气做爱岂不更好。这不是春膳的目的吗？阿连德这样谆谆教诲。是的，在这张名为“情欲”的餐桌上所摆放的一切，外表远比口味重要，你只要有几个唬人而讨巧的菜谱、几件精致漂亮的餐具和满满的爱意就足够了。

确实有些东西，天生就是性感的。昏暗的灯光，或者仅仅留下烛光，就算再木讷的人也会明了心意吧。温暖的质感和颜色总是让人容易动情，比如暗红色、暖紫色、粉色和橘色，将这些色调的轻薄羊绒或者有立体浮雕感花纹的织物铺在桌面上，任何一张餐桌都可以立刻变得香艳起来。那些冷冰冰的极简设计和黑白灰色调不知道能不能激发艺术家的激情，但稍微有点华丽感，且不俗艳低廉的东西，却总能让人的肾上激素不由得升高。金色的刀叉、装着琥珀色香槟的华美古董水晶杯、盛放牡蛎和贝类的银色托盘，还有花瓶里盛放的花朵，不是雏菊也不是绣球，而是属于夜晚的牡丹或玫瑰，它们都有种丰腴而性感的美。将餐桌布置成这样的女主人，想必也是秀色可餐的吧。

至于桌上的食物，就按照阿连德写的去做吧。苹果是诱惑的象征，鳄梨能激起内心的情欲，草莓、樱桃、葡萄和无花果都是性感的，软软多汁的口感和娇艳鲜嫩的颜色，仿佛带着某种暧昧的隐喻。鱼子酱和任何海鲜贝类都是催情的圣物，其实所有食物在她的笔下都有催情的效果，而且容易烹饪。最后别忘记“这场情色大宴的 happy ending（完美结局）”——甜品。巧克力就很好，阿连德毫不掩饰地指出，巧克力酱的催情效果在于在情侣手指上舔舐的感觉，不过她亦狡黠地提醒你，如果真想这么做，最好把酱涂在自己身上，这样可让对方把卡路里吃到肚子里……

对不知如何以情欲餐桌的布局网住情人的 M 小姐，我最终决定送给她这本《阿佛洛狄特：感官回忆录》，当然，作为闺密，我也借给她尽量多的华美餐具并亲自示范摆放秘诀。在她和心上人约会后第二天的中午（显然起得很晚），M 小姐便兴奋地来汇报了——

“他敲门，打开房门看到的就是客厅里点了蜡烛的餐桌，上面有爱马仕羊绒披肩华丽客串的桌布和用红玫瑰与樱桃巧妙摆放的花饰，他的眼神立刻就变得充满赞赏而温存了。

“我还照你吩咐，买了 Baccarat（巴卡拉）水晶红酒杯，好在就需要两个啊，要不真的破产了，但这东西真的提气！让他对我的生活格调刮目相看。

“菜完全是按照书上来的，用虾混合白葡萄酒、月桂叶、柠檬片和海盐做成了让人情欲大张的虾戳，把它们戳在牙签上，摆放在装饰了薄荷叶子的银盘里，他一下就被这道菜美艳的外表迷惑了。

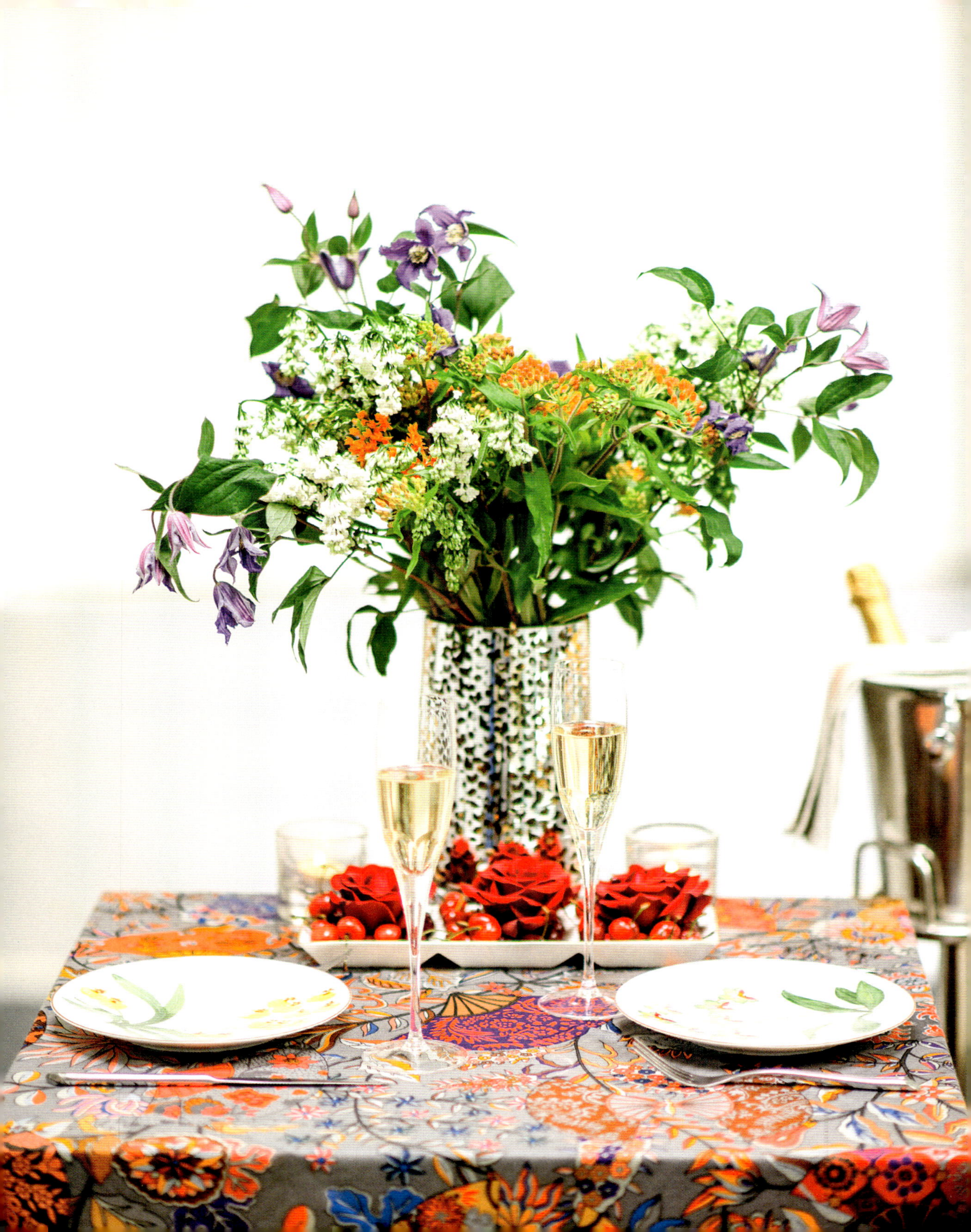

“然后是装在纯白色浮雕纹路汤碗里的超级春宴的奶油迷魂汤。在吃卖相奢华但制作超级简单的龙虾大菜时，他已经有些心猿意马了……

“当然，还有甜品，完全没有技术含量的巧克力慕斯配性感树莓，在我用手指将蘸好的树莓送到他唇边之前，并没忘记把那本《感官回忆录》往床底下更深地踢了半米……

“一切都完美极了！

“只是……”

“只是什么？”

“只是，当一切尘埃落定，硝烟散去后，我处女座的强迫症发作了。整晚都在他身边无法入眠……想的是我那120支纱埃及棉贡缎床单上的巧克力酱和酒渍到底能不能洗掉啊……”

◀ 这条爱马仕的羊绒大披肩铺在桌面上带来十足的香艳效果，暖橙和紫唤醒情欲，柔软顺滑的质感更让人感到奢华沉迷。

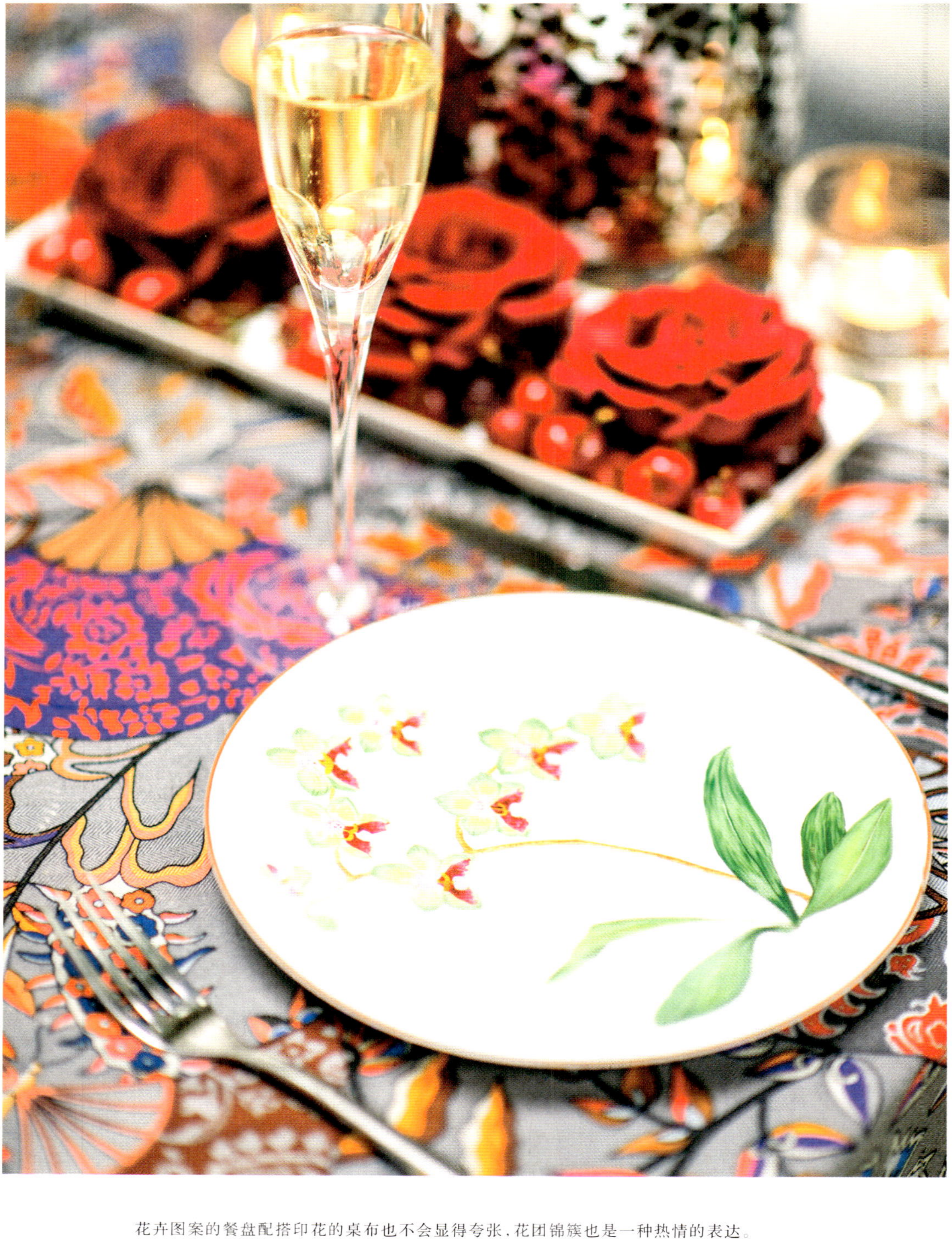

花卉图案的餐盘配搭印花的桌布也不会显得夸张，花团锦簇也是一种热情的表达。

让 餐 桌 变 得 性 感

CREATING A ROMANTIC ATMOSPHERE

华 美 才 性 感

关于性感的定义很多，怎样都可以达到目的，但我还是要说，华美也许和性感的距离最近。用暗色调衬托宝石般闪耀的色彩，寻找有奢华质感的桌布、餐具和烛台，纤细娇贵的水晶杯，这些都可以直白地表达性感和情欲。而其中餐刀和水晶杯是最值得投资的部分，它们可以让饮酒和用餐整个儿变得不同，也让女主角的格调更高贵。关键是，就像M小姐说的那样，只需要准备两个人用的，这不会让你破产的。

就 用 红 玫 瑰

红玫瑰确实比较老套，但它本身就代表爱情，这一点无法取代。我知道你也不喜欢那些情人节里和满天星或粉百合组合在一起的红玫瑰，不要那样，其实只要一两枝，无论是斜插在花瓶中还是把花朵摘下来与水果重新组合成小花饰都别具心思，可以化俗气为灵气。

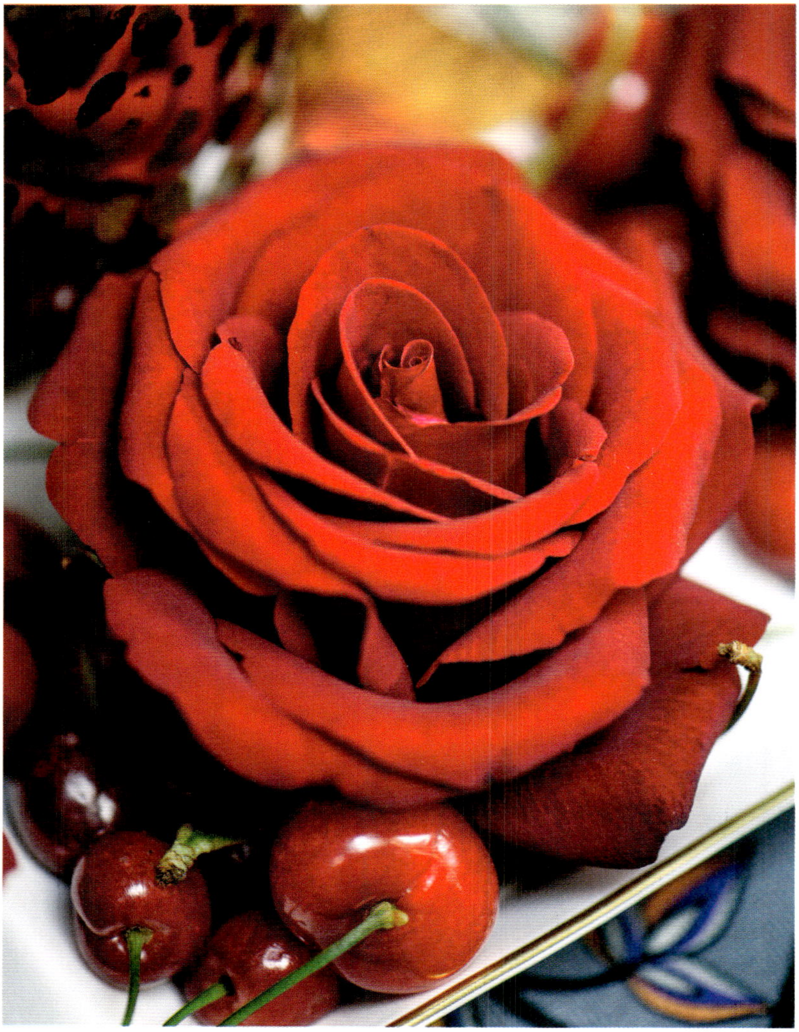

就是普通的红玫瑰，与熟透的樱桃一起摆在小盘子里，装饰感极强，百无聊赖时拈起一颗放在唇边，也是种美妙的姿态。

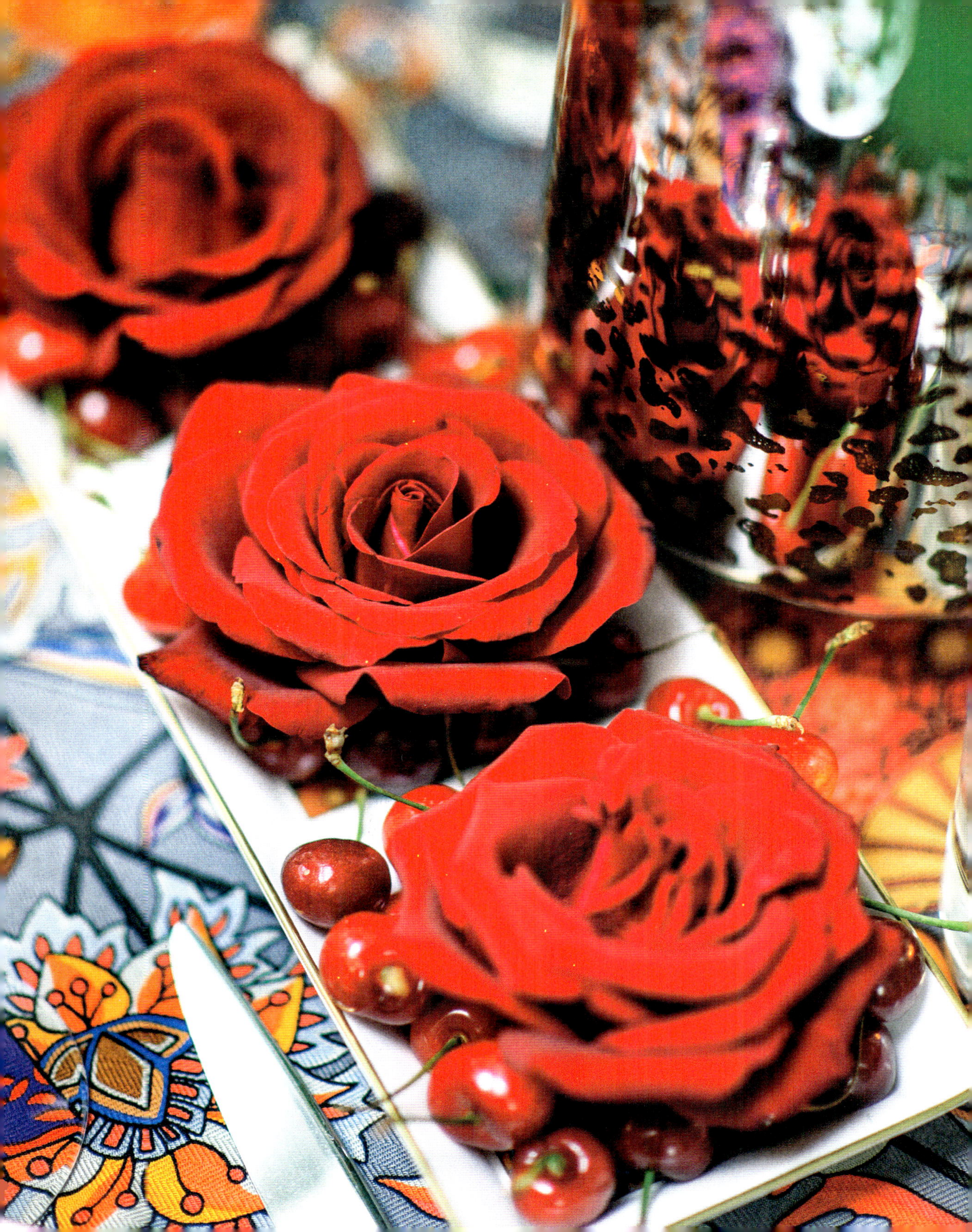

尽量简单

华美不等于繁复。用充满细节的餐具饰品，但整体要保持简约和随意的感觉。这里面有两层意思：一是从视觉风格上，越是华丽的用具越要用清晰明快的摆放方式来衬托，才不会感觉 too much（太过）。二是为了节省时间，花太多的时间在烹饪或摆放餐桌上，都不是情欲餐桌的最终目的。用心于餐桌的确可以让他感到被重视、被暗示，但同时那份妙不可言的漫不经心，能帮你保住矜持，不会显得猴儿急。

PART 2

不仅是一顿顿的饭，
还是一场场的欢聚

IT'S MORE THAN A MEAL,
IT'S A TIME FOR CELEBRATION

小小的，美美的

SMALL AND SWEET

有时候我想，就这样一起玩儿着，让我陪着她慢慢长大，当她转身跑开，不再对我有所依赖和索求，不再张开小手要妈妈抱抱的时候，这些对餐桌和厨房的爱、对花朵的情感，会一直陪着她。

小叶子任性地要玩我修剪花枝的剪刀，被拒绝后大哭。我板着脸，很严肃。她伸出两只小手，哭着要妈妈抱抱。我不理睬她。她就站在桌前，哭得湿答答的，小脸通红的。她缓缓缩回了小手，脚往后微微挪了半步。我的心却揪了一下，生怕她下一刻会转头跑开，不再理我。随即她又怯怯地伸出了双手，我上前把她揽入怀中，像抱住一团小小的湿漉漉的棉花糖。我好怕这样的索求稍纵即逝，她对我的依赖也许只是短短的瞬间。

然后，她便安静地看着我把刚从花市买来的鲜花一枝一枝修剪掉多余的叶子，插入瓶中。过了一会儿，她忽然指向书架高处一个小小的陶罐，咿咿呀呀地说："叶叶，花瓶，叶叶要花瓶。"我一下明白了，即使刚才她上前争夺剪刀也并不是顽皮，只是想学着我的样子，打理这些花枝，让它们美美地绽放在瓶中。我取下了小罐子，又给她找了一把安全的小剪刀，她便在一旁捡起我剪掉的小花枝，像模像样地修修剪剪，摆弄起了那些花朵。

不知是从哪一时刻开始的，无论是我布置餐桌，还是插花，小叶子都愿意一起参与，也会用过家家的餐具和乐高玩具，摆上一桌有花花的晚餐或下午茶，端着小盘子，学着我们的样子，用木头叉子美滋滋地“吃点心”。有时候我布置餐桌，她坐在儿童椅里，看着我忙忙碌碌地摆盘弄花，会喃喃自语地说：“妈妈弄得真漂亮！”这些都让我惊讶、惊喜，又有些感动。我想象不出她将来会是什么样子，过着什么样的生活，但看到美的东西会开心、会觉得快乐，有这样的心，想必将来的生活也会很容易感到愉快吧。

从叶子开始吃第一口食物，到她能坐在餐桌旁和我们一起用餐，我给她准备的餐具基本和成人是一样的，只是成人碗碟中小小的、美美的那些。她也不曾有各种卡通的、塑料的、颜色鲜艳的碗碗盘盘，只因为我觉得，那并不好看。我不觉得儿童的审美和成人有太大区别，那些刻意营造出的粗劣的可爱和刺目的艳丽也许只是大人心里想象出的儿童世界。有意思的是，小叶子也从未打破过一个瓷碗或玻璃杯，她其实很小心，会和我们一样，懂得珍爱这些美丽的东西。

叶子过生日，为她的小派对我设计了独特的餐桌布置。一大清早，便去菜市场搬回了很多盘绿绿的嫩嫩的麦苗，还有各式各样的迷你多肉小盆栽。并不是要布置花园，而是要把它们摆上餐桌。由小叶子的乳名到她的样子，都让我想到这些萌萌的嫩绿的小苗儿，把它们摆在桌子中间，再把俏丽的玛格丽特小菊花点缀其中，一簇一朵，像一条长长的桌上花园，散发着植物和花朵的清香。还有仿真的小动物藏匿在“花园”之中，孩子们连同大人，都好开心地寻找，惊喜地发现一只可爱的小猫、漂亮的小鸟或是呆萌的蜗牛。当派对结束，孩子们还可以把自己喜欢的小动物装在准备好的小竹篮里和糖果一

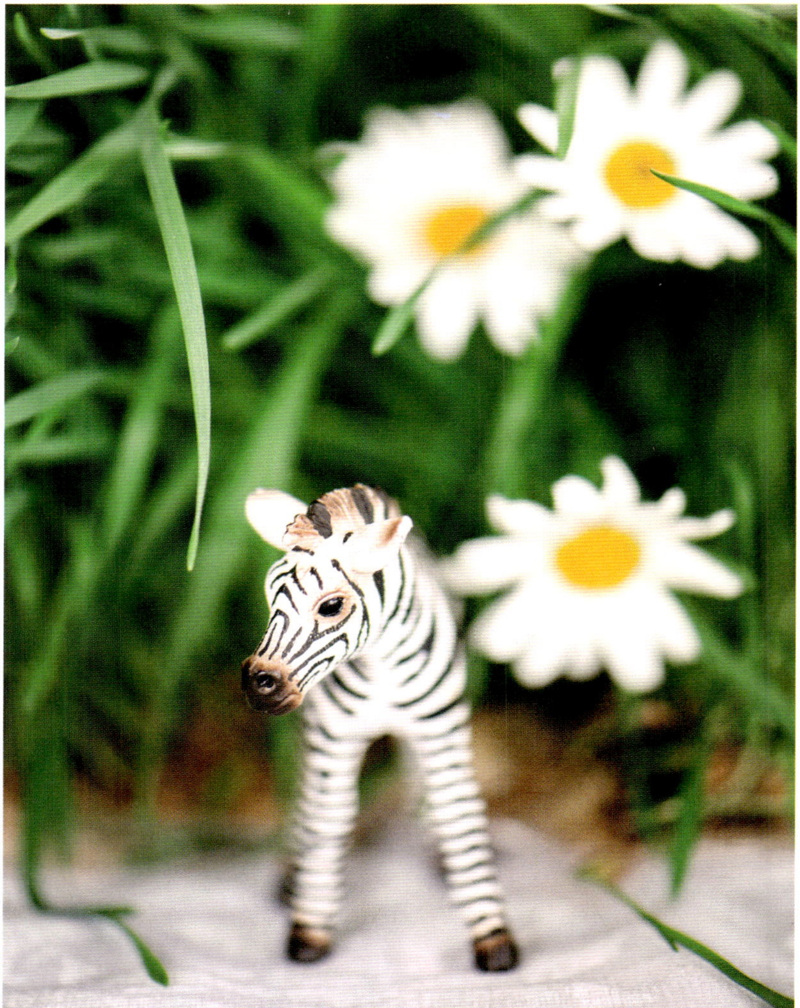

用麦苗和小花布置成的桌面花园，还有仿真小动物出没，不仅让孩子们感到新奇有趣，也让大人们乐在其中。

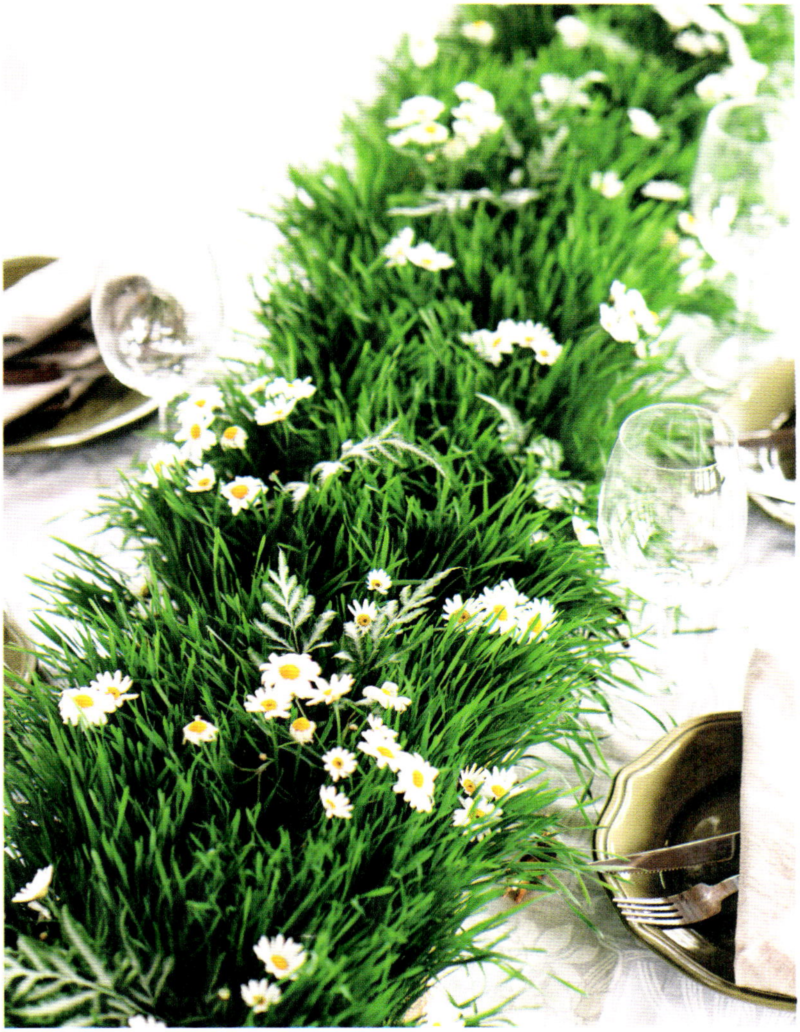

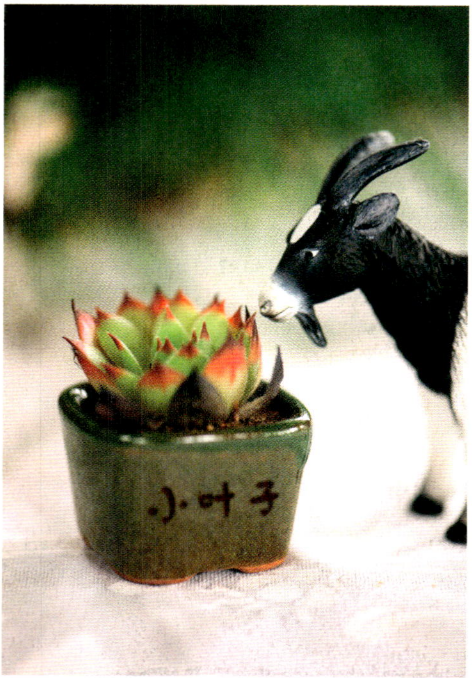

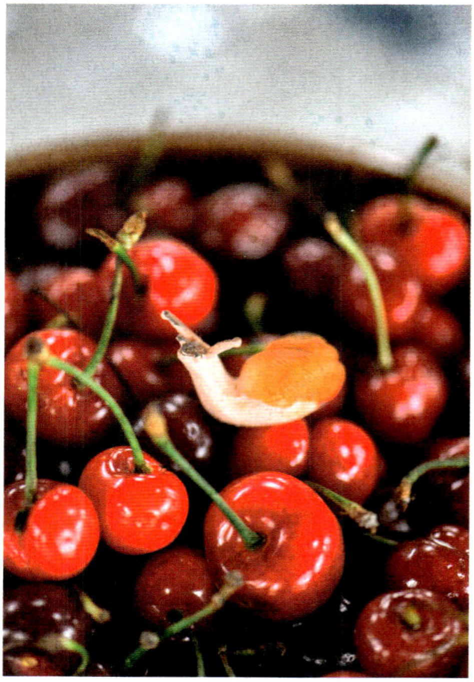

小小的多肉盆栽，是桌面装饰，也是用来排列座位的“名卡”。

水果里也会发现可爱的蜗牛，让小朋友在选取食物时充满乐趣！

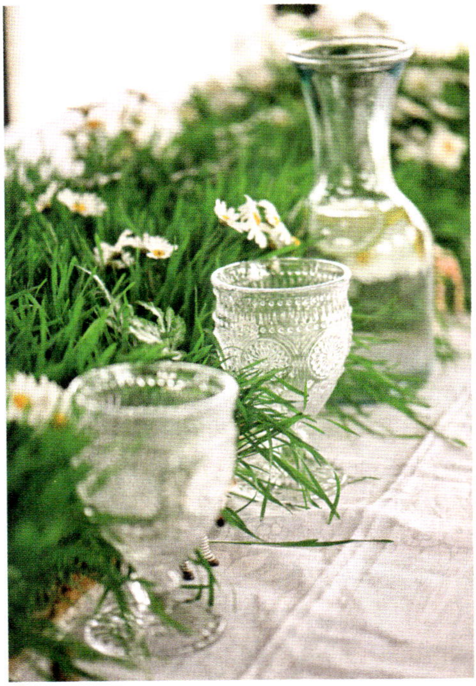

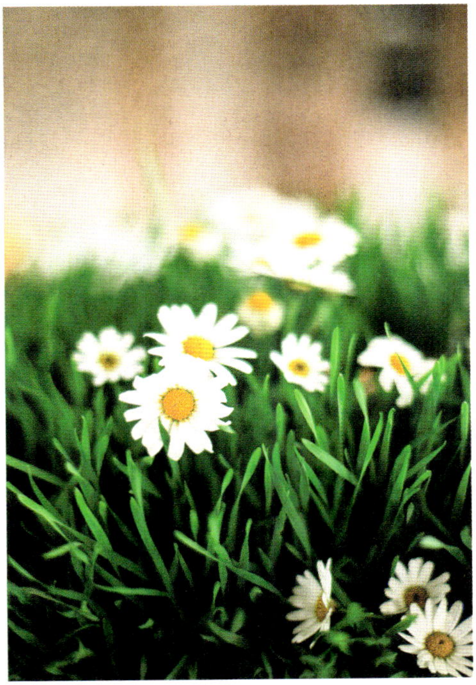

这场在朋友耀扬的“乡舍”中举办的聚会确实如在田园间的一场游戏。

起带走，与叶子一起分享生日的快乐。而那些可爱的迷你多肉，不仅可以放在盘子里当成装饰，还可以在花盆上用马克笔写上来宾的名字，当作餐桌的“名卡”，而且，那小小的肉肉的样子，恰恰就像婴孩娇憨的模样。

随着叶子一点一点长大，从躺着到坐着，从睁大眼睛看着到能伸出小手开心地摆弄餐桌上的花草、餐具，这些我爱的，也渐渐成了能在她眼睛中闪耀的火花。有时候我想，就这样一起玩儿着，让我陪着她慢慢长大，当她转身跑开，不再对我有所依赖和索求，不再张开小手要妈妈抱抱的时候，这些对餐桌和厨房的爱、对花朵的情感，会一直陪着她。但我也并不是总会有时间和心思与小叶子一起玩耍。每月到了杂志要截稿的日子，我都会很忙，忙到即使周末也没有时间为叶子做一顿美丽的早餐。甚至有的时候，早晨离开，她还在熟睡，晚上回来，她又已经睡着。我轻手轻脚地推开房门，看看她熟睡的小脸和肆意伸展的小胳膊小腿，然后到她每天玩耍的地毯上坐坐，看看她当天画的画儿或刚刚翻过的书本，有时候还会发现，那里有她用过家家的餐具和乐高玩具，摆出的一桌有花花的晚餐或下午茶，想象着她认真地摆弄着那些杯杯碟碟，用乐高插出食物和花的样子，然后端起小盘子，学着我们的样子，用木头叉子吃着“点心”，美滋滋的……

美呀美呀小小饭桌

IDEAS FOR A CHILDREN`S PARTY

不光要他们喜欢，也要你喜欢

为孩子布置聚会的餐桌其实要谨记一点——不光要他们喜欢，也要你喜欢。常常看到那些很“儿童化”的布置，充满了颜色杂乱的气球、做工粗糙的塑料餐具、丑陋的小玩具，也许公认这就是给孩子们布置聚会的标准样式，孩子也不会拒绝，但糟糕的色彩和给人廉价感的用具绝对缺乏美感。用心想一个让你和孩子都觉得充满创造性的、令人愉悦的餐桌布置吧，上面有色彩明亮且精致的餐具、美味易分取的食物和有趣的饰品，还可以用桌布和鲜花烘托气氛。

分享礼物

任何孩子的聚会，都要考虑给每个来参加的小朋友准备一份小礼物。传统的goody buckets（糖果桶）里面是一些糖果和小玩具，这些是永远不会过时的选择。不要用那些廉价的塑料包装，可以选一些小孩玩的铁皮小桶或小竹篮子，也可以是漂亮的纸盒或

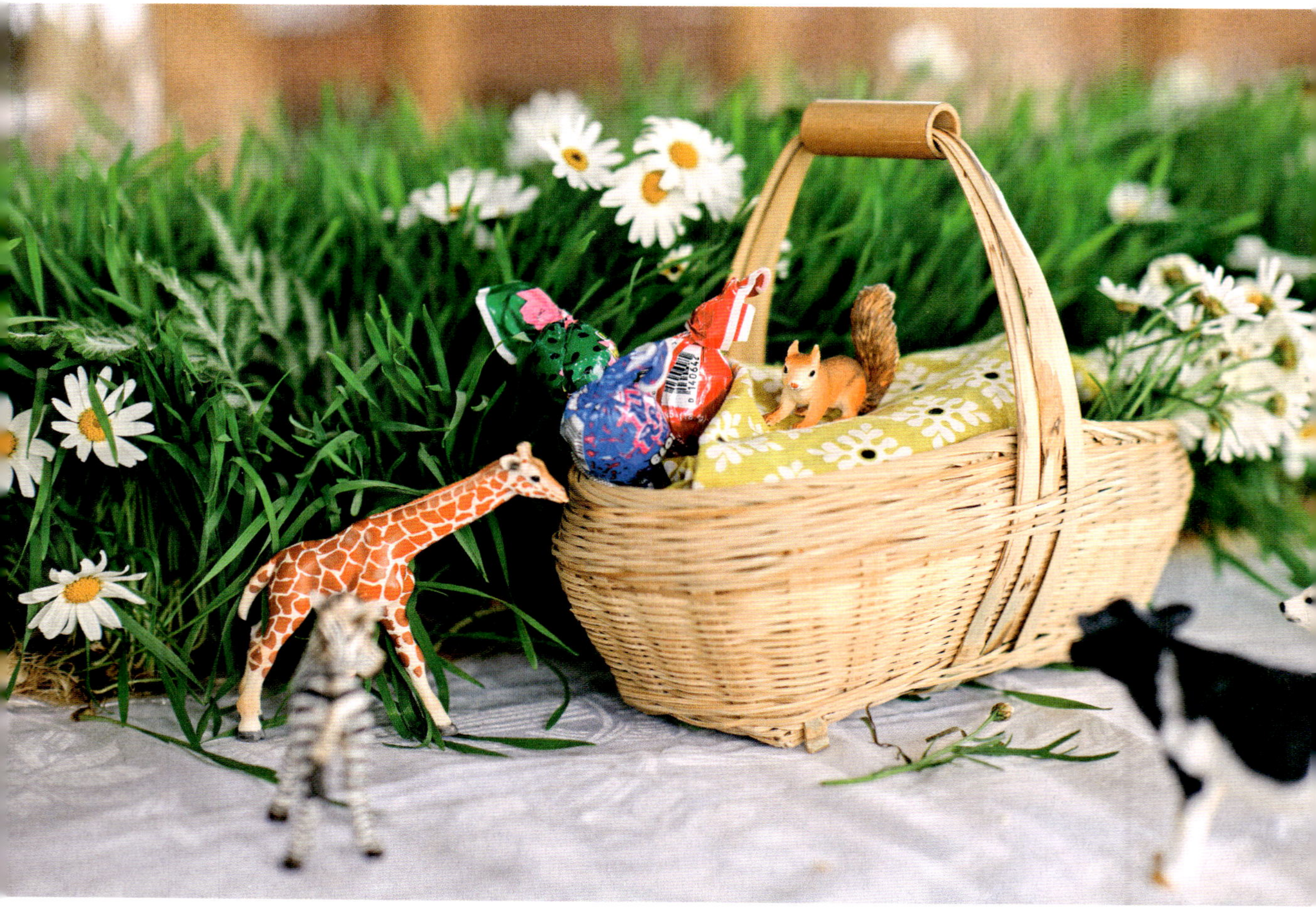

每人一份，把糖果放入小竹篮，既美观又环保，小朋友们还可以把桌面上喜欢的小动物一起带回家。

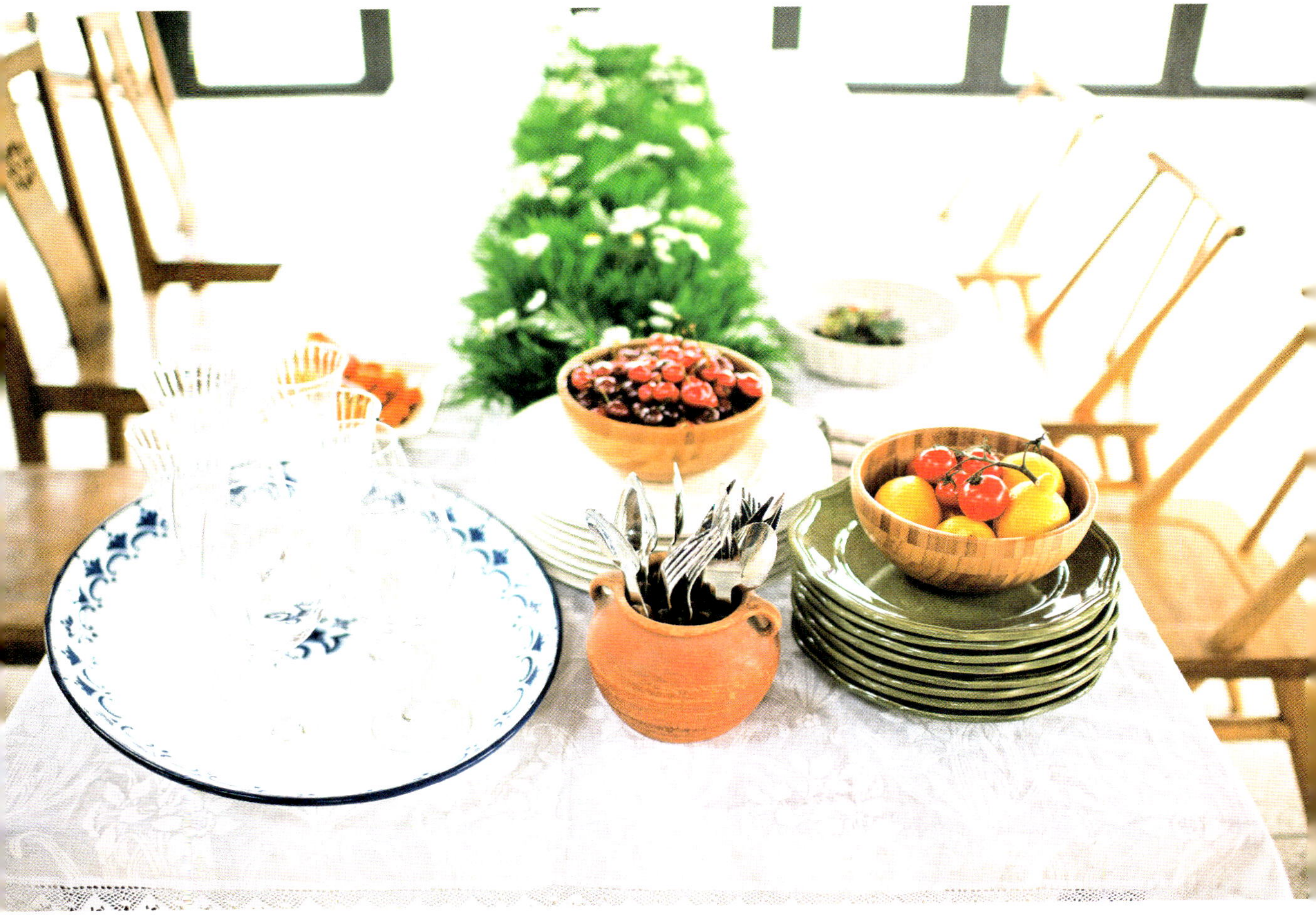

孩子的派对没必要摆放得整整齐齐，自助的形式更轻松欢快，把餐具堆放在餐桌一头，也节省了布置餐桌的时间。

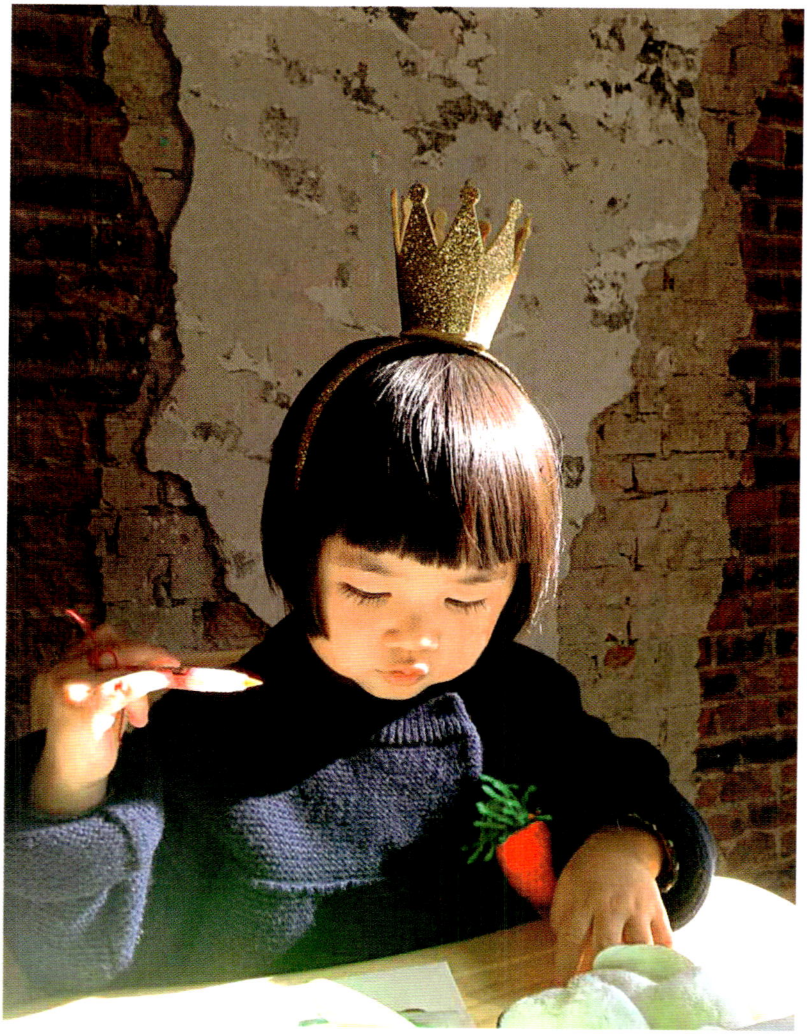

从叶子一岁到两岁，在无数小朋友的聚会上，和她一起享受着美好时光。

布袋，这些都是可以循环使用、玩耍的玩具，而且也很环保。如果更加用心，可以在每份礼物上用一个独特的标签写上小朋友的名字，可以是一个由字母连接的珠串，也可以是一张手绘的卡片。

简 便 好 操 作

不得不承认一点，给孩子举办聚会是很难控制场面的。想想五六个孩子玩闹成一团的场面，啧啧，还是给自己留条活路吧。让一切在美丽的基础上，做到简便好操作。我在家里准备了大量搪瓷餐具，不仅设计美观，还具有很强的复古感，还有那些质地厚实且小的陶瓷杯碗，也不容易碎。安全不易破损的用具仍然是儿童聚会的首选。现在很多家居店里都可以买到很好的塑料、树脂碗碟，色彩明快，无毒，且造型和图案都很有设计感。还有带防水涂层的印花桌布，既美观，又容易打理。另外，聚会所提供的食物也应该是小份儿、容易取食的，可以把它们分别盛放在可爱的小碗里，让孩子可以随时方便地拿到，又不会把所有的食物弄乱。在筹备派对的细节时，不妨让你的孩子也参与进来，一起定主题，一起挑选、布置、写名卡和邀请函，这本身也是聚会乐趣和成长的一部分。

花园里的早午餐

BRUNCH IN THE GARDEN

一边做菜一边吃，聊聊天，弄弄花，喝喝酒，
有舒服的椅子、好看的餐桌餐具，混着混着，
就到了下午茶的时间。

园子中央是一张巨大的彩色长桌，这是园子的男主人尹齐亲手制作的。那些具有波普风格的圆形和波纹被分割、拼色、组合，经画家的手，这些来自建材市场滞销的廉价瓷砖宛若新生，甚至被拼出了独特的装饰主义风格。在桌子周围，是春天里开得正热闹的花树：榆叶梅、杏花、白玉兰、连翘、李子花、粉玉兰，地上刚冒出芽的是菠菜苗、嫩葱和韭菜，还有盛开在各处的紫色的二月兰和紫花地丁。小孩子蹲在花丛里采花，衣服和头发沾上了淡淡的甜美花香。上午十点半，尹齐正在摆弄一大早从市场上搬回的修理房顶的石棉瓦，一会儿的工夫，他又转身出发，要去村子里买几株石榴苗。女主人细毛则正在洒满阳光的厨房里准备早午餐的食物，孩子们刚刚睡醒，在花园里玩耍，而我，正在那张美丽的彩色大桌前插花、摆盘，美美地布置餐桌，为美好的一天画出漂亮的底色。

一到周末，微博和朋友圈里晒得最多的就是去某热门餐厅和朋友一起晒太阳享用Sunday Brunch（周末早午餐）的照片，那些配着刁草和辣根的烟熏三文鱼散发着强烈的诱惑，

番茄沙拉佐马祖里拉奶酪有着清新的味道，还有香喷喷的德式炸猪排、香煎鹅肝与红酒烩鸡挑逗着你的食欲，闪闪发亮的焦糖布丁让一切都染上了阳光的颜色。这并不是新的时髦，而是在19世纪就从英国开始风靡的时尚。从那时开始，起床越晚，就越代表着是有钱的精英阶层，而Brunch这个合成词，恰如其分地表达了这种生活方式——Breakfast（早餐）与Lunch（午餐）组合在一起，既不是早餐，也不是午餐，慵懒闲散之感跃然纸上。

有人刻薄地说，讲英文的国家都做不好美食，但他们的长处是，创造了很多弥补吃不好正餐的附属品。英国人轻松地发明了Brunch这个美妙的词语，而真正让它像龙卷风一样，迅速成为一种时髦的生活方式的，却是美国人。一方面也许是因为仅仅依靠鱼排、薯条当正餐的英式厨房不足以支撑如此丰盛的场面，另一方面，英式有板有眼的节奏正像巴赫的平均律那样一丝不苟，能留给早午餐的放松空间少之又少。而在大西洋那头，在能把新奥尔良黑人音乐与欧洲白人文化糅合形成爵士乐的美国，则更适合“早午餐”这个“混血”的孩子痛快地成长。据说在20世纪30年代，美国的时髦人士就会为了一顿Ambassador Hotel（大使酒店）的奢华Brunch，特地搭乘火车头等包厢前往芝加哥。如果那时候有Twitter（推特），可以想象，他们一定也会找到最好的角度拍出美美的照片，发送，让所有人羡慕他们的悠闲和前卫。而今，美国新一代白富美的代表人物Gossip Girl（绯闻女孩，美剧《Gossip Girl》的主角们）则大声喊出——像我们这样的上东区富豪，才不会在周末的早晨躺在床上读报、喝咖啡虚度时光，早午餐就是我们的早餐，有香槟做伴，有时髦的衣裙，有闺密，也有情敌。她们热衷于扎堆儿的地方是纽约被誉为“早午餐女王”的莎拉贝思·莱文（Sarabeth Levine）女士创建于1981年的Sarabeth's餐厅，无论是《绯闻女孩》还是《欲望都市》（*Sex and The City*）里的女郎

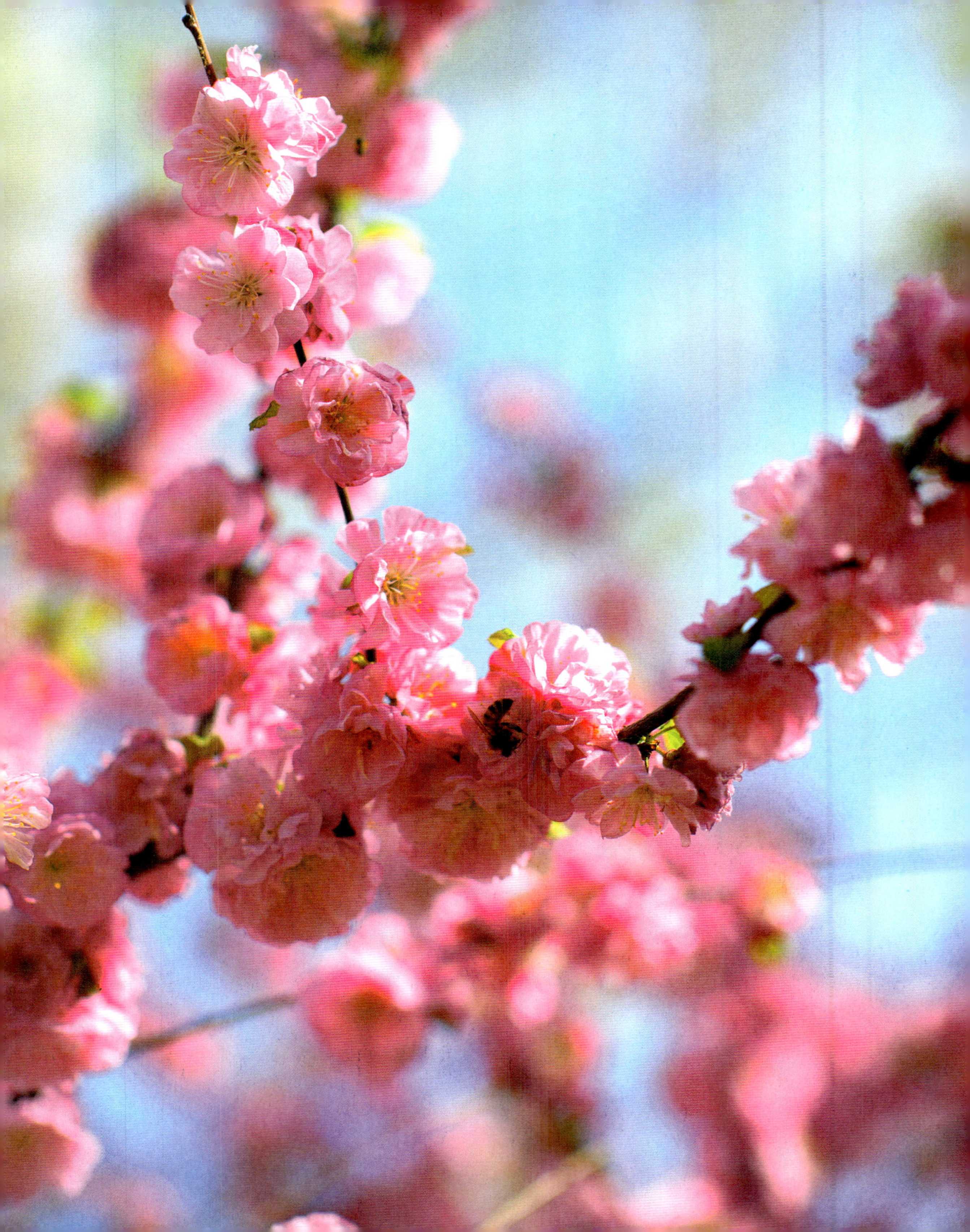

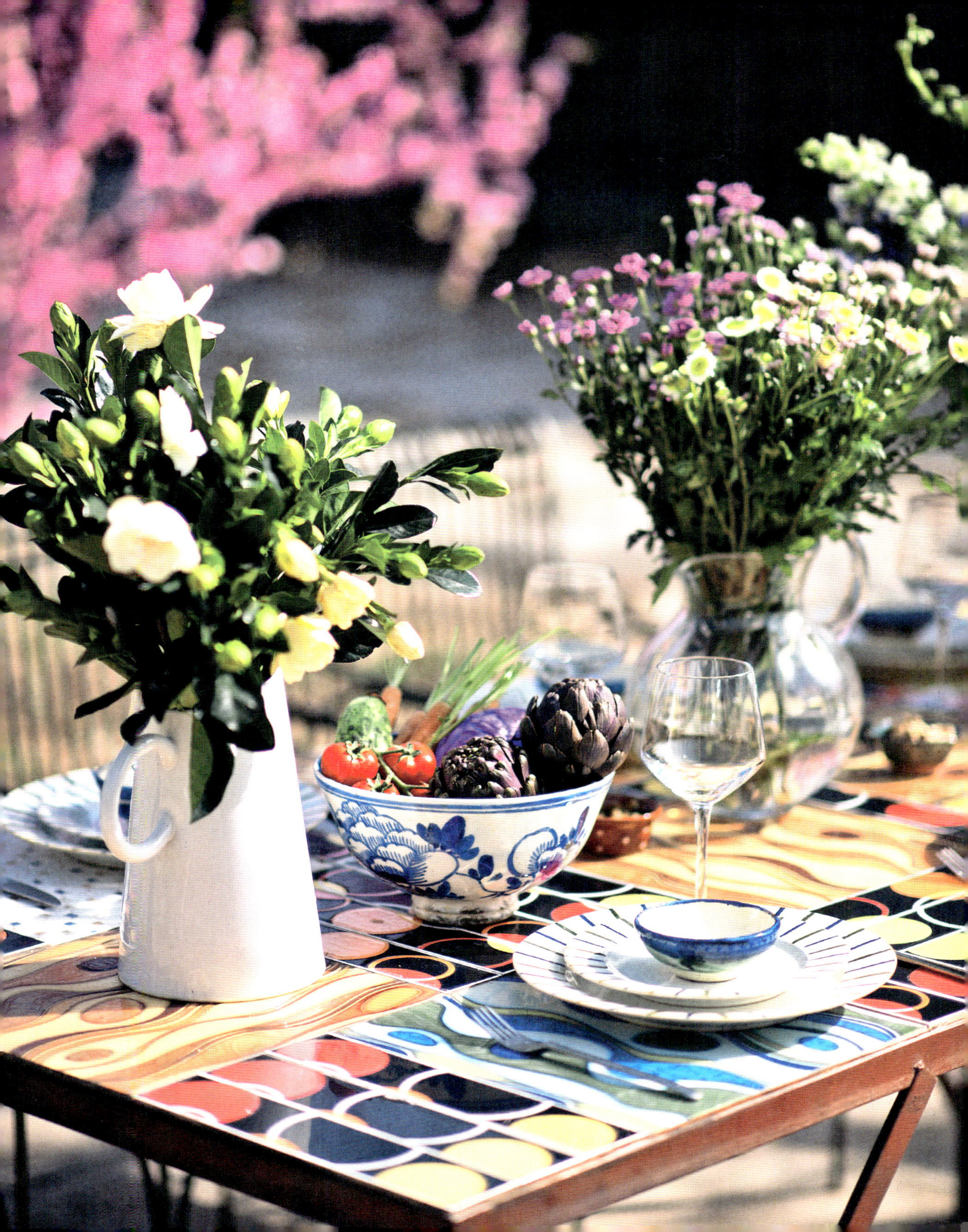

们，都常常出现在这里，这无意中让等位的队伍又加长了一百米。

那些前一晚参加派对刚刚醒酒的女郎，此时需要一杯低度数的鸡尾酒“回魂”；每天朝九晚五闷头工作的白领，迫切地想和好友分享丰盛的美食和热辣的八卦；而对于爱人、孩子和父母，则需要一段轻松而悠长的时光，一起共享其乐融融的氛围。生物钟把大家的胃一起唤醒在上午十点之后，让 Brunch 穿梭在早餐的简易清爽和午餐的浓烈厚重之间。“舒缓无压力的节奏”、“丰盛却轻松的美食”、“香槟和鸡尾酒”、“八卦和好友”，这些关键词构成了 Brunch 的精髓，无论你是把它当作私人时光来享受，还是当成一种社交形式，都是最从容和放松的节奏。

而像我们这样有小孩子的家庭，更喜欢呼朋唤友地在家里进行早午餐。这样的早午餐聚会是最轻松的了，它既没有像对午宴那样过高的期待，又不必到最后一分钟还在准备菜肴一起上桌。大家轻松围坐，一边做菜一边吃，聊聊天，弄弄花，喝喝酒，有舒服的椅子、好看的餐桌餐具，混着混着，就到了下午茶的时间。就像这天，当我摆盘停当，细毛的美味陆续上桌时，他们的女儿樱桃欢呼着爬上座椅，尹齐的石榴苗已经扎实地栽在了小院的土地上，水汩汩地从一条黑色皮水管里流进树苗周围新培的土窝，一点一点渗入土壤，冒出细小的气泡。

居住于伦敦的作家、家居和园艺设计师卡罗琳·克利夫顿－莫格（Caroline Clifton-Mogg）曾说过：“一眼看过去，会客早午餐的餐桌要散发出欢迎的气氛。”想要达到这个目的有一个最简单的办法：在已经布置好的餐桌上摆放些食物，提醒客人，美味之旅即将开始。与光秃秃的餐桌和空着的瓷盘相比，只有在食物参与进来后，一张餐桌的布置才算完整，也更能让人感觉到主人的热情。于是，在摆放好盘碟的餐桌上，有装在小竹篮子里的面包、码在各种美丽的搪瓷和陶质盘子中的水果，还有一个很乡村很传统的蓝白花纹的大陶盆，里面装的是各色新鲜的蔬菜，如水粉静物画一般，既是完美的桌面装饰，在养眼之后，还会变成餐盘里美味清新的沙拉。

从吃着粘满香脆杏仁片的可颂面包、自制的甜橙酱、新鲜的水果开始，慢慢吃到用橄榄油和香草醋拌的蔬菜沙拉、从西班牙带回的火腿，再吃到我最拿手的蜜汁烤翅，还不过瘾，细毛挽起袖子，从地里采来鲜嫩的菠菜和小水萝卜。小水萝卜的那种桃红色看上去迷人极了，是调色板上都找不出的艳丽。洗干净，咬一口，脆脆的，满口的清香。菠菜用热水轻轻焯过就好，放在煮得软硬合适的面条里，加一点台湾的鲜味酱油膏、一大勺雪白软糯的猪油，趁着热度拌匀，就是一道简单却丰厚的美味。

时光仿佛带着一种童年时暑假才会有的气息，悠长、缓慢又昏昏欲睡。太阳从偏东到正中，又渐渐西斜的时候，我们依然懒散地倚在舒服的椅子中，喝着小酒，闲聊着。樱桃用小铲子在玩树坑里的水和泥巴，随时吸引她的，还有地上刚冒出的各种小花。五个月大的小叶子则在树荫下香甜地做着美梦。无论有多少时光，在这里也只是瞬间的消遣。这时候，面前的彩色大长桌上又摆满了我国宝岛台湾的竹炭花生、法国的马卡龙和我们自己烘焙的各种花色的杯子蛋糕，还有装在搪瓷盘子里的冷冻的大甜柿子，黄澄澄的颜色一如它去年秋天挂在枝头般明亮。茶杯茶壶一一摆出，被滚烫的水冲刷过，再泡上一壶新得的明前龙井。没一会儿，院子里又渐渐飘出了煮咖啡的香气……

轻松惬意的早午餐

A RELAXING BRUNCH

半自助式早午餐

开放式的厨房也是客厅，一群朋友端着香槟杯，自己斟酒，听着音乐说说笑笑，随手捏起大餐盘里摆好的各种精巧的小食，再切一片木头小案板上的黑胡椒牛肉放进嘴里，等待着主人不断颠动的平底锅里马上就要出锅的美式炒蛋……如果说早餐是收拾行囊准备出发，午餐是去征服眼前的高山，早午餐则更像是漫无目的的逛街，走走停停，优哉游哉。多花一些时间在享受布置餐桌的过程上吧——用一些简单新鲜的花朵，随意插在花瓶或大杯子中就好；无论是把盘碟分别摆放好，还是只是将它们成摞地摆放在桌子的一角，都没问题；刀叉餐具也可以直接放在罐子或杯子里，让客人自己取用；包括食物，也可以用大号的盘子或碗盛放，让大家享受自助和分享的乐趣。这既减少了自己的工作量，又营造了轻松的氛围，这才算是掌握了早午餐的精髓。早午餐的餐桌布置不宜过于花哨，但要热情、迷人并舒适无比，就像前文所说，别忘记在布置好的餐桌上摆放一些现成的食物，例如一些自制的果酱、装在小陶罐里的黄油、装在玻璃大扎里的鲜榨果汁或放在篮子里的新鲜面包……不用着急，你可以一边和朋友聊天一边在厨房里做菜，这些食物会静静地待在桌面上，替你向每个来客微笑，问好。

把餐桌搬到户外

在户外用餐的好处是，尽管打破以往布置餐桌的常规，可以用旧床单当作桌布，也可以把花园中的盆花直接搬上餐桌。甚至把秋日的落叶撒满餐桌，间或装饰一些粗树枝做成的烛台，让季节感直接入味。户外用餐时所有的装饰品要和环境相互呼应，用陶器代替细腻的瓷器，用木质或竹质的餐具代替华丽的银器，把那些娇气的水晶花瓶也留在屋内吧，用陶土小花罐和搪瓷壶当作花器就足够了。水果和蔬菜除了被吃掉，还可以把它们当作装饰品。那些颇具建筑美感的洋蓟和茴香头摆在碗里相当漂亮，各种菜瓜也是很有体积感的道具，堆放在一起颇有丰收之感，对切、去掉内瓤之后，甚至还能当作插花容器。

再体贴一点

所有的一切都在提醒你，早午餐很轻松，在户外用餐可以更加随意。但随意是客人享受的一种气氛，要让这种“随意”舒服得体，则是主人更该花心思的。首先是座位。无论是北欧风格的原木座椅，还是庭院感觉的藤椅或铁艺座椅，上面一定要有厚厚的软垫和靠垫，让每个人都感觉舒服是最基本的要求，甚至大于美观。然后要想到餐桌上是否要有遮阳伞，或者有一片浓浓的树荫，因为阳光并不是任何时候都让人感觉愉悦的。夏天还要考虑用不用准备户外用的驱蚊蜡烛或者大功率的户外电扇。飞虫较多的季节，要考虑食物是否需要罩上一些专用的纱罩。

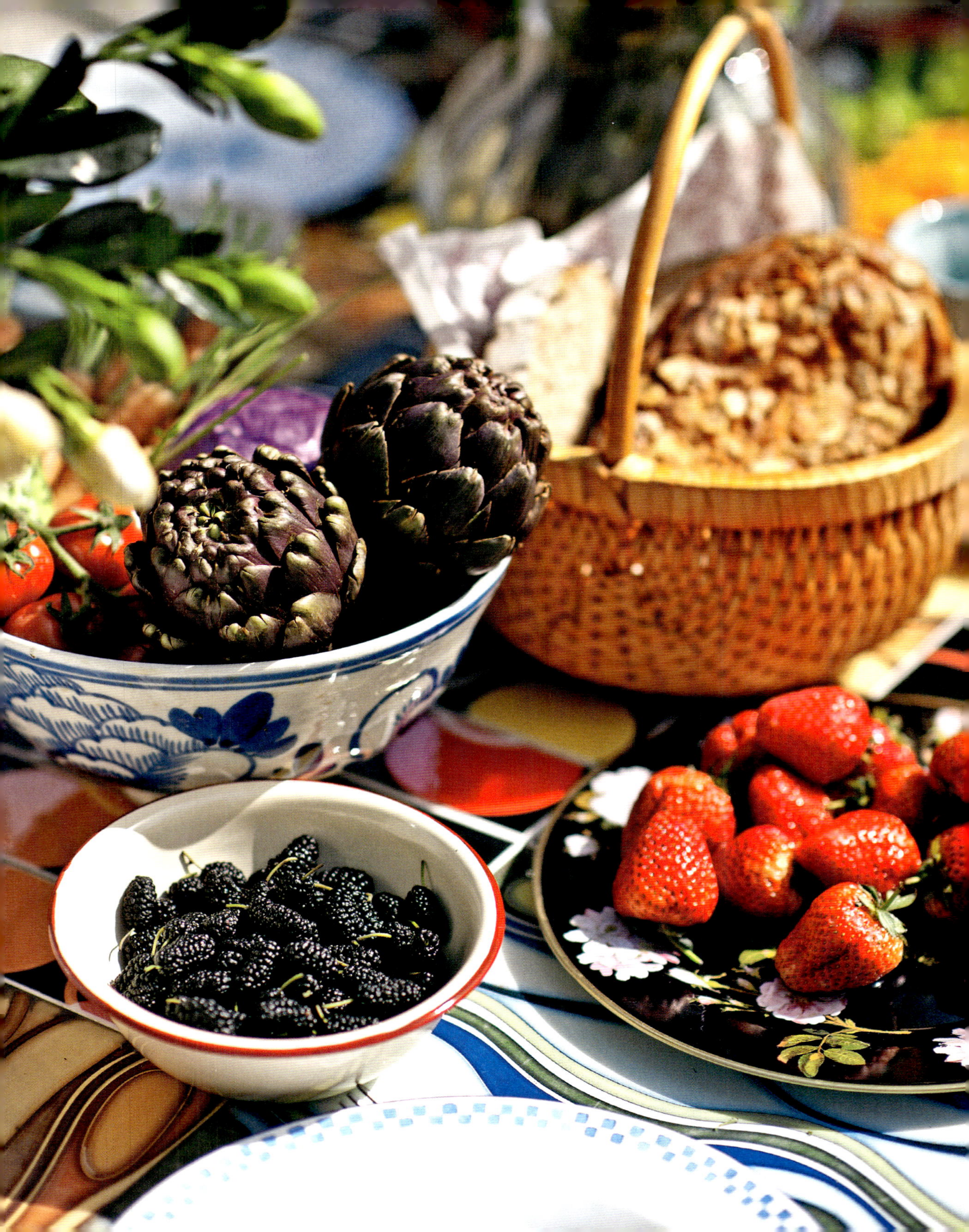

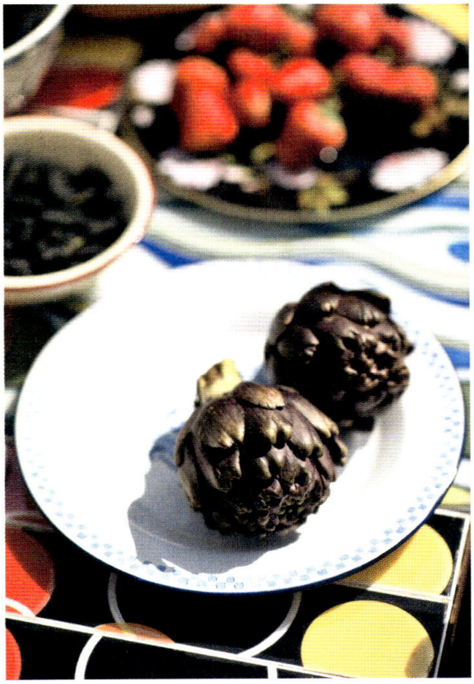

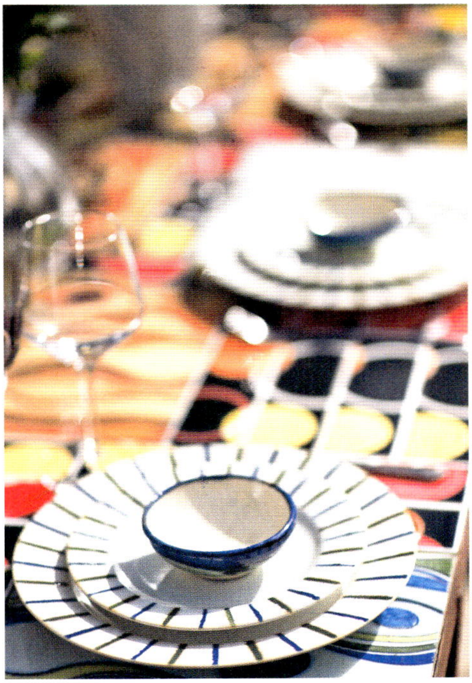

外表很有装饰性的朝鲜蓟摆放在餐盘里或装饰在陶瓷盆里，很有乡村风情，同时，它又是很好的开胃菜。

◀ 在花园的餐桌上，蔬菜、水果都是最好最自然的装饰，而且让人愉快的是，还可以把它们通通吃掉！

美丽的粗陶器皿更适合户外，白色、蓝色和咖啡色的搭配仿佛带来了地中海的阳光。

一 起 等 待 的 春 日

WAITING FOR SPRING

一桌人各自默默滑手机的局面像北京雾霾的天气一样灰色、压抑而令人沮丧。但在这样一个等待春日的午餐桌上，有美丽的鲜花、可口的食物、漂亮的餐具，谁又愿意去对着无聊的手机屏幕呢?

窗外是北京二月末的天气，依然灰色寒冷，却暗暗酝酿着巨大的暖意。收音机开着，池子里各式各样碧绿、嫩黄、莹红的芽儿，尖儿，果儿，都已经冲洗干净，鲜嫩地滴着水，瓦罐里的素高汤也已经突突地冒出了清香的热气，肥美的鳕鱼已经被腌制了整整一天，等待着被推进热热的烤箱，吱吱地冒出油泡儿。此时的小叶子正在她的小床上安静地睡着，这小小的婴孩似乎知道一会儿即将到来的热闹，于是悄悄把觉提前睡好。

这个季节，菜市场和花卉市场里，都有了大批的鲜货。刚冒芽儿的小菠菜，幼嫩的叶子和粉红的根楚楚动人，顶着黄花的刚刚长出的小小黄瓜苗即被摘下，让我家阿姨看到直说作孽。还有水灵的芥蓝、鸡毛菜、豌豆、春笋，一派生机盎然，让人看了便想微笑。花市里也一下丰富了起来，洋牡丹正当季，颜色不下十几种，龙胆依然清新，还有第一次见到的绿色的康乃馨、近乎灰白色的银叶菊，让流连于其中的我，久久无法确定自己的心思。

平时很少有机会可以在午餐时和大家相聚，中午从来都是匆匆忙忙的简餐或联络同事的聚餐。周末的聚会也常常为了准备得更充裕而选择晚餐，但这样的季节，这样一个等待春天的时刻，我脑子里出现的画面是明亮的——花儿在阳光下呈现出它们最美的颜色，所有的食物也都是在自然的光线下，经过精致的烹饪，让每个人感受到蔬菜的新鲜碧绿、烤肉的焦香肥美。

今天来的客人除了老友细毛、尹齐一家，还有新朋友——协和医院的张羽医生和她可爱的小女儿。要是放在以前，我们可能几乎没有什么机会相识，但微博真是个好东西，因为同样爱旧货、爱瓷器而使我们聊到一起，直到相约围坐在一起吃饭、面对面地谈笑。她在微博上的名字是“协和张羽”，头像有着很专业的笑容，让人敬畏。当门铃被按响，开门的一瞬间我发现，她本人比照片上漂亮、生动很多，医生的威严不复存在，那一刻，更是一见如故。

小女孩们自然地跑到一边去玩儿了，完全不用操心和照顾。启开香槟，一道道菜上桌，话题也随之而来。平日大家花太多时间在网上了解社会和生活，用键盘与人交谈，在餐桌上也常常出现一桌人各自默默滑手机的局面，那感觉就像北京雾霾的天气一样灰色、压抑而令人沮丧。久而久之，人变得枯燥而麻木，似乎忘记了怎么与人面对面地交流，而恰恰是面对面地聊天，感受对方的语言、神态和各种微妙的信号，才能激活人的生动和新鲜。我们的话题从网络上“下载”到饭桌上，就像走进了一座熟悉的城市，却因为与友人同游，惊讶地发现了更多有趣的角落……阳光一点一点透进玻璃窗，在屋里绽放，落在盘子里、茶面上，在刀叉交错间跳跃、闪耀，然后又悄悄地溜走。

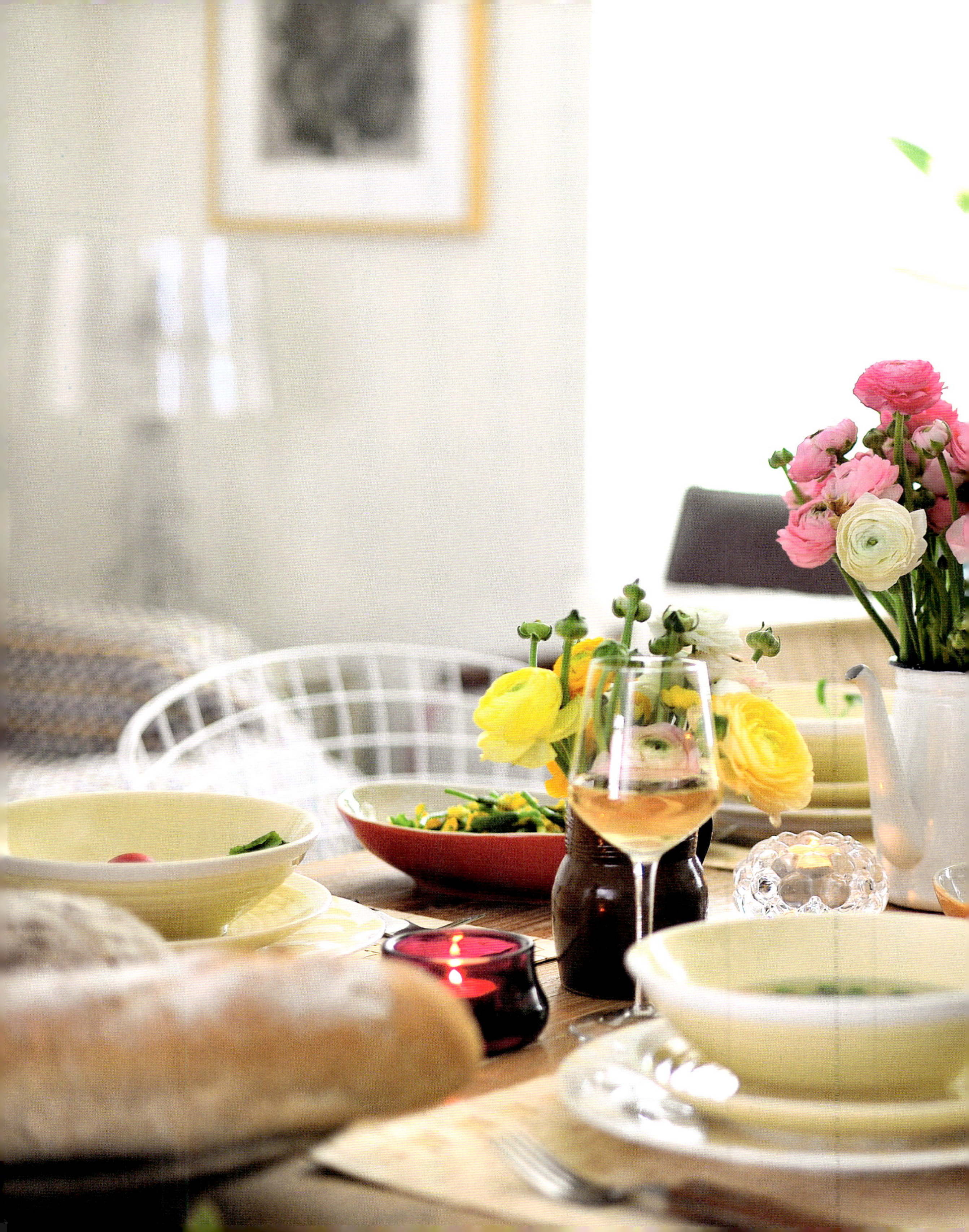

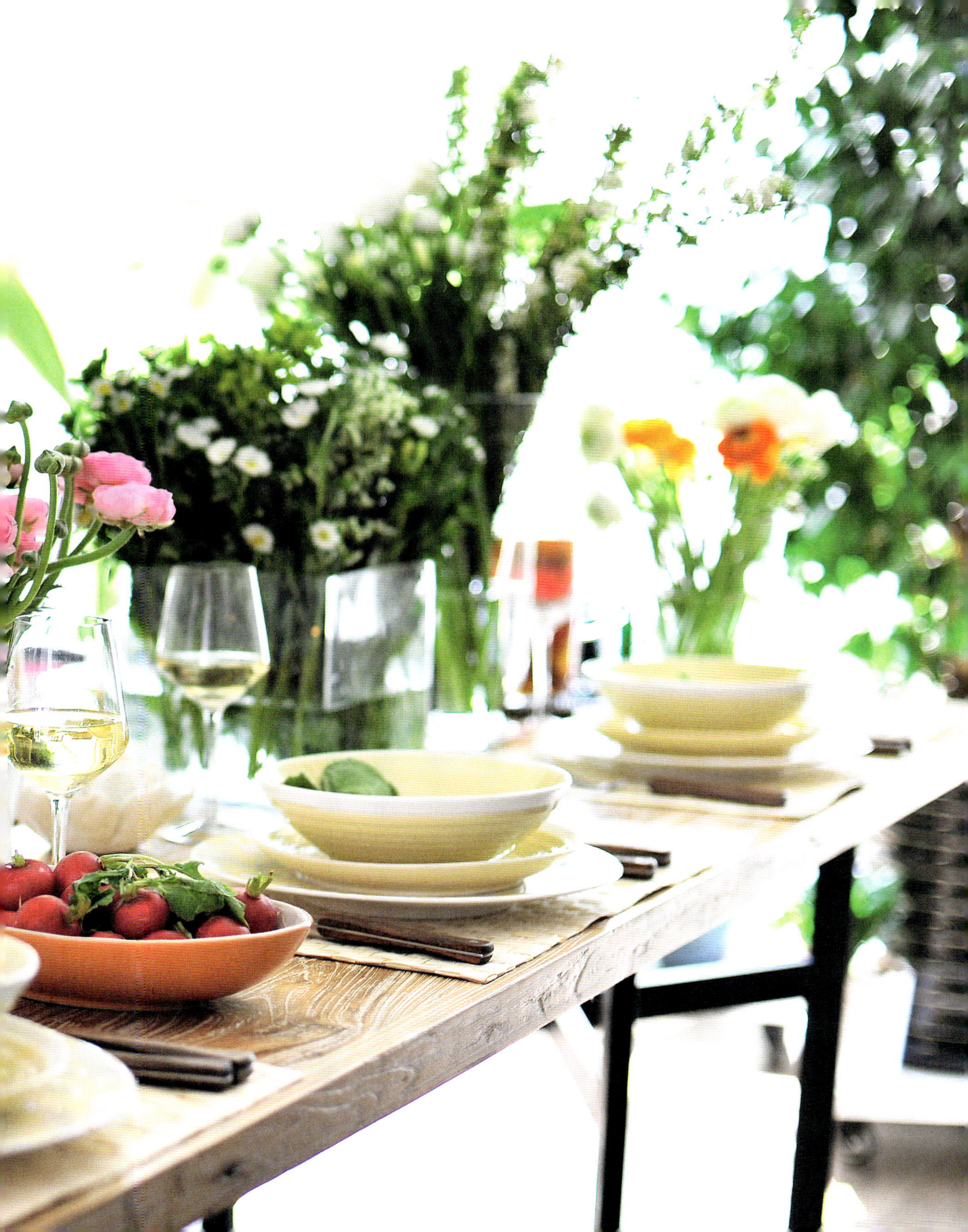

餐桌上明亮的黄色和粉色的洋牡丹灿烂美丽，花朵图案的餐巾和玻璃杯让人心情也亮堂起来。看到装饰在餐盘里新鲜可爱的小萝卜，每个人都不禁发出惊叹，仿佛一下被带入了有视觉和味觉双重感受的春天——春心荡漾，正是今天餐桌的主题。吃的菜也是素的，且新鲜清淡。但这一餐，准备的时间却比以往任何浓油酱赤的大鱼大肉都要长。那些小嫩芽、嫩叶，需要一根一根地择菜和清洗，还有用七种蔬菜慢煲四个多小时的素汤，上好的鳕鱼也用简单而神秘的私房酱料腌了二十四小时。烤好的鳕鱼肉嫩且紧致润滑，焦香入味，被细毛和尹齐这样品遍全球美食的刁嘴评为“最好吃的烤鳕鱼”。另一道大受美赞的菜是头盘的桂花梨汁浸樱桃番茄。这是之前去三摩地素食餐厅吃饭时吃过并念念不忘的一道小菜。餐厅的老板唐香香亲自传授制法，小番茄去皮，与樱桃一同用梨汁和桂花酱腌渍一天以上，出来的味儿除了樱桃和番茄本身的味道之外，还有淡淡的桂花香和梨的清新感觉，放一颗在嘴里，从舌尖到心脾都润润的。唐香香的一句话给我留下深刻印象，她说，这是一个“糖拌西红柿”的速成时代，已经难得有谁乐意用二十四小时的耐心去等待，只不过是一颗颗小番茄的美丽蜕变了。然而，至少在我和我的朋友这里，花时间用心思去做一道菜，用它来表达某种爱，是真的快乐的。

培根烤金针菇出炉了，色相红亮，味道喷香。培根的油脂和咸鲜味儿被热力渗入金针菇中，简单的食材搭配在一起，经过最简单的烹饪，往往效果却很好。尹齐望着盘子直搓手。他当时正在患过敏性哮喘，几乎失语，被医生禁了酒肉。他哑着嗓子请求细毛帮他抽出里面的金针菇吃吃。一边的张羽看不过去了，说你吃点肉吧，没事儿。那边话音还没落，这边尹齐立刻遵医嘱动起手来。管她是不是妇产科医生呢！

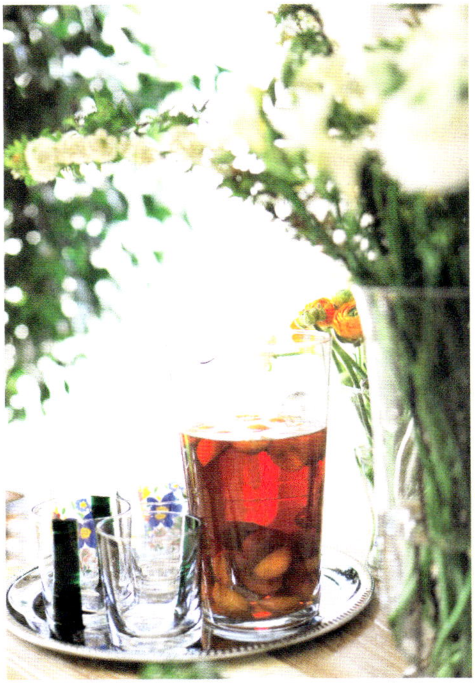

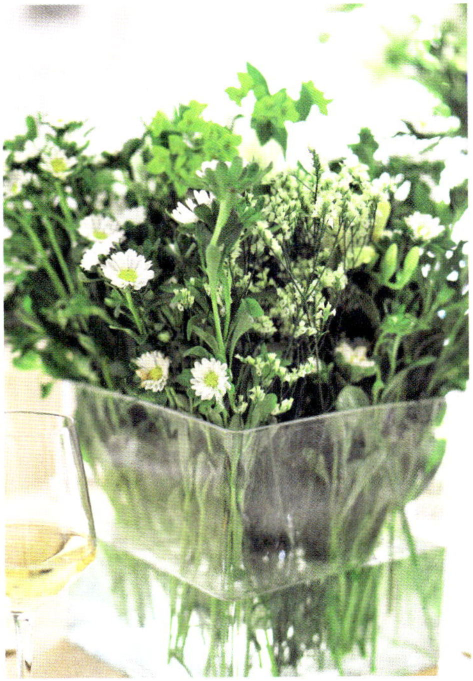

印花玻璃杯和自制的金橘红茶都让春天的感觉无处不在。

就像路边采来的小花，不用费心打理，随便插在瓶中就好了，轻轻松松。

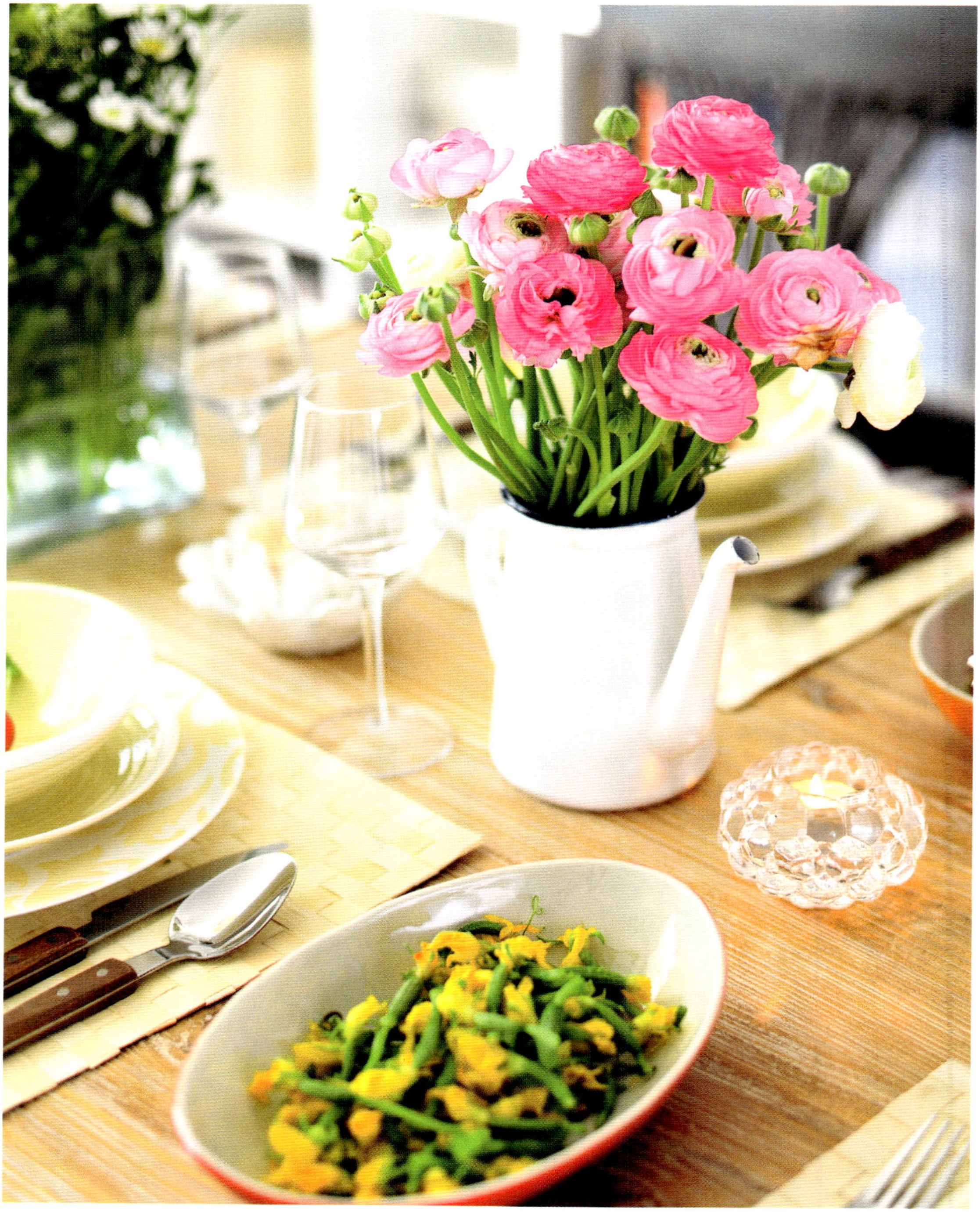

不一定非要用花瓶插花，搪瓷茶壶也可以拿来当花器，烘托轻松随意的家庭气氛。

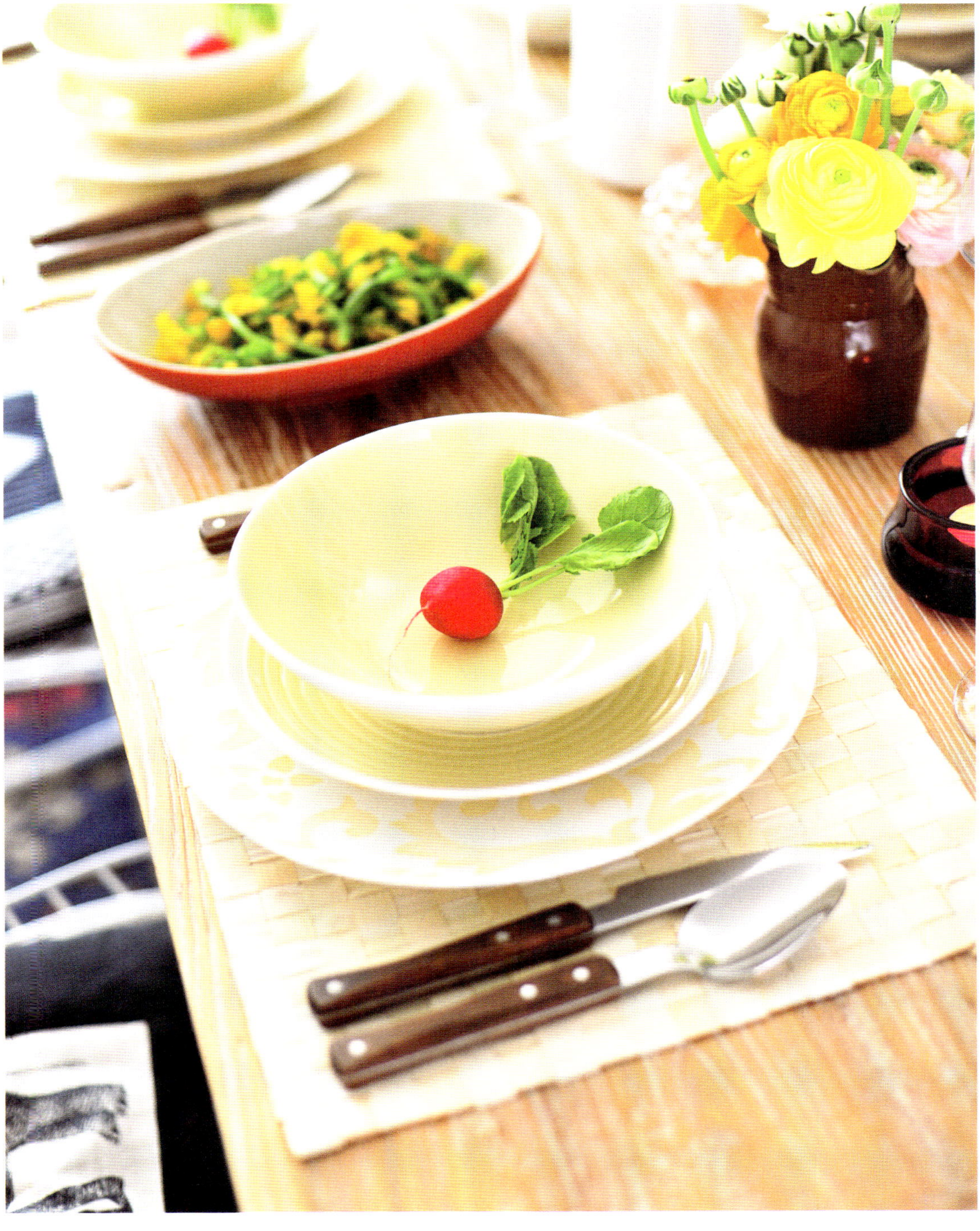

用新鲜艳丽的小萝卜作为餐盘装饰，不仅漂亮，且很容易就把客人带入对春天视觉和味觉的双重感受中。

春光明媚的午餐桌

A LUNCH TABLE IN SPRINGTIME

美丽的餐桌让大家团聚

好像自从长大以后，就很少再有一家人一起坐下来吃午餐的时候了。但这种习惯其实非常值得保留。不去看电视，也远离手机，在周末与家人或朋友一起享用一次阳光午餐——看着他们眉飞色舞地聊八卦，小孩子两眼放光地描述学校的游戏和趣事，哪怕是父母对邻居发的牢骚，都会是生动有趣的话题，让你更接近他们的世界。但能够吸引大家围坐过来不愿走开的前提是，要有一个非常美丽且具有吸引力的餐桌布置。想象一下，当你精心地熨好桌布，摆上鲜花，把每天都用的餐具装饰起来，还有可口的食物、漂亮的餐巾，谁又愿意去面对无聊的手机和电视屏幕呢?

不复杂，不凌乱

午餐相对于晚餐，是比较简单的一餐，布置不那么复杂，也没那么多规矩，虽然也会用到鲜花、茶蜡、桌布，但总体的氛围是轻松和随意的。可以选那些手工陶器或粗一些的瓷器，不必十分精美。餐盘有的有边沿，有的没有，那些没有的，就是适合午餐使用的随意款式。

色彩上也要选一个轻盈且简单的方案。让背景尽量干净简约，餐桌保持桌面的本色或只用一块白色的桌布就很好。盘子的色彩和花朵呼应，采用同样轻柔的黄色、白色、灰粉色或自然色，这些搭配起来怎么也不会杂乱。

来自春天的花朵

什么季节用什么花是最容易让人融入餐桌氛围的方法。春天可选的花太多了，例如洋牡丹、蔷薇等都是应季的灿烂小花。文心兰其实在什么季节都有，但它明黄的颜色却永远让人想到春天，是在迎春花开放之前的最好的替代品。一瓶合时宜的鲜花让桌面立刻有一种 dressed up（精心装扮）过的感觉，另外需要注意的是，如果花的香气很浓烈，那在你坐下开始吃饭前要把它们挪开，并且保持你的布置低于用餐者坐下交谈时的视线高度。

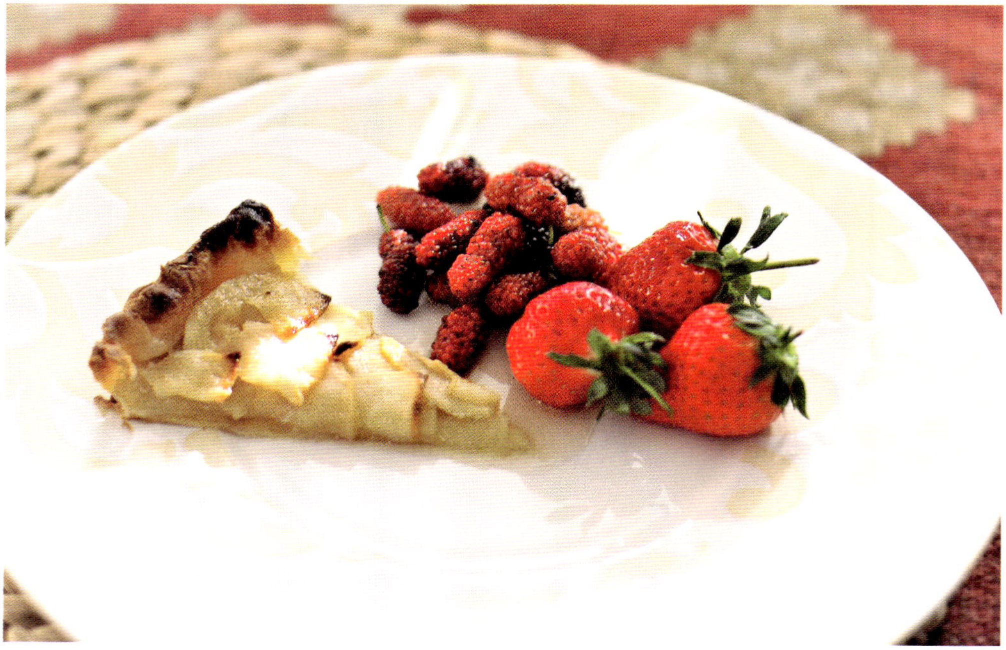

桑葚、草莓、亲手烘焙的苹果派，伴随着午后阳光和有着淡淡花香的蜂蜜，让春意盎然的感受达到顶峰。

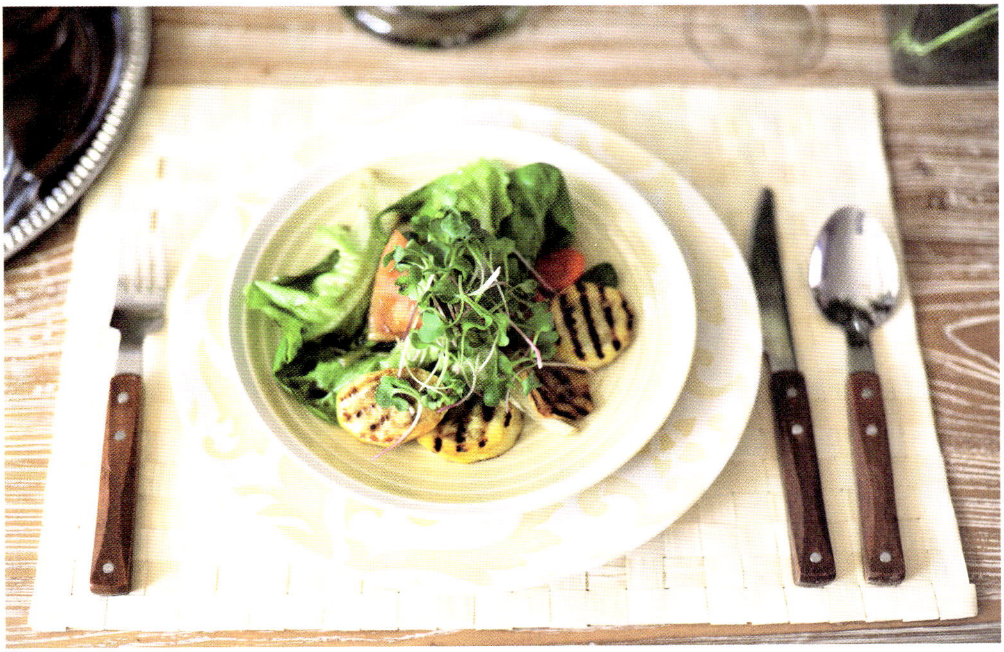

沙拉的颜色和餐盘很搭调，品尝春味的同时，也在观赏春色。

夏　夜　欢　宴

A SUMMER GALA

每当回忆过去时，依然会想起那时的觥筹交错、推杯换盏，那些温柔而美丽的细节，在彼此心里还会漾起涟漪，变换成唇边的一丝笑意。

在花卉市场，我被一间根雕店中堆在桌子下面的几块沉木吸引。自然的深褐色，枝角清晰，纹理生动，其中的“漏”也恰到好处。向店员询价，说这是没有加工的原材料，不出售。死磨硬泡一番，最终以按斤称的价格全部拿下。

拉着小推车才把这三条沉木从地下车库搬回家，擦去上面的浮尘、土渣，抚摸着骨感的枝干，开始幻想着它未来的各种可能性。

寻找这些树干，缘于几天前和 Patrick 的见面。Patrick 经营着北京一家有名的家居艺术机构和私人会所 Dara Lifelounge 私享家，他的会所和他本人一样，有一种惹眼、时髦且明朗爽快的风格。那天他喝着咖啡，忽然说，老几位真该聚一聚了，要不你来张罗，就在我这儿，咱们赶紧的吧。好啊，说着我环顾了一下四周，在会所二楼，有一间漂亮的天光餐厅，还有一间和开放式厨房相连的圆桌餐厅，一般来说，他的各种宴请都在这

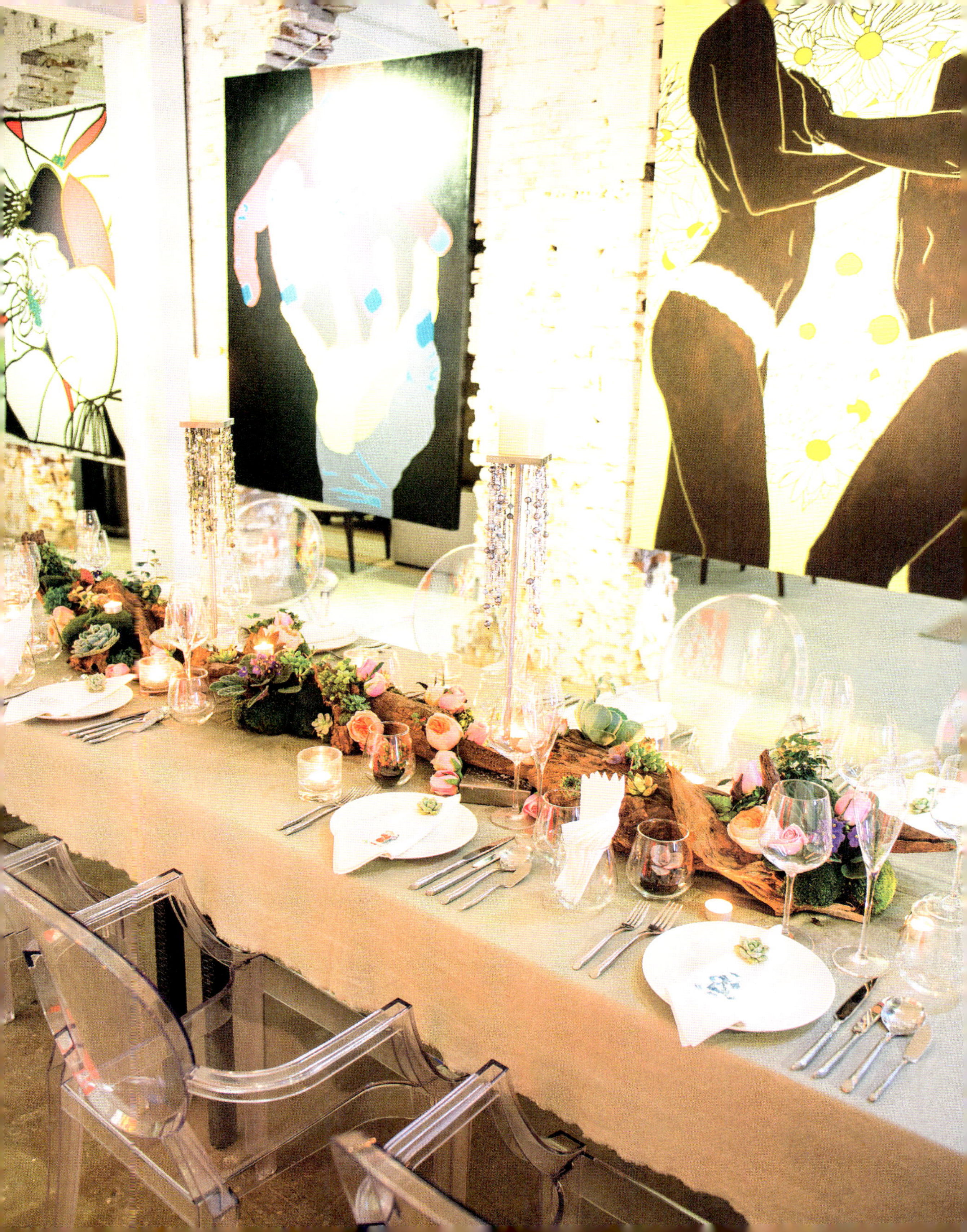

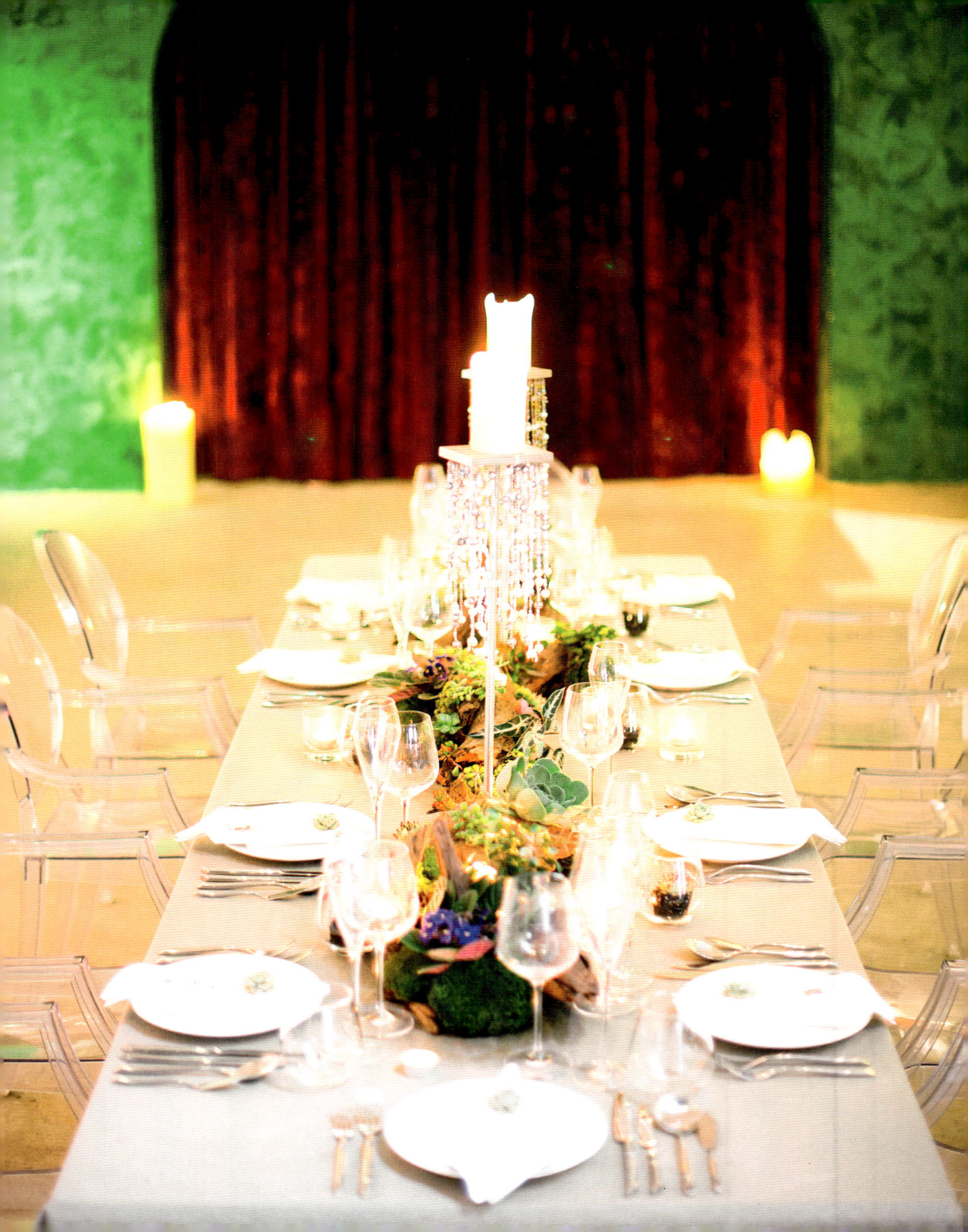

两间餐厅里进行。但过于常规的形式总是对我缺乏吸引力，于是目光继续转，下到一层画廊，那里正在展出的是画家兰一的作品，其中两幅梅花格外抢眼，一幅蓝色的，一幅红色的，鲜艳的色彩和张扬的笔触在冷色调高挑水泥结构的空间中，热烈、神秘，有一种动人心魄的力量。不如把餐桌搬到楼下来，就在这些画中间怎么样？我提议。Patrick犹豫了一下，他说从来没有在这个位置摆放过餐桌，不过，为什么不呢？就在这儿了！

我周围的朋友都具有某种共性——喜欢新鲜独特的东西，喜欢即兴，喜欢美好的形式感。所以当我发出这场“夏夜花园欢宴”的邀请时，立刻就得到了他们热情而欢快的回应。或者说，让我们着迷的不仅仅是美食和美酒，更多的是与之相关的其他的东西——那些理所当然的邀约借口，面对面直白而不加掩饰的赞赏和惊叹，让人无负担的小小放纵和沉迷，暗藏在一杯、一碟、一餐、一酒中对情意的珍重和表达。

当时正值五月伊始，立夏已过，北京的天气却反常，一直没有真正热起来。期待中初夏的鲜花、树木、暖风、冷酒就像漫长的序曲，总也迎不来高潮。我想象着初夏夜晚于我的感觉，思考着是以一组一组不规则的透明玻璃花瓶中插放深红色牡丹来装饰桌面，还是以树木、植物、各种花草来组成大胆而神秘的花园。前者是我有把握的布局，基本的样式在脑海中清晰呈现，真实的效果也会美轮美奂。而后者是从未尝试过的想象，或者说，在没有看到那些真实的树木枝干和与之组合的花草前，一切都只是设想。

◀ 枯木、苔藓、多肉植物和各种花草、鲜花，夏夜充满神秘色彩的花园于餐桌之上徐徐展开，给每位客人都留下了深刻的印象。

每次筹划朋友的聚会，我都会如此费一番心思，即使再随意的小聚，也希望让他们在不经意中感受到一些新意。可以说，这是我的一种执着，一种摩羯座特有的固执和认真。而且，随着年龄的增加，越发觉得能聚在一起的朋友是多么难得。时光易逝，经常走着走着，一些曾经很近的朋友，就渐渐走散了，但每当回忆过去时，依然会想起那时的觥筹交错、推杯换盏，那些温柔而美丽的细节，在彼此心里还会漾起涟漪，变换成唇边的一丝笑意。

而晚宴在任何文化里，都是隆重而精致的终极盛宴，发出晚宴的邀请甚至让人心里有一点点紧张，它既不像早午餐那样懒散随意，也不像午餐那样简单。菜要有隆重的大菜，甜品不但必不可少，而且最好有几种选择。Patrick 的主厨和我商量晚宴的菜单——清爽的黄瓜冷汤作为开始，然后是鞑靼三文鱼和香煎澳带作为开胃前菜，优质的小牛肉作为主菜，之后是各种莓果和烤蛋白组合的甜品，所有的食材、搭配以及色彩、造型都配合夏夜主题，清爽而丰盛。

各种细节在两天内纷纷确定，而我的寻找也在走了几家花卉市场，看了很多根雕花艺，直到遇到那几条原始的沉木时瞬间明朗。对的，就是它们。一直懵然的幻想一下清晰了，美艳的牡丹在意念中灰飞烟灭，尽管当时那几条干枯的树干落满了尘土，尽管它们脏兮兮的样子和精致的法式美食毫不搭界，但我知道，就是它们了。

“时光凋零陨落，仿佛蜡炬成灰。山川和树林，正当时，正当时。”叶芝笔下黛绿色的森林、花园、夏夜、仙人、铃兰花，像画面，像密码。跟随着这些讯息，继续拼凑我脑海中的幻想。

宝石花、冰灯玉露、白牡丹……这些有着动人名字的多肉植物有着奇妙而娇憨的姿态。还有非洲紫罗兰、铜钱蕨、网纹草，对的，还有一大包碧绿湿润的苔藓。把苔藓植入沉木天然的“漏”之中，再分别嵌入多肉植物和各种花草，一丛一簇，疏密有致，生机勃勃。随着一点点的完工，整条枯木像被魔法棒点过，瞬间被赋予了生命。仿佛还缺少让它们彻底绽放的一笔？是玫瑰！淡粉色的奥斯丁玫瑰有着多重繁复的花瓣，就像中世纪贵妇层层叠叠的裙摆，它们彻底激发了这座神秘花园妖娆的魔力。当闪亮的餐具严格规整地排列好，香槟杯和红酒杯各就各位，蜡烛一盏一盏被点燃，洁白的亚麻绣花餐巾叠放得当，最后一朵“白牡丹”轻放在餐巾之上，一切就绪。

烛光跳动闪耀，伴着舒伯特《a 小调大提琴奏鸣曲》（D.821），原本冷静理性的画廊被夏夜美丽的餐桌变幻出浓浓的梦幻气氛。踩着点儿准时到达的是李艾。认识她十几年了，从名模到名主持，这几年见到她反而更多是在电视上、照片里。她笑着指着自己的脸说，这是刚刚在出租车上才化的妆。本来素颜赴约，路上忽然刷出 Patrick 发在朋友圈里提前曝光的餐桌照片，惊呆了，这么美，必须“盛妆”配合呀！果然是很摩羯女的做派。粉红的香槟开启，闺蜜庄雅婷到了，随后是伊岚，只要有她们在场，就会有延绵不绝的欢声笑语。和我搭档的摄影师柴利增和他的太太 Flora 也到了，这是 Flora 生完宝宝后第一次参加晚上的欢聚，宝宝到来后全新的生活让大家的话题有了更多延伸……我们一起举杯，北京初夏的夜晚依然有几分凉意，但此刻，在这张长长的餐桌旁，鲜花和芳草，正当时，香槟和笑靥，正当时。

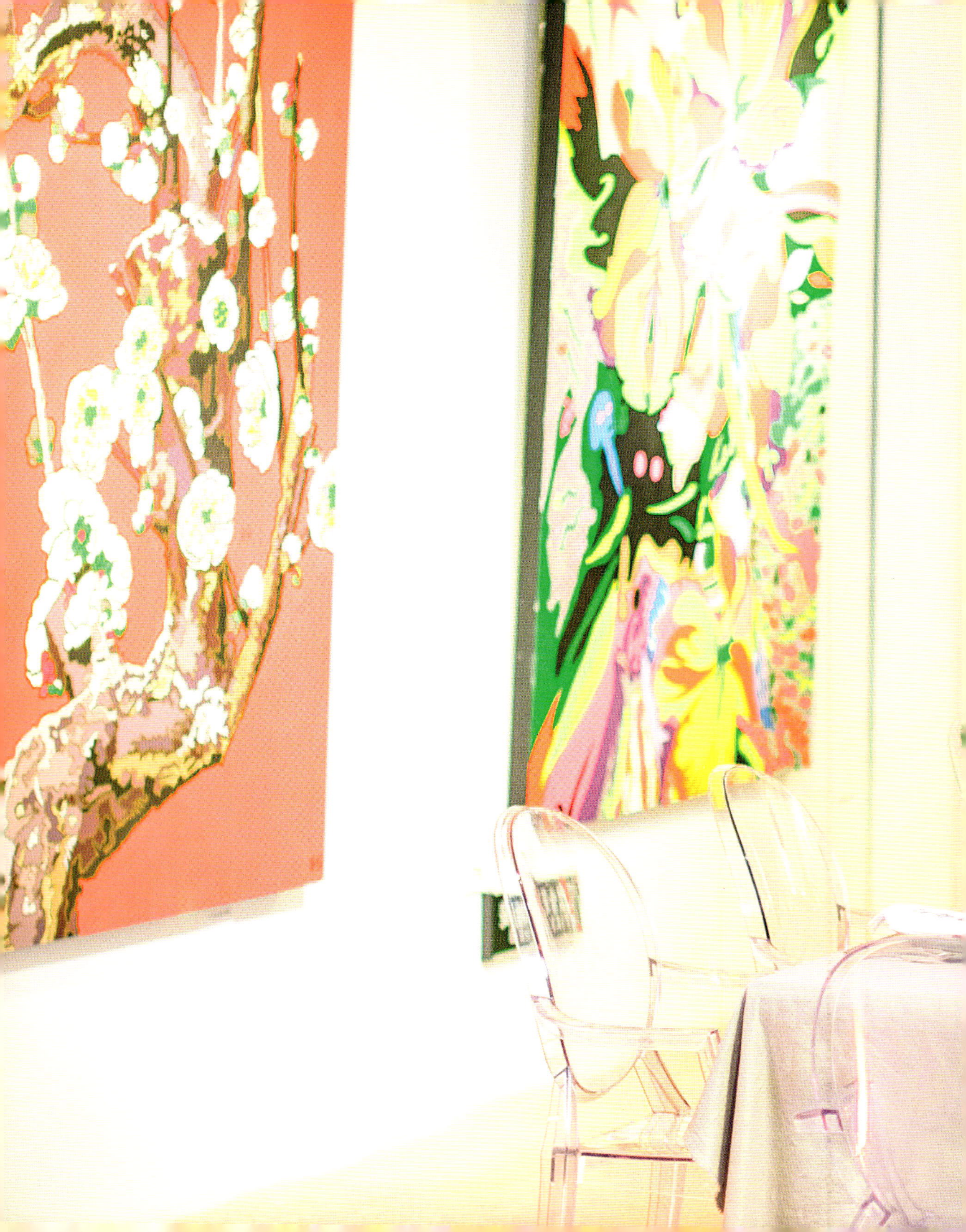

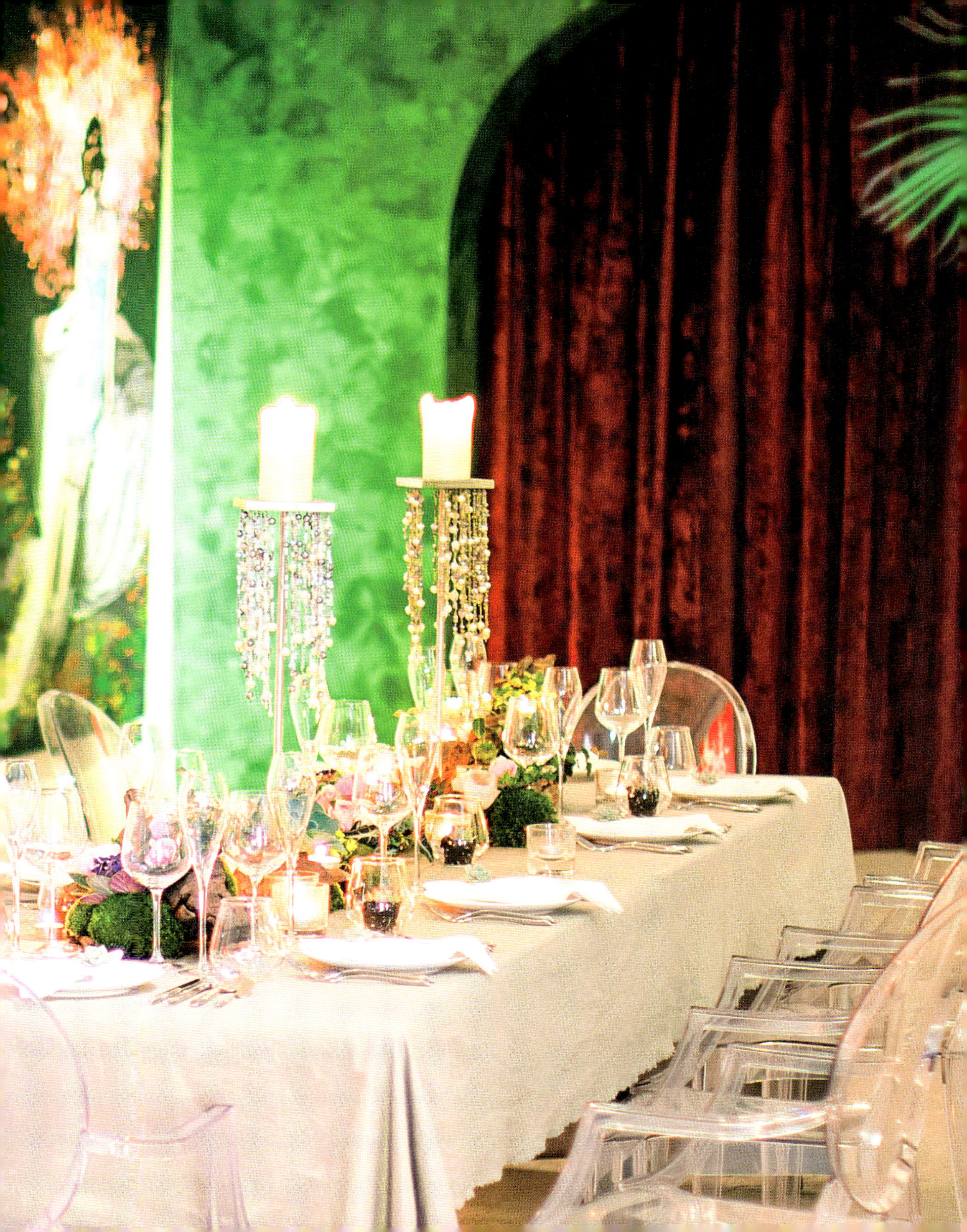

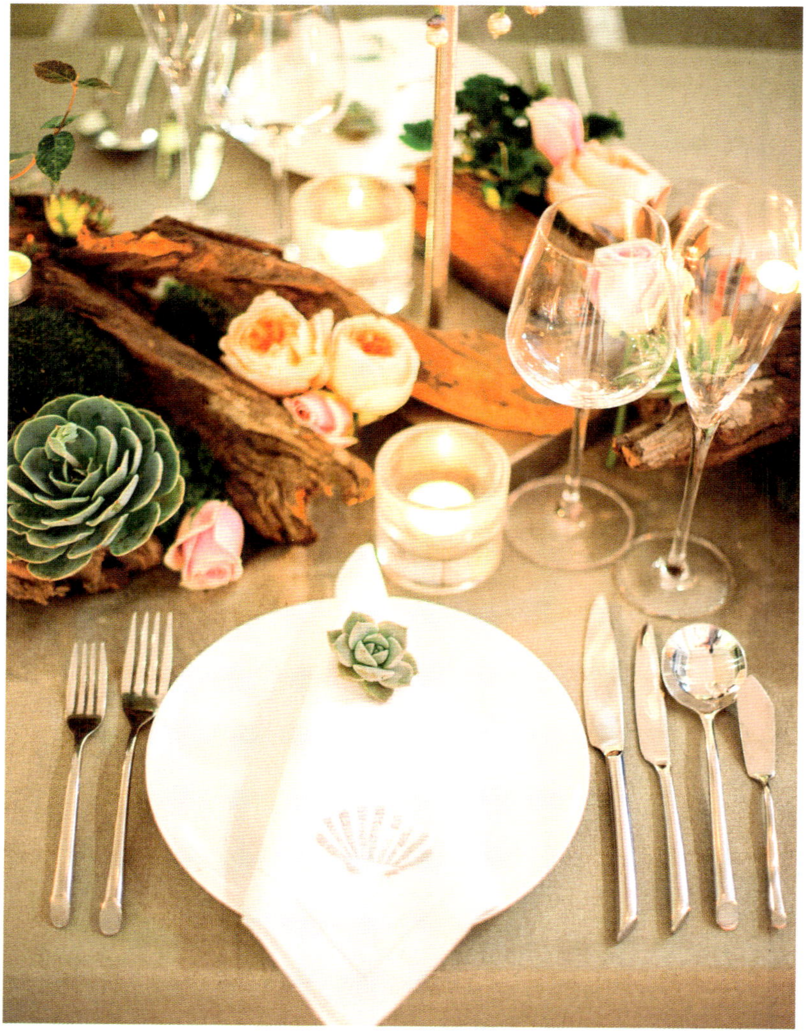

餐盘上装饰的“白牡丹”和桌面装饰相映成趣，还可以让客人带走继续种植。

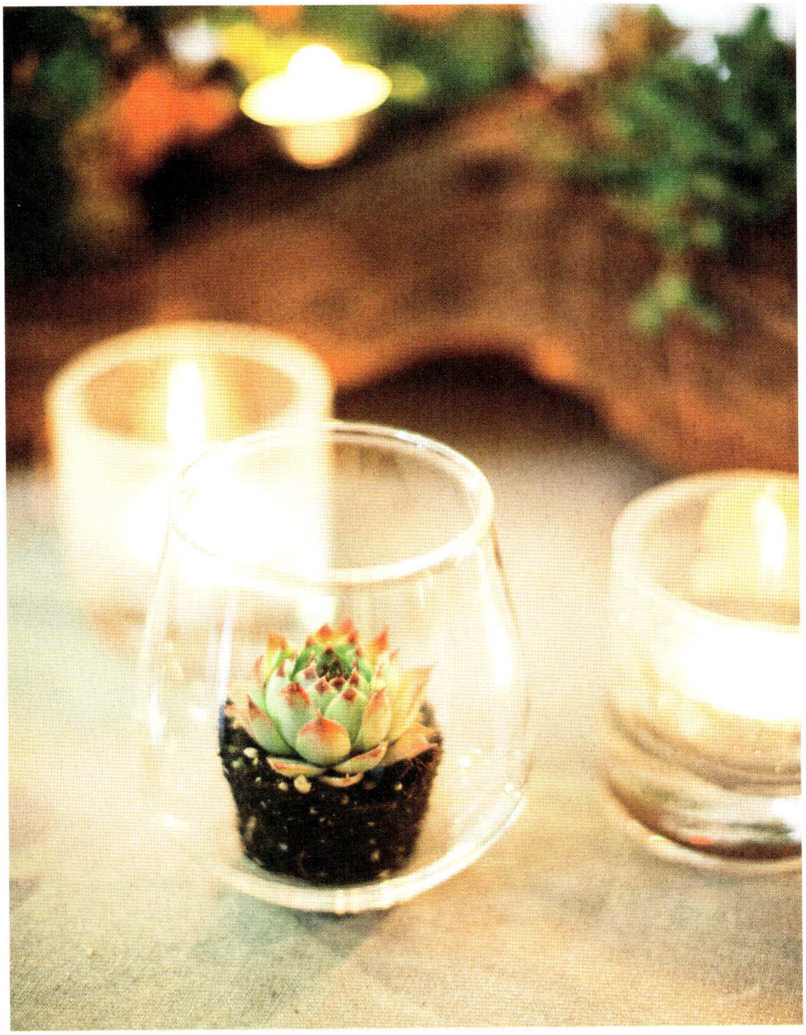

连土一起装入玻璃杯的多肉植物看上去像一块小小的杯子蛋糕。

晚 宴 的 魔 力

THE MAGIC OF A DINNER PARTY

奢华是晚宴的基调

这里所说的奢华并不是金钱上的堆砌和昂贵，而是用心。花很多时间在设计和筹备上，让每个客人感到难忘——难忘主人的殷勤和周到，难忘精彩的餐桌设计和别致的细节，难忘丰盛的美食甚至是席间或热烈或优美的佐餐音乐。所有的一切表现出主人的一种精神上的慷慨，要知道，晚宴餐桌不仅是一个舞台，更是主人的作品，取悦客人，同时也令自己陶醉。

使用最好的餐具

毫不吝惜地使用你最好的餐具、银器、玻璃器皿吧，尤其是酒杯。当一排高低不同的酒杯摆放整齐后，蜡烛在上面反射出无数的光芒，即使再寡淡的餐桌也让人像喝了酒一样目眩起来。“讲究气氛的餐桌上，要布置许多酒杯，以便饮用精心挑选来搭配不同菜肴的各色葡萄酒。理想状态下，应该先上白葡萄酒，然后是两到三种红酒，如果你的客人值得如此慷慨相待的话。”伊莎贝尔·阿连德在她的《阿佛洛狄特：感官回忆录》里如是说。

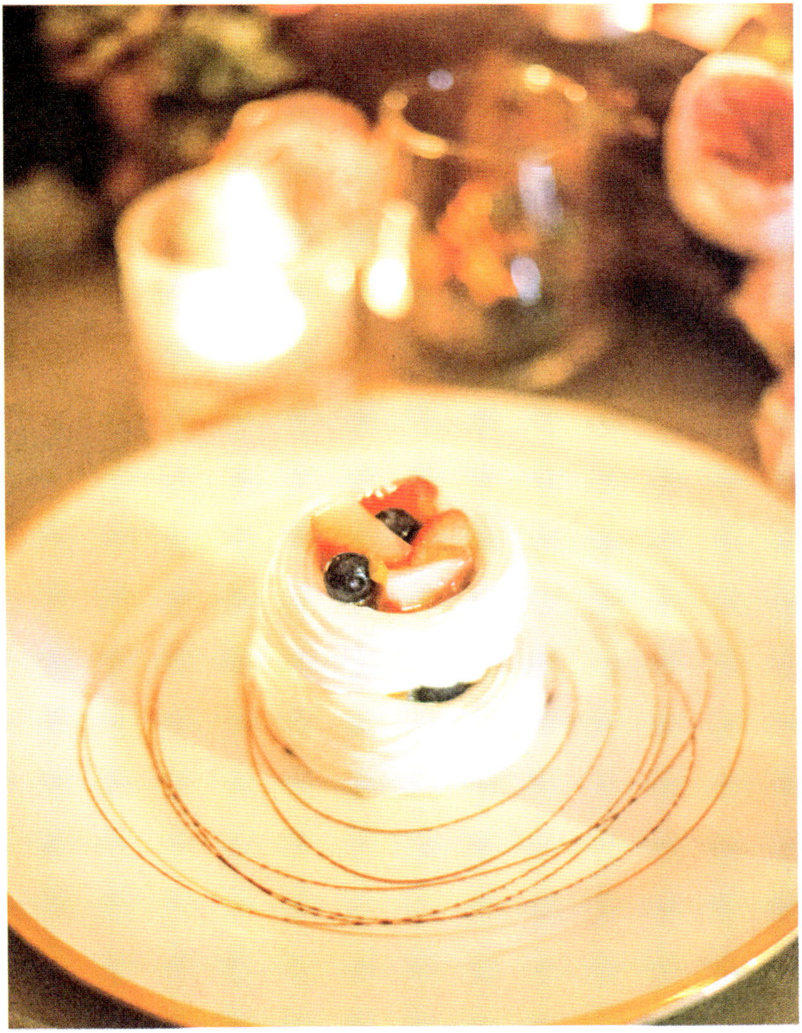

厨师长为晚宴专门设计的充满夏日色彩的甜品。

在细节上花心思

布置一张让人难忘的晚宴餐桌并不是很难，只要有颇具心思的细节。在这个夏夜欢宴的餐桌上，除了枯木与花草的结合外，在其他地方，亦有很多与之呼应的细节。比如餐巾上装饰的白牡丹多肉植物，还有一些小朵多肉，干脆连带原花盆里凝固成杯子状的土壤一起放进玻璃杯，与小茶蜡比肩摆放，让客人惊讶地以为是巧克力杯子蛋糕上装饰的花朵。在拥有很多装饰物的餐桌上，要注意一个原则，就是保持餐桌的一目了然。客人的目光应该能从装饰物上跃过，而不应该被阻拦，就像这张长桌上，大多数蜡烛是低矮的茶蜡或圆柱矮蜡。而制造层次的蜡烛则高高在上，被高挑的蜡烛台托起，同样不会隔断客人的目光。

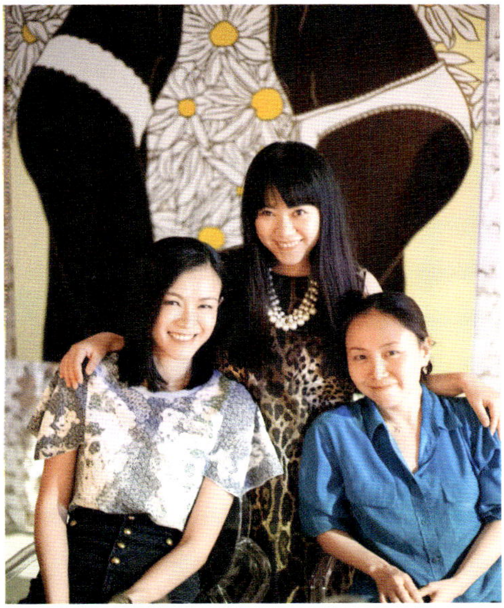

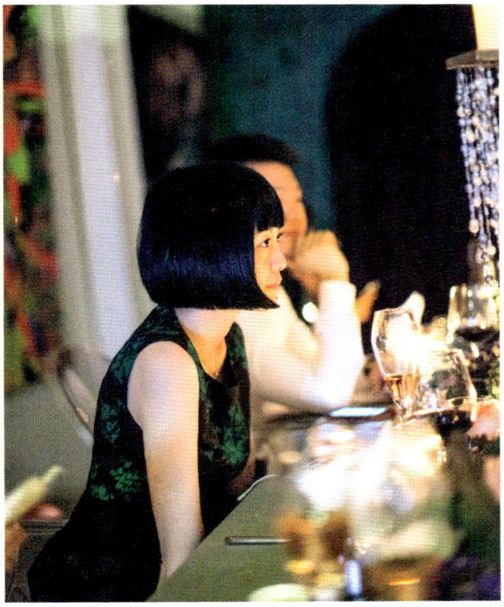

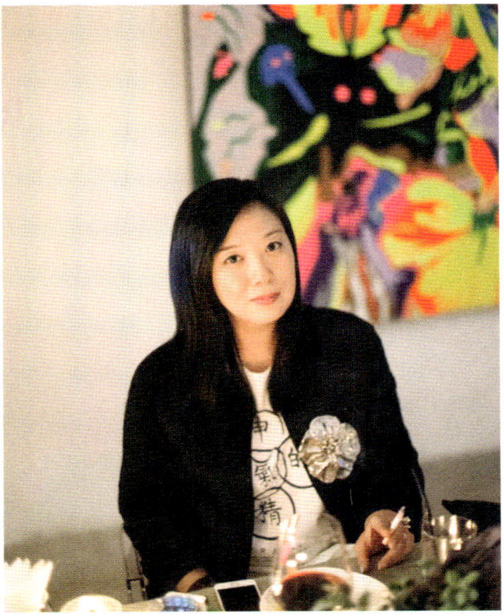

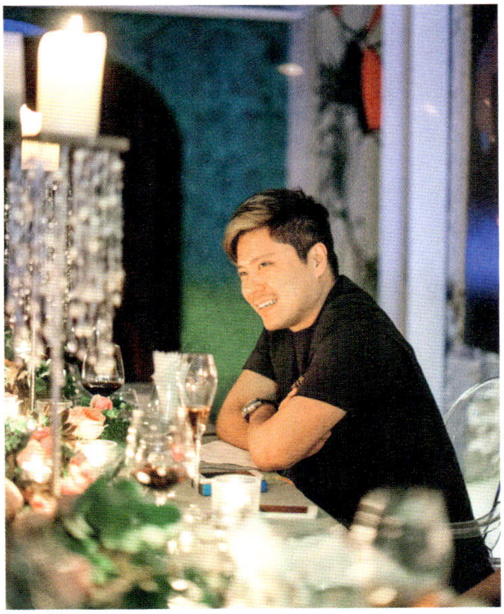

李艾、Flora 和伊岚
庄雅婷

曾焱冰
Patrick

节日，一起快乐

A TIME FOR CELEBRATION

那年的万圣节，北京居然下了大雪，桌上布置着各种橘色的果实和南瓜做成的装饰，盘子里装着软香浓郁的南瓜派；圣诞节的记忆则锁定在了小叶子出生的那年，红色花纹的桌布和装饰的松枝让人难忘；新年的餐桌最能给人带来希望，红色的LANVIN（浪凡）跳舞娃娃、金色的盘碟，一切都是喜欢的、希望的样子……

清晨的大雪扑打在车窗上，雨刷器奋力地刷着，发出唰唰的响声。2009年的10月31日，万圣节前夕，北京意外地飘起了大雪。在花卉市场和菜市场，我找到了红色的火龙珠、玫瑰，黄色的大花蕙兰以及小金橘、玉米、红梨等一大堆原本毫不相干的蔬果，将它们"跨界"组合后，变成了两棵奇妙的花果树。将花果树摆在长条的餐桌上，配上橘色的烛台，节日气氛浓得出奇，尤其在这白茫茫的大雪天，很温暖。

第一次在万圣节请朋友来家里吃晚宴，来的都是和我要好的姑娘们。她们有的打扮成了歌甜人美的八十年代歌后，有的戴着护士帽上演制服诱惑，还有的则摇身一变成了有着尖尖耳朵的性感小野猫。桌上的大餐从暖暖的南瓜汤开始，到超级万圣甜品拼盘结束——我亲手做的草莓慕斯配黄桃、树莓、杏仁瓦片，还有不可缺少的奶油南瓜派、涂了橙色糖衣的曲奇。记忆中食物的味道渐渐模糊了，但那些餐桌上无处不在的浓烈色彩却一直生动地储存在大脑深处。那一夜，如果从夜空看过来，在一片白茫茫的夜色中，是一面透出浓烈的橙色光芒的窗，从里面传出的欢声笑语在夜空里回旋。透过窗户可以看到，当时桌上蜡烛的火焰因众人的大笑而抖动，大家频频举杯，一大瓶香槟没了，三瓶红酒没了，两瓶瑞典绝对伏特加也没了，还有在各种广东话、上海话、闽南话、北京话的背景音中，那些喝高了胡言乱语的豪迈女们……

时隔一年，在同样的餐桌上，万圣节的气氛却完全不同了。依然到处都是主打的橙色和黑色，但多了给小朋友准备的多层糖果架：第一层是橘子味的软糖，第二层是黑色的甘草糖，然后是金灿灿的巧克力。黑色的餐巾叠成三角形状，在餐盘里对角摆放，放眼望去像南瓜人巨大的牙齿，还有餐巾上面点缀的小鬼脸南瓜巧克力，格外俏皮。同样是南瓜造型的还有分散在房间各处的纸灯笼、蜡烛以及布偶，虽然还是万圣节，却更应该被称为南瓜节，因为它被布置得是那样有趣而可爱，是一个为孩子们准备的节日。刚刚一岁多的樱桃和小方块儿，两个蹒跚学路的小女孩，在她们人生中的第一个万圣节吃到了甜蜜的糖果，还记住了南瓜的笑颜。

关于圣诞节的记忆则锁定在了小叶子出生的那个冬天。

期待、疼痛、欣喜、忧郁、焦虑、幸福，一个婴儿的来临，让人生变得全然不同。值得庆幸的是，生活不存在天翻地覆的改变，我依然是过去的我，喜欢花朵，喜欢朋友，

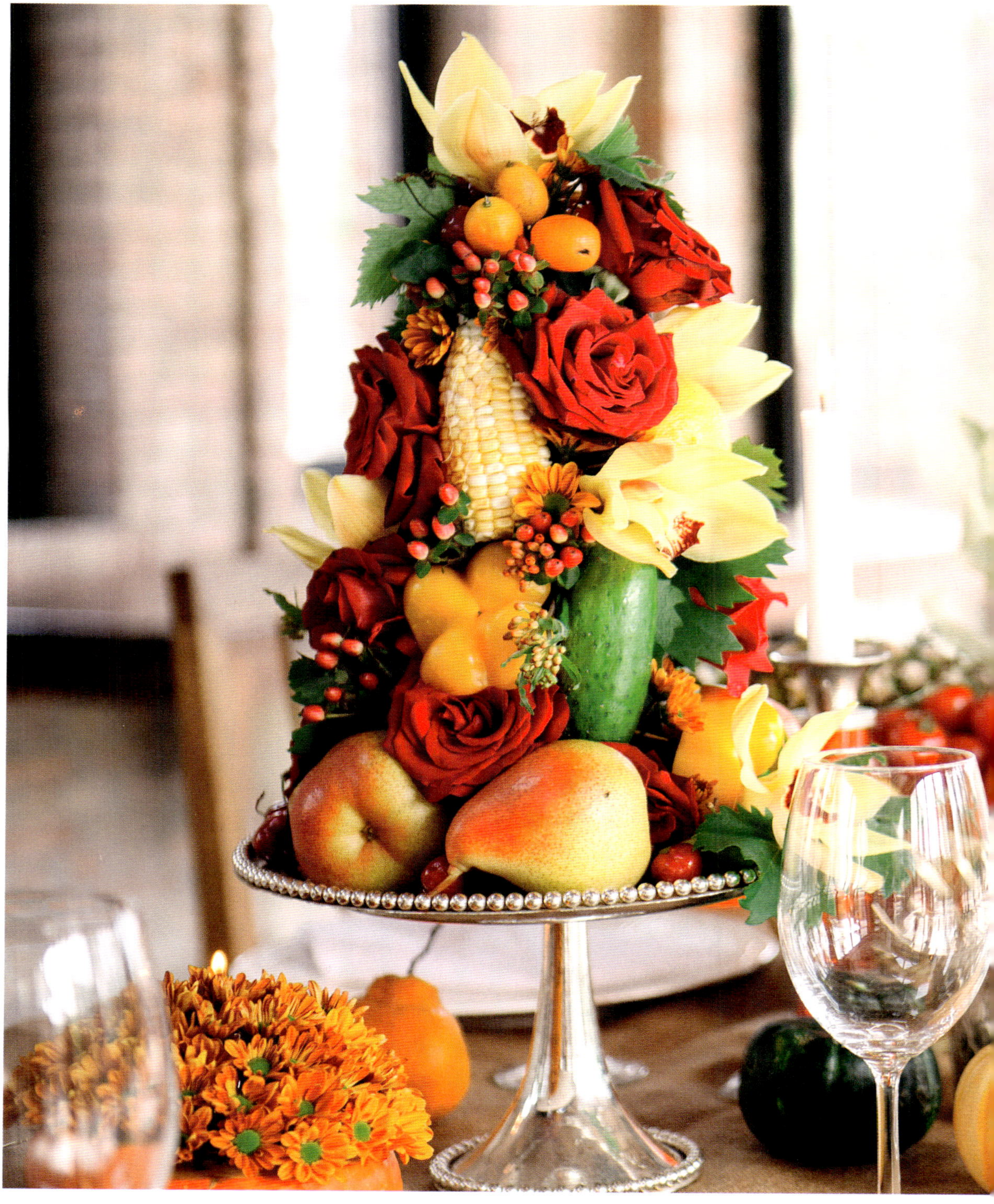

无处不在的橙色是万圣节的标签，丰盛、繁复而热烈的装饰是庆祝节日最好的表达。

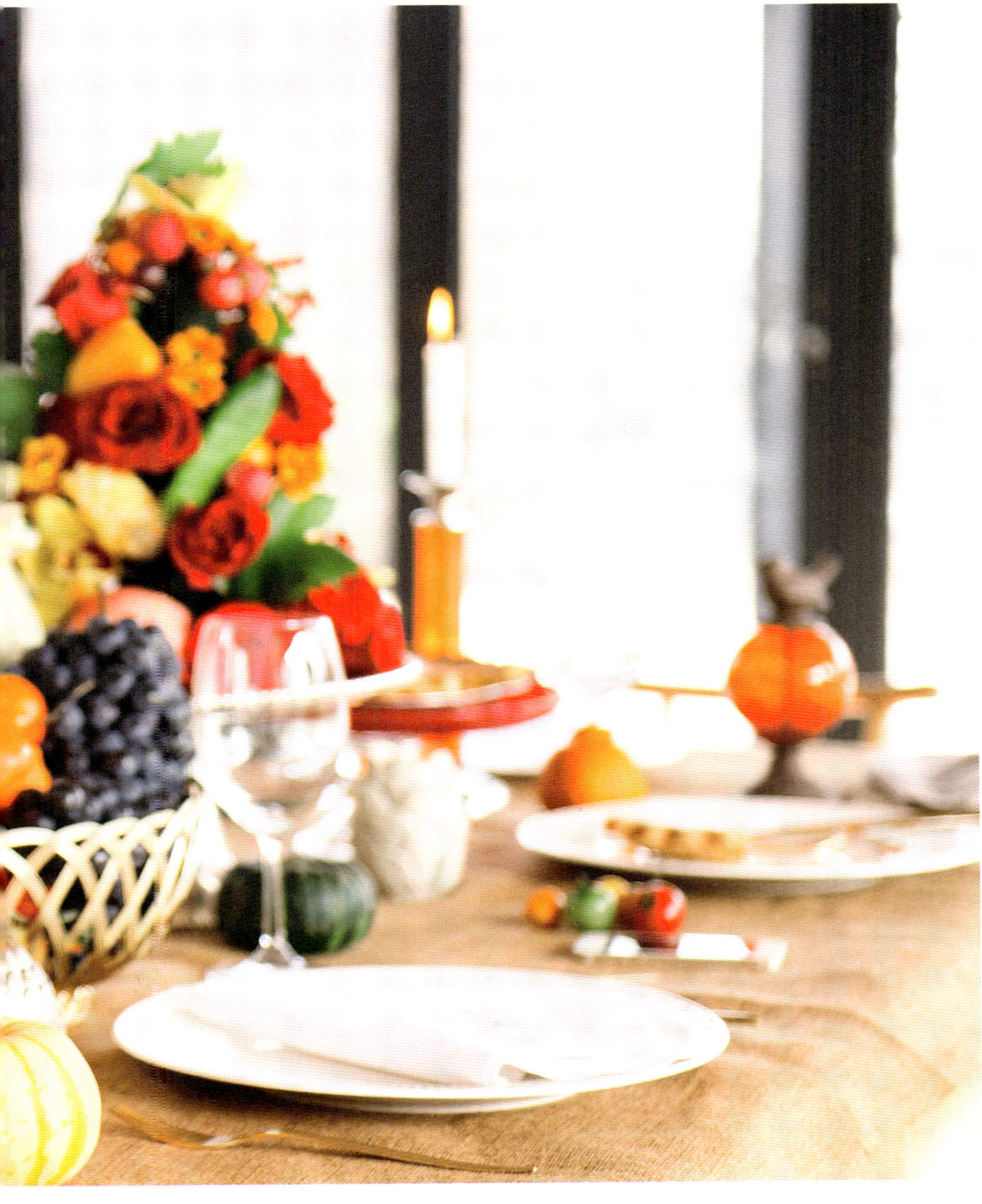

喜欢漂亮的细节，喜欢一切形式感动人的东西。那时候，唯一困扰过我的，是一种力不从心的惶恐。刚刚生完小叶子一个多月，过去于我轻而易举的瑜伽动作，在那时却成了难题。身体和气力上的羁绊让人有些忧郁，但我知道，这要靠内心的力量去击溃，恢复完全的自己，变成更好的自己。

发出圣诞节午宴的邀请前，我下了半天的决心。太久没有动手做饭和操办聚会了，家里又有了新的变化，新成员的到来让空间变小、杂物增多，但就在翻出收藏的各种杯碗盏碟、买到新的桌布、列好菜单的一瞬间，我好像又满血复活了。生命在于折腾，不折腾的时候永远不知道自己有多少能量。从网上订了各种圣诞装饰物，给每个人选择圣诞礼物，从我的花艺师那儿订来鲜花，摆好盘子、刀叉，给水晶香槟杯斟上琥珀色的美酒，为小叶子穿上红红的节日新衣，一切都还是那么美好。在设计菜单时，就想好以简单快捷为原则。头盘是最容易的酸奶油酱配烟熏三文鱼、两种火腿、经典拌菜，然后有多米诺骨牌烤土豆、柴鸡汤娃娃菜，还有圣诞气氛浓烈的蜜汁烤小排、海盐煎大虾。最后是我拿手的香甜浓郁的圣诞巧克力蛋糕配英国伯爵茶。这些全是多次做过的，对于我这个当时刚出月子的产妇来说，是给自己找了一条轻松之路。

那个中午，冬日的阳光毫不吝惜地洒满了整个房间。北欧风格的红色花纹桌布明快而热烈，被我反过来用，不会太抢美食的风头。餐盘里装饰的松枝很有圣诞气息，从圣诞老人的故乡芬兰背回的驯鹿烛台也终于等到了这个节日，还有银色的蜡烛杯和瑞典的水晶酒杯，一切都显得丰盛，并带着小小的华丽。此时已经快三岁的樱桃跑去和一个多月的小叶子说着只有她们才懂的话。一丁十四岁的女儿带来了自己亲手烘焙的细腻绵软的海绵蛋糕。我和朋友们聊着天，产后与世隔绝的疏离感和小小的忧郁一扫而光。所幸，我拥有这么多美好的朋友，他们对生活的从容是给当时的我最好的强心针。这些人从来没有输给过繁忙、平淡、压力和疲惫，不仅兼顾事业和孩子，更让生活的趣味、自身的完善从未遗失。或许生活从来不是只有漂亮的颜色，但他们总能从中提炼出最亮眼的色彩。

在这之后，还有过无数次的节日相聚。无论是摆放着 LANVIN 穿红裙的跳舞娃娃、金色盘碟的华美的新年晚宴，还是银装素裹、像被雪花覆盖一般的圣诞餐桌，或是有着传统味道、以兰花装饰的优雅中国年晚宴，一切都是喜欢的、希望的样子。用心布置出一张张美丽的餐桌，因为那不仅仅是一顿顿的饭，还是一次次难得的欢聚。桌上的花朵、盘中的美味、别致的摆设，无不在表达——节日，大家一起快乐！

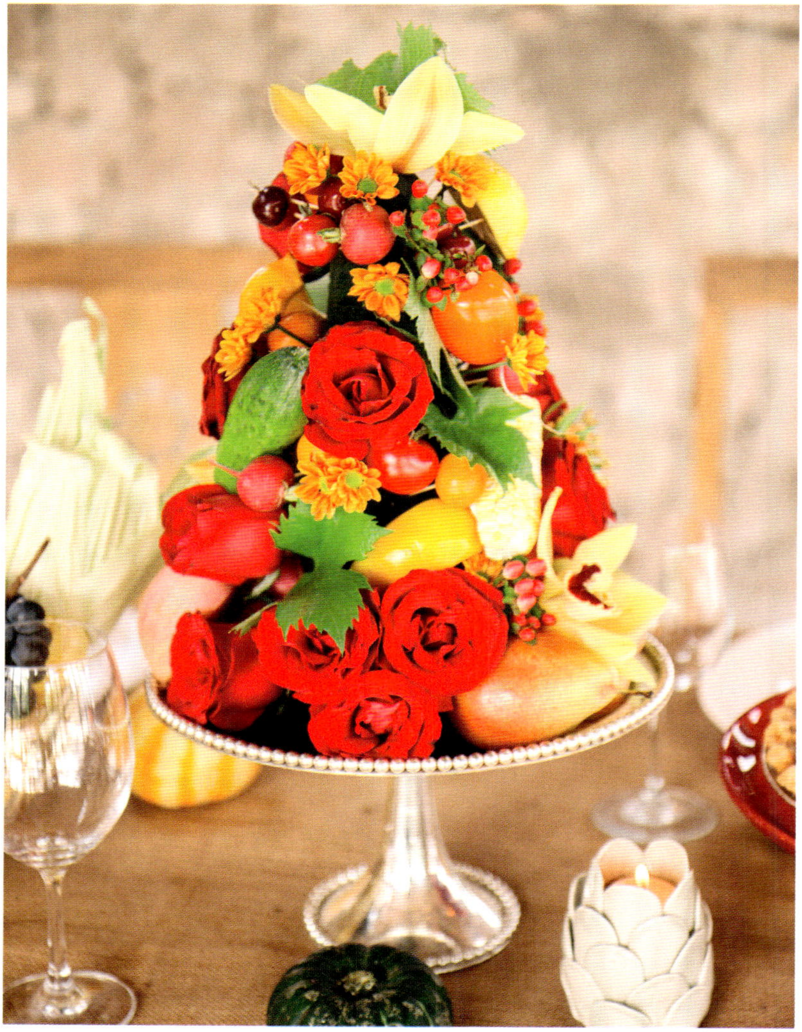

用各种蔬菜、水果和鲜花组成的花果树既寓意丰收，也是万圣节的另一层含义。

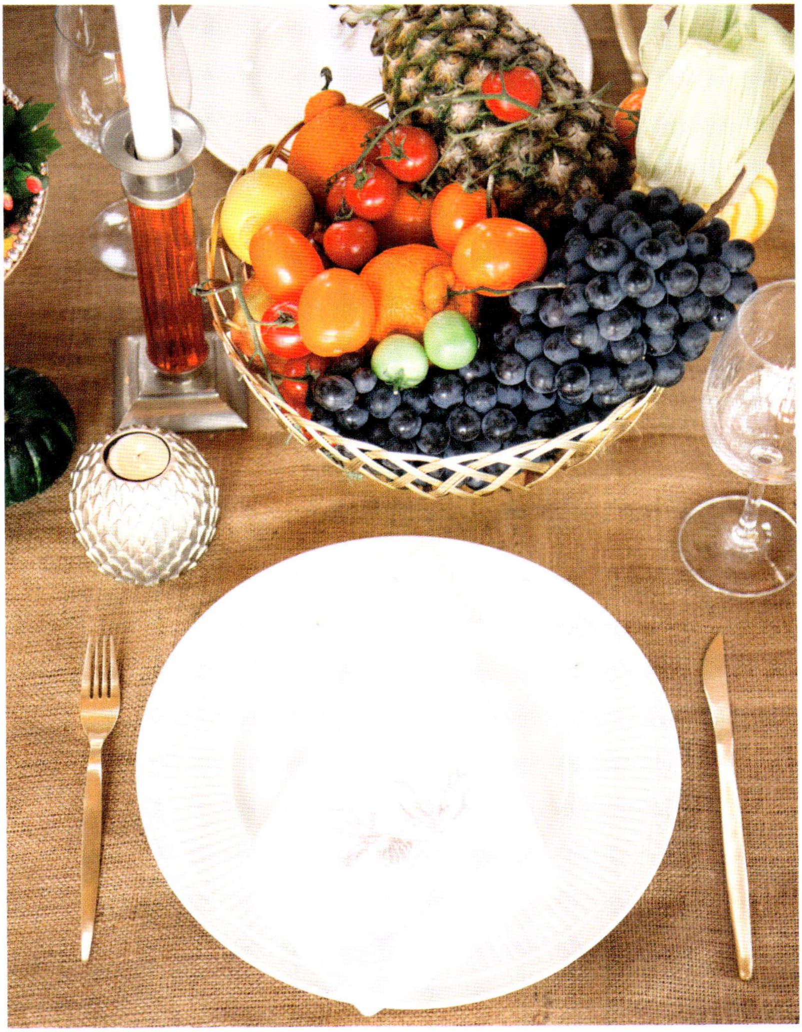

本色的粗麻桌布，配合金色的刀叉、水果筐和橘色的烛台，每个细节都完美呼应。

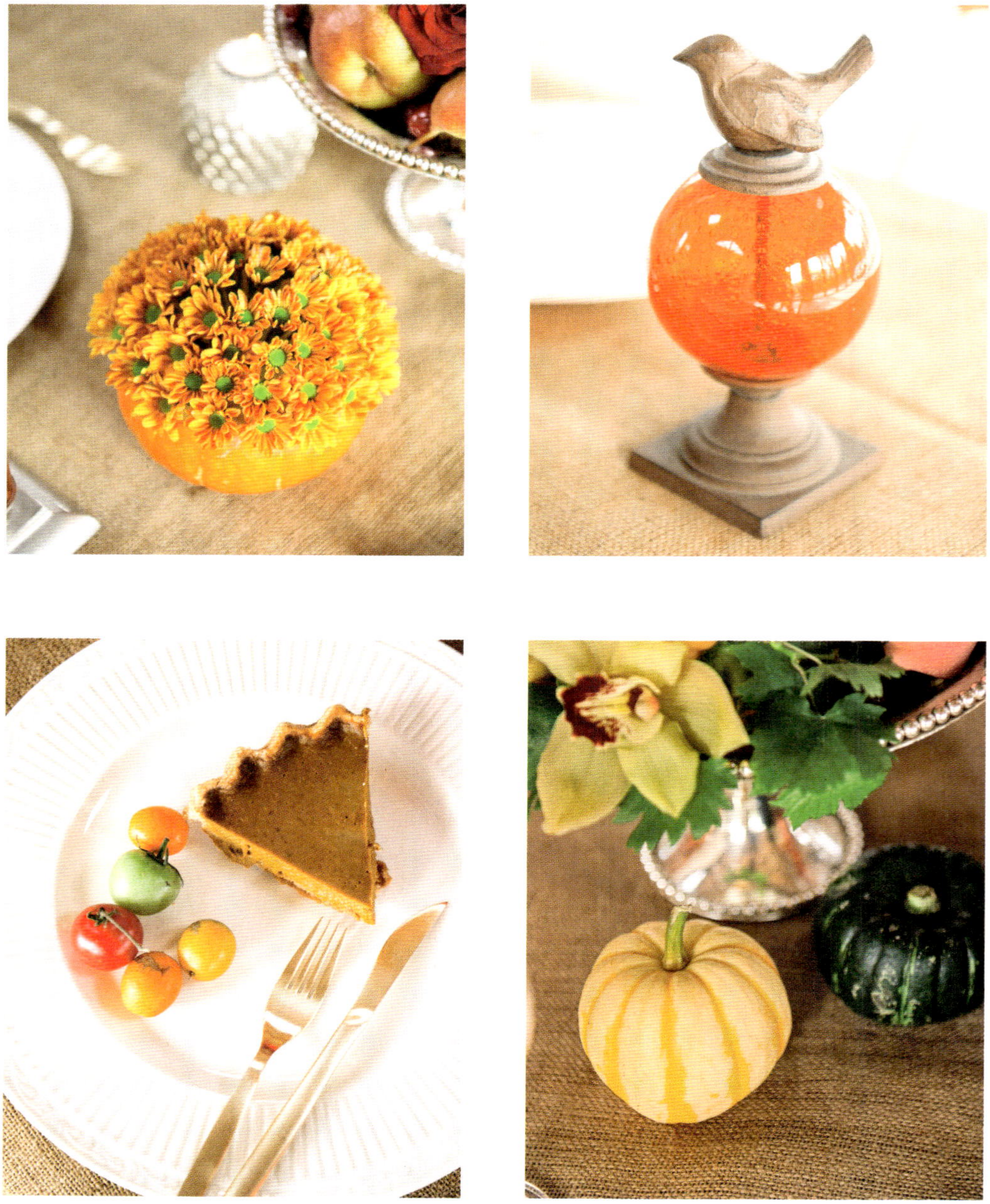

无处不在的万圣节精彩小装饰。

华美而应景的节日餐桌

F E S T I V E T A B L E S

节日和菜单

为了庆祝什么样的节日，这个节日的来龙去脉、文化典故，这些是定下餐单和布置餐桌前要思考的。听起来有点学究儿，但让我们兴致盎然的不正是这些有意思、有故事的细节吗？当我们知道 1621 年，清教徒们庆祝的不只是他们的第一个丰收年，更想借此表达对当地印第安人的感激之情，因为是印第安人教会了他们如何在这片土地上寻找新食物，比如玉米、南瓜和火鸡，我们便可以以烤玉米蛋糕、用南瓜做桌面装饰，以及分享装在烤鸡造型的瓶子里的美酒来欢度感恩节；了解了民间“吃年糕，年年高”这样的风俗，我们便可以在腊月里开始准备汤年糕、酒酿年糕、毛蟹炒年糕等各种创意菜肴来欢度中国年……应景是节日宴请重要的因素，也是最有发挥余地的创意空间。

一点儿夸张和炫耀

随着门铃被按响，房门打开，如果映入客人眼帘的是摇曳的烛光、摆放妥当的精美

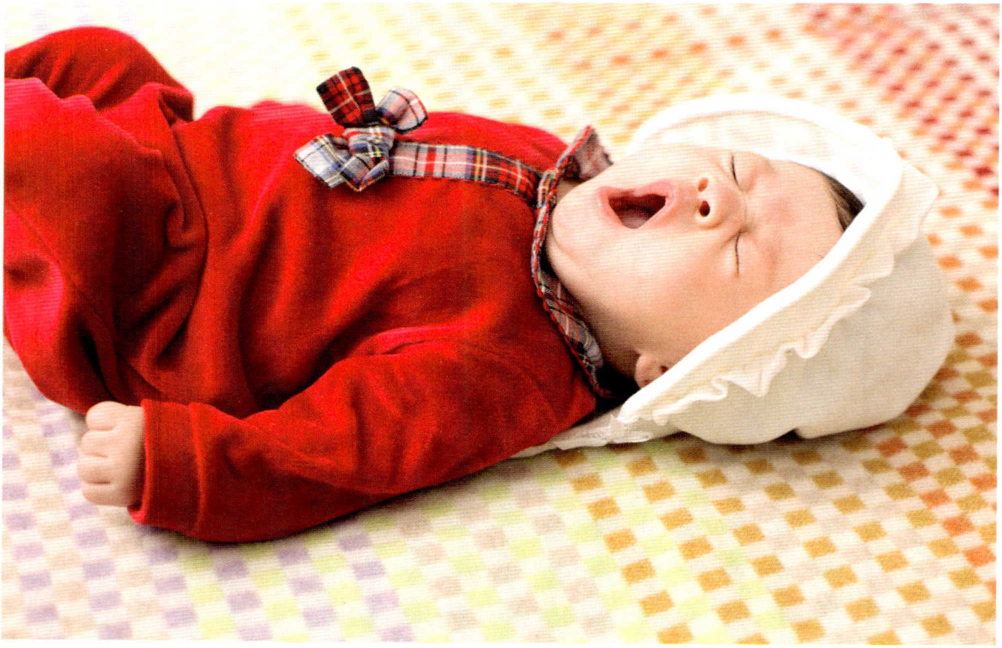

一个多月的小叶子也被打扮成了新年娃娃。（摄影：黄鹭）

餐具、美丽的插花和闪耀着柔和光芒的烛台，那你的客人的第一感受一定是非常惊喜并感觉到被宠爱、被尊重。既然邀请朋友来，就一定要多花些功夫去布置一张完美的餐桌，让他们感觉到能参加你的聚餐，是多么幸福的一件事。把你珍爱的那些昂贵的餐具都拿出来吧，还有平时不舍得用的细腻的亚麻桌布和水晶酒杯。无论布置桌面还是设计菜品，有一些小小的夸张甚至炫耀感。以最精美的用品和最优质的食材，体现出你的最高水平，才是一场宴请恰如其分的做法，让每个前来赴宴的人都感受到十分的尊崇。毕竟，让你的客人感觉快乐，才是你如此倾力准备宴请的目的。

让人欢喜的细节

我喜欢在长餐桌上摆放高低不同的几个插花，最高的插花会放在桌子中间，或者摆在一旁放置酒水饮料的地方。它们会非常吸引客人的视线，让人一下融入美好的气氛，但在就餐时，我会悄悄把它们挪开，只留下矮矮的插花，这样不至于遮挡客人交谈的视线。室内的灯光会稍微调暗，即使主要光源仍然是灯光，蜡烛也仍是最适合晚上宴请时烘托气氛的必备之物。另外，布置好的漂亮的餐桌一旦开始用餐，很快就会被打破格局，变得杂乱起来，因而，在餐桌以外的地方也摆放一些呼应主题的装饰物就显得格外重要。比如万圣节的南瓜装饰，可以在沙发侧面或花盆里也点缀一些；圣诞的松枝，可以在化妆间和客人挂衣帽的地方反复出现，还有厨房的窗台上，可以摆放一些当日主要的蔬果做装饰，会有意想不到的效果。这些小细节不仅会给人留下更深的印象，还有助于增加宾客间交流的谈资。

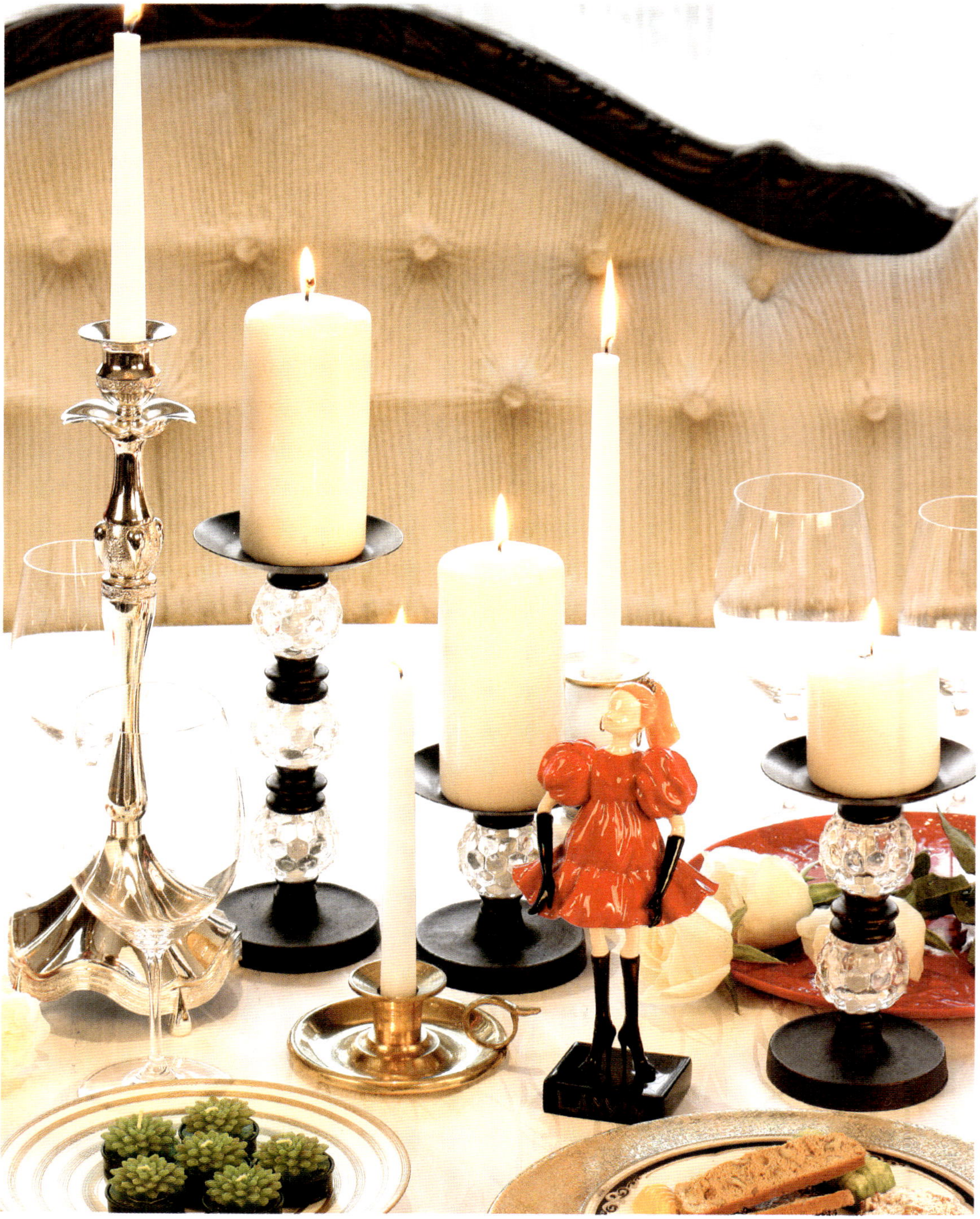

新年餐桌上的 LANVIN 穿红裙的跳舞娃娃。（摄影：王笑飞）

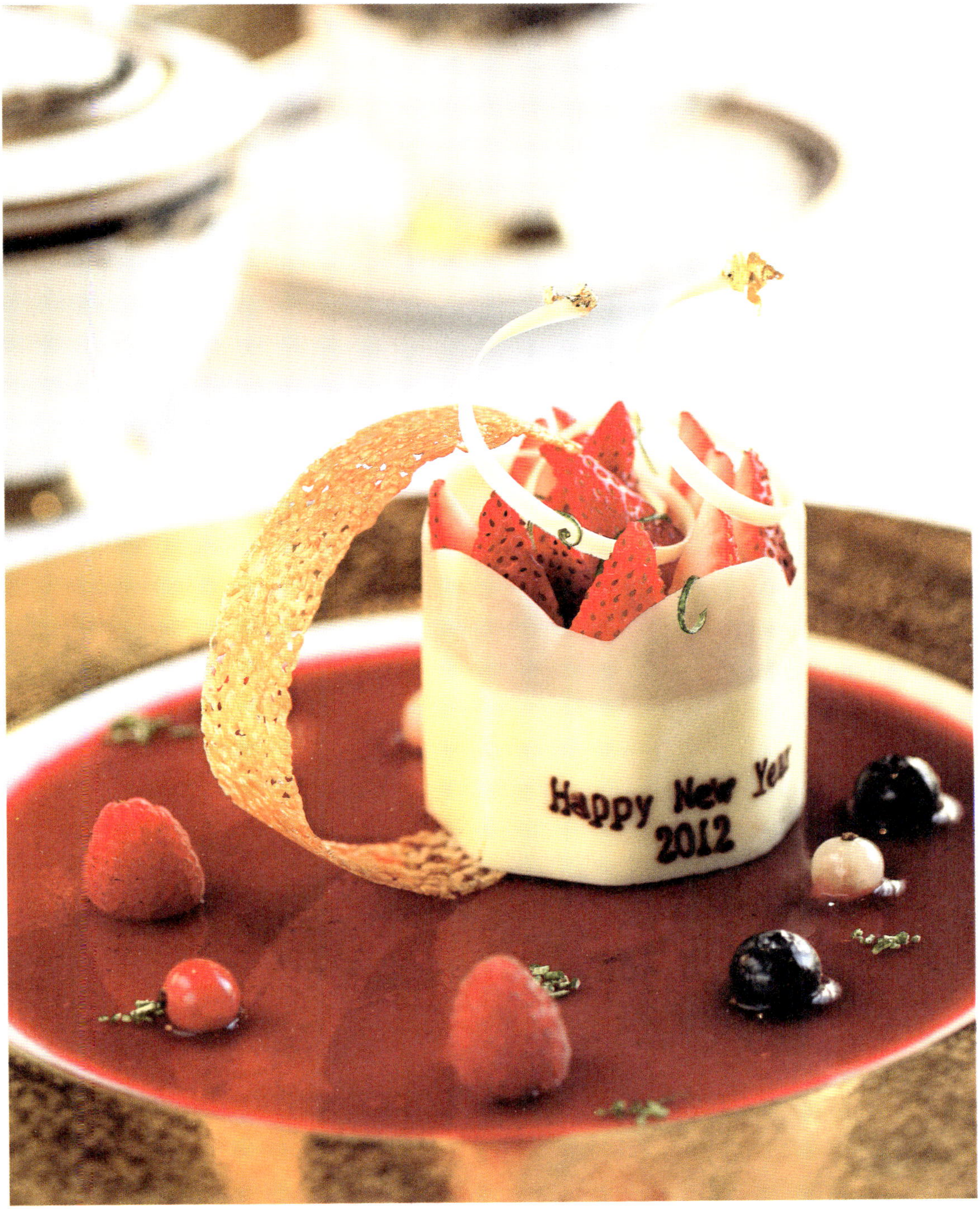

新年是红彤彤、金灿灿的，象征着新的一年有好运气。（摄影：王笑飞）

PART 3

关于餐桌布置
你想知道的事儿

ALL YOU NEED TO KNOW
ABOUT TABLE SETTINGS

寻找优雅又聪明的待客之道

CREATIVE IDEAS FOR ELEGANT AND AFFORDABLE HOSPITALITY

想拥有漂亮的餐桌，但预算和储物空间有限，这并不是让人尴尬的问题，而是我们都要面对的现实。精美的瓷器只是生活中的锦上添花，在家招待客人也不再是“头等大事”，而只是我们日常生活的一部分。重要的并不是拥有多少套名贵的餐具，而是有一颗热爱生活、能感受到生活细微之美的心。

好吧，就从现在开始，即使什么都还没有，只要按照我总结的经验去做，就能布置出一张让人羡慕的餐桌。这并不需要花上一大笔钱，只要拥有最基本的餐具，再加上搭配的心思、技巧和热情。

有　全　能　餐　盘　吗？

IS THERE REALLY A SET OF TABLEWARE SUITED FOR EVERY OCCASION?

答案是有。只是也许你不会甘心真正理性地购买。

尽管我的储藏柜里有多套餐盘，但最常使用的只是一套简单的白色带蓝边的盘碟。它几乎适用于各种季节和聚会，只要搭配不同的酒杯、花器、餐巾或餐垫，就会有不一样的感觉。事实上也是如此，包括前菜和主菜的两件套餐碟，你只要有两套就足够了——一套是细腻简洁的骨瓷质地，一套可以是乡村风格的陶瓷质地。它们足够应付你的日常三餐和基本宴请。除非是结婚礼物，现在已经很少有人去购买整套的包括甜品碟和汤盆、汤碗在内的餐具了，因为宴请对我们来说不再是什么重大事件，而是日常生活的一部分，那些有创造性的桌面布置才是最吸引人的。

请在冲动购买前考虑一下你实际需要的数量。如果你的客厅最多能容纳六个人一起用餐，那就不必非要购买八件套或十件套。粥、汤、面和布丁是否能用一个碗搞定？那些有巨大边沿和盖子的西式汤碗究竟能用到几次？在大城市的房价飙升到了五万一平方米甚至更高的时候，少几个不实用的碗也是一种生活品质的提升。另外，选择白色的餐具是永远不会错的。尽管拥有不一样的质地和设计，但却可以轻松地混搭在一起使用，不仅能很完美地衬托食物，还能和桌上任何物品搭配，把出彩的部分交给餐垫、桌布、

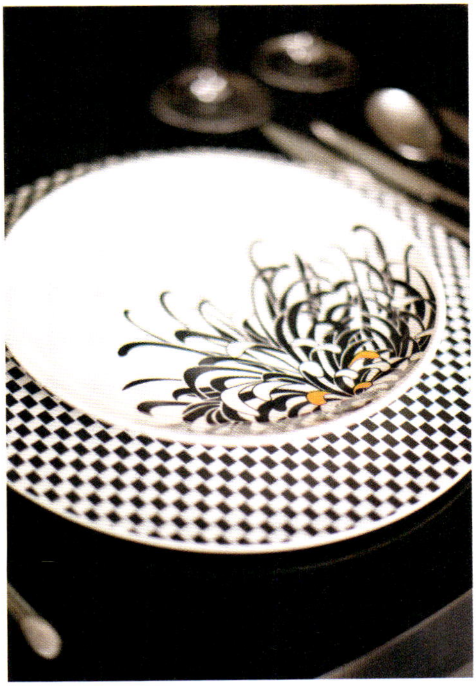

白色的餐具几乎适用于任何宴请。

装饰盘是用来衬托餐盘的，作为餐垫的替代品。

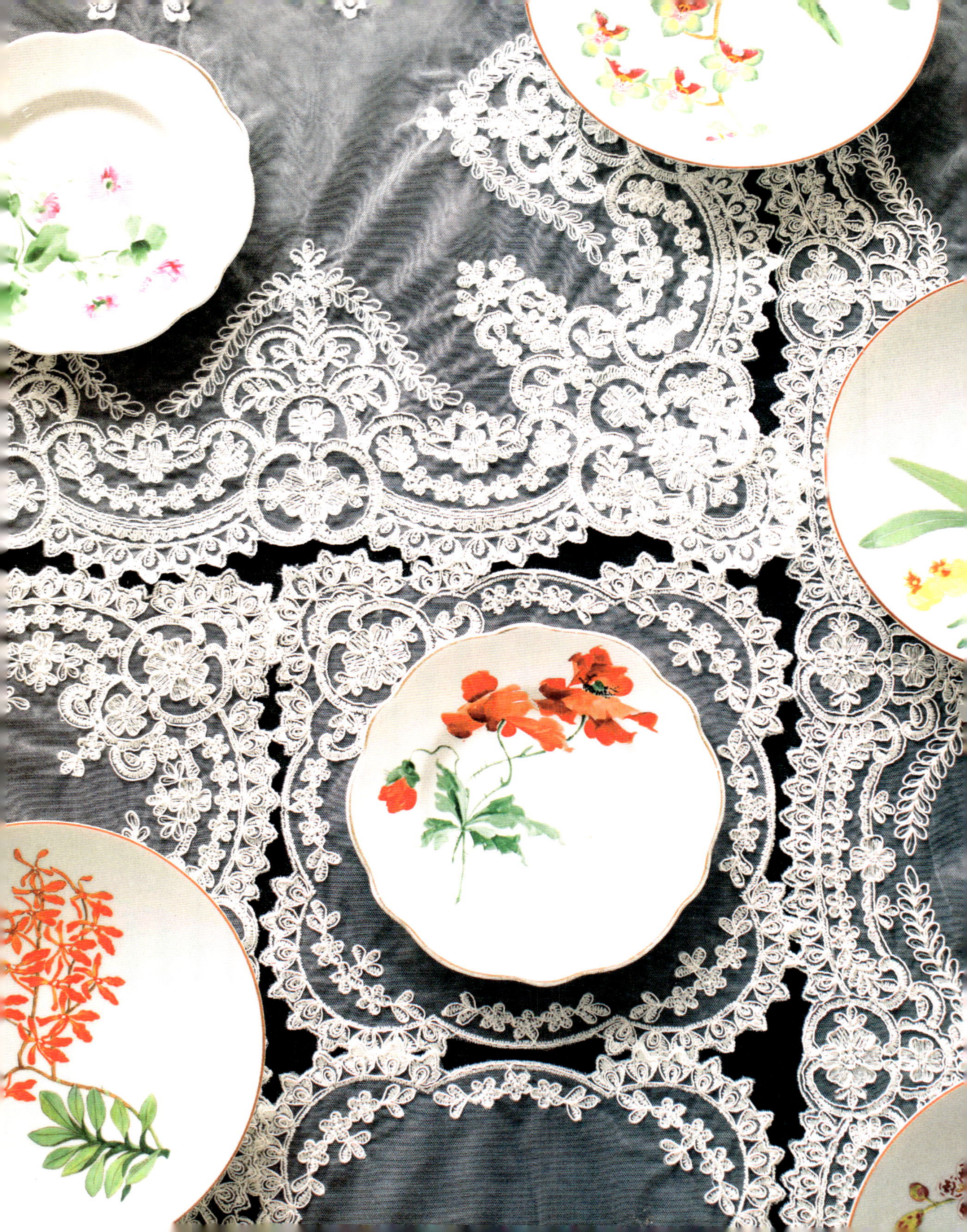

甜品盘和杯子们去发挥吧。

但如果你偏爱彩色的或有图案的盘子，并且想收藏尽量多的款式，那最好让它们之间有某种关联的主题。比如有相同的色调——同样的海洋色系、大地色系，让不同色彩的餐盘容易配搭。再或者，让它们之间有类似的图案关联。我曾在瑞典的跳蚤市场买过一套八个手绘花草图案的古董甜品盘，后来又在巴黎福宝大街的爱马仕店购入了一套同样花卉主题的点心盘，虽然它们的绘画手法和质地完全不同，价格更有着天壤之别，但放在一起使用，不仅不唐突，还很有趣味。

另外，在你的餐具收藏中，可以考虑增添一些古董瓷器。在旅行中，带回一套19世纪或更古老的盘子或碗，在就餐的同时欣赏旧时的美，并谈论一些关于过去的话题，是非常有乐趣的事情。那些旧货市场上的东西不会很贵，只要你眼光好，果断把它们背回来，和新的餐具混搭使用，会大大提升你的餐桌品位。

◀ 一套是来自瑞典跳蚤市场的手绘瓷盘，另一套是来自爱马仕的设计师系列，花草图案将它们连接在一起。

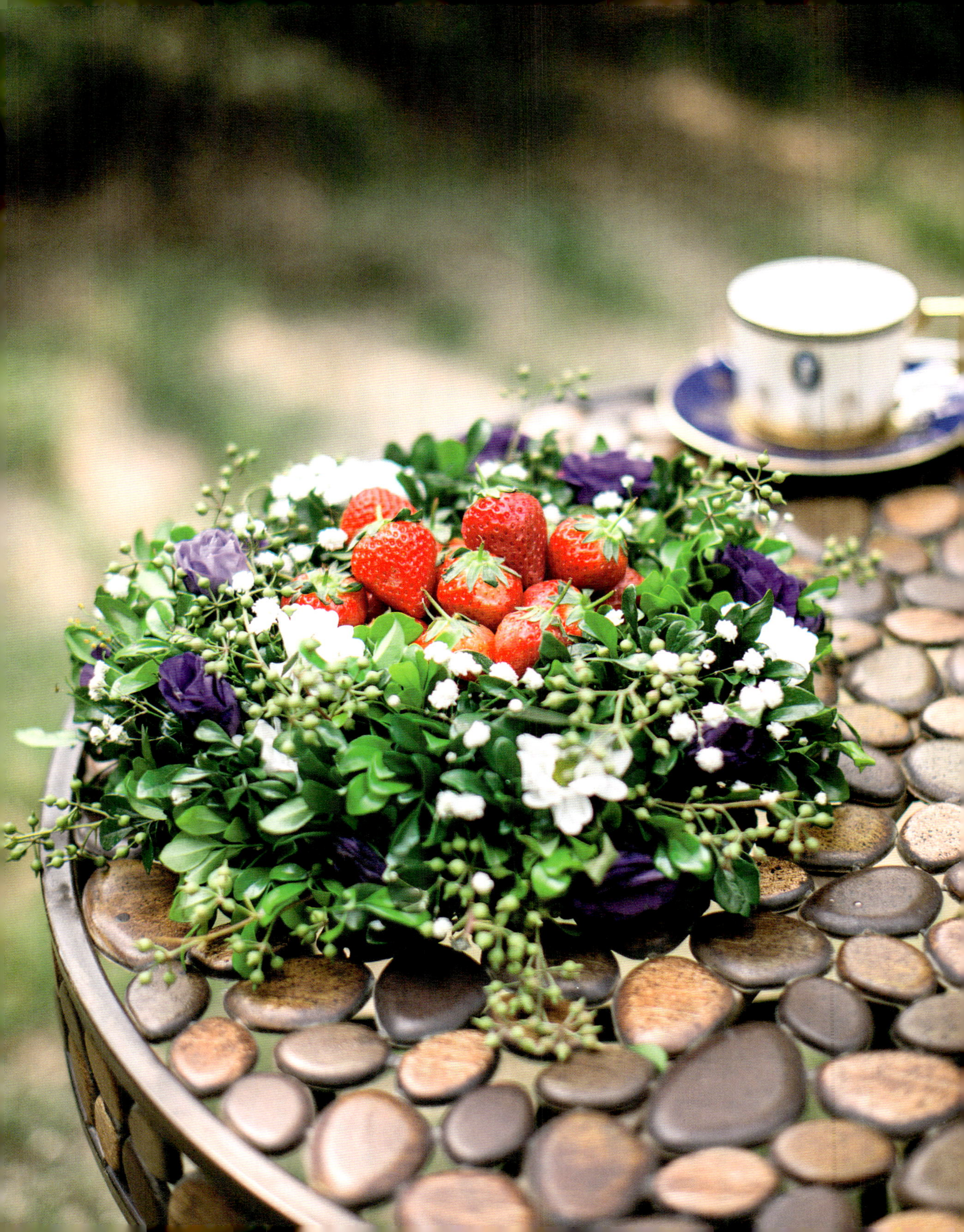

什么容器都可以插花

EVERY CONTAINER CAN BE USED TO ARRANGE FLOWERS

有时候，越是用不是花器的“花器”盛放鲜花，越容易给人留下深刻的印象。从奶杯、白兰地杯、彩色玻璃杯、各种瓶子甚至试管，到陶瓷碗、铁皮小桶或藤编的小篮子，无所禁忌。桌面上的鲜花能够让桌面迅速变得有气氛，而对这些花的要求就是——看上去要像没特地打理过的样子。这就好像T型台上模特慵懒的“起床妆”，每根看似随意、杂乱的发丝，其实都是经过精心梳理的。一束简单却精致随意的鲜花，也许要花费你更多的时间，但它远比刻板整齐的插花看上去时髦得多，即使再高级、再时髦的晚宴，也不例外。

如果是圆桌，可以在中心摆放一个花篮或插花，或者摆一组高低不同的玻璃器皿，在其中插上鲜花，要点就是从各个角度看过去，都一样好看。如果是长桌，需要摆放一组以上的花，那么可以重复一个主题：可以是一个简单的花瓶，里面插满雏菊，也可以是一组两三个玻璃瓶，每个里面有一两枝花。布置桌面的鲜花不必名贵珍奇，它们吸引人的地方在于够新鲜。除了鲜花，草、蔬菜、水果或者盆栽的小型开花植物，都可以是桌面装饰的主题，把它们搭好、扎好放在瓶子中，或把盆栽直接放进好看的碗或盆里，都是出其不意的桌面布置。

◀ 在下午茶餐桌上，用鲜花插成的花环作为盛放水果的“器皿”，是个漂亮的好主意。

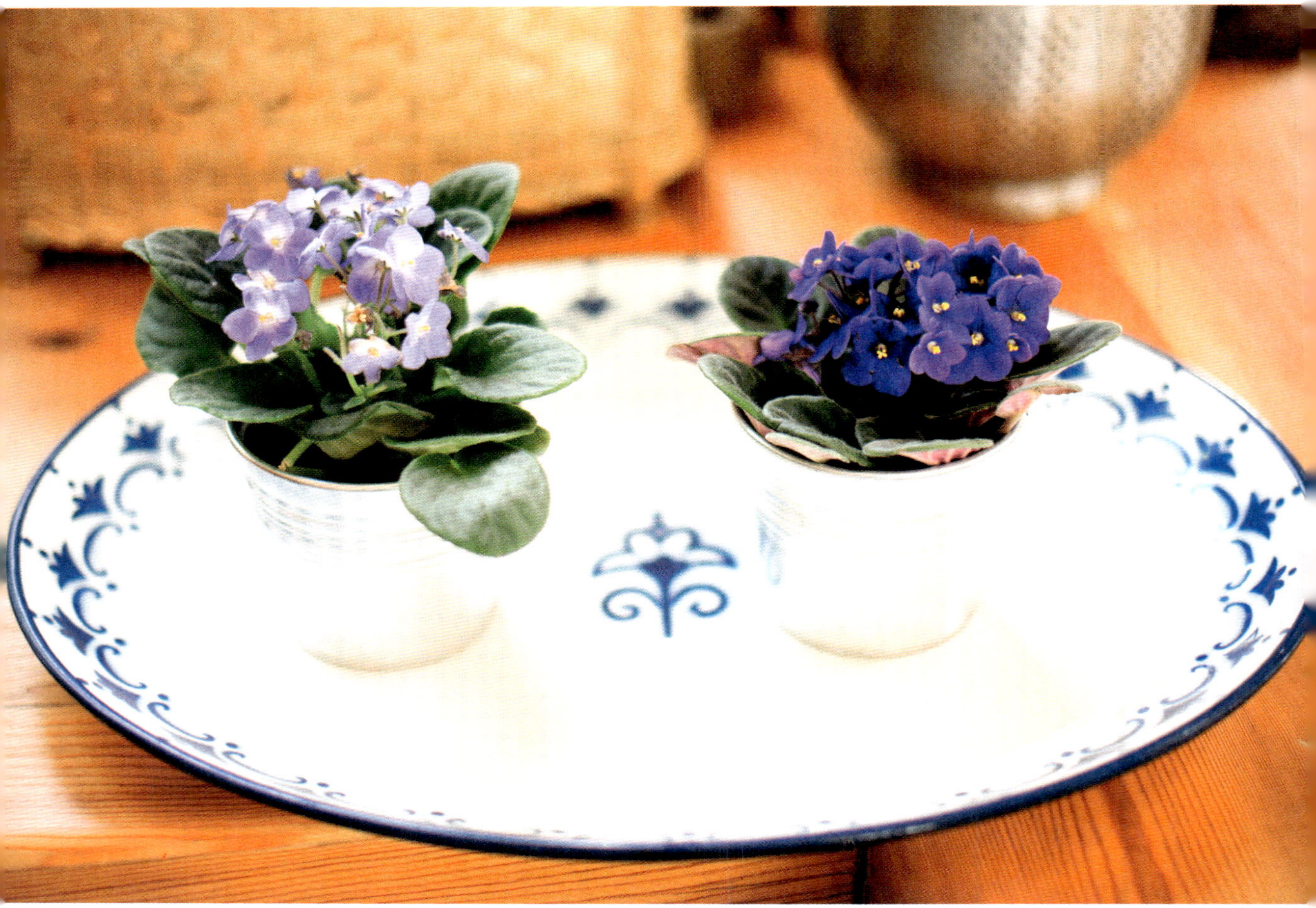

餐桌上除了用鲜花插花，摆放一些小型开花植物也是很好的想法。布置完餐桌后还可以继续用来装饰居室。

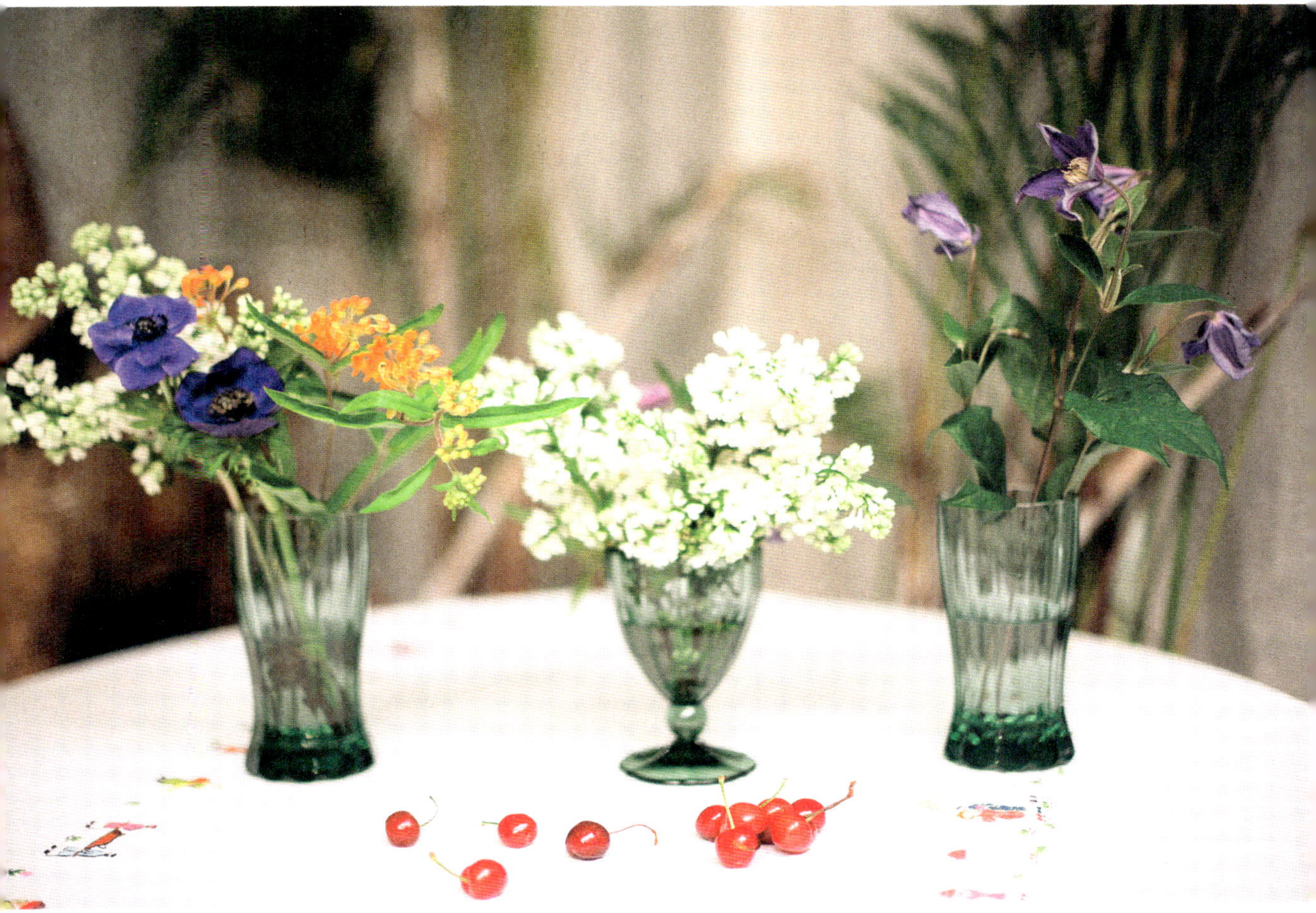

同色系的水杯和酒杯摆放成一组夏日主题的小插花，像一首清新跳跃的钢琴曲。

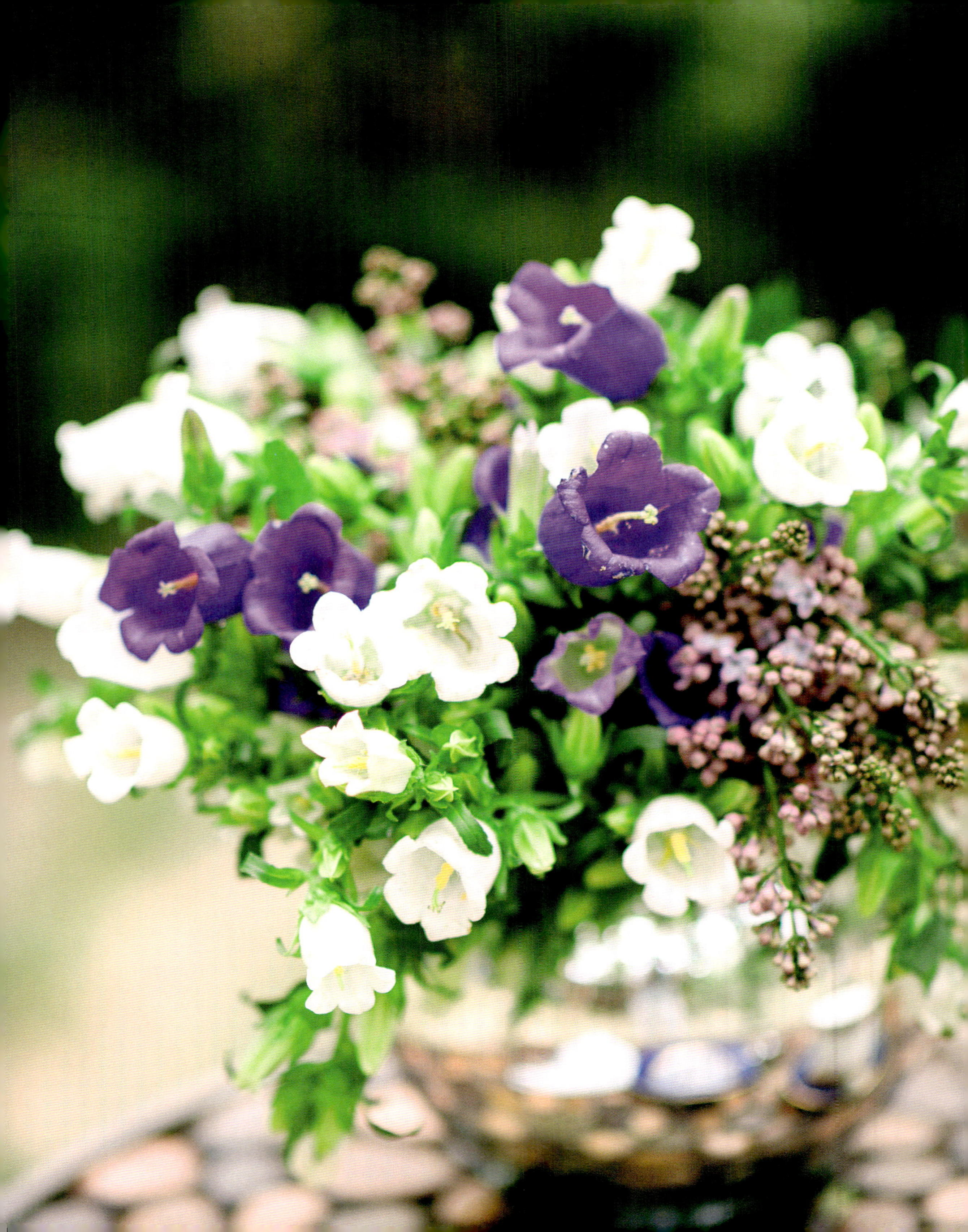

对于桌面的鲜花布置，重要的原则只有两点，我在之前的文章中已经反复提过：首先是不要用过于芳香的鲜花来干扰食物的味道，还有就是不要让客人在花丛中“捉迷藏”。花卉的摆放要么高到可以从它下面看到桌子对面，要么低到可以从花朵上面看到对面的用餐者。如果有非常大型的花卉设计，那么在开餐前应该把它挪到餐桌一旁。另外，具体如何摆放鲜花，是在长桌中间铺满，还是简单地点缀，这要依据当日菜品的数量和用餐的方式而定，分餐制的西餐可以让鲜花占据桌面很多的面积，但需要分享食物的中餐则要留出桌面给菜肴摆放，鲜花只能是零星地点缀。

◀ 让花瓶和桌面在质感上形成对比，粗糙的石头表面和精致光滑的花瓶碰撞出让人印象深刻的视觉效果。

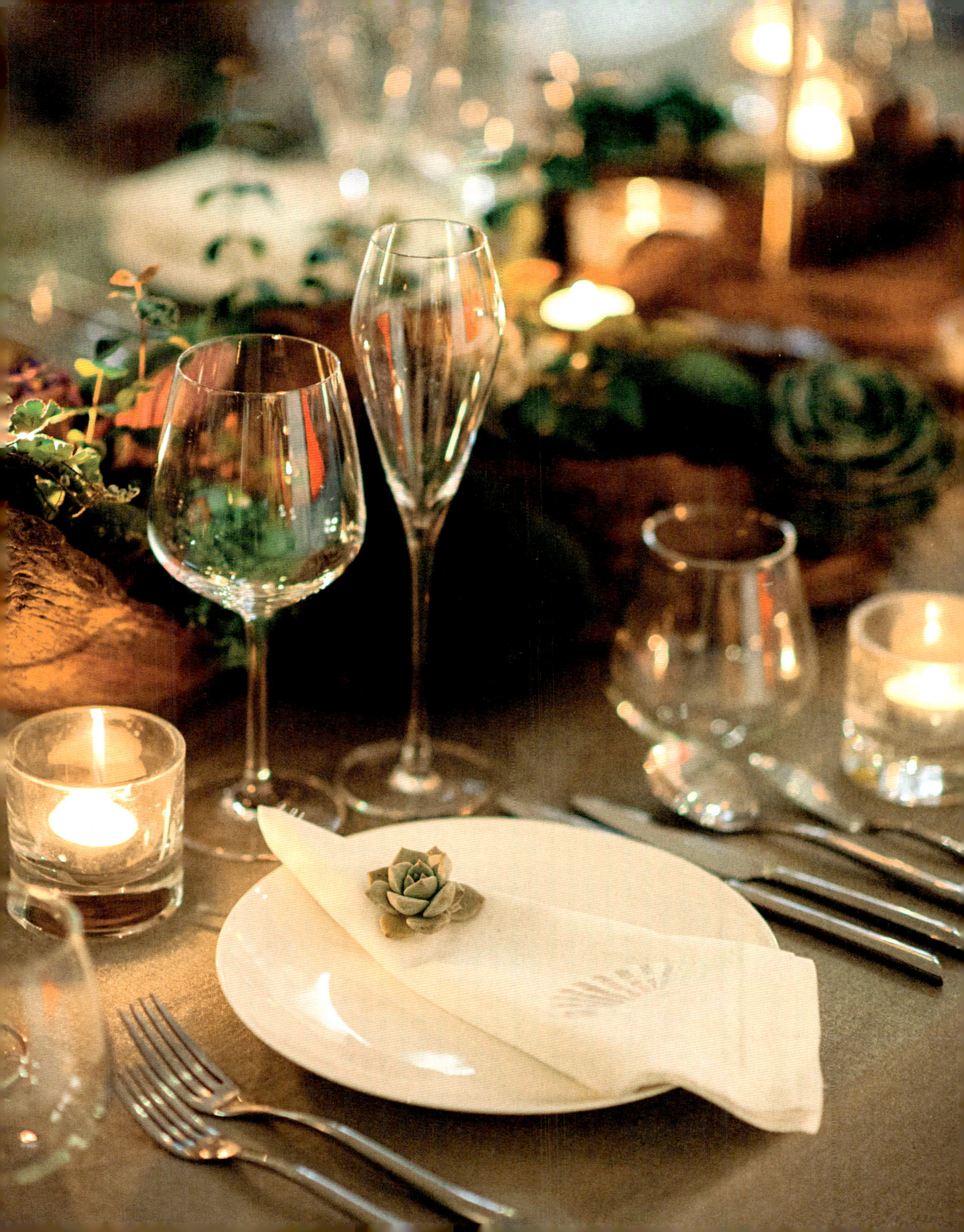

用 蜡 烛 点 燃 气 氛

USE CANDLELIGHT TO CREATE A LOVELY ATMOSPHERE

“烛光晚餐”在我们的意识中有点被矫情化了。它并不应该是二人世界煽情的专利，而是在每一次与朋友的聚会中，无论室内还是室外，无论是否配合其他灯光使用，它都是一种最好的调节气氛的照明方式——不仅能照亮餐桌，衬托饭菜和人的面容，而且当客人看到餐桌上摇曳的烛光时，还能感受到主人的热情和期待。

蜡烛和灯光配合的最佳平衡点便是“不亮也不暗”，这需要不断的尝试，根据季节、时间、光线的不同。那些台灯、落地灯或墙壁上的侧灯都可以配合蜡烛使用，对餐桌唯一非常有杀伤力的是房间内的顶灯，一旦将它打开，桌上的一切一览无余，变得简单粗暴。

可选择的蜡烛种类实在太多了。那些古典的枝状烛台可以和小茶蜡配合使用，制造高低不同的层次感；小茶蜡不仅可以放在蜡座里，也可以放置在任何可爱的容器中（但要注意别被点燃或爆裂）；传统主义喜欢在餐桌上用乳白色的蜡烛，而且不喜欢锥形的蜡烛；彩色蜡烛在时髦的聚会中配合桌布或鲜花使用有出奇好的效果。在使用蜡烛时，只需要记住两点：和桌上的鲜花一样，烛台要么足够高，要么足够低，不要让它遮挡入座后的用餐者交谈的视线；另外就是，芳香蜡烛永远不要出现在餐桌上，它的气味会干扰食物的味道。

◀ 蜡烛是晚宴上最重要的光源，即使有其他光源，它依然是点燃气氛的关键。

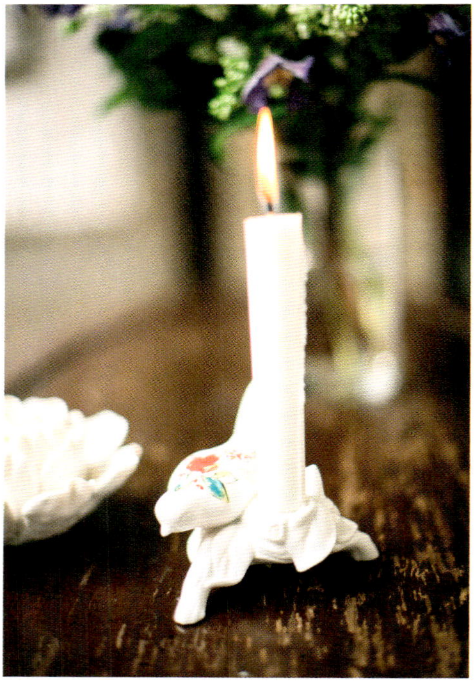

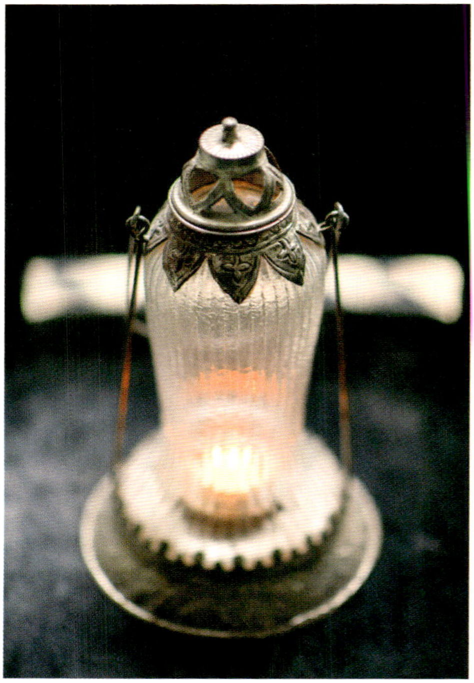

造型拙朴的花朵和小鸟，无论在白天配合阳光使用还是晚上与灯光呼应，都很有雅趣。

一盏古典的蜡烛灯给晚餐餐桌增添些小华丽，即使白天摆放也是很好的装饰。

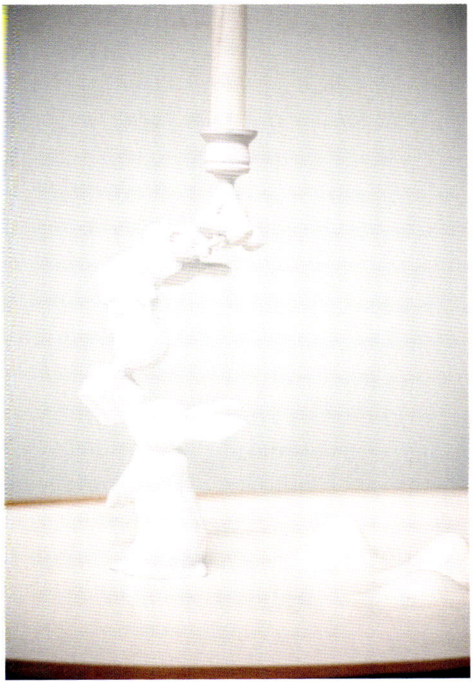

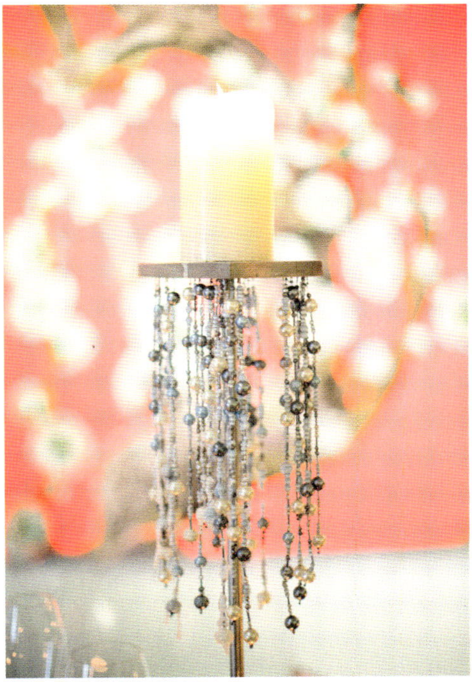

来自设计师斯蒂芬·约翰逊（Stephen Johnson）的仙境系列烛台 Wonderland-Rabbit 给平凡的生活增添一些梦幻的想象。

从蜡烛上滴落下来的蜡珠便是这个烛台的设计灵感，下面这些珠串和实际的蜡珠混合在一起，自然生动。

请买你买得起的最好的杯子

BUY THE BEST GLASSES YOU CAN AFFORD

当举起酒杯的一刹那，手中感受到的分量感和质感，轻轻碰撞时发出的声响，瞬间让一顿饭的格调变得不同。不管是Riedel（醴铎）、Rona（洛娜）还是Baccarat（巴卡拉），它们除了代表梦幻，还代表不菲的价格。但如果你认为喝一杯酒能让一天变得美好，那就请购买你买得起的最好的杯子吧。当你想到，餐桌上的水晶酒杯，就像女人脖子上的珠宝，不仅可以让整个人都变得熠熠生辉，还可以代代相传，那便可以说服自己，哪怕两个两个地开始收集，这肯定是不会让你后悔的事。

玻璃餐具可以给平放餐具的桌面增加高度、层次和亮点，是成功布置桌面的关键。而且精彩的玻璃餐具永远都不嫌多。无论是一个设计简约的现代水杯，还是17世纪经过吹制工艺而制成的高脚酒杯，都能找到适合的餐桌风格，与其他餐具搭配得默契而出彩。除了那些昂贵的高级货，也可以去跳蚤市场寻找一些古董玻璃杯，不必成套，一两个华丽复古的杯子就足以让整个桌面变得与众不同。

你还可以灵机一动，用酒杯当花器。一排小巧的平底杯，装上简单的一两朵花，就能成为可爱的焦点。当然，用鸡尾酒杯装各种甜品也是不错的主意，无论是布丁还是草莓慕斯，或葡萄和鲜虾制成的开胃小食，都是优雅又美妙的设计。

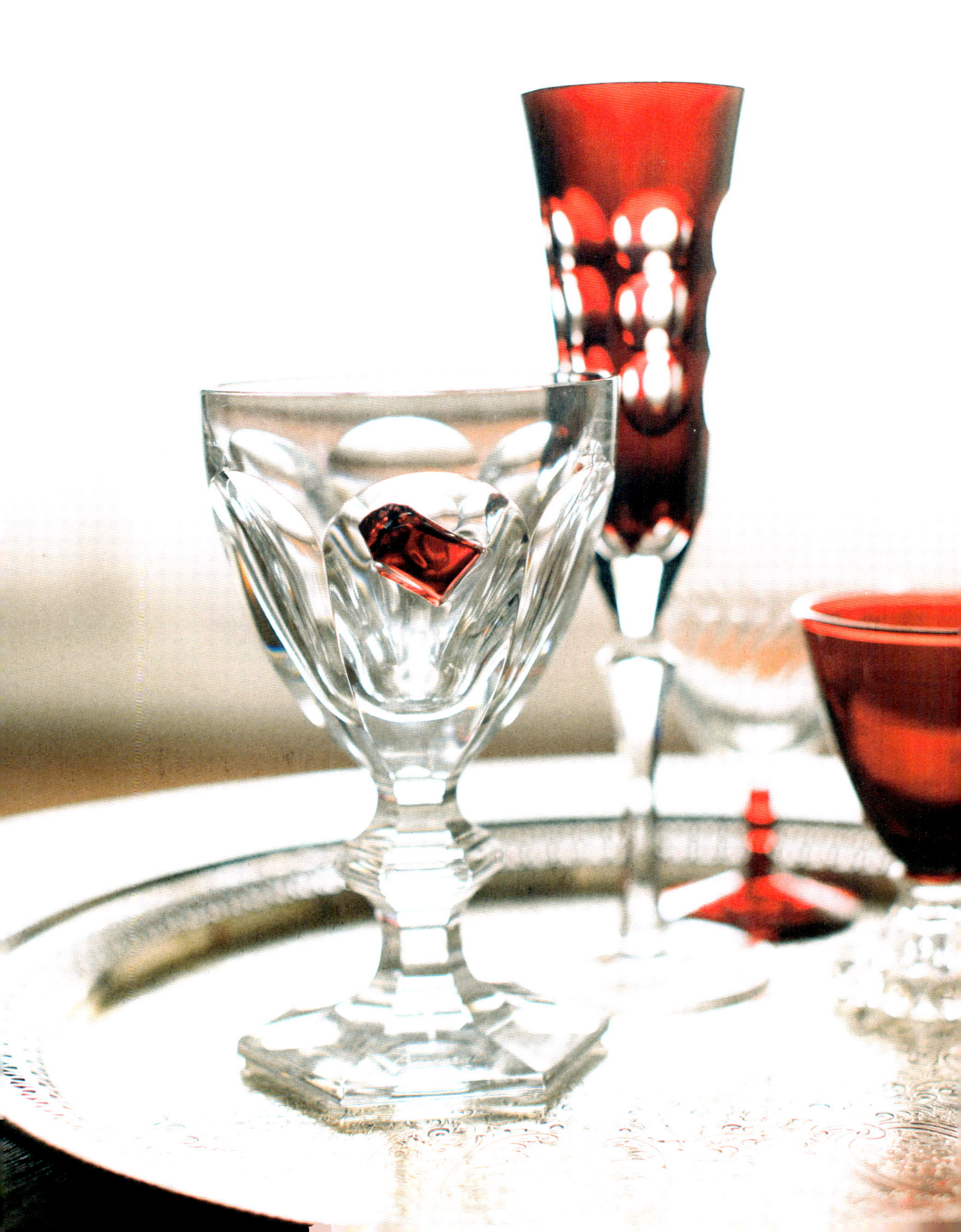

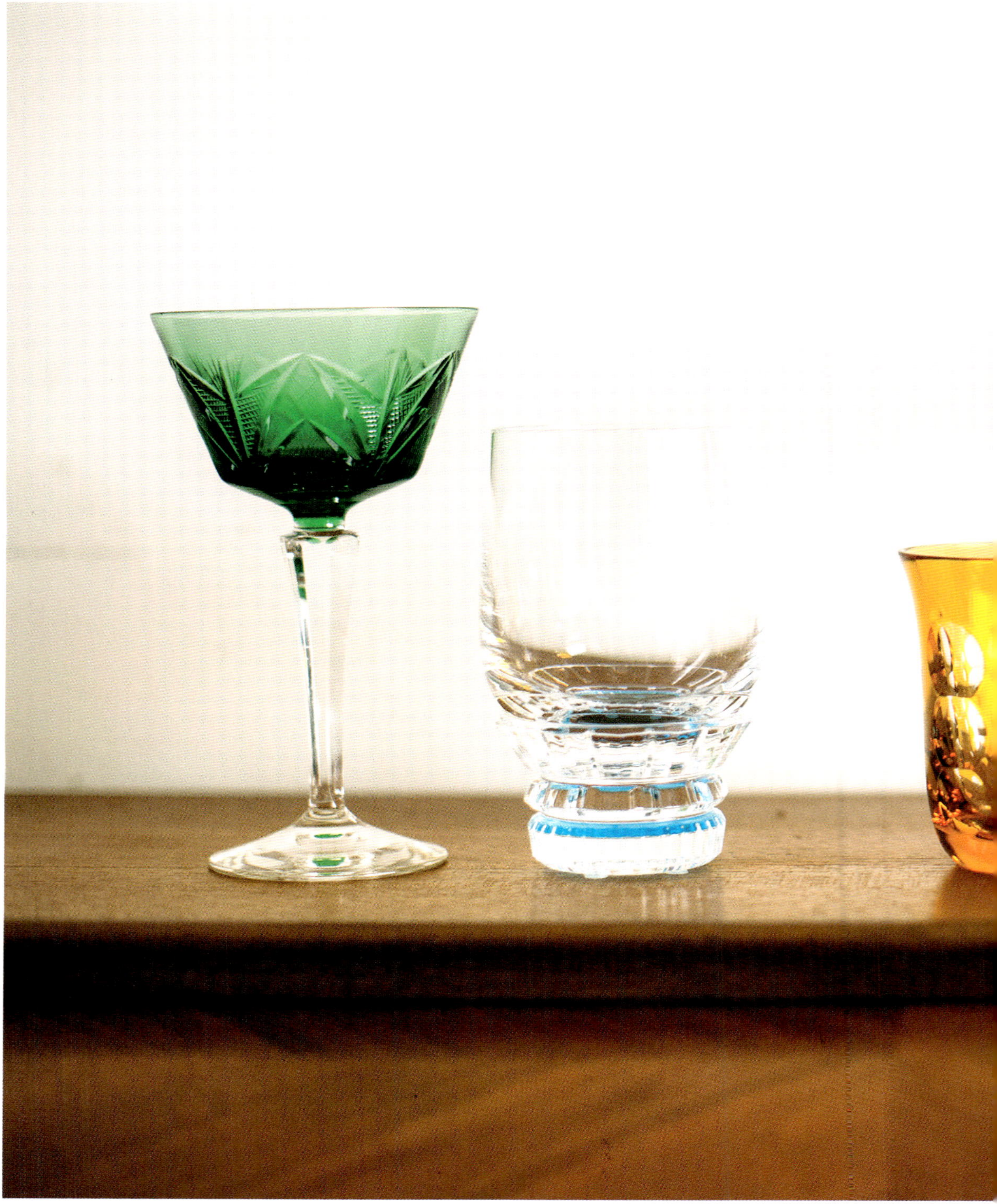

彩色水晶杯是节日的宠儿，也可以轻松地让不同季节的餐桌有很明确的色彩主题。

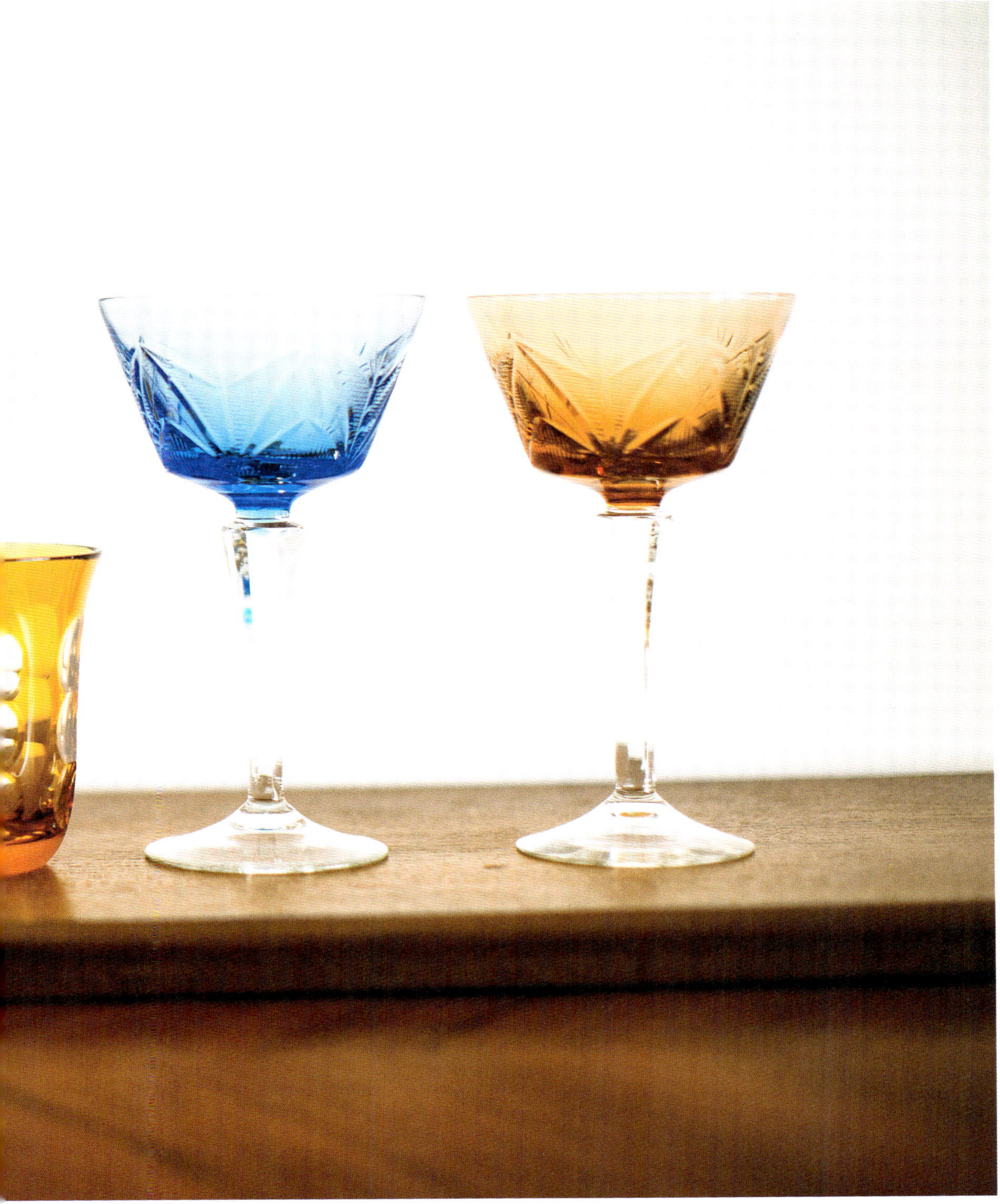

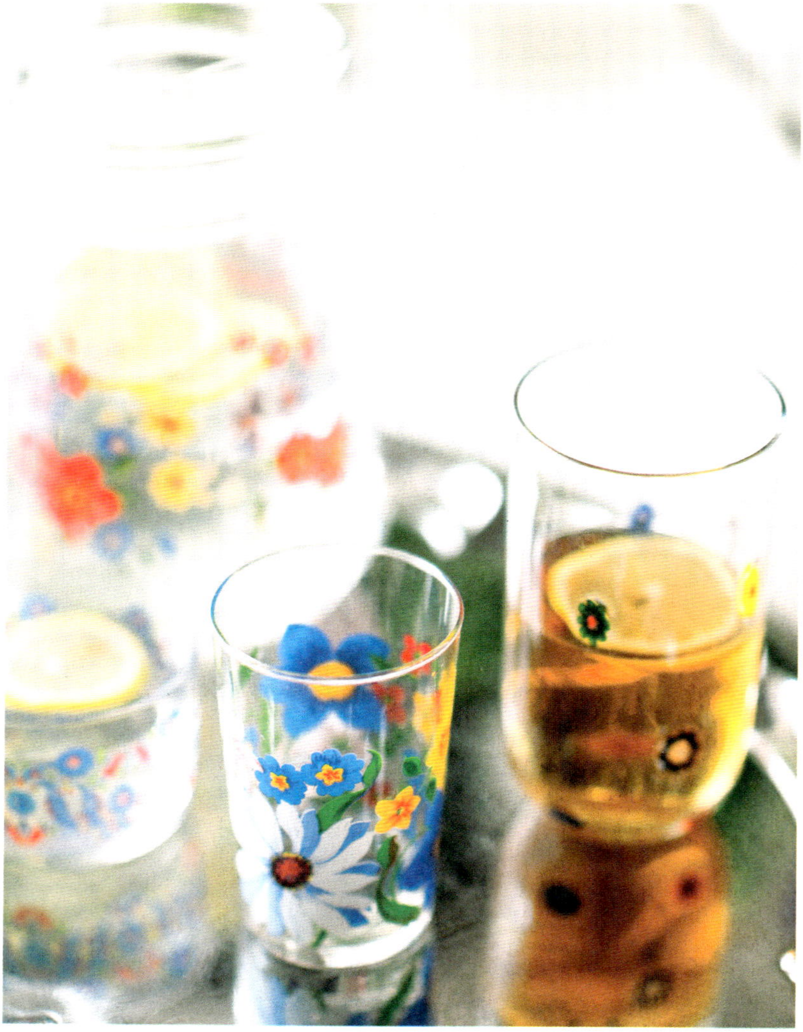

有着不同品牌和历史的玻璃杯，是花卉图案让它们不分彼此。

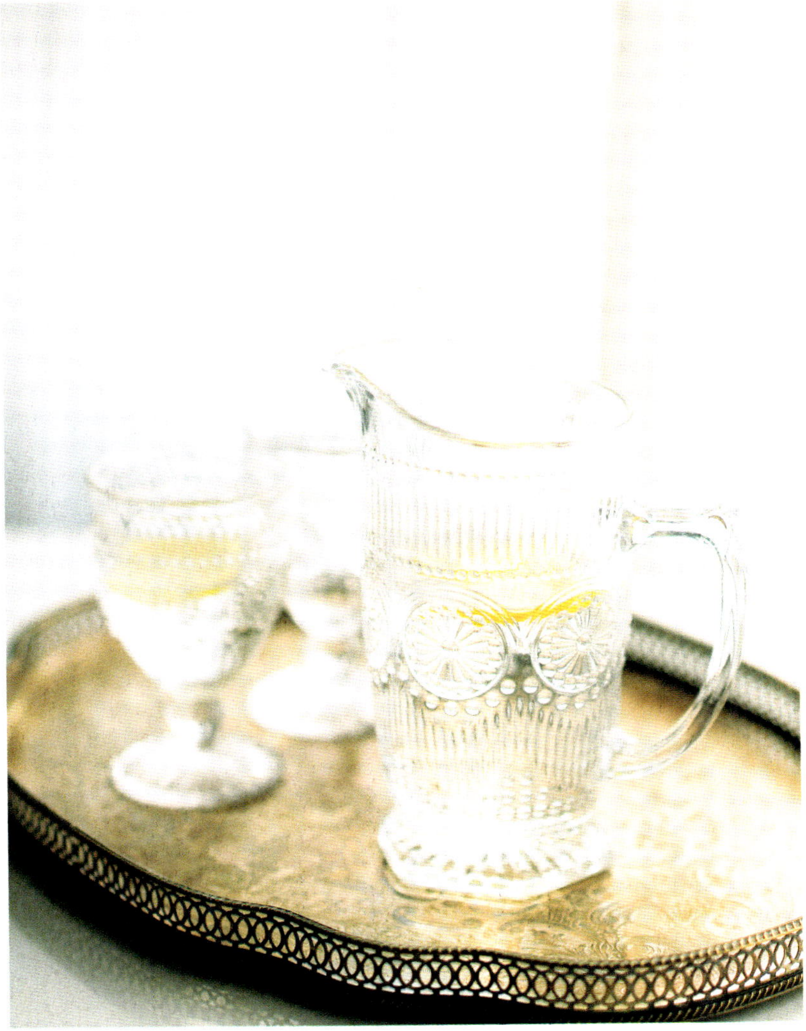

一大瓶水是每张餐桌都需要的，一个设计不平淡且百搭的凉水瓶是必备品。

不需要额外购买桌布

YOU DON'T NEED A PROPER TABLECLOTH

桌布很重要，当然，在我看来，桌上的一切都很重要。但也确实，用桌布的人越来越少了，人们不愿意把时间花在浆洗、熨烫桌布上，一切生活用品的流行或消退，都是源于生活节奏的改变。但对于只有一张大餐桌的我们，桌布能轻松营造百变的餐桌风格，这也是事实，它非常实用，并总能起到画龙点睛的作用。

按照传统的社交礼仪规则，桌布下垂的尺寸，早餐时应为 15~20 厘米，午餐时应为 20~30 厘米或更长一些。但真的无所谓，布置餐桌不是考试，也没有教官会去用尺子量，更何况，有些人非常讨厌桌布下面露出桌脚，有人又完全不接受全包式铺法。按你的喜好来就好，或者按照这个通用准则——无论什么场合，桌布平均下垂到 30 厘米左右就可以了。

其实并不需要额外花钱购买很多桌布，将旧的印花床单或各种材质的大披肩铺在早餐桌上，一样可以让每个清晨都有新鲜的感觉；装修剩下的壁纸也可以是一次性餐桌布

▶ 虽说不用额外购买桌布，但用爱马仕的羊绒披肩当桌布确实有些过分。不过，用大围巾客串桌布确实是好办法，这点毋庸置疑。

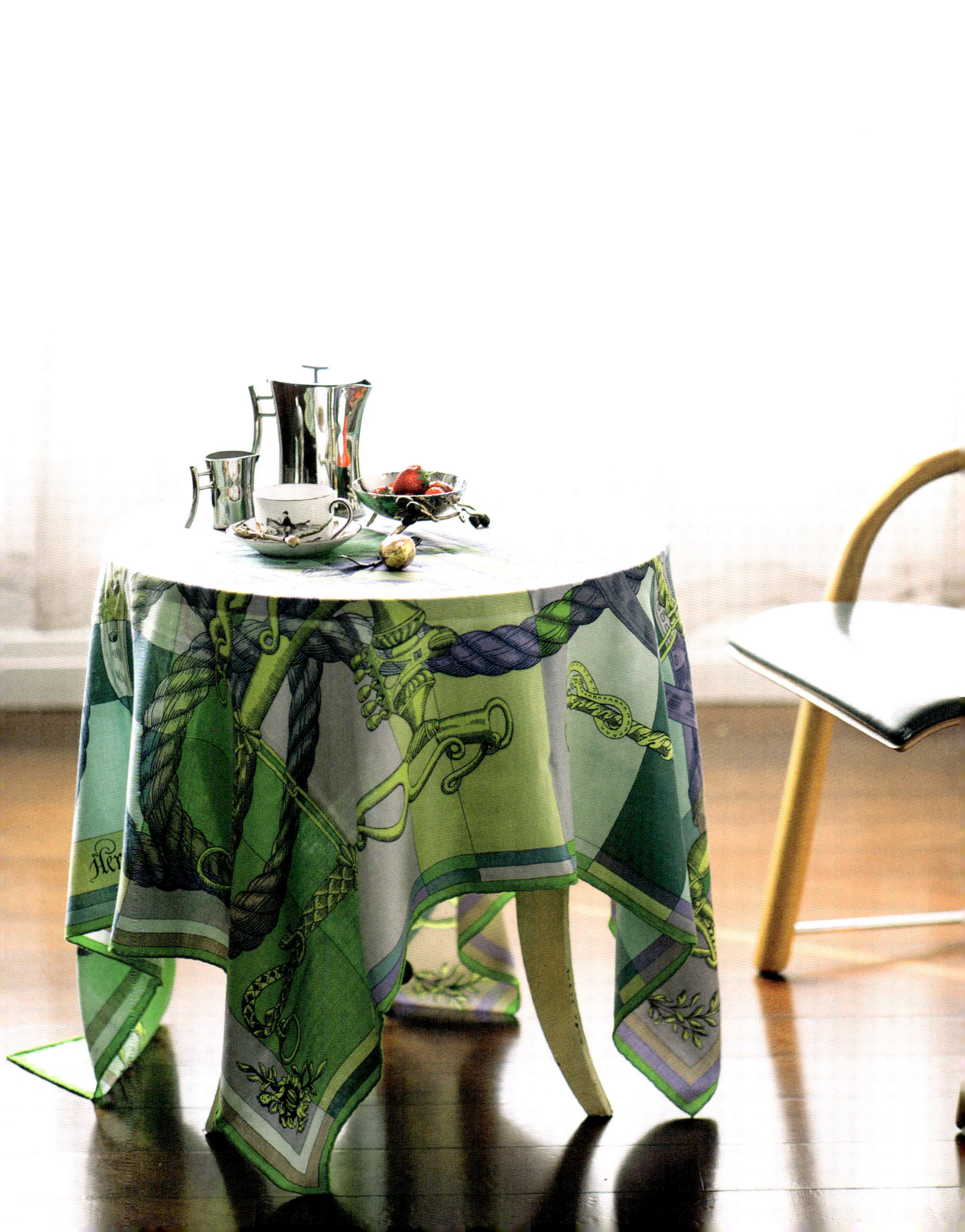

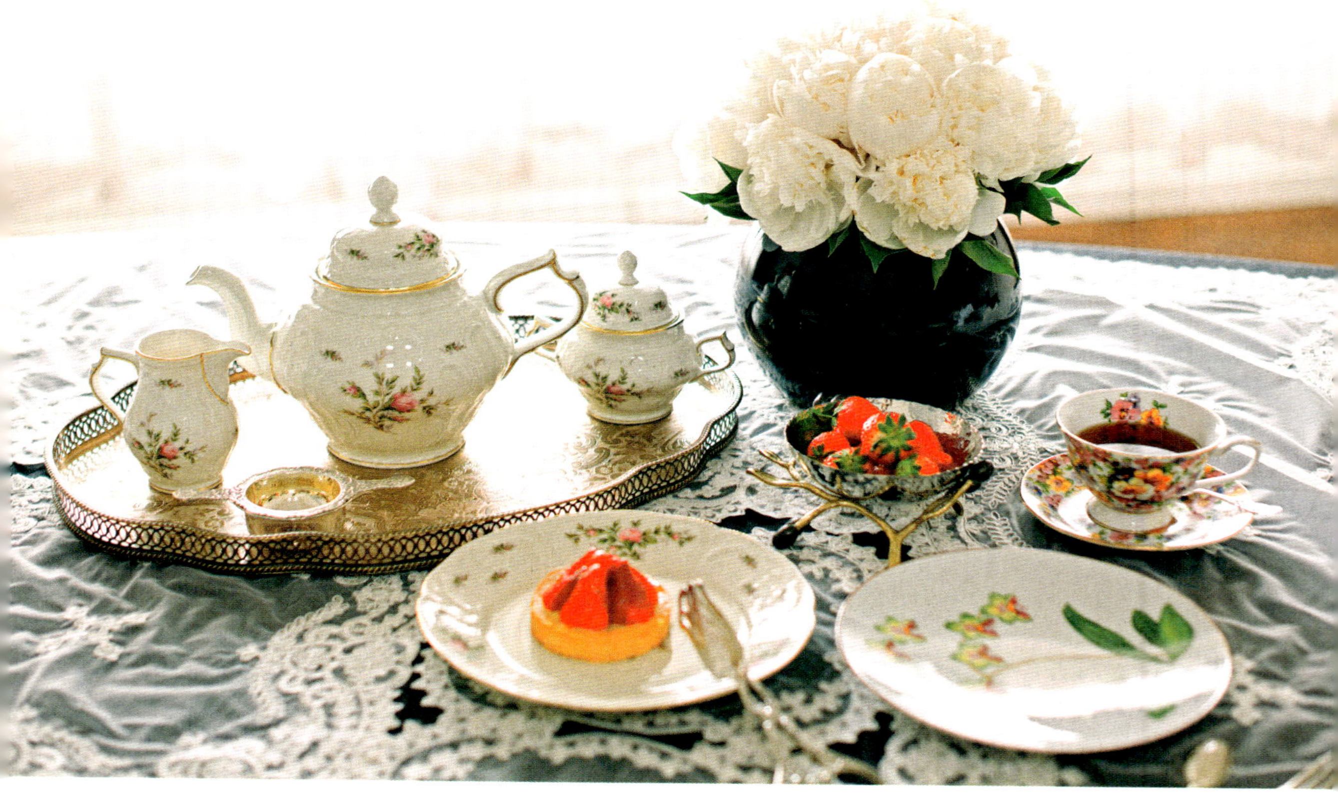

用厚重的深灰色毛呢面料打底，将小块的透明蕾丝茶巾相互拼接码放在上面，创造出一种全新的下午茶桌风格。

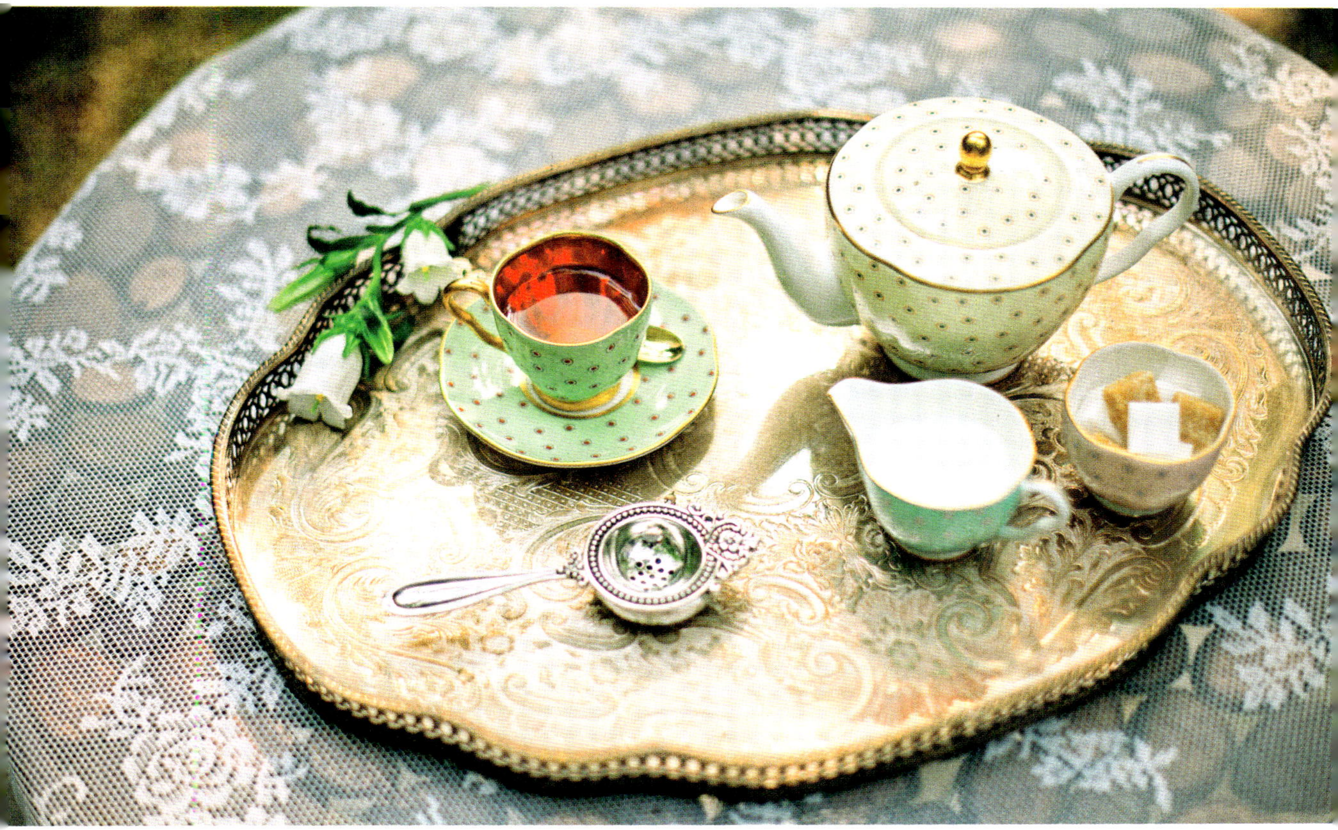

粗糙的石头桌面，却用精致的蕾丝当作桌布，运用强烈的质感对比是我喜欢的餐桌游戏法则。

置的道具，把它铺在餐桌上，会有意想不到的效果；在面料市场淘来的精致的白色蕾丝将它铺在室外粗糙的木条长桌上，强烈的对比让餐桌格外迷人。还可以试试把桌布叠铺的效果——我收集过很多欧洲跳蚤市场上的手工钩花的茶巾，这些茶巾流行于20世纪，现在已经很少有人使用，就连Paper Doily（茶巾）这个词组，也让年轻一代觉得陌生，认为是老奶奶才知道的词汇。它们一般比餐桌要小，把它们叠铺在有大桌布打底的餐桌上，下面的桌布也许是深色的丝绒，也许是同样白色的亚麻布，或呈现对比之美，或感受呼应的精致细节，让下午茶餐桌有一种既现代又复古的情趣。把餐桌和桌布当成一种装扮游戏，随你想象，怎么好玩怎么来，毕竟，铺着硬挺的雪白桌布的正式晚宴，对于我们来说，并不是日常生活的常态。

餐垫和餐巾

PLACEMAT AND NAPKIN

餐垫和餐巾是餐桌上经常被省略，但其实很有效果的小物。前者可以轻松改变餐桌的气氛，让同样的餐具呈现出不同的风格，后者除了实用价值外，也是装饰桌面的一个精致的细节。

我比较喜欢天然材质的餐垫，像棉、麻、竹、草、木，这些材质的餐垫总给人一种清新自然的风格，连带盘碗中的食物都仿佛变成了纯粹的有机食品，让人产生信任感。而那些有着五颜六色图案的塑料餐垫就算了吧，它们除了能避免掉落的食物弄脏桌面外，实在让人感觉很廉价。现代的设计师更开发出一些新鲜材质的餐垫，比如皮革、金属，这些能带给餐桌时髦的感觉，往往小小一块儿，便让人耳目一新。

我们现在的很多便餐，都不再用织物餐巾了，取而代之的是漂亮的纸质餐巾。这些有各种图案和色彩的纸质餐巾简便好用，但传统的熨烫得整整齐齐的织物餐巾的优雅感，仍然不可取代。餐巾摆放的位置从中世纪的披在用餐者的左臂上，到后来转移到用餐者的前胸部，到 19 世纪，才转移到膝部。而长度也从“如浴巾一般”变为 24 英寸（约 60 厘米）左右。晚餐餐巾的尺寸最大，而午餐为 43~50 厘米，下午茶为 30 厘米。要说餐巾其实还是大一点更舒适好用，也显出一种非凡的气派。1979 年开张的时尚界传奇餐厅

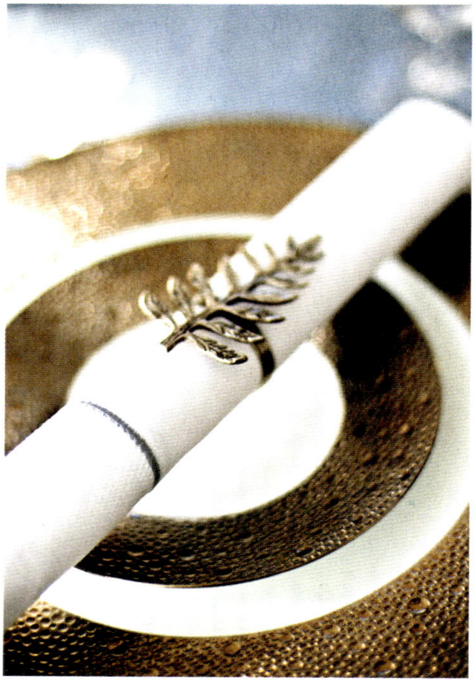

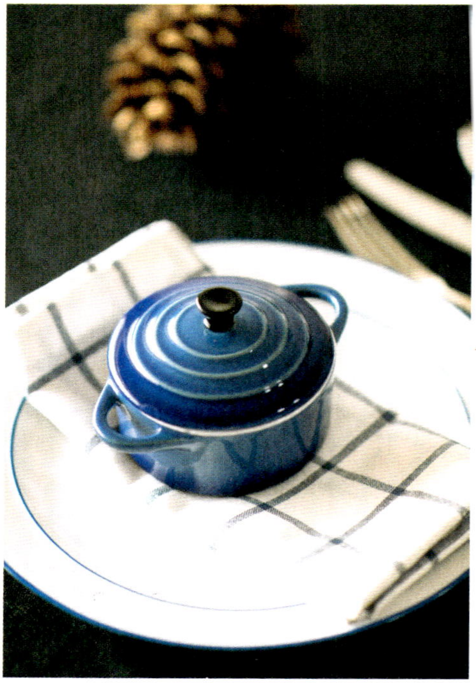

餐巾和餐巾环就像餐具的首饰，在这个圣诞餐盘上，银色的叶子和银边餐盘呼应，点缀出白色圣诞的强烈氛围。

这块蓝格子的棉麻布其实是宜家卖得很便宜的擦碗布，但用它来冒充餐巾配搭这个盘子和小汤锅，是不是同样很完美？

Mr. Chow 纽约店的每一处细节都被业内人士津津乐道，其中与 Lalique（莱俪）出品的双排玻璃门、Richard Smith（理查德 · 史密斯）设计的悬空雕塑、Giacometti（贾科梅蒂）的青铜落地灯相提并论的，是店内 28 英寸（约 71 厘米）长的餐巾。

另外，如果你已经不再是个婴儿，却还把餐巾系到脖子上，会被认为是不礼貌的。我们现在的做法通常是把餐巾对折叠放在膝部，开口的一面朝向自己，以方便用下层擦拭嘴角，再以干净的一面覆盖。餐巾的材质当然还是以选择天然柔软的棉麻为佳，合成纤维会在膝盖上打滑，客人不断地弯腰捡起落地的餐巾，并且把脸擦得更花一定不是你想看到的。

基本餐具和额外餐具

CUTLERY: THE BASICS AND THE EXTRAS

现在很多家庭的日常饮食受各地美食文化的影响，制作食物的灵感多元化，也使得用餐时不再单一地只需要筷子和勺子。如果说挑选筷子我们可以从材质、产地、样式、环保程度来判断，那么，五花八门的刀叉类餐具，我们又从何选起呢？

一般中国家庭使用到的基本西餐餐具，无非是标准的刀、叉、汤匙。要知道，在西方世界，一直到18世纪，有了这三件餐具，人们才能够以我们所谓的礼貌而又实用的方式，处理并享用所有的食物。至于那些鱼刀、带尖的葡萄柚勺子等等，都是在19世纪后期到20世纪才出现的"新食器时代"的工具。当我们选择一套基础的西式餐具时，别被太多的设计迷惑。要知道，餐具无论做成什么样子，如果不方便用来吃饭，那还是很让人郁闷的。好的餐具拿在手里手感要平衡，容易抓握，重量适当。刀刃要容易切东西，还要够宽，好将食物推到叉子上。而叉子齿距要恰当，齿够锋利。勺子的曲线要舒服，还要够深。这些是餐具应该具备的基本"美德"，除此之外，才是不同材质带来的视觉感受。当你有了这些基础款后，可以根据家庭的饮食习惯添置一些额外的餐具。比如常吃红肉的家庭可以准备牛排刀，以白肉为主的家庭有了鱼刀匙(sauce spoon)自然更方便，甜品叉和茶勺虽然不是必备，但如果有，在下午茶聚会上还是显得很有格调的。

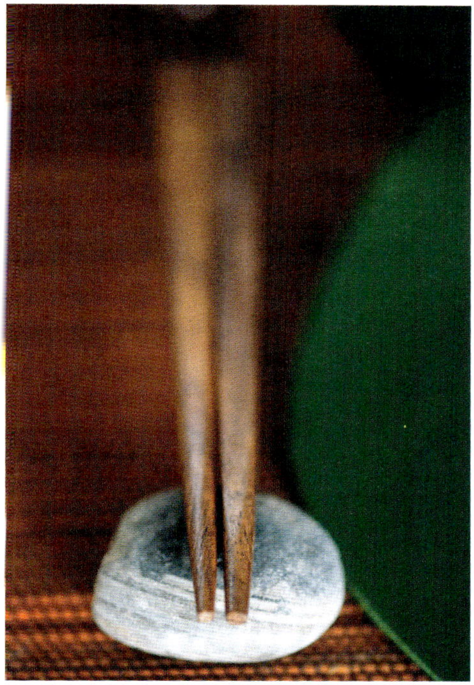

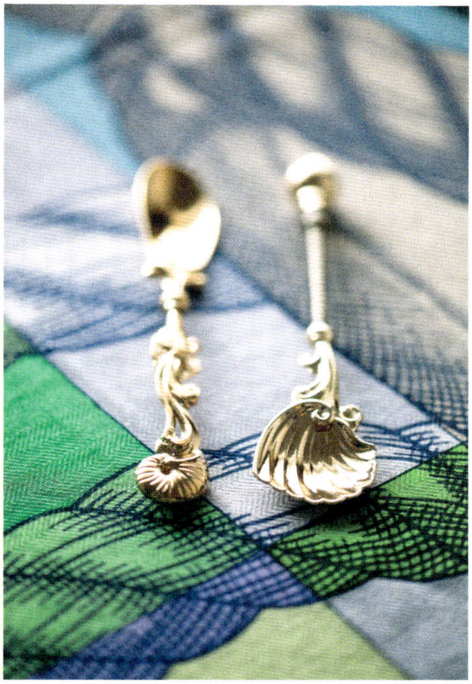

有很多精美的筷子架出售，但像这样从河边捡来的鹅卵石当筷子架也别有风情。

茶勺如果和下午茶餐桌的主题相配合，也会成为被人赞叹的最吸引人的细节。

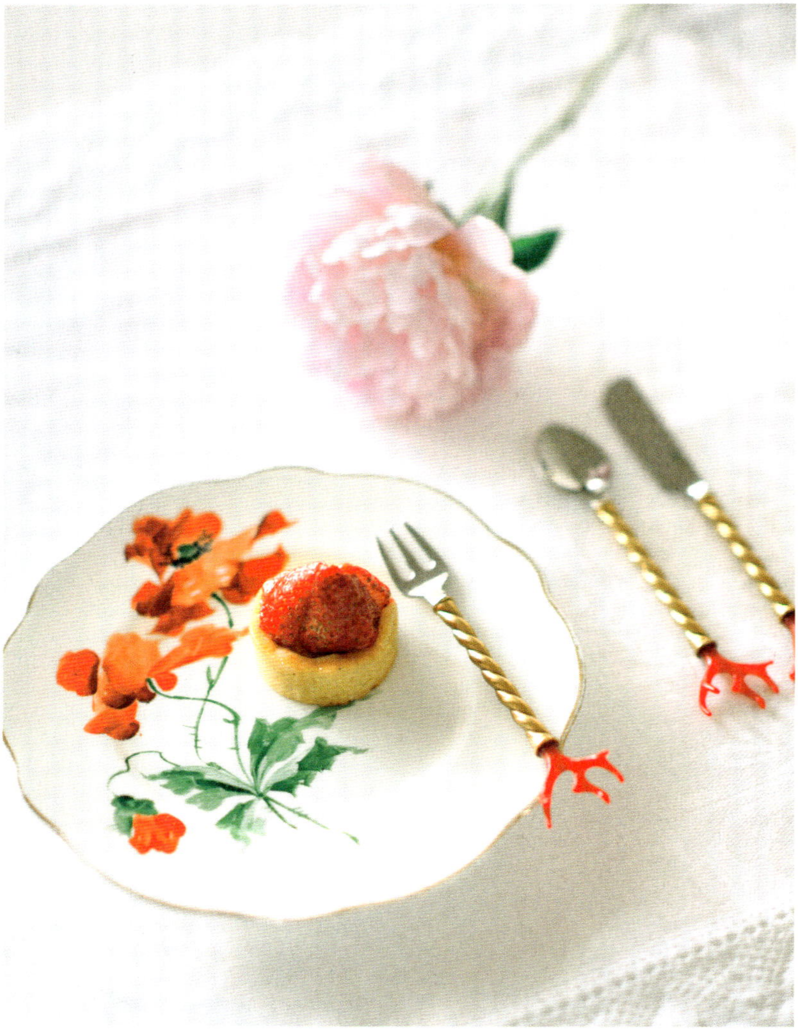

甜品刀叉不是家庭必备，但拥有一套这样的珊瑚镶嵌把柄的甜品刀叉能让下午茶格调猛烈提高。

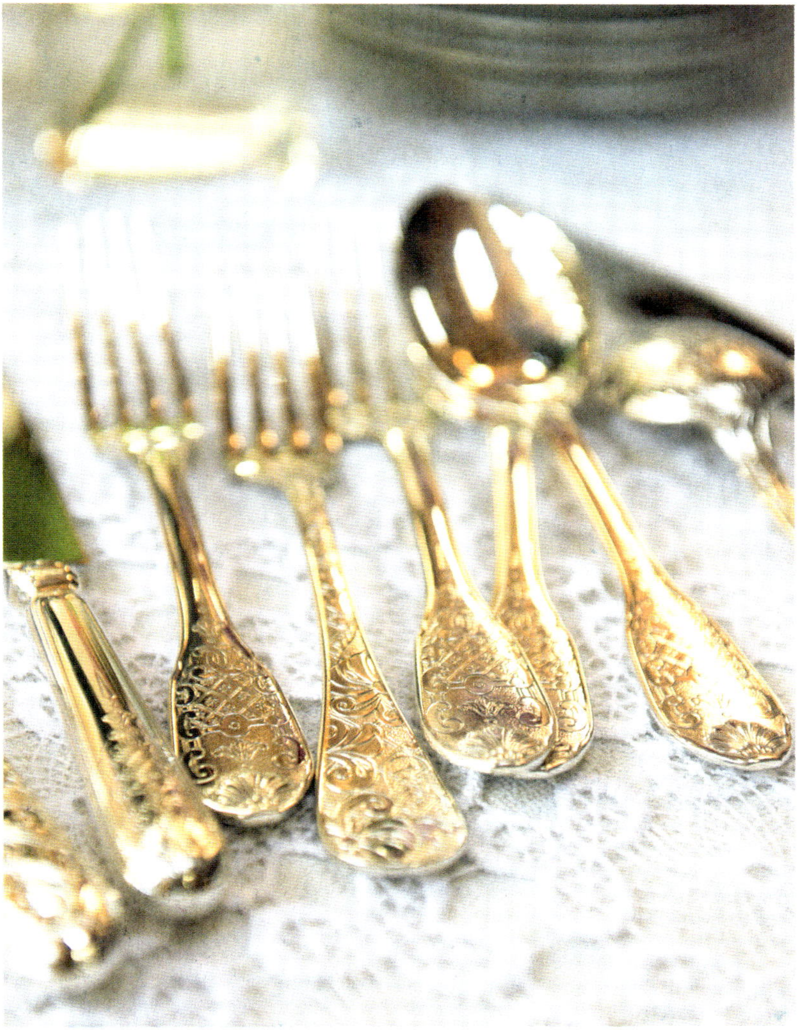

像这种Christofle（昆庭）的带有雕花的银质餐具，对大多数欧洲家庭来说，也只有吃圣诞大餐时才舍得拿出来，但如果拥有，会是可以世代相传的宝贝。

小心照顾你的餐具

TAKING CARE OF YOUR TABLEWARE

每次我在微博上贴出早餐或家宴的照片，总有人会问，这么多碗，怎么洗?

这个问题虽然煞风景，但挺实际，答案就是——你家里需要有一台好使的洗碗机和一个训练有素的阿姨或自己。洗碗机帮你解决大部分家常的餐具，也就是那些不太贵的、简单易得的基础款。但如果遇到古董餐具或珍贵的餐具，则一定要手洗。这包括古董的瓷器、玻璃制品，以及银器和骨把的餐具。一则是因为洗碗机的清洗容易让古董器皿上的图案褪色，表面被腐蚀，二是容易造成玻璃制品表面的划痕和磨损。不仅是古董玻璃杯，那些手工玻璃、切割玻璃也同样要手洗，并且最好装在塑料盆中，而不是直接放在容易磕碰的搪瓷或不锈钢水盆中。洗干净后，好的玻璃制品应该用传统的亚麻布擦拭干净，这样才能保持其光亮，并且，无论好的还是便宜的玻璃杯，最好都杯口朝上存放，这样虽然会进灰尘，但最容易破损的部分——杯口，得到了有效的保护。另外，刀叉餐具也要小心照顾，洗好后，要擦拭干净，保持干燥，这样才不会使它们失去光泽。

▶ 高级的水晶杯以及古董玻璃杯最好手洗，以免表面被划伤。

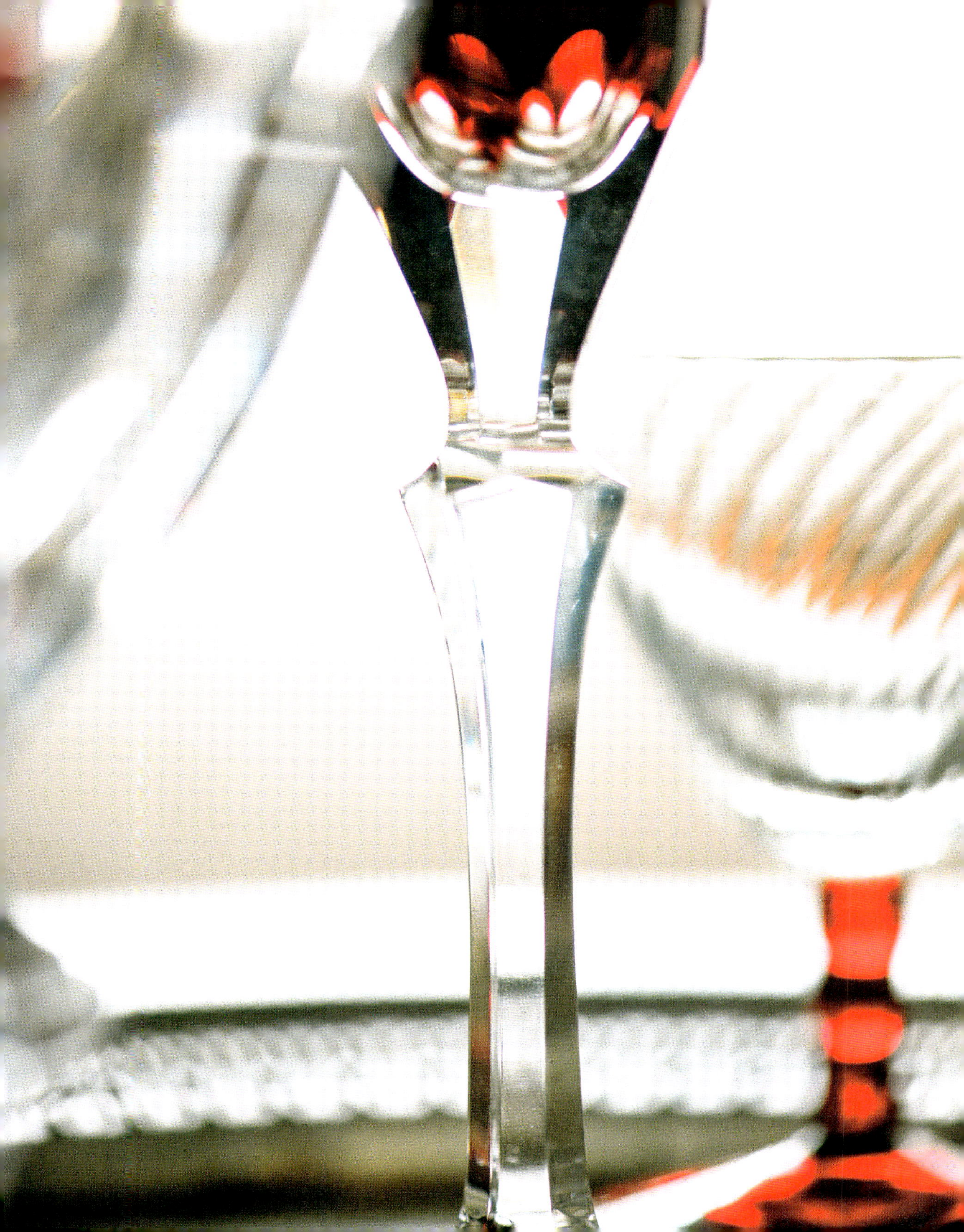

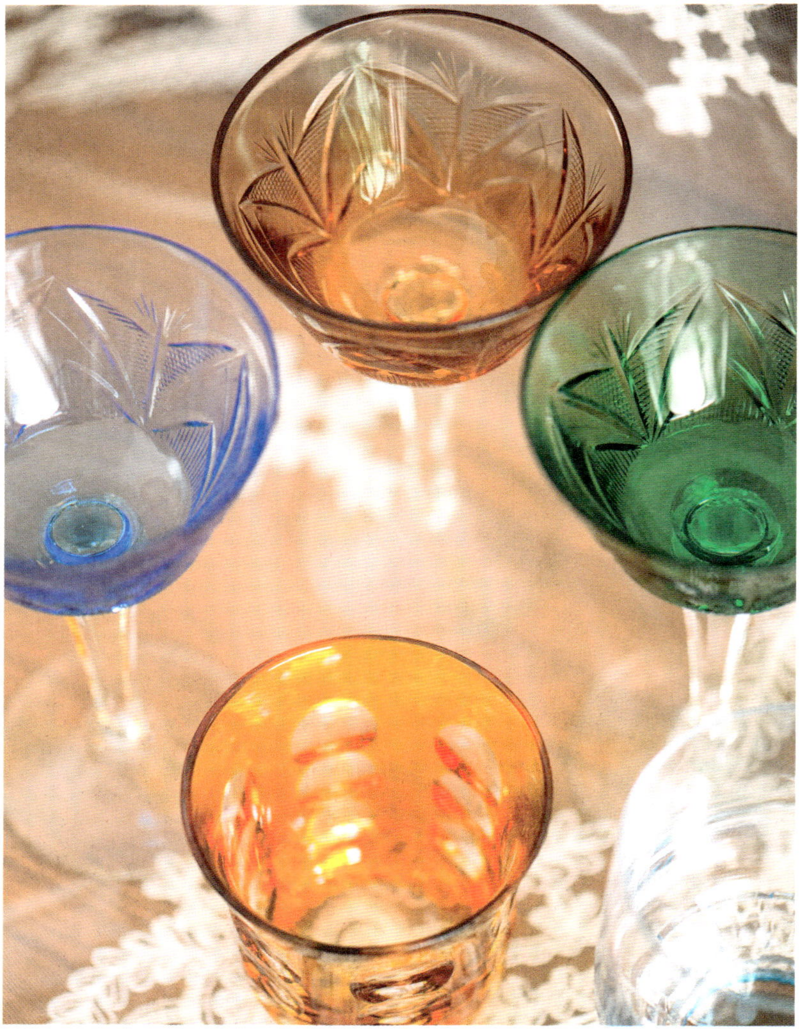

玻璃杯一定要杯口朝上存放，取拿时也尽量避免直接捏杯口。

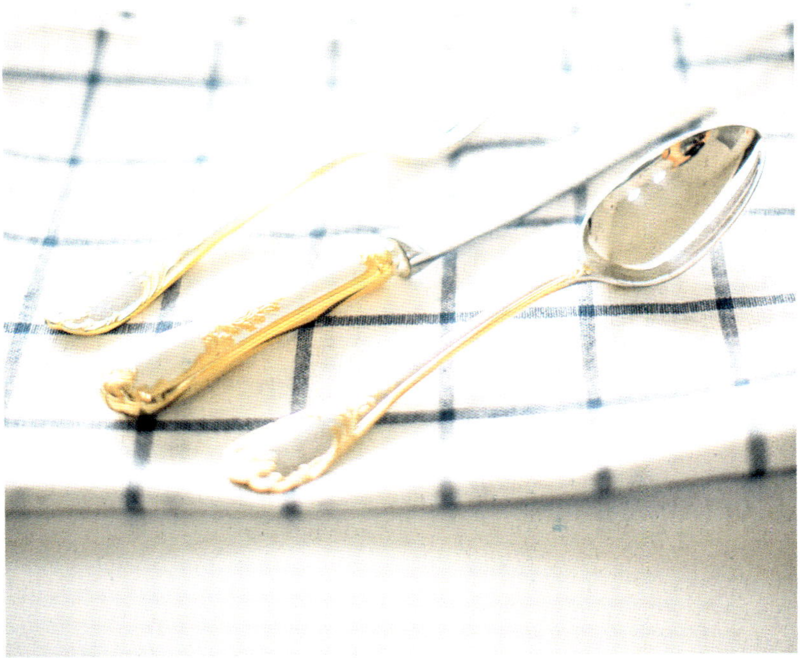

无论是银质还是钢质的餐具，清洗后都要用棉麻布擦干，这样才能令其永远光亮如新。

西 餐 摆 盘 江 湖

A HISTORY OF WESTERN TABLE SETTINGS

生活在这样一个分秒变换的时代，即使严格的西式餐桌摆放方式和礼仪，也在逐渐根据饮食习惯和生活节奏而改变，甚至因审美的变化而变化。

从 11 世纪到 16 世纪初期，欧洲的餐桌上还是一片狼藉。餐具还是奢侈品，不曾被广泛使用，人们在对着嘴灌完汤后，随便用手撕扯下几块肉送到口中，再在衣服或桌布上蹭蹭黏糊糊的手指——是的，这些曾经都是国王的宴会上的场景。查理六世（Charles VI）的宫廷宴会恶名昭彰。法国人文主义作家蒙田（Michel de Montaigne）也曾坦白地说："我很少使用勺子和叉子……吃得忙乱，几次咬到了自己的手指头。"

一直到文艺复兴时期，这种局面才因由"新资产阶级"的上位得以逐渐扭转。大量餐桌礼仪的著作相继出版，人们开始规范自己的举止，餐桌也变得空前浮夸华美。路易十四（Louis XIV）虽然仍坚持用手抓饭，但他的侍从会为他摆上专用的盘子，放上他并不会用到的勺子和叉子，国王的餐刀用一块折叠的餐巾遮盖，据说，这种"摆遮盖"就是"摆桌"说法的由来。

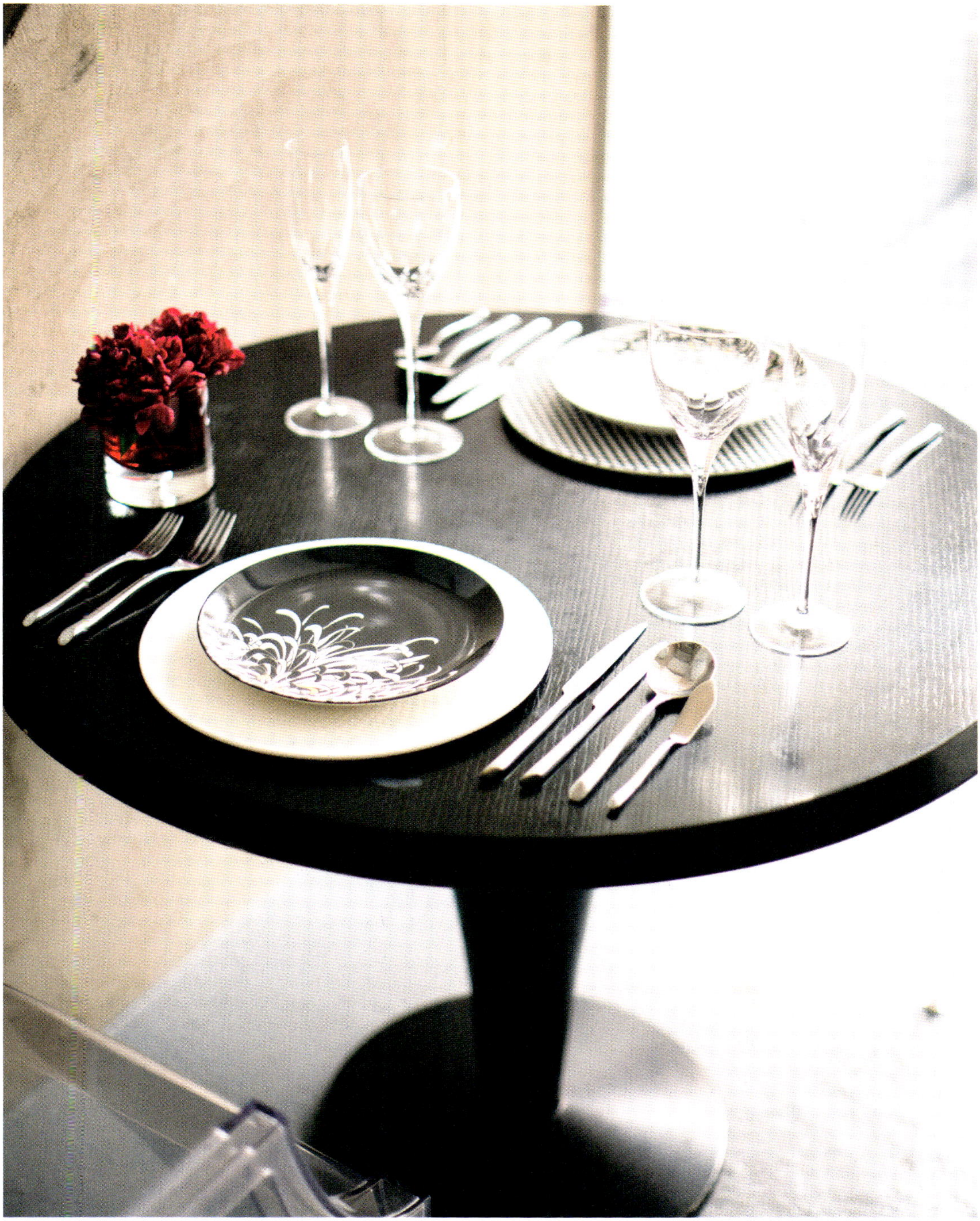

一些时髦的餐厅，由于空间限制不设置面包盘，而是将黄油刀在内的所有餐具从外到内一一排列。甜品叉勺会在上甜品的阶段提供。

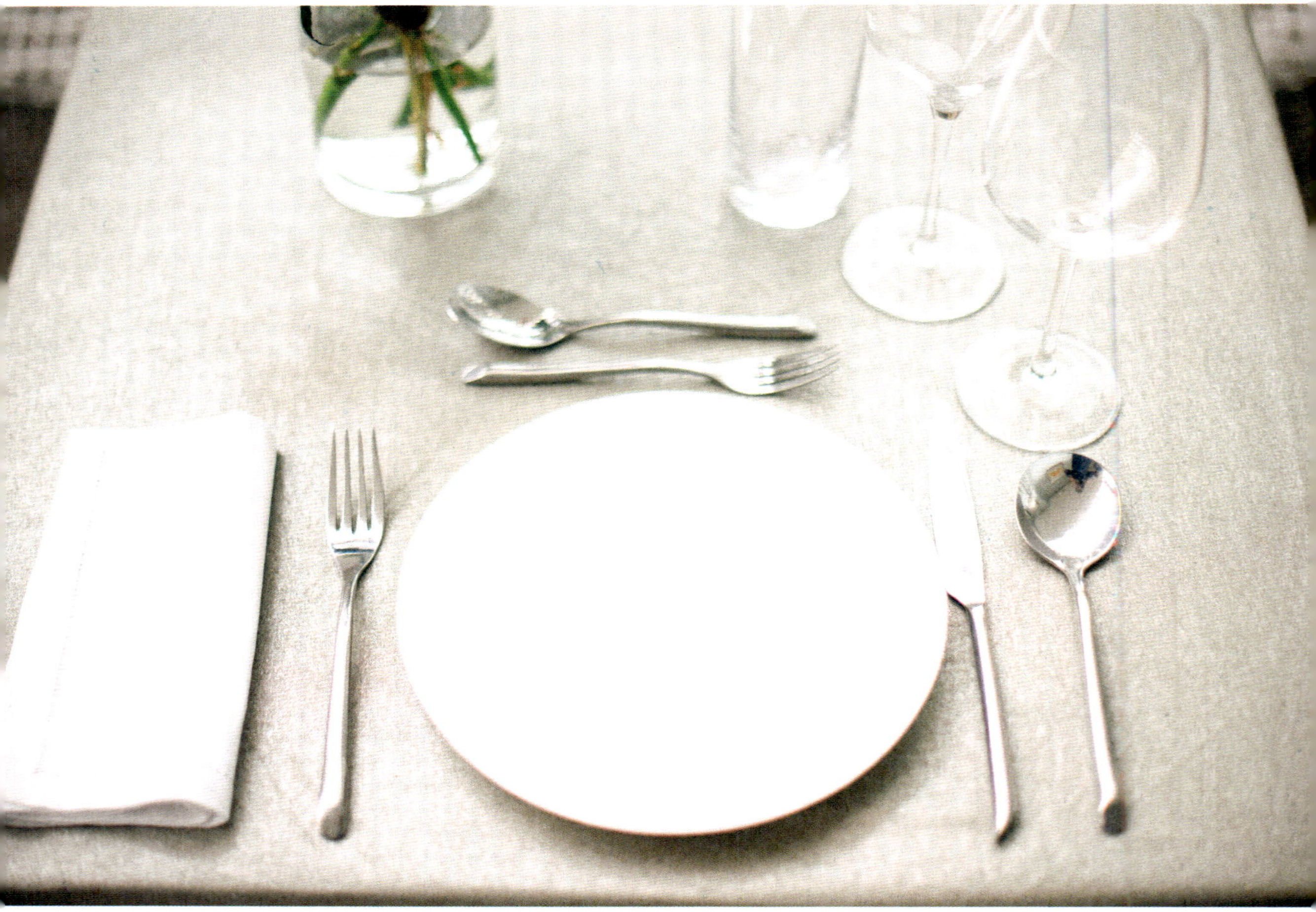

这是可以适合任何非正式西餐的国际通用基础摆放方式。餐盘对准用餐者入座后的正中位置，餐叉在左，餐刀和汤勺在右，甜点叉勺在盘子的上方，叉子和勺子的柄对着手的方向，利于拿放。

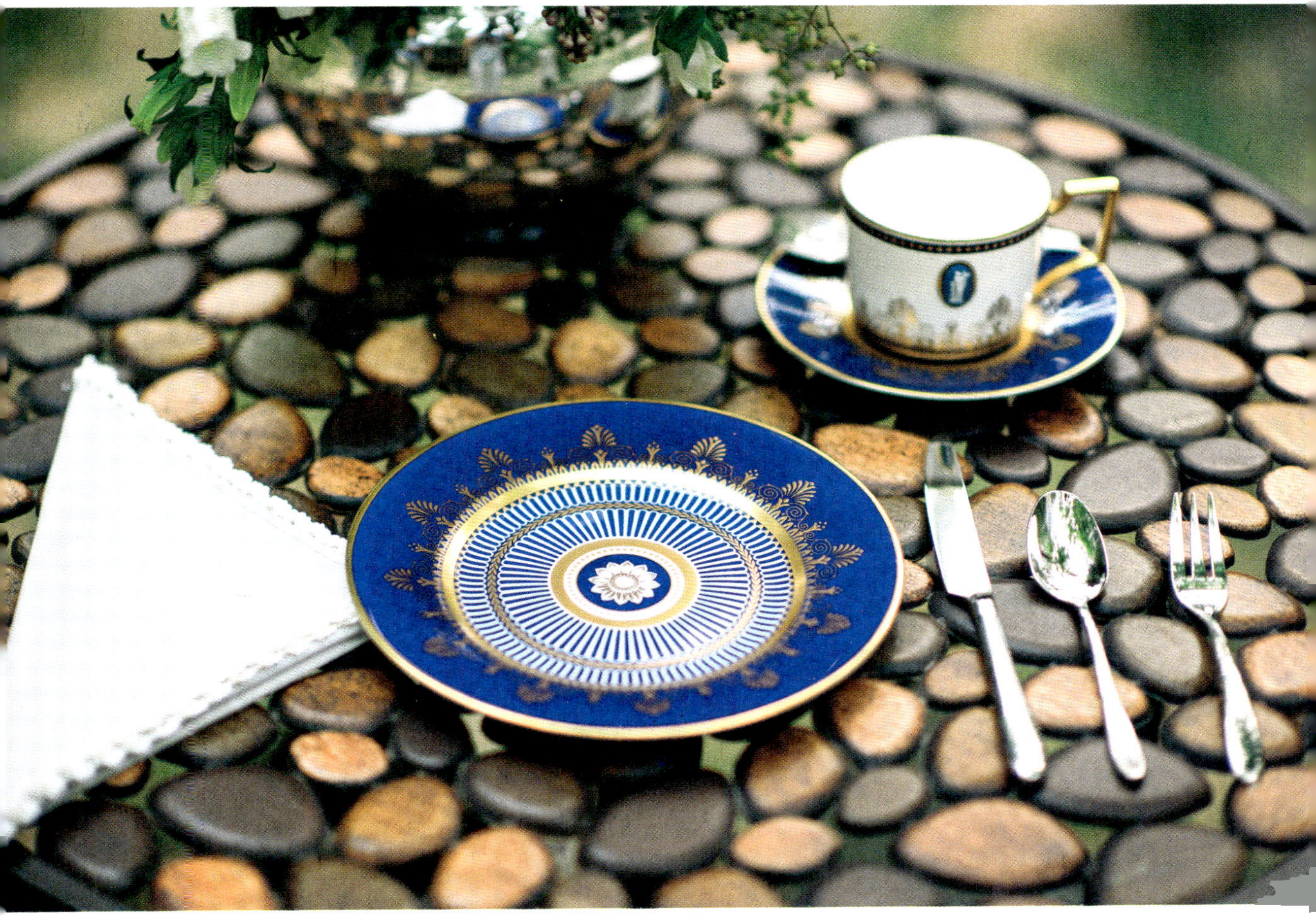

正式的英式下午茶需要每个人面前有一个甜点盘、一套茶杯茶托茶匙、一把糕点叉、一把用来切司空的茶点刀、一把吃特别的奶油蛋糕的勺子和一小块折成三角形的小餐巾。所有餐具都要放在盘子的右侧，餐巾放在左侧或盘子的上方。

罗伊·斯特朗（Roy Strong）在《盛宴》（*Feast*）一书中说，在16世纪宫廷宴会上，会将糖和其他成分混合，制成复杂的雕塑，经过染色、镀金，摆到桌子上，而为了把这种大型雕塑运送到宴会桌上，甚至需要把门加大尺寸。坐在桌子两边的客人想要说话，得靠传递小纸条才行。到了19世纪鱼刀等"新食器"的时代来临，精英们精简菜单、重新规范餐桌礼仪，桌面装饰的重点从鲜花蜡烛转换成了每个人面前实用的餐具。单盘变成了双盘甚至三层盘，酒杯也开始排列成行。而大洋彼岸的美国在叫响《独立宣言》后，仍然沿用欧洲移民带来的文化，但他们也把自己的节奏混入其中。因而，在西餐的餐桌上，你知道餐具的摆放顺序是左边叉，右边刀，无论想用到多少餐具，都可以按照上菜的顺序，从外侧到内侧，一一摆放在盘子两边。同样，这也是用餐者的使用顺序，最先用到最容易取到的。尽管如此，你依然会对一些问题感到困惑，比如牛油盘（butter plate）应该放在侧面还是侧上面？牛油刀到底横放还是对角线斜放？餐桌上到底是否都应该提供盐和胡椒以及黄油这类的东西？

这些其实对应的正是文化差异。先说摆盘。牛油盘是英国人发明的，他们把它摆放在餐叉的左侧，如果提供牛油刀，则可以把它横放在面包盘中间，刀把朝右，刀刃朝下，和桌子的边缘平行。到了美国，人们更倾向于把牛油盘或沙拉盘放在左上方，位于餐叉上方，而不是侧面。牛油刀会放在牛油盘的对角线位置，刀把朝右，刀刃朝上。或者将它横放在面包盘上右1/3处。但到了法国，即使他们将面包直接扔在桌子上，既没有牛油盘也没有牛油刀，当然也没有牛油，那你也不用生气地指责他们为什么这么做，这和法国人爱"炫富"、爱"怀旧"的情结有关。

在法国历史学家让－马克·阿尔贝（Jean-Marc Albert）的《权力的餐桌》（*Aux*

tables du pouvoir）中有这样一个故事：拿破仑曾和他的外长塔列朗说："把饭菜弄得象样一些，你们要挣一个花两个，不够了去借，我最后结账。"他把餐桌当作一种外交工具，请一切对法兰西有价值的人来吃饭。塔列朗是个很会作秀的外交家，一次晚宴，仆人端来一条极大的鲑鱼，到桌子附近时却不小心弄翻了盘子。在当时，鱼是宴会头等奢华的大菜，众人哗然。但塔列朗不动声色地叫人又端来一条一模一样同样硕大的鲑鱼。这个"事故"是精心安排好的，为了展示的是皇帝的实力。

说得有点远，但法国人确实爱"炫富"。再回到面包上。中世纪时，贵族们用餐，会用不发酵的粗面包厚片垫在桌子上，上面摆放他们所食用的高级精细的面包。我们现在所使用的盘子正是来源于此——这种垫在下面不发酵的硬面包渐渐被木块代替，然后转变为锡器和瓷器。而以法国为代表的欧洲大陆的人不用面包盘的做法正是一种缅怀封建时代贵族旧时光的情绪。另外还有一种版本是说，在正式宴会中所使用的白色亚麻桌布相当昂贵，而这样随意将面包扔在桌面上的做法，是要故意摆出一种满不在乎的有钱人姿态，表示自己财力雄厚。

另外，法国人还习惯将餐具正面朝下扣在桌子上，并且他们使用大汤匙而不是圆形汤匙。有时候，法国人会用到餐刀架，这样主餐刀就可以放回到桌子上，因为在完整的法餐中，上甜品前会有一个上奶酪的环节（英国是在甜点和奶酪之间二选一），在这个时候，餐刀可以再次使用。

但生活在这样一个分秒变换的时代，即使严格的西式餐桌摆放方式和礼仪，也在逐渐根据饮食习惯和生活节奏而改变，甚至因审美的变化而变化。比如，英国奢华宴会服务公司“The Admirable Crichton”的设计师约翰尼·罗克斯伯勒（Johnny Roxburgh）就说过：“在一张偌大的桌子上，摆上一大片餐具，看起来会不舒服。相反，我们更喜欢分两次布置餐桌，到甜点时间将勺子和叉子收走。”同样，也可以每上一道菜，摆放分发一次相应的餐具，这样可以让窄小的桌面看起来更清爽，用餐者亦感到更方便。为了让摆上装饰品后的桌面保持整洁，约翰尼还不喜欢用牛油盘：“有人及时更换补充餐具要比把面包放在盘子一侧好得多。另外，最好是每份餐具都配有盐和胡椒，不一定装在传统的盐盅里，可以使用任意一款漂亮的器皿，不需要盐勺。”（引自卡罗琳·克利夫顿－莫格的作品《Set with Style》。）

就像评价人一样，不要轻易用对或错去评价一种餐具的摆放方式，这也许基于不同的文化，也许是时代发展和饮食变化而产生的新的摆放方法，就像亘古以来人类继承的语言文字有着严格的传承，但也依然会不断有新的词汇加入，无论你是否愿意接受。

与这些变化相对，在西餐摆盘中永远不变，需要严格恪守的清规戒律，除了左叉右刀、从外到内的顺序之外，还有一个重要原则是，每样东西的摆放都要“稳、正、匀”。摆在中心的餐具要在正中间，餐具之间的距离要相等，视觉上要平衡。一位英国老祖母曾经教授孙女严格的餐桌礼仪：所有盘子上的刀叉手柄都与桌子边缘对齐，另外摆在每位客人面前的所有餐具，总宽度应该为 60~70 厘米，她认为，这种密度方便客人交流，感觉更舒适。这让人不禁想到，在诺贝尔颁奖的千人盛宴上，除了卡尔十六世·古斯塔夫（Carl XVI Gustaf）国王和王后拥有 70 厘米的宽度外，其他人一律 60 厘米排开，看着各位社会名流肩并肩地挨在一起还是颇有些喜感的。

中 式 餐 桌 慢 优 雅

THE ELEGANCE OF CHINESE TABLE SETTINGS

好的餐桌摆放形式是符合人体工学、让人使用方便的，就像好的礼法也是符合全人类文明进程的，走到哪里都会适用，其中并不存在很大的东西方的差异。

喜欢引经据典、在中国几千年文化里找渊源的人可能也很难找到一套流传下来的关于中式餐桌摆放的规矩。记录秦汉以前礼仪文化的著作《礼记》中提到了一些关于宴席食物摆放的要求，大意是：带骨肉放在净肉左方，饭食放在用餐者左方，肉羹则放在右方，调味品放在面前的位置……但中餐体系庞大，各地有很大的差异，经过千百年的流传，也无法对现实有借鉴意义。现代中餐的摆桌摆盘，一方面是依据饮食的传统，比如餐间饮茶、用餐者分享食物、需要调味品佐味、会有汤羹等等。另一方面是根据餐具的具体使用习惯，像筷子、筷子架、湿巾碟这些器物都有很强的独立性。

在中式摆盘中，中国人崇尚“对称”和“平、直、正”的审美，即餐具之间距离要相等、视觉平衡，这一点全世界都是共通的。日常吃饭请客，需要的是每人一个骨碟，这个骨碟也可以和西式餐具中吃前菜的餐盘通用，骨碟摆在用餐者正中间的位置，距离桌子边缘大概两指（1.5~2 厘米）。此外还需要一个味碟、一副汤碗和汤勺以及筷子和筷子架。

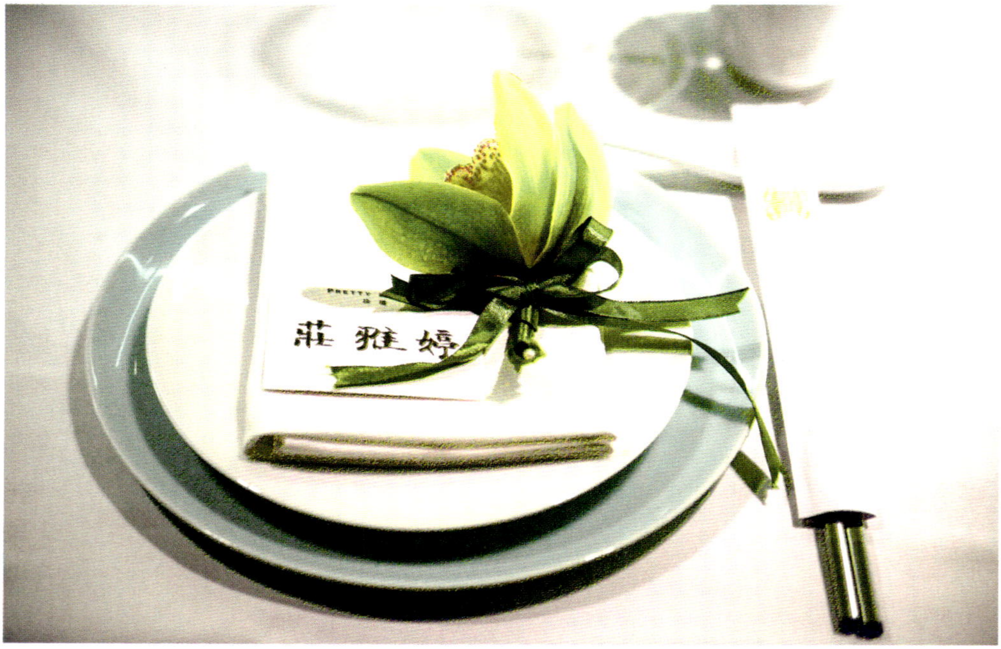

用丝带缠绕的蕙兰装饰餐盘精致典雅，以毛笔书写名卡，很注重传统礼节。（本篇摄影：袁小涵）

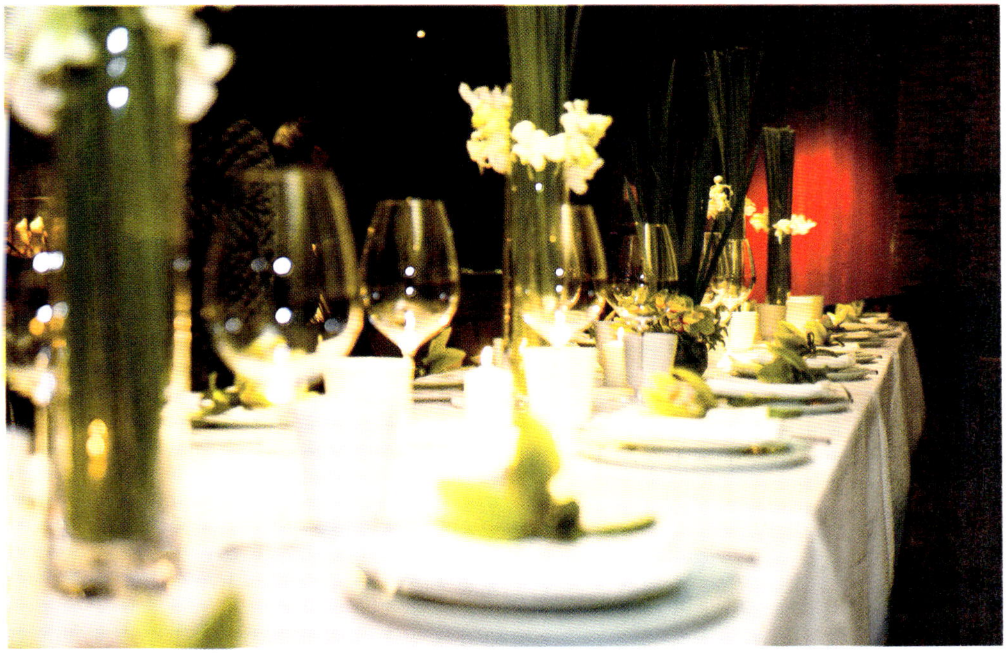

中餐也可以用长桌来呈现，花卉装饰不要太占地，要留出摆放菜品的空间。

茶杯最典型的是用没有把手的那种，摆在右上方或者筷子旁边都是没有问题的。筷子架如果是动物或人物造型，那么头部要朝左摆放。在正式的宴请中，还会用到湿巾碟，放在骨碟的左侧，千万别拿错了邻座的湿巾，会很尴尬。

近年来，很多中国家庭日常饮食都发生了很多改变。以前只钟情于煎炒烹炸的传统烹饪方式，现在也逐渐开始接受使用烤箱烤制食品菜肴、用搅拌机进行食物加工、以沙拉的形式生食蔬菜水果，还有代替传统白酒，饮葡萄酒成为主流，就连分享式的用餐习惯也被更方便卫生的分餐式强烈冲击着……这些改变让中式餐桌也变得界限不再清晰，很多西式的摆盘形式被借鉴进来。就像在这本书里，虽然没有特别布置过一个纯粹的中餐餐桌，但很多布局只是换一双筷子，同样成立。这一点和礼仪相同，好的餐桌摆放形式是符合人体工学、让人使用方便的，就像好的礼法也是符合全人类文明进程的，走到哪里都会适用，其中并不存在很大的东西方的差异。

礼仪方面，老人会从小教导我们，主宾座离门最远、面对门，主人座则靠近门；茶壶嘴不能对着任何人，鱼头则要对着主人；有眼力见儿的年轻人要主动为其他客人斟茶，斟茶次序按照年长、尊贵程度来排列；胳膊肘不上桌；筷子不用时要放在筷子架上，不能横放在饭碗上；尽量少夹菜，保持自己的盘子干净，夹了的菜就不要再放回去；主人应先向客人祝酒，客人亦要敬主人酒以表示感谢；碰杯时，酒杯低于对方的酒杯，以示谦卑和尊敬；起身去夹菜和在盘中翻翻拣拣，甚至将筷子伸到别人面前夹菜都是非常粗鲁的行为；湿巾是用来擦手的，再热也不能擦脸……

郭德纲曾给他儿子写过一段话，其中提到——喝汤不许吸溜，吃饭不许吧嗒嘴，要闭上嘴嚼。筷子不许立插米饭中，因为象征香炉，只有死刑犯的辞阳饭才这样插筷子。吃饭时，手要扶碗，决不许一只手在桌下。家有客人，要谨记茶七、饭八、酒满。客人添饭时一定不能说：还要饭吗？必须问：给您再添点儿？上人家里串门，敲门时先敲一下，再连敲两下，急促地拍门属于报丧，本家必不悦……尽管这位相声演员平时口中尽是笑谈，但这几句却字字箴言，就像他自己所说："规矩可以不遵守，但不能被毁灭。"

然而，让人感到遗憾的是，近年来，在媒体上频频爆出中国游客因为吵闹喧哗、举止粗鲁而被外国餐厅拒之门外的事件，让人误以为中国餐桌无礼仪，老祖宗握碎了家法棒在九泉之下恨得咬牙切齿。但从另一方面想，正是这些让人觉得颜面尽失的事情的发生，才会刺激更多的人去重视和重拾餐桌礼仪。古话说"仓廪实而知礼节，衣食足而知荣辱"，就像西方人所说三代才能培养出一个贵族，我们在经过了贫穷和文化断裂后，也要经过三代人的吃饱饭和重建认知结构，才能恢复美好的礼仪吧。所谓优雅，并不是一时强摆出来的做作姿态，而是建立在知识和规则的基础上的一种由内而外的从容的美感。

从知识层面讲，中餐喧闹，除了一些人本身嗓门大、举止粗鲁的硬伤外，还有一些认知上的误区。比如，中餐讲究主宾不入座，客人不能入座，因而在主人请你当主宾的时候，略表谦逊即可，万万别推搡扭捏，仪态尽失，还让其他人陪着罚站；敬酒酒杯低于对方是表示敬意，但如果对方明显比你年龄小或职位低，或仅仅因为他是主人你是客人、他是男人你是女人，也不必一层低过一层地推让；还有在中餐馆中常常看到扭打成一团的场面，不是打架，而是争着埋单（肯定还不是大单）。这又何必。如果事先约定

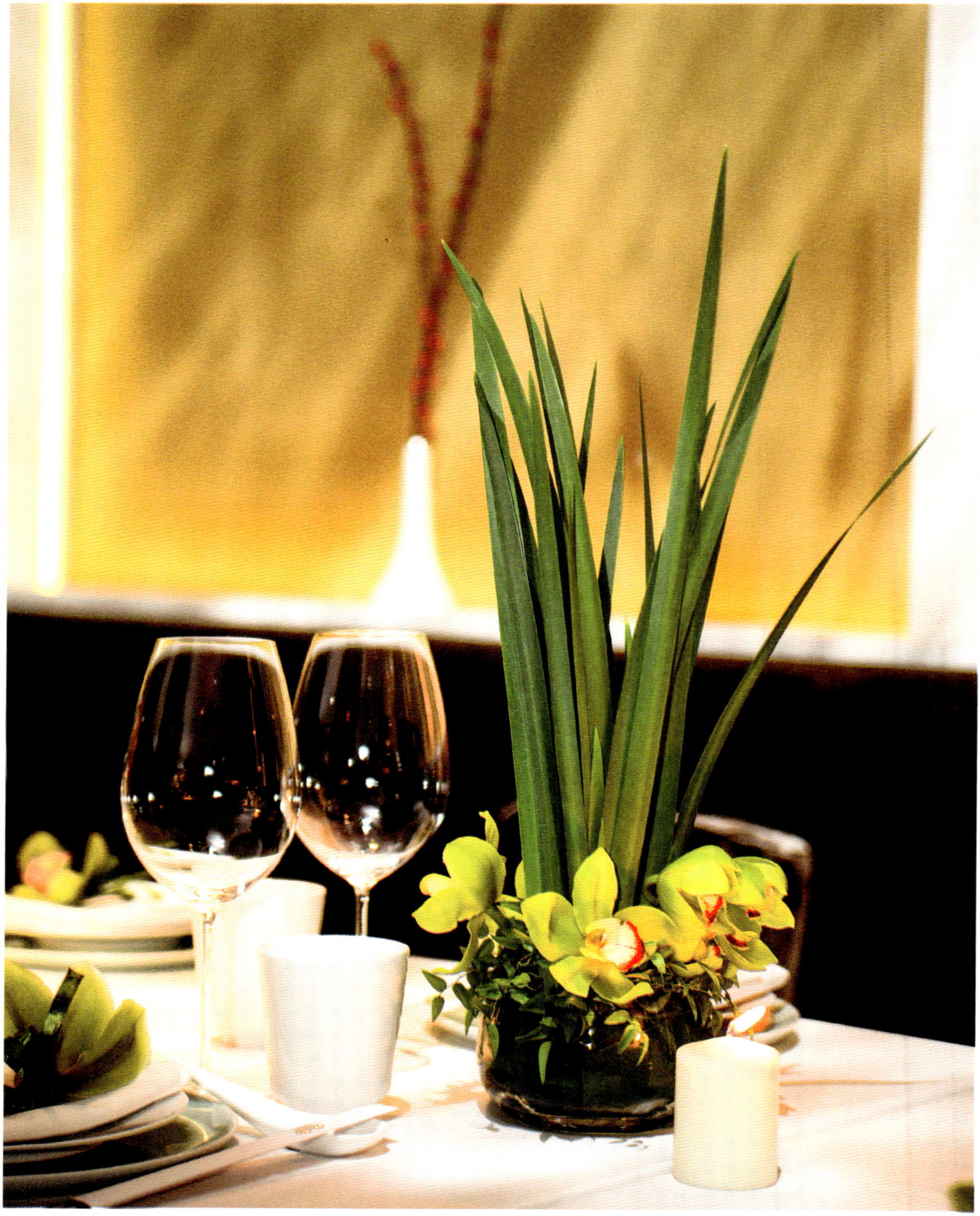

优雅而有东方意境的兰花作为中餐桌的主题花卉非常恰当。

好谁请客，客人不要去抢，以免驳了主人的面子，主人亦可在宴请结束前默默埋单……

想讲礼貌却因认知不够而弄巧成拙是一种失礼，而不讲究灵活性也会成为笑谈。梁实秋曾在《吃相》中描写一位女士，喝汤时“真能把上下唇撮成一颗樱桃那样大，然后以匙尖触到口边徐徐吮饮之。这和把整个调羹送到嘴里面去的人比较起来，又近于矫枉过正了”。在所有的礼仪中，都有一些模糊的界限，正所谓审时度势，什么场合做什么姿态。比如通常大家认为，中餐不要吃得盆干碗净才表示主人提供的食物充足富余，但在家宴中，的确是吃光所有的东西才会让主人高兴；替人夹菜是很体贴友爱的行为，但在上菜的时候夹一次也就够了，毕竟现在都讲究控制饮食，你不知道其他人是否在节食；在服务费很高的餐厅里，服务员会殷勤地帮你更换骨碟，但如果明明面前的骨碟还很干净，却任由他更换，尽管没错，却不符合现代人环保的精神，礼貌地拒绝也是一种优雅的姿态。

养成好的餐桌礼仪是一个既快又慢的过程。“快”在要尽快认识到礼法上的欠缺和不足，而在日常的每一餐中有意识地观察、学习、应用。从无意识到有意识，不熟练到很熟练，会是一个进步很快的过程。而慢有两层含义，一是要放慢生活节奏和放松心态，凡事不急不慌，慢慢来。在外用餐，本来就是一个慢慢享受的过程，在餐厅大声叫喊服务员、暴躁地催菜，在自助餐厅一次取食很多，甚至无序哄抢食物，这些是起于心急、节奏急、怕吃亏，是一种贫相和贪相毕露的做法。另一方面，在照猫画虎学会了一些基本礼仪后，更深层次地去顾及他人感受、服务他人、懂得赞美和欣赏，达到自然流露出从容优雅、有教养，要从生活水准和意识形态两方面去慢慢提高，这也许还需要两代人到三代人的努力，但为了我们将来可以获得更多的尊重和自由，请不要停住脚步，这一切努力都值得。

顽童与餐桌的战争

HOW TO TEACH PERFECT TABLE MANNERS TO CHILDREN

餐桌礼仪不是让孩子戴着脚镣舞蹈，而是灰姑娘的水晶鞋，把孩子最天真美好的部分连同他们古灵精怪的热情一起安放其中，用最自然最舒服的方式展现出他们闪闪发亮的一面。讲述让孩子从小就懂得的餐桌礼仪，以及如何帮助他们养成这些习惯。

在餐厅里，我们都有过这样默默崩溃的时刻——邻桌的孩子不停打闹、上蹿下跳、互相追逐；孩子把盘子或碗敲得叮当乱响，挑拣食物或把食物当作玩具；席间一同就餐的孩子不停打断大人谈话，大声尖叫、娇纵顽劣……

每当这种时候，邻桌的人总是心里恨恨地想，如果是我的孩子，一定臭揍一顿！但孩子在餐桌上没样儿，并非抽他两个嘴巴，然后告诉他一堆条条框框就可以解决的。多观察就会发现，那些可以安安静静、举止得体的孩子，都是在平日里就受到过良好的言传身教，有愉悦的生活环境，并时刻被成人礼貌对待着的孩子。反之，没有被好好尊重过的孩子是不会理解那些抽象词汇的含义的。

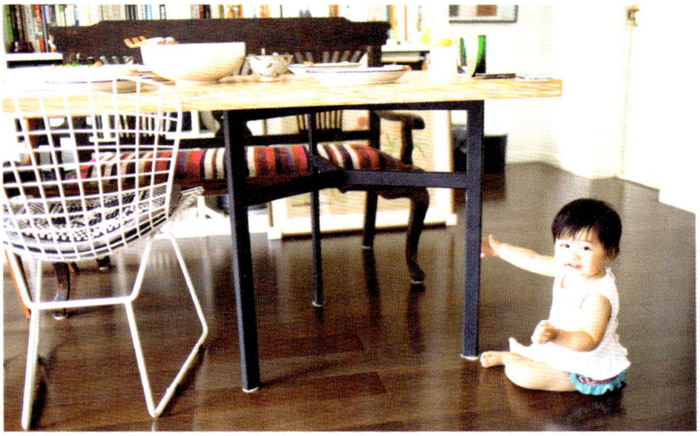

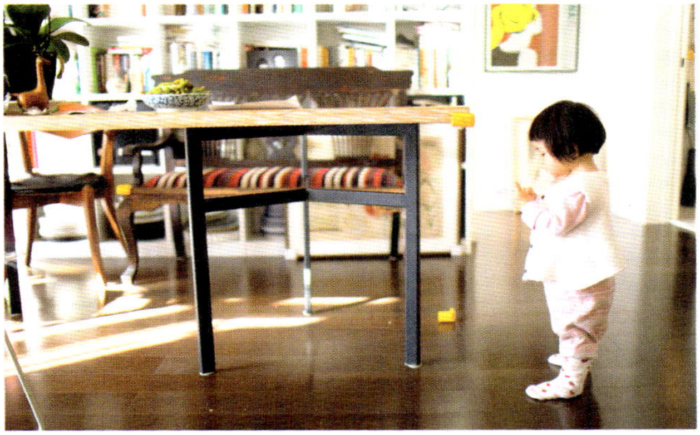

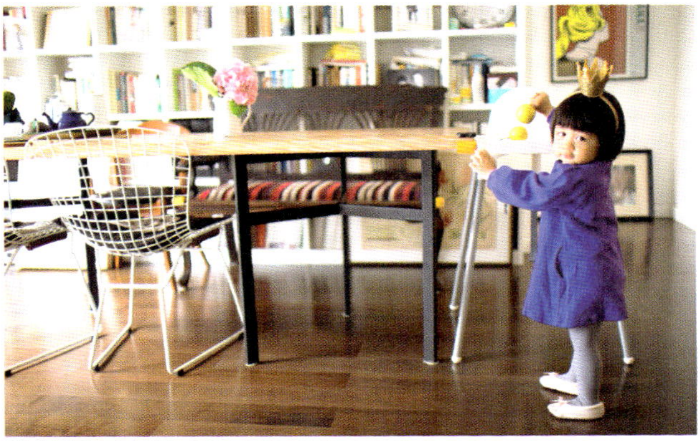

家的核心是一张让家人欢聚的餐桌，以这张餐桌为女儿的参照物，记录她不断的成长。（摄影：黄鹭）

“礼法并不是为了看着漂亮，礼法的真意是理解生命中的一些本质。”日本知名平面设计师山口信博如是说。就像我们了解，残酷是生命的真相，因而我们懂得要珍惜那些被我们剥夺生命而得来的食物。在西方的餐桌上，饭前会为上天赐予的食物祈祷，在东方，亦以不可掉落饭粒和剩余食物为重要的用餐礼节。自私是人的本性，克制自己为他人着想则成为重要的礼仪。谦恭、隐忍、注重礼节——不打搅别人，让他人感到愉悦是其中的本质……

对于幼童，在日常生活的每一餐中培养的礼仪，并不仅仅是教会他们这些规矩，而是通过这些细小的行为方式，告诉他们一种与人、与世界相处的模式，并通过这些获得自信和他人的尊重。英女王皇室家庭总管亚历山德拉·梅瑟维（Alexandra Messervy）女士这样诠释礼仪——拥有好的礼仪的全部目的，是为了建立自信。因为它可以使其他人感到舒服、自然。

同样，对于孩子的教育和培养，也并非是粗鲁的命令和强加的过程，而是在尊重他们、为他们着想的基础上，让他们从懵懂的模仿，到能体会出其中的美好真谛。

一起就餐是为了愉快

这么说听起来有点白痴，谁不知道用餐是为了愉快呢？但事实往往本末倒置，在我们过多专注于严格训练孩子用餐礼仪、培养用餐好习惯时，常常忘了让他们首先感受到，吃饭是一个享受愉悦的过程——这才是我们的出发点。那些懂得享受用餐乐趣的孩子总能在举手投足间做到得体大方，而缺乏用餐礼仪的孩子更多时候甚至不知道他们为何会出现在餐桌前，为何总在这种时候被父母教训，更不知道他们究竟该用什么样的态度去对待食物或周围环境。

拍电影有几条定律——不要碰小孩，不要碰动物，不要碰水。确实，这些都是最难掌控的部分，但电影可以避开小孩，可作为生活的导演，我们必须面对我们的孩子。在这部戏的脚本中，就要从心底认同，教会孩子餐桌礼仪的目的，不是在外出吃饭时做给别人看，也不是在家里拿着游标卡尺度量孩子在餐桌上的一言一行就够了。餐桌礼仪不是桎梏，不是让孩子戴着脚镣舞蹈，而是灰姑娘的水晶鞋，把孩子最天真美好的部分连同他们古灵精怪的热情一起安放其中，用最自然最舒服的方式展现出他们闪闪发亮的一面。

教养首先要讲道理

一次吃饭时，一个孩子不断大声地打断我们的对话，对她的妈妈以及其他人大叫——吃饭的时候不可以说话！

场面尴尬。作为父母，是粗鲁地呵斥她大人说话小孩不要搭茬儿，还是含糊地说大人可以说话但小孩不可以？这似乎都不合理。难道不是她的老师或父母曾经这样要求她吗？是否有必要先给她解释清楚，吃饭的时候为什么不能说话？

是的，吃饭的时候为什么不能说话呢？

难道吃饭的时候不正是大家交谈的最好时机吗？这条规矩的形成也许起因于老师或

父母希望孩子尽快专心吃完食物，并且不要被饭粒呛到，但这并不合乎生活常理。日本小说家、评论家宫本百合子在她的著作《新教养》中提到，教养要合乎道理，这是非常重要的事。烦琐而不得要领的教养，是最差的。因而，吃饭不能说话这条规矩应该稍作修改——嘴里含着食物的时候，请不要说话。

教养首先要讲道理。实际上，无论是拿筷子的方式，还是左叉右刀、从外而内的餐具摆放顺序，都是符合人体工学的。千百年来形成的礼法，一定是最方便、最有效率的章法。无论中西，上菜的顺序、品尝美味的讲究，又都包含着对人类味觉的深入研究。我们为什么要告诉孩子，先品尝清淡的前菜，味重的荤菜要在海鲜之后，而甜品压轴？因为这样才能享受到味觉丰富的层次。又为什么拿酒杯的时候只能捏住杯脚？喝勃艮第酒的酒杯杯口窄，而喝波尔多酒的酒杯杯口宽？这里面关于化学和生理学的原理可以等他们长大点儿后再慢慢讲解。但你要做的是，教给孩子之前，自己要深谙其中的道理，即使像不能抖腿斜眼、筷子不能插在米饭上、不能敲盘子敲碗这些要求，虽然尽可以大喝一声，少废话，这就是老祖宗留下的规矩！但其实，这一切也是和社会文化与心理学有着千丝万缕的关联和典故的。

不被打扰的孩子才懂得安静

在餐厅里，我们会遇到这样的孩子——像有多动症一般，一直处于不安的状态。对父母说话高声而无理，甚至尖叫，把食物乱丢，把杯盘弄得乱响，还会撒泼哭闹。

我们也会遇到这样的孩子——一直专注地吃着面前的食物，小手的动作甚至还笨笨氏、萌萌的，但却很努力地吃完食物。想要什么的时候会向父母提出请求，会和父母交流，但不会音量过大或一直打断大人的谈话。

这两种孩子从生下来都是一无所知，并没有谁对餐桌礼仪或用餐规则天生就懂，但发展到如此极端的两个方向，必然有其中的原因。我们把镜头再推过去仔细观察，会看到第一个孩子的妈妈一直在絮絮叨叨地问孩子吃这个不、吃那个不，要擦手、要喝水、要撒尿，不要摔筷子、不要敲碗、要坐直。那个孩子刚吃一口米饭，妈妈便塞过来一口青菜，刚要喝水，妈妈又叫着擦擦嘴，而孩子的父亲一直在玩手机，与这对母子的交流几乎为零。而第二个孩子的父母则穿戴精致得体，一边用餐，一边轻声愉快地交谈，他们的目光时常会落在孩子的身上，但很少去打扰他，只在他最需要的时候及时而到位地提供帮助。如果孩子要说什么，他们总会转过目光，注视着他认真倾听，并耐心地和他交流。

就像前文所说，被好好尊重和礼貌对待的孩子，才会同样礼貌待人。同样，在日常生活中不被随意打扰的孩子，才能够懂得安静和专心。从儿童心理学的角度讲，专注力是幼儿发展的第一要素，成人的过多指令和频繁干扰会阻碍专注力的发展；不能懂得他们内心的需求，错误的教育手法和无效的沟通方式，都会让孩子因为无路可走而变得焦躁——他们除了以发脾气和搞破坏为手段来发泄和引起关注外，别无他法。做一个简单的置换游戏，假设你是那个被一万只苍蝇嗡嗡嗡包围住的可怜虫，三分钟被人摆弄一下头发、抹一下嘴角，两分钟被纠正一次坐姿，并不断地让你吃这个、吃那个，要这样、不要那样，你还不能掀桌子也不能起身就走，不可以以成人的方式表示抗议，怎么办？估计也只能号啕着满地打滚儿了……

为孩子外出用餐做足准备

经常看到一些年轻而时髦的父母带着他们一两个月甚至更小的婴儿一起吃饭、喝咖啡、晒太阳，小宝宝也许只是躺在婴儿提篮里，或依偎在大人怀里睁大眼睛吃着手指好奇地看，但最好的家庭教育，不正是一家人在一起，愉快地吃很多很多顿饭吗？

千万不要因为怕麻烦而放弃带孩子出门。在餐厅里看各式各样的人，观察环境，感受轻松欢乐的气氛，都是潜移默化的启蒙。只是当你决定带小宝宝出门时，准备工作要做仔细，这样才能让吃饭变成一个令人愉快的过程。

首先是餐厅选择。对于婴幼儿来说，希望他们接触的环境是明亮宽敞、充满阳光的，不那么嘈杂，雅致干净，尤其是气味上要清新自然，用餐的客人也是彬彬有礼的——好的审美和举止对小宝宝都是正面的熏陶。那些提供周末早午餐的西餐厅会是很好的选择。这些餐厅在入夜后也许是正式的 Fine Dining（高级餐厅），不适合儿童，但周末早午餐则不同，没那么正式，用餐的人群也会包含很多家庭。

当小宝宝会走路之后，则可以选择一些有花园、户外走廊或专门设有儿童活动区域的餐厅。耐性差是小孩子的天性，当他有些坐不住的时候，可以带他出去放放风，寻找点其他乐趣。而在他能吃东西后，要在选择餐厅的时候着重考虑，是否有提供适合小宝宝食用的安全可靠的食物，毕竟，和大人一起享用美味才是出去吃饭的根本。

至于绝对不要选择的地方，一类是非常正式的高级餐厅（尤其是晚餐），无论是否有明文规定，带低龄的孩子去都是不礼貌的；有酒吧性质的餐厅，吵闹的音乐和狭窄的环境也不适合儿童；洋快餐店实在是摧毁味觉和健康的地方，建议远离；火锅店、烧烤店一类有不安全因素的餐厅更不适合孩子。

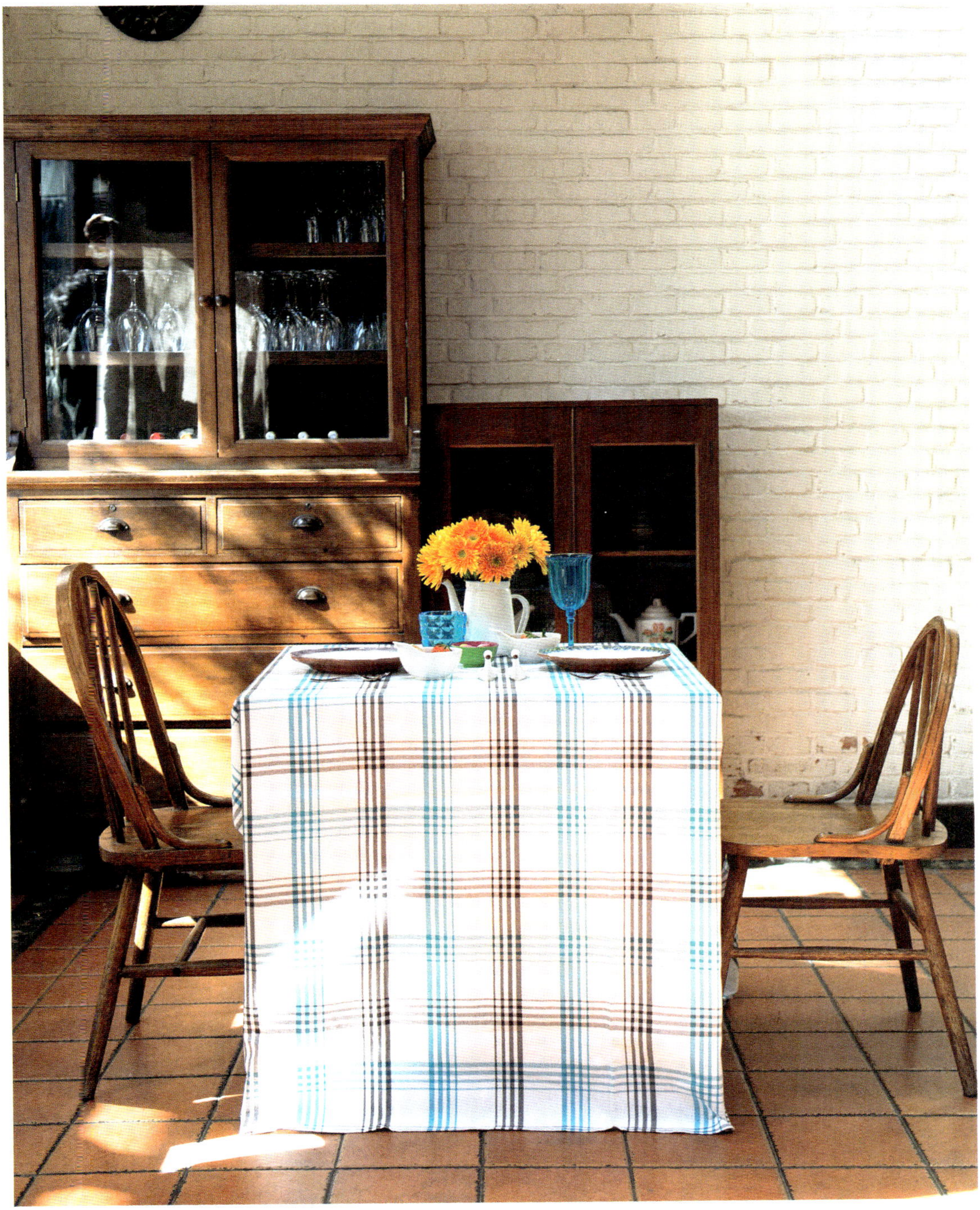

为孩子举办的派对，也要有漂亮的餐桌布置，让他们感受到在餐桌上的时光，是愉快美妙的。

此外，一些对孩子友善（children-friendly）的餐厅，会提供可爱且不易碎的儿童餐具，对于不单独提供餐具的地方，要根据自己孩子的情况决定是否随身携带专属的杯盘勺筷。还有用餐时间，即使爱丽舍宫的总统晚宴也会严格规定时间不超过55分钟，更何况小孩子的天性使然，不可能安安静静地一直坐着，所以要考虑到餐厅上菜速度和用餐时点菜的数量。如果是和友人相聚畅聊的饭局，就干脆把孩子放在家里吧。

餐桌礼仪就是日常的教养

保罗·福塞尔（Paul Fussell）在《格调》（*Class: A Guide Through the American Status System*）一书中提到，人的生活品位随着他的成长一旦形成之后，一般不会再发生大的改变，即使经由有意识的熏陶和训练似乎也收效甚微。这也是你很难看到通过一两个疗程的“贵族礼仪培训课”就能培养出贵族一样。尤其是在经历过天灾人祸、传统文化曾经严重断裂的中国，重拾礼仪更是一个急迫却也漫长的过程。如今迅速成长的中产阶级父母会格外看重下一代的教养养成，希望他们的孩子可以在餐桌上举止优雅，在社交场合待人接物彬彬有礼，成长为社会中的“新贵族”。但这一切又真的急不得，比如我们讨论的餐桌礼仪，说白了，实际上都是日常的教养，它们并不独立存在，也不会像餐巾布一样，只短暂地展示于餐桌之上，而是整个家庭生活水平、成员教育程度和教养综合熏陶的呈现。

因而餐桌礼仪的培养，不应该仅仅限于在餐桌之上。一言一行具体的身教，胜于空洞乏味的言传。就像简单的请、谢谢、对不起，每个成年人都会教给孩子，但孩子更直观地感受到的不是这些词汇的应用，而是父母对待服务人员的态度。为他人着想是一个宽泛的概念，在降低了嗓门、打喷嚏知道遮住嘴巴后，在餐桌上是否会倾听别人的谈话则是潜移默化中教养的体现。筷子刀叉的使用方法可以通过严格的管教来传授，但吃相中的贪相和贫相则是更细微之处的流露。

在遇到孩子失礼于人的时候，我们总是先想到，你丢了我的脸。但要知道，他并不会为了你的面子而活。教养并不是只针对孩子，要时刻透过孩子的行为反思自己的举止。

也不要喋喋不休地去说这样不可以那样不可以，而是去做。一个温和谦恭的父亲，不会教出对人颐指气使的女儿；一个举止优雅的母亲，也不会有粗俗莽撞的儿子。一个顽劣的孩子，反射出的实际上是父母的粗鲁和不自知。

因而我们也会说，养孩子也是一个不断自我修正的过程。与其说，孩子，你要为我争气！不如说，孩子，我会为你争气！

全世界通用的餐桌礼仪

在我们的印象里，总有个误区，觉得西餐的规矩更多一些，而中餐不必那么讲究。但其实，先秦汉以前的各种礼仪就已经写成了一部《礼记》，其中关于餐宴中的诸多规矩细致到惊人："毋咤食，毋啮骨，毋反鱼肉，毋投与狗骨。毋固获，毋扬饭……"翻译成大白话就是：吃饭别吧嗒嘴；不要大口啃肉；吃多少夹多少，别再放回去；狗也有尊严，别把自己不啃的骨头扔给狗；不能爱吃什么就猛吃，更不能因为烫嘴就扇风吹气……这些东西放在今天，依然是完全通行的标准，而且，如果细细想来，其实无论中餐西餐，好的礼仪，全世界通用。

比如说手脚。在中国，老祖宗留下的规矩是，吃饭时，手要扶碗，决不许一只手垂在桌下，当然，也不能胳膊肘上桌子，空着的手，轻握在桌边，小孩可以放在膝盖上；双脚要平放，脱鞋或叉开双腿都很不礼貌；不翘腿，不抖脚。在西方，这些规则都可以直接翻译，分毫不差。

再说坐。无论中西，坐如钟，便是要正、稳。椅子要深坐，不靠椅背，整个人腰背挺直。在任何文化中，歪斜的坐姿或瘫软趴下都是不入流的表现，挺拔而不僵硬为最佳。

具体到吃饭，不管哪国人，主人（或长辈）不开动，客人（或晚辈）不能吃；中式饭碗要端起，不低头扒饭，西餐餐叉送嘴边，不为食物而折腰；喝汤不出声，中式汤烫不要吹，放凉一点再喝也不迟；从小学会把食物分成一小口一小口吃，不撕咬、整块啃，吃相不野蛮，不要打扰到别人；一只手一次只做一件事，轻拿轻放，不撞杯子不撞盘；吃相要干净，保持自己的碗盘餐具整洁；无论西式自助还是中餐分享，不要一次取食太多，不可挑挑拣拣，筷子不能伸到别人面前夹菜，不能把喜欢的食物都揽到面前；勤擦嘴，不喜欢吃的东西要悄悄吐在纸巾中；吃饭只能在餐桌上，不能满餐厅乱走，坐下后不可换座位，提前离座要征询大人同意；嘴里含着食物不说话；桌上够不到的东西不要伸胳膊去拿，请旁人帮忙传递，中餐转盘，小孩不可擅自转动，而应该请父母代替夹取食物。

这些规矩，都是从小便应该熟知的，它就像音乐或艺术，是一种非语言的交流方式。掌握这种技能，就犹如让孩子瞬间拥有了好的歌喉或神奇的画笔，无论是在金发碧眼的国度，还是在我们古典的东方，都可以顺利与人交往。文明的礼仪，实际上是一本全球免签的护照，能帮孩子走得更高、更远。

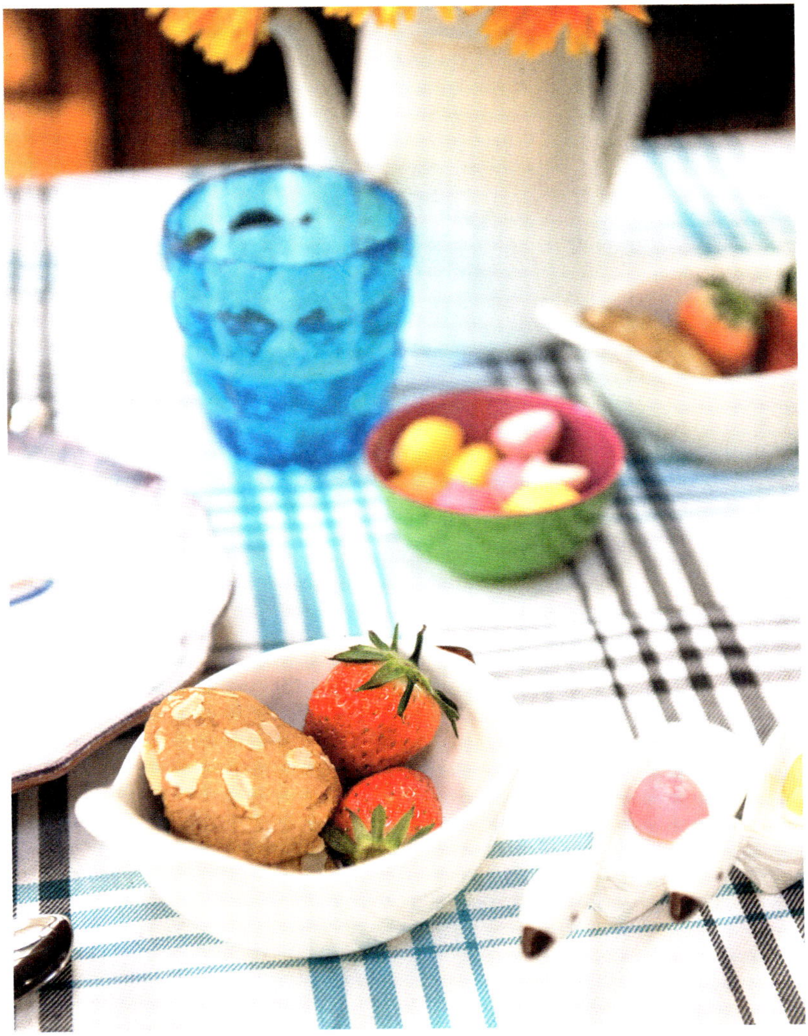

帮孩子们把食物分成小份儿，让他们取食方便，是有助于他们拥有良好用餐习惯的第一步。

“救火”和“应急”

在说完所有这些之后，还要说一件事。

要知道，孩子毕竟是孩子，他们都是天使和恶魔的混合体，或者说就像来自蓝星的生物，平时再有教养的孩子也会有这样的时刻——也许是身体不舒服，或者是情绪不佳，再或者只是忽然想念自己的星球而有些伤感，在你完全无法掌控的某个点上，他失控了。

这时你要做的肯定不是当众训斥孩子，那只能让场面更糟。先稳定住自己的情绪，放松，要知道大家虽然被打搅都会不愉快，但文明社会中的人们，对于难以掌控的低龄幼童还是会有宽容之心的。迅速而平静地把他带离餐厅，哪怕是舍弃还没有端上桌的龙虾或鹅肝，到一个安静的、不会打扰到其他人的地方等他稳定情绪。温和地对他。这时最怕的是大人的慌乱和紧张，至于如何让自己在这种尴尬的时刻泰然自若？

旅行作家，且育有一个非常出色的女儿的英国绅士马克·格雷厄姆（Mark Graham）曾告诉我，当年他在带着三岁的女儿外出偶遇状况时，心里默念十遍让自己镇定的“秘密口诀”是：我默默忍受了那么多年吃饭时听熊孩子吵闹，现在终于该是你们偿还我的时刻了！

▶ 最好的家庭教育，就是和孩子在一起，愉快地吃很多很多顿饭。

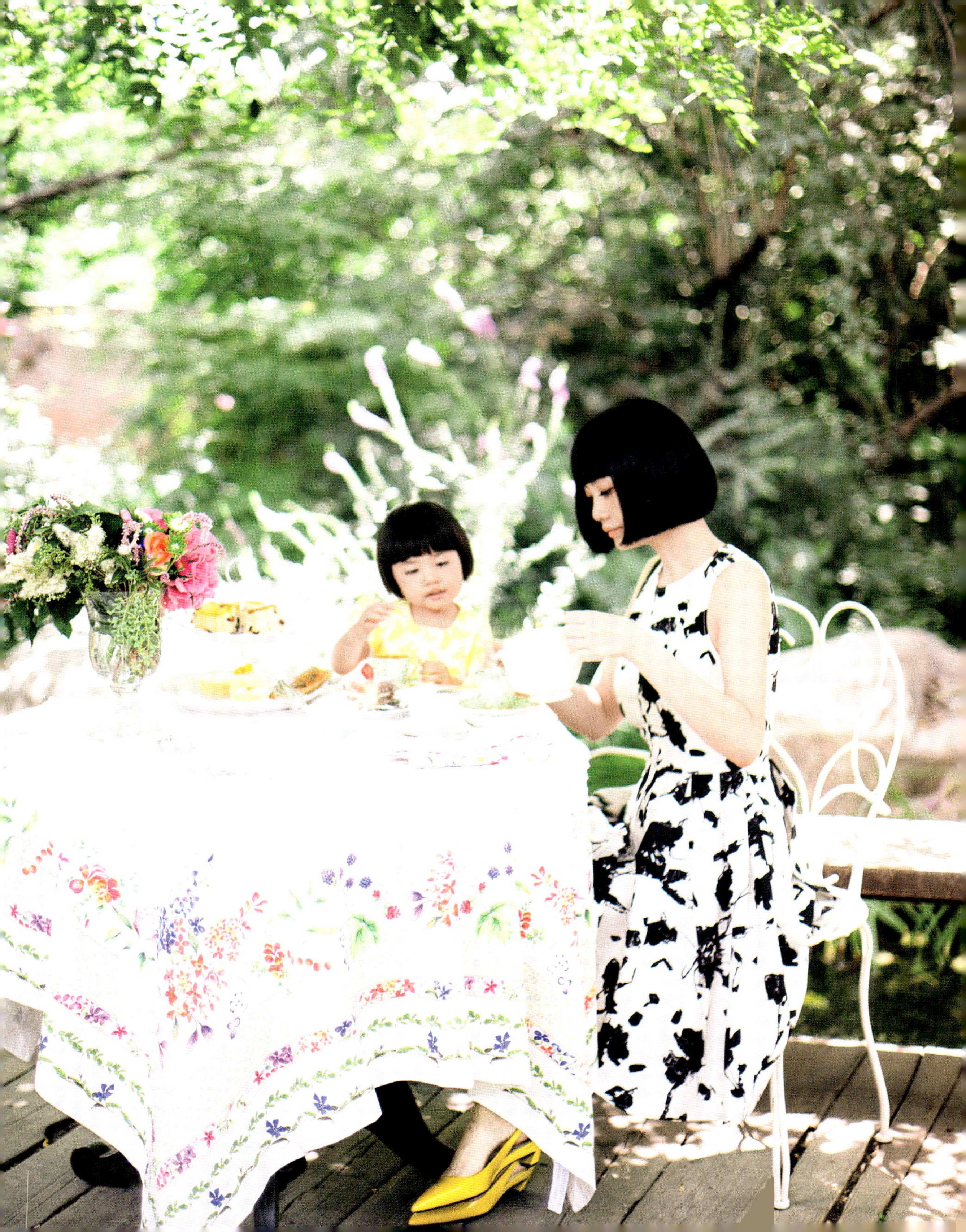

镜头对准一朵粉色洋牡丹上的水珠，下午的阳光在上面折射出亮闪闪的光。调焦，按下快门。咔嚓。这是 2011 年的春天，在我家的餐桌旁，我的朋友——著名时尚摄影师柴利增拍下的第一组关于春天的聚会。

在那之后的三年中，一切缓慢地继续着。

花开的时候，我们会聚集到乡村小院中，与满树樱桃花共进早午餐，顺便记录下春日的暖意；树林里刚刚被金黄的落叶铺满，我们便一起野餐，拍摄下藤篮边的雏菊、盘中的酱肉和一杯杯的美酒；还有在各种各样的餐桌上，为不同的欢聚，布置的那些长长的花桌，镜头拍摄下的是大家一起举杯一起玩乐的笑脸……一切缓慢地继续着，悠长的时光被镜头一幕一幕定格，这里面凝集的不仅仅是一顿一顿的餐饭，还有我和朋友们在一起的欢乐时光。

这本书从开始策划到最后出版，经历了一个漫长的过程。还记得最初由闺密庄雅婷提出这个想法时，我觉得有趣。渐渐去留意、学习、积累后，却从中发现了更大更精彩的世界——这个世界的核心便是一张属于家庭的餐桌，围坐的是我们所爱的家人、朋友，上面摆放的一花一草、一杯一碟、一餐一饭，便是我们生命中一点一滴爱意的凝结。

在这本书制作的过程中，我得到了很多很多朋友的鼓励和帮助。我的图书经纪人张国辰先生一直以他不紧不慢的速度对我进行关注、指点和适时的催促；与我合作的摄影师柴利增在三年中自己的事业突飞猛进，但永远以最优先的时间和专业的态度和我一起工作；经营着一家有名的瓷器商店"一鸿艺居"的一鸿和一丁，总是在新品到店的第一时间便想到我，并为我精选了无数美丽的瓷器；好友细毛、耀扬、Mia、李溯、姚雨杭总会在我需要时为我提供最及时的帮助；"Pretty Petals 珍瓏花局"的花艺师胡锐先生和杨小凡小姐更是以他们高超的技艺给了我最有力的技术支持；还有中信出版社第六分社社长王菲菲女士，我永远记得我们在咖啡馆里的那次见面，很多细小的信息让我获得了巨大的启发。

当我敲下最后一个字，结束了这三年来缓慢的进程，以我所能尽到的最大努力完成这本小书时，我脑海里想到的是，我庆幸自己可以拥有这么多美好的朋友，并有机会在这里用文字、图片记录下我们一起度过的最好的时光。我所能感谢到的人只是很小的一部分，甚至没有更多的篇幅提到永远默默支持我的先生。当然还有我可爱的女儿小叶子，如果没有你，可能两年前这本书就会面市，但那会是多么空洞的一本书啊，是你在这两年多的时光里，让我的生命有了更多生动的感悟。还有，那些我惦记的朋友们，这本书里会有你们的身影，有那时的觥筹交错、推杯换盏，会让我们再想起彼时的快乐和忧伤，想起我们一直一直都还在一起。此刻，无论你身在何处，如果你看到这些和你有关的文字和故事，希望我们可以一起举杯，饮下这杯由时光和爱酿造的美酒。